Y0-BZZ-679

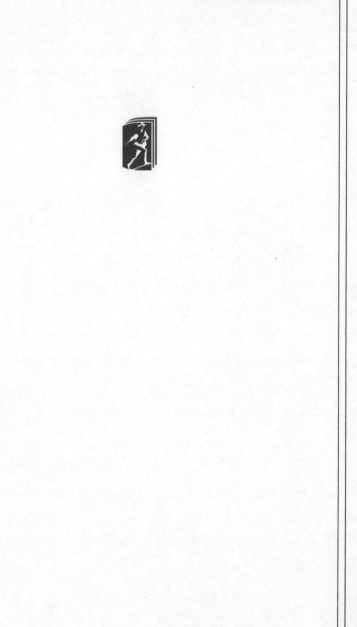

VANITY FAIR's

SCHOOLS
FOR
SCANDAL

The Inside Dramas at 16 of America's
Most Elite Campuses—Plus Oxford!

EDITED BY

GRAYDON CARTER

with an Introduction by Cullen Murphy

SIMON & SCHUSTER PAPERBACKS

New York London Toronto Sydney New Delhi

Simon & Schuster Paperbacks
An Imprint of Simon & Schuster, Inc.
1230 Avenue of the Americas
New York, NY 10020

First Simon & Schuster trade paperback edition August 2018

SIMON & SCHUSTER Paperbacks and colophon are registered trademarks of
Simon & Schuster, Inc.

For information about special discounts for bulk purchases, please contact
Simon & Schuster Special Sales at 1-866-506-1949 or business@simonandschuster.com.

The Simon & Schuster Speakers Bureau can bring authors to your live event.
For more information or to book an event, contact the Simon & Schuster Speakers Bureau
at 1-866-248-3049 or visit our website at www.simonspeakers.com.

Interior design by Ruth Lee-Mui

Manufactured in the United States of America

1   3   5   7   9   10   8   6   4   2

Library of Congress Cataloging-in-Publication Data is available.

ISBN 978-1-5011-7374-5
ISBN 978-1-5011-7376-9 (pbk)
ISBN 978-1-5011-7375-2 (ebook)

CONTENTS

CONTENTS

CONTENTS

FOLLOW THE MONEY

INTRODUCTION

By Cullen Murphy

George Bernard Shaw once said that the only time his education had been interrupted was when he was in school. Mark Twain was made of nimbler stuff, maintaining that he'd actually never let schooling get in the way of his education. Schools have always been good for an easy contrarian laugh.

And yet we can't take our eyes away. There's a reason why schools drive the plots or provide the setting for novels and movies known to everyone—from *The Catcher in the Rye* and *A Separate Peace* to *Infinite Jest* and *Prep*; from *Goodbye, Mr. Chips* and *The Prime of Miss Jean Brodie* to *Rushmore, Animal House*, and *Fast Times at Ridgemont High*. It's not only the magical elements that make *Harry Potter* so compelling. It's also, even mostly, what's familiar—the familiar environment of a school.

The investigations collected in *Vanity Fair's Schools for Scandal* were published in the magazine over a period of 25 years. Each of them focuses on events at a particular institution. All of them, taken together, reveal why schools of one sort or another—public or private, secondary or post-secondary, old or new, rich or poor, nonprofit or for-profit— make for natural targets of journalistic opportunity.

First, schools are closed systems—not entirely, but significantly. As subjects, they have boundaries to them; the boundaries may even come in the form of actual walls, with Gothic crenellations and wrought-iron gates. Every school is a compact world unto itself—with its own history and traditions, its psychology and myths, its *ancien regime*, its Young Turks, its successes, its failures, its ambitions. Every school has its own rules, written and unwritten. Every school also occupies a particular place in the world—sometimes a shifting place—and every school nurtures (or clings to, if only by the fingernails) a sense of identity and status. Every school, finally, has its secrets: either known to all but never spoken of, or known to just a few until a moment of searing revelation. To a writer, for all these reasons, a school offers a form of locked-room mystery.

So that's one characteristic that schools have to offer. Then there's the flip side. Yes, schools may constitute their own little worlds—but they're also a point of intersection for just about every social phenomenon on the planet. School is an institution that everyone attends—no other institution can say that. Every day the outside world ventures into classrooms and onto campus in the form of flesh-and-blood human beings from every part of society. The questions central to education— what do students need to know? how should they be taught? who should do the teaching?—are difficult enough, and elicit no sustained agreement. But schools of every kind, at every level, also have to contend with the state of the economy; with wealth and poverty; attitudes toward sex; attitudes toward gender; attitudes toward disability; the prominence of athletics; changing family structures; race and ethnicity; counseling and medication; addiction to drugs and alcohol; the legal system; crime and punishment; state and federal mandates; standardized testing; changing technology; changing modes of transportation; legal and illegal immigration; politics and political correctness; and much else. Add to this the fact that many of the people involved are at different stages of emotional and intellectual development; are changing rapidly on both the inside and outside; and, no matter how exemplary, are several increments shy of maturity. And that's just the students.

Think of it as a recipe. In a small pressure cooker combine every known ingredient. Tighten the lid. Bring to a boil.

The 18 articles collected here cover a wide range of subject matter—from the secretive management of multibillion-dollar endowments (as in the case of Harvard) to the secretive management of private clubs (as in the case of St. Anthony's Hall, at Columbia); from events on campus that have brought criminal charges for defensible reasons (as in the case of St. Paul's School) to events that have led to charges for indefensible ones (as in the case of the Duke University lacrosse players); from episodes that have made headlines across the nation (as in the case of the rape allegations at the University of Virginia) to activities that by design are almost never exposed to public view (as in the case of the infamous Yale secret society, Skull and Bones). Now and then the articles venture into obscure nooks and crannies—the art thefts at Transylvania University; the lethal, envelope-pushing endeavors by an Oxford sporting club—but they also describe the complicated public collisions of truth and ideology, law and press, passion and process.

Context is essential. Bring any one issue to the foreground, and many other issues are sure to emerge from the shadows. Sarah Ellison's 2015 account of the *annus horribilis* at the University of Virginia, "Shadows on the Lawn," provides a classic case in point. The precipitating event was the publication of an article in *Rolling Stone* magazine ("A Rape on Campus," by Sabrina Rubin Erdely) in which an anonymous student, referred to only as "Jackie," recounted firsthand a horrific episode—her gang rape by members of a campus fraternity. The article appeared at a moment when campuses nationwide were grappling with documented episodes of sexual misconduct—not a problem confined to colleges and universities, by the way—and gamely attempting to deal with the problem through on-campus judicial proceedings (mandated by federal law) and broad efforts at education and awareness.

The *Rolling Stone* report lit a match to dry tinder. But no sooner had it appeared—sparking protests against sexual violence on campuses everywhere, and a criminal investigation by authorities in Virginia—than cracks in the story began to appear. Jackie's account came under scrutiny, and so did the magazine's editorial process. The cracks widened with every passing day, and in the end *Rolling Stone* retracted the article. A story about an alleged rape on campus had now become a story about something else: a story about shoddy journalism, about anonymous sources, about fact-checking. But that too was just one facet of the larger reality. As Ellison looked further into the events, drawing on her own experience as a UVA undergraduate, she enlarged her canvas. To understand the texture of life at the university—the dynamic background that allowed the *Rolling Stone* article to find credence on campus in the first place—she delved into the history of coeducation at the school, the social structure on campus, the mixed record on race, the nature of governance, and what even casual visitors have perceived as a clubby ethos ("girls in pearls and guys in ties") with lingering traces of an old aristocracy. Ellison allowed readers to see the university for what it is—an institution with a specific history but also one, like any institution, that absorbs and reflects the surrounding environment.

Or consider Nina Munk's "Rich Harvard, Poor Harvard," from 2009, her riveting description of a financial earthquake that shook the Harvard endowment—and of the behind-the-scenes turmoil among the men and women paid (very well) to manage it. Endowments are not as straightforward as they are sometimes portrayed. "Endowment" is often used as shorthand for "unaccountable wealth," and there's no question that some colleges and universities are very wealthy. Harvard's endowment stands at more than $36 billion. But endowment money isn't just socked away. It makes possible expenditures that the institution could otherwise not afford (including vast amounts of financial aid). Money spent from endowments also amounts to a redistributionist transfer program from past generations to future ones. Because it pays for a huge proportion of operating expenses—and because you can squeeze only so much out of it every year if you want to milk the principal indefinitely—an endowment, properly managed, is a special subset of the investing art.

Bill Gates and Carlos Slim can afford to gamble with their wealth, if they choose. Harvard cannot. And so, when the 2008 financial crisis caused its endowment to plummet—by 30 percent in a few short months—Harvard was thrown into the worst financial crisis in its history. On a campus where ambition can be pharaonic—new buildings erected at Harvard since 2000 have added square-footage equivalent to the Pentagon's—vast projects had to be canceled. Layoffs and attrition claimed thousands of jobs—a reminder that, in communities all across postindustrial America, hospitals and universities are among the most reliable employers. As Munk points out, all of this cutting back occurred in a context where officials seemed incapable of saying what they meant. In academe, nothing ever gets the axe—programs are "re-aligned" or "resized" or "re-calibrated." There are no "problems"—only "challenges." The political correctness we hear so much about is often seen, simplistically, as a weapon used by the Left against the Right. Judging from the language used at Harvard, the true target is reality.

Once again, context: this time in the form of William D. Cohan's "Big Hair on Campus," a 2014 report on the now-defunct Trump University, a venture launched by a man who has reached the White House and one that, according to New York State's attorney general, Eric Schneiderman, amounted to nothing short of out-and-out fraud. Trump University, Schneiderman alleged, was, in essence, a glorified pickpocketing scheme. It charged as much as $35,000 for what the attorney general considered worthless real-estate seminars that stoked delusional hopes of easy street. When he brought suit against the venture, he charged outright that "Mr. Trump used his celebrity status and personally appeared in commercials making false promises to convince people to spend tens of thousands of dollars they couldn't afford for lessons they never got." Trump's university was a scam, Schneiderman said, and Trump paid a hefty penalty (while admitting no wrongdoing and continuing to claim he would have won the case) when he settled for $25 million. The Trump University case was egregious, but it did not arise in isolation: the context is the rapid and massive expansion of for-profit educational programs throughout the country—most of them legitimate, but few subject to the scrutiny and oversight that traditional schools receive.

Trump also took advantage of a deeply rooted American character trait—the unshakable belief in the power of education and the possibility of self-improvement. In Trump's case, self-aggrandizement also came into play. Cohan quotes many exchanges between Trump and Schneiderman as they waged a public war of words over the lawsuit, one that spilled over into the tabloids. The attorney general came out ahead, noting at one point that Trump "seems to be the kind of person who goes to the Super Bowl and thinks the people in the huddle are talking about him."

Many of the episodes covered in this book deal with scandals that revolve around sex. The infamous "senior salute" at St. Paul's. Predatory teachers at St. George's. Accusations of rape and cover-up at the Air Force Academy. An affair and a lawsuit in the upper reaches of Stanford University's business school. There are other episodes. As I write, damning reports have just been issued by Choate Rosemary Hall, in Connecticut, and St. Paul's School, in New Hampshire, detailing accusations of sexual assault or abuse of students by numerous teachers over the course of several decades. You could be forgiven for thinking that schools, with their built-in imbalances of power and age, and their cloistered inner lives, must be more susceptible to scandal than other institutions.

They are not. Governments and corporations contribute mightily to the annals of impropriety. By volume and consequence, they are probably worse offenders. But time and again we turn our gaze back to schools—for reasons that, in a backhanded way, underscore the special place schools occupy in our minds.

They are, first of all, accessible—we feel close to them. There aren't many of us who cherish a personal relationship with Monsanto or the Securities and Exchange Commission, and there are even fewer who can breach the protective shell around, say, the Defense Logistics Agency or Goldman Sachs. But schools are woven into the fabric of our lives in an intimate way.

Second, we give schools our implicit trust to a degree we're reluctant to do with other institutions. Sending children, even if they're budding young adults, into their care is the obvious mark of that trust. The trust isn't a blank check—there is more and more regulation, more and more oversight—but it remains substantial, and it's real. The very idea of education is premised on trust.

And third, rightly or wrongly, we expect more from schools than we do from big business or big government. When it comes to standards of conduct, standards of honesty, and standards of care, schools represent a first line of defense. A breakdown here portends a breakdown everywhere else.

In "Shadows on the Lawn," Sarah Ellison described the University of Virginia as "a petri dish of issues facing society at large." The observation could apply to any school and its problems—or "challenges," if you prefer.

Within these pages, then, are vivid and deeply reported stories of schools facing scandal. And in this period when scandal is both epidemic *and* endemic in Washington, D.C., we could do worse than to try to learn from these cautionary tales that occur in more traditionally "manageable" and nurturing settings—places that many of us still regard as seats of wisdom, pride, and promise.

—May 2017

SECRETS & RITUALS

YALE'S SKULL AND BONES CLUB

"POWERFUL SECRETS"

By Alexandra Robbins

JULY 2004

T here are certain sure signs of spring at Yale. Dogwood trees blossom across New Haven. The daffodils on Old Campus bloom. Freshmen turn their speakers to face the courtyard and blast music while they kick Hacky Sacks and throw Frisbees on the green. And a certain group of upperclassmen participate in a quiet but frenzied one-night ritual known simply as Tap Night.

Each of Yale's six major secret societies elects its members on the same night in April of the prospective members' junior year. In April of 1965 and 1967, respectively, John F. Kerry and George W. Bush received the same fateful call to the same mysterious organization: the undergraduate club perhaps mythologized more than any other by the outside world, Skull and Bones.

It's no secret that Skull and Bones, which elects 15 Yale juniors annually to meet in a crypt-like headquarters called "the Tomb," is no mere college club. The fact that the 2004 presidential election is a Bones-versus-Bones ballot raises eyebrows not just because it brings to light that, despite their ideological differences, both candidates come from the same echelon of American society but also because it's a bit astounding that a club with only about 800 living members has seen so many of them reach prominence. Conspiracy theorists are having a field day speculating about the group that has been called everything from "an international mafia" to "the Brotherhood of Death."

They are not completely wrong. Skull and Bones really is one of the most powerful and successful alumni networks in America. Alumni, or "patriarchs," return often to the Tomb, where connections are made and favors granted. Some classes have "Pat Night," an event where patriarchs mingle with "knights" (undergraduate members) and circulate job offers. Among its roster, Bones counts three U.S. presidents, two Supreme Court chief justices, and scores of Cabinet members, senators, and congressmen. Bonesman president William Howard Taft named two fellow Bonesmen to his nine-man Cabinet.

More good news for the fanatics: there is a strong link between Bones and the C.I.A. In Bush and Kerry's day, the agency was known as an "employer of last resort," says a Bonesman from the 1960s, since so many Bonesmen went on to join. "If you couldn't get a job elsewhere, you could go there if you wanted to." Because of the high numbers of Bonesmen in the C.I.A. and in the Time Inc. empire (*Time* magazine co-founders Henry Luce and Briton Hadden were members), these organizations were "explicitly willing to take" Bonesmen seeking employment.

Many Bonesmen who had become C.I.A. operatives and government officials returned to the Tomb and discussed highly classified matters, as National-Security Adviser McGeorge Bundy reportedly did.

"The things that fascinated me at Pat gatherings were the level of penetration . . . and how open they were about talking in the Tomb," says a Bonesman who graduated in the 1980s. "They talked about foreign operations at the time, the stuff that became Iran-contra. The level of trust was startling. It was like once you were trusted enough to get in, people just talked openly."

Other illustrious alumni include Pulitzer Prize–winning biographer David McCullough; former *New York Times* general manager Amory Howe Bradford; actor James Whitmore; Morgan Stanley founder Harold Stanley; J. Richardson Dilworth, manager of the Rockefeller fortune; former Major League Baseball deputy commissioner Stephen Greenberg; and Walter Camp, the father of American football. During World War II, Bones' Henry Stimson, the secretary of war who often consulted fellow Bonesmen railroad heir W. Averell Harriman and poet Archibald MacLeish, hired four other Bones members for his War Department— Robert Lovett as assistant secretary of war for air, Artemus Gates as assistant secretary of the navy for air, George Harrison as a special consultant, and Harvey Bundy as his special assistant. In this respect, those in the conspiracy crowd who link Skull and Bones to the building of the atomic bomb are not entirely off base: Bonesmen were involved with its construction and deployment.

To be sure, it is an elite group. But while some members come away only with close friendships and peculiar college memories, others take Bones so seriously that they purposefully spread self-aggrandizing rumors about the society to fuel a culture of mystery. Some go as far as to threaten reporters. "The guys who take it really seriously are typically the ones who have lived the myth—the second- and third-generation Bonesmen who campaign to get in, and once they get in it's almost a religious fervor," the 1980s Bonesman says. Many Bonesmen spoke for this article only on condition of anonymity because, as one puts it, "I don't want to get in trouble with those guys." (Neither the White House nor the Kerry campaign returned repeated calls for comment.)

On April 28, 1967, the current president of the United States [George W. Bush] felt a clap on his shoulder. Contrary to numerous reports, Bush was not tapped by his father (although alumni occasionally participate in "tap"). By the time he got to Yale, Bush had several relatives in Skull and Bones, including his father and grandfather, but it was David Alan Richards who was assigned to tap him, likely because they both lived in the residential college Davenport. Richards met Bush in the Davenport courtyard, wearing his Tiffany gold Skull and Bones pin. "I was told that was my man. I smashed him on the shoulder, barked at him, 'Go to your room,' and followed my instructions," says Richards. "Now it's a matter of some embarrassment because I'm such a Democrat."

(A knight tells a prospective member to go to his room in a nod to Yale's early days, when Tap Day was held in a courtyard in front of an audience of hundreds. Once in private, the Bonesman intones, "At the appointed time tomorrow evening, wearing neither metal nor sulfur, nor glass, leave the base of Harkness Tower and walk south on High Street. Look neither to the right nor to the left. Pass through the sacred pillars of Hercules and approach the Temple. Take the right book in your left hand and knock thrice upon the sacred portals. Remember well, but keep silent, concerning what you have heard here.")

Richards's Bones experience—he was a knight in the class of 1967—intersected both Bush's (1968) and Kerry's (1966). "I have the odd feeling of being a center of the hinge," says Richards, now a real-estate attorney in New York. Of the election process, he says, "It's like picking the American soldiers for a World War II movie—one Jew, one Italian, one American Indian. You want a mix. You don't want everyone to be an Andover preppie who played lacrosse. Did we feel pressure [to elect Bush]? Are you aware of legacies when you're voting? Yeah. But he was well known to two intersecting circles. In my club there were three members of the fraternity D.K.E. and three people in Davenport, and he had the legacy going back several generations. I don't think W. was particularly interested in joining, but it was part of the family life. Do I believe reports that his father encouraged him to do it, as opposed to going into an underground [society] to drink? It's likely. I suspect family pressure was put on him."

Some of those relatives, including Bush's father and grandfather, attended his initiation in the Tomb, says Richards. "All I will say about his initiation," another patriarch who was present says, "is that he caught on pretty quickly and I was pleased with his response." The society is so secretive about Bush's time in Bones that the scrapbooks from his year—each class keeps candid brown-paged scrapbooks to memorialize the experience—have been sealed so knights can't read them. "If those scrapbooks were as obscene as ours were, it's a good thing for the White House and for the society," a Bonesman of that period muttered.

Bones largely presented a departure from Bush's usual college escapades. No alcohol is allowed inside the Tomb, and much of the time inside is spent on debates and delivering "life histories," or oral autobiographies. When George H. W. Bush gave his life history in the fall of 1947, he focused on his military service, married life with Barbara, and his hope to "have an impact in public service," one of his clubmates says. George W. Bush, by contrast, spent most of his presentations in the Tomb speaking about his father—reportedly in "almost God-like terms."

Life histories, as well as initiation rites, the rumored "Connubial Bliss" ritual, and the twice-weekly meetings, all occur in the Tomb. The Tomb has been the Skull and Bones haunt since 1856, when Daniel Coit Gilman, the founding president of Johns Hopkins University, incorporated Bones as the Russell Trust Association, now re-incorporated as RTA. A three-story Greco-Egyptian monolith of brown sandstone, "the T," as Bonesmen refer to it, sits on High Street in the middle of the Yale campus. No non-members—"barbarians," in Bones lingo—are allowed to enter. Inside the Tomb, the halls have been decorated by renowned architect John Walter Cross (a Bonesman) with pieces by distinguished painters such as J. Alden Weir (a barbarian). Dozens of skeletons and skulls grip the walls, surrounding such items as a mummy, gravestones— including one labeled "Tablet from the grave of Elihu Yale [the school's namesake] taken from Wrexham churchyard"—and war memorabilia.

The dining room, which members call "the boodle," is the most impressive chamber in the Tomb, decorated with engraved silver and bronze skulls and 30-foot-high windows that overlook a lush courtyard. The room is blanketed by portraits of the most illustrious Bones alumni, including William Howard Taft; Supreme Court chief justice Morrison Waite; Kerry's classmate Dick Pershing, who was killed in the 1968 Tet offensive; and, as of 1998, former president George H. W. Bush. The skulls and crossbones stamp everything from skull-shaped crockery to exit signs printed with letters composed of tiny skulls. Light shines through the gaping eye sockets of skulls bordering otherwise elegant fixtures. There are grand fireplaces on either side of the room which double as goals for the violent soccer-hockey hybrid Bones sport known as "boodleball."

One of the most avid boodleball players of his year was John Kerry. Kerry, along with Dick Pershing, David Thorne (a publishing executive in Massachusetts), and Fred Smith (the founder of FedEx) played boodleball as often as possible. The game, which involves a half-deflated ball and frequently leaves Bonesmen bleeding, is supposed to be played in the dining room only after it is cleared of couches and other furniture. "The four of us were the core of the boodleball group," says Thorne. "Freddie Smith was a maniac, and Dick broke his toe once. There were a lot of very hard obstacles in the way and we didn't bother moving them."

Kerry came to treasure his boodleball teammates more than the men on his college teams. By all accounts Kerry, who may have felt like an outsider as a Catholic at St. Paul's, his extremely Waspy Episcopalian prep school, thrived at Yale. He was president of the Political Union, a debater, and an athlete who played soccer, ice hockey, and lacrosse. He was friendly with about half a dozen members of his 1966 Bones class before they entered Bones, and was tapped by his St. Paul's friend John Shattuck, who would go on to be an assistant secretary of state under Clinton.

In the Tomb, Kerry bonded closely with the other knights and often steered conversations toward Vietnam and politics. Kerry helped Smith resurrect Yale Aviation, once an influential naval-air-reserve unit founded by Bonesmen during World War I. "Bones was one of the most meaningful parts of his life because of the focus and intensity that came from that experience: the regularly scheduled meetings, the amount of time you formally and informally spend with a group of people that created a bond, and a focus you don't get out of other activities like athletic teams. He remains very close to the guys. Most of us would go out of the way to help each other, no questions asked," says Thorne, Kerry's closest friend and former campaign manager, who became Kerry's brother-in-law when Kerry married Thorne's twin sister, Julia. (Kerry's second wife, Teresa, had become the daughter-in-law of a Bonesman when she married her first husband, Senator John Heinz.)

Other Bonesmen say Kerry was "delighted" by Skull and Bones because it built and cemented strong friendships. Fellow Bonesman Chip Stanberry (1966) was Kerry's partner for three years on Yale's debate team, but he says the friendship didn't grow close until they went through Bones together. "We think of politicians as garrulous and backslapping. John was private and reserved. He was shy to jump into a crowded circle of four guys having a beer. People therefore mistook him as aloof," Stanberry says. In the protective environment of the Tomb, however, Kerry "relaxed, he was more natural. He broke out of whatever that shy, reserved part of his person was. John took it seriously, and it meant a lot to him. Of course, John took everything seriously."

As are all matters relating to Bones, the origin of the society is shrouded in mystery. The most plausible story has Yale student William Russell, later a Civil War general and Connecticut state representative, studying abroad in Germany in 1832. He returned to Yale dismayed to find that Phi Beta Kappa, until then a secret society, had been stripped of its secrecy in the anti-Masonic fervor of the time. Incensed, Russell grabbed some big men on campus, including future secretary of war Alphonso Taft, and formed an American chapter of a German society. The group was founded on the legend that when Greek orator Demosthenes died, in 322 B.C., Eulogia, the goddess of eloquence, arose to the heavens. Originally called the Eulogian Club, the society holds that the goddess returned to take up residence with them in 1832.

Hence the importance of the number 322 to Bones members— Kerry has used 322 as a code, and Thorne uses 322 as his phone extension; W. Averell Harriman used it as the combination of the lock on a briefcase carrying dispatches between London and Moscow—and the obsession with the goddess Eulogia. Members open a shrine to her at Thursday- and Sunday-night meetings, and regularly sing "sacred anthems" about her.

Both 322 and Eulogia are central symbols in the society's initiation. When an initiate approaches the Tomb for the ceremony, the front door creaks open and knights immediately cover his head with a hood. After a brief stay in "the Firefly Room," a pitch-black living room in which his hood is removed to reveal the lit cigarettes the patriarchs wave to resemble fireflies, he is whirled throughout the building and the grounds.

The heart of the ceremony is in Room 322—the Inner Temple, or "I.T." There, a group of knights (led by a distinguished patriarch known for the evening as Uncle Toby, dressed in a distinctive robe) awaits the initiate, wearing masks and various costumes, including the Devil, Don Quixote, Elihu Yale, and a Pope with one foot sheathed in a monogrammed white slipper that rests on a stone skull. Other knights are dressed as skeletons, and patriarchs line the halls, where their solemn duty is to yell so loudly they scare the new member.

One by one, each neophyte is led into the I.T., where he's shoved around to various features of the room, including a picture of Eulogia, and forced to do things such as read a secrecy oath repeatedly, kiss the Pope's foot, and drink "blood" from "the Yorick," a skull container usually holding red Kool-Aid. Finally, the initiate is shoved to his knees in front of Don Quixote as the shrieking crowd falls silent. Quixote taps him on the left shoulder with a sword and says, "By order of our order, I dub thee Knight of Eulogia."

Soon after initiation, each knight is assigned a Bones name, which the society will call him from then on. There are three ways to acquire a nickname: receive one from a patriarch who wishes to pass his down, as Bankers Trust head Lewis Lapham (father of the *Harper's* editor of the same name) passed "Sancho Panza" to political adviser Tex McCrary; accept a traditionally assigned name, such as "Magog," which is given to the knight with the most sexual experience (Robert Alphonso Taft and William Howard Taft each earned this distinction); or choose your own (McGeorge and William Bundy chose "Odin," Supreme Court justice Potter Stewart—who swore in George H. W. Bush as director of the C.I.A. and vice president—chose "Crappo," W. Averell Harriman and Dean Witter Jr. were "Thor," and Henry Luce opted for "Baal"). John Kerry likely came close to earning the name "Long Devil," the traditional tag for the tallest man in the club, but narrowly missed—Alan Cross, now a doctor in North Carolina, is taller. Kerry chose his own name, but Bonesmen are keeping it quiet. George W. Bush, unable to come up with his own name, was dubbed "Temporary" and never managed to decide on a replacement.

At the end of the school year, the new group of 15 is whisked away to Deer Island in the Saint Lawrence River, 340 miles from New York City; the 50-acre private island was given to the society by a Bonesman at the turn of the 20th century. Both Kerry and Bush returned to the island as seniors. Kerry's group prepared to go to Vietnam. (Kerry spent his time there rewriting his class oration in a rustic cabin by candlelight.) Bush's club spent their time digesting the news that Bobby Kennedy had been shot.

When the knights return from summer break, they almost immediately launch into the activity that a knight from Prescott Bush's class once called "a wonderful sensation." Perhaps the most prevalent rumor about Bones is that initiates must lie naked in a coffin and masturbate while recounting their sexual histories. Naked coffin exploits aren't officially on the Bones program, but part of the rumor is not too far from the truth: at successive Sunday meetings, each knight has an evening devoted to him for the activity known as "Connubial Bliss." In a cozy room lit only by a crackling fire, in front of 14 clubmates lounging on plush couches, he stands before a painting of a woman named Connubial Bliss while the knights sing a sacred anthem about romance, ending with "so let's steal a few hours from the night, my love." Then he is expected to recount his entire sexual history.

Apparently this ritual has remained unchanged since the acceptance of women into the club in 1991. A group of Bonesmen led by William F. Buckley Jr. (Bones name: Cheevy) obtained a court order blocking initiation of the society's first female members, claiming that admitting women would lead to "date rape" in the "medium future." Approximately 83 women have since been admitted, despite feverish lobbying by W.'s uncle Jonathan Bush, whom a fellow member called a "fanatical Bonesman." Neither Bush's nor Kerry's daughters are members, however. Kerry's daughter Vanessa wasn't tapped in 1998, and last year Bush's daughter Barbara decided to join Spade and Chalice, an underground (less formal, tomb-less) society.

For all the mystery and conspiracy theories surrounding Skull and Bones, the club's deepest secret may be its most obvious: the bonds between Bonesmen often supersede others. "For some people, Skull and Bones becomes the most important thing that ever happened to them, and they tend to stay involved," a patriarch told me. Indeed, the year spent as an undergraduate in the club is really only the beginning of a lifetime membership that can, depending on how it is used, reap enormous benefits.

As his father and grandfather had done before him, George W. Bush called a Bonesman when he was looking for his first job out of college. Although Robert Gow wasn't hiring at the time, he still took on Bush as a management trainee at his Houston-based agricultural company Stratford of Texas. In 1977, when Bush formed his first company, he turned to his uncle Jonathan Bush, who lined up $565,000 from 28 investors. One investor brought in approximately $100,000: California venture capitalist William H. Draper III, a Bonesman. Even Bush's Rangers baseball deal involved a Bonesman—Edward Lampert (Bones 1984) was an initial investor.

Bonesmen used to grant favors if a fellow member began a conversation with the code phrase "Do you know General Russell?" By the time he was running for president, Bush didn't have to ask. In October of 2000, Stephen Adams (Bones 1959), who owns Adams Outdoor Advertising, spent $1 million on billboard ads in key states for Bush. When asked a few years ago why he had made such a large contribution to someone he hadn't met, Adams replied that the shared Bones experience was a factor. Even a 1970s Bonesman who tried to quit the society admitted he would readily help a fellow Bonesman "just because of Bones. Because we did go through something really weird together."

Bush apparently feels the same way. One of the first social gatherings he held in the White House was a reunion of his Skull and Bones 1968 clubmates, and within the past two years he held another reunion, this time at Camp David. One of Bush's early appointments as president was Robert McCallum Jr. (Bones 1968), now associate attorney general. (In 2002, McCallum, whose Justice Department civil division includes attorney and 1984 Bonesman David Wiseman, filed pleadings in U.S. District Court asserting an executive privilege that would make information on presidential pardons more secret than in the past.) Among Bush's other Bones appointees are Bill Donaldson (1953), chairman of the Securities and Exchange Commission (and onetime director of the Deer Island Corporation); Edward McNally (1979), general counsel of the Office of Homeland Security and a senior associate counsel to the president; Rex Cowdry (1968), associate director of the National Economic Council; Roy Austin (1968), ambassador to Trinidad and Tobago; Evan G. Galbraith (1950), the secretary of defense's representative in Europe and the defense adviser to the U.S. mission to NATO; James Boasberg (1985), associate judge of the superior court of the District of Columbia; former Knoxville mayor Victor Ashe (1967), the first mayor appointed to the board of directors of the housing-finance company Fannie Mae; Jack McGregor (1956), a nominee for the Saint Lawrence Seaway Development Corporation advisory board, the same waterway that is home to Deer Island; and Bush's cousin George Herbert Walker III (1953), ambassador to Hungary. Frederick Smith (1966) was reportedly Bush's top choice for secretary of defense until he withdrew from the running because of health reasons.

Bonesmen say the president values the society because it became an extension of his family: the Bush-Walker web in Bones includes at least 10 members, including those who, like Reuben Holden (Bones name: McQuilp), married in. Donald Etra, a member of Bush's 1968 Bones club and a close friend who regularly visits the president, says Bones is important to Bush because "loyalty and tradition is important to the family." But Bush views Bones, he adds, "as a private matter which he does not discuss. The president believes there's still a realm where privacy counts."

Bones loyalty runs deep in John Kerry too. In 1993, Kerry, who, like Bush, has participated in several reunions with his clubmates, organized a meeting and a visit to Arlington National Cemetery on the 25th anniversary of Dick Pershing's death. When Pershing died, Kerry wrote to his own parents that Pershing "was so much a part of my life at the irreplaceable, incomparable moments of love, concern, anger and compassion exchanged in Bones that can never be replaced." After the trip to the gravesite, 10 members convened at a Washington hotel to talk about Pershing, Bones, and one another. "It was very, very moving and poignant," says Chip Stanberry. "It was neat that John went to the trouble to make it happen, and 30 years later we were able to pick up with each other, immediately identifying, feeling a connection." Kerry has also been back to the Bones Tomb a few times and once delivered a speech there. "When he's got a little time, he stops in. Most of us do," Thorne says.

On at least one occasion, Kerry took on a more involved Bones role. In 1986, Jacob Weisberg, now the editor of *Slate*, was taking time off from Yale to intern at *The New Republic*, in Washington, D.C., when he received a call from Kerry's secretary. "Senator Kerry wants to see you in his office," the secretary said. "He won't tell me what it is about."

Weisberg showed up at the senator's office at eight A.M. Initially, Kerry made small talk while Weisberg wondered why he was there. Then Kerry tapped him for Bones. Weisberg, who hadn't known Kerry was a member, was stunned.

"Senator Kerry," Weisberg said, "you're a liberal—why do you support this organization that doesn't admit women?"

Kerry listed his efforts to assist women throughout his career. "I've marched with battered women. I've supported women's rights. No one can question my dedication to women." Weisberg said he wasn't interested. Kerry replied, "Promise me you'll think about it before saying no."

When Weisberg called Kerry back, his call went straight through to the senator. He rejected the offer, and Kerry, Weisberg recalls, said he was disappointed.

Kerry's fellow Bonesmen say the senator considers Skull and Bones a valuable part of his college life and a source of lasting friendships—but no more than that. "I don't think it plays a significant role in his thinking or in his circle of advisers," says Alan Cross. Indeed, a glance through notable figures in Kerry's life reveals only the Bonesmen whom he knew before they were tapped. And Kerry, as an anti-war Vietnam veteran, publicly railed against fellow Bonesman McGeorge Bundy in testimony before the Senate Foreign Relations Committee in 1971.

"[Kerry's] family carried the name Forbes, but John was never comfortable as a part of the Establishment," says Thorne, who adds that the 1966 group wasn't the "elite Establishment type." "He achieved what he achieved on his own. His is a life marked by intellectual and other kinds of achievement, not by who you know. That's just how he was."

Thorne has friends in both the Kerry and Bush families, and has discussed the Bones-versus-Bones election with Kerry and with first cousin Brinkley Thorne, one of Bush's fellow 1968 Bonesmen, who has remained close to the president. When I asked David Thorne why Kerry dismisses inquiries about the society, he said the Bones face-off is simply a source of amusement. "It's kind of an amazing coincidence, and so much elitism can be drawn from it. The accusation of all the mysteries attributed to Bones—is this the big one?" Thorne laughs. "I think John feels it's not relevant to the election, like marriage or divorce. It's a private matter. Bones is no less meaningful to George than it was to John, and I'm sure they both know of their own experience and they acknowledge that."

Certainly neither man is speaking about Bones in public. "It's a secret," Kerry deadpanned when Tim Russert asked him about Bones on

Meet the Press. "It's so secret we can't talk about it," Bush responded when Russert asked him a similar question in February 2004.

Despite political differences, most members view the upcoming election with a mixture of pride in the society and embarrassment at the increased scrutiny. As they see it, Bones will have a White House connection either way. "It's a win-win situation," says a 1960s Bonesman. "If there is a goddess, it looks like she is smiling on them both."

"EXTREME OXFORD"

By Brett Martin

FEBRUARY 2004

H

idden among the cow pastures and rolling meadows of Somerset, in the Southwest of England, Middlemoor Water Park features a muddy man-made waterskiing pond, a go-kart track, and a shack selling beer and snacks. But on November 24, 2002, Middlemoor's main attraction was somewhat more exotic: in a clearing behind the gravel parking lot stood a replica of a trebuchet—a medieval catapult—looming like an oil derrick against the sky. Twenty-six feet tall at rest, made of steel and rough timber, the trebuchet was, according to its builder, a onetime motorcycle salesman and scrapyard owner named David Aitkenhead, "a big, evil, savage-looking contraption." On this day, the machine was being prepared to violently hurl willing human beings several stories high and into a net 100 feet away.

It was a warm day and a crowd of at least 30 had gathered to watch the trebuchet in action. Most were Oxford University student members of the Oxford Stunt Factory, a private alternative- and extreme-sports club. They had arrived in a caravan organized by the head of the club, David "Ding" Boston. The majority had come as spectators. A handful, however—including an enthusiastic 19-year-old freshman biochemistry student from Bulgaria named Kostadine "Dino" Iliev Yankov—were intent on taking a turn.

The proceedings got rolling as the first daredevil was placed in the trebuchet's sling and then flung in a perfect, arcing parabola into the center of the net, which sat atop 26 stout telegraph poles on the other side of the clearing. Four more successful throws followed. "There was a half-hour between jumps," remembers Boston, who was videotaping the event from a position beyond the landing area. "It was really a question of keeping yourself busy as they adjusted the weights."

Finally, it was Yankov's turn. "I was looking through the video lens," says Boston, "and I saw the same thing I had seen on the previous throws except that, the moment when I expected him to come into the viewfinder, there was nothing. And then, milliseconds later, a very dull, heavy thud."

Yankov's body had missed the net by inches and come crashing to the earth, where he now lay in a broken heap. "You expected to see one of the bearings broken, or a wheel rolling away, or the net hanging, or something," Boston says. "But there was just Dino, on the ground, making the most ghastly, guttural sounds."

A helicopter arrived and rushed Yankov to a hospital in Bristol. But the catapult had sent him on a trajectory equivalent to being thrown over a house. By 7:30 P.M. he was dead. Aitkenhead and his partner, Richard Wicks, were arrested eight days later and were eventually charged with manslaughter. Their trial will take place sometime this year.

The sad story made a few headlines in the English papers and would likely have died as a three-line item in "news of the weird" blogs around the world if it hadn't been for the fact that Aitkenhead and Boston share a distinguished pedigree. Both men served time in the Dangerous Sports Club, a gathering of brilliant and adventurous souls that came together in Oxford in the late 70s and, in a burst of imagination, mischief, and style, more or less invented the world of alternative sports. In the decade when it burned brightest, the D.S.C. pioneered hang gliding, invented bungee jumping, sent a grand piano down the slopes at Saint-Moritz, Switzerland, and generally raised a good deal of witty, iconoclastic hell on several continents before going the way of all things that start out new and exciting and then inevitably run their course. The trebuchet accident was a tragic coda to this history, though exactly when—and if—the saga of the D.S.C. came to an end is among the most contentious questions of all.

At the beginning, middle, and end of any history of the Dangerous Sports Club is the inspiring, infuriating figure of David Kirke, its chairman, guiding spirit, and only member-for-life. In many ways, Kirke is the prototypical Oxford man. Born in 1945, he was the eldest of seven children. His father was a schoolmaster, and his mother was a concert pianist. The family wintered in Switzerland and summered in France, employed 15 servants, and drove around in a vintage Rolls-Royce—all at the last moment of British history when it was possible to enjoy such luxuries and still be considered middle-class. In 1964, Kirke entered Oxford's Corpus Christi College to study psychology and philosophy.

He was pursuing a graduate degree in 1977 when, along with fellow Oxford graduate student Edward Hulton, he set off for Saint-Moritz to give the famous Cresta Run toboggan track a whirl. The two men shared a distaste for anything in sport that smacked of professionalism. "What we hated was the way that formal sports had all these little, important bourgeois instructors saying, 'You've got to get through five-part exams to do this,'" Kirke says. The Cresta—exciting, but not truly dangerous—didn't cut it. Looking elsewhere, the two traveled to the Swiss resort of Klosters and met a young man named Chris Baker, the genial, ski-bum scion of a department-store family in Bristol, who was experimenting with hang gliders.

The first generation of gliders had only recently begun to arrive from California. It was a signal moment for do-it-yourself adventurers. "Hang gliding was a very significant departure," says Hugo Spowers, an engineer and ex–racecar designer who later concocted some of the D.S.C.'s more fantastical devices. "It set the tone for an awful lot of possibilities whereby the boundaries of human experience could be pushed back, for very small sums of money, by amateurs."

For Kirke, Baker's flying machines were a revelation. "Awestruck," he writes in his sprawling, unfinished history of the D.S.C., "we realized that someone out there . . . had built something that was so beautiful, so absolutely beyond bureaucracy and so totally dependent on using one's faculties that it was a work of art within an infinite frame." With characteristic bluster, Kirke convinced Baker that he was an experienced flier. After a fine takeoff and a less than fine landing, the men retired to a bar. There, over drinks (it's safe to assume that nearly any significant conversation concerning the D.S.C. was held over drinks), the idea of a Dangerous Sports Club was born. It would be committed, says Baker, "to going and doing somewhat silly or dangerous things which were fun and would annoy bureaucrats." In true Oxonian style, there would even be a club tie: a silver wheelchair, with a blood-red seat, set on funereal black.

Back in Oxford, the new club's members set about planning a series of "away days": a "Tesco Cresta Run" down very steep hills in shopping carts (this, 20 years before *Jackass*); running with the bulls at Pamplona while riding skateboards and carrying umbrellas; an aborted attempt to jump a car across Tower Bridge's open drawbridge. These were interspersed with more ambitious trips, including hang-gliding expeditions off of Mount Olympus (the first ever from that peak) and Mount Kilimanjaro. The abiding principle on all of these outings, says Kirke, was "one-third recklessness of innocence, tempered with two-thirds recklessness of contempt."

Meanwhile, the club's twin motifs of formal dress and abundant champagne were quickly set, and its growing reputation was attracting an eclectic group of Oxford undergraduates that included Alan Weston, an engineering student who went on to become one of the U.S. Air Force's top rocket scientists; Tim Hunt, who is now an agent for the Andy Warhol Foundation for the Visual Arts; and Phillip Oppenheim, a future member of Parliament and Treasury minister. "It was a very bleak period in England," says Xan Rufus-Isaacs, an early member who is now an entertainment lawyer in Los Angeles. "Thatcher had taken over. There was the whole punk movement. There was a very nihilistic atmosphere. And David was saying, 'Let's go do some stunts and stuff.' It seemed to be something interesting and different and, apart from anything else, humorous."

The press predictably ate up the image of renegade bluebloods, but it was only half true. The D.S.C. included the upper crust (Xan Rufus-Isaacs is more properly Lord Alexander Rufus-Isaacs, and another member, Tommy Leigh-Pemberton, who later died in a car accident, was the son of the governor of the Bank of England) but also members from the middle and working classes. Still, the class symbols were a potent form of branding. "We consciously pushed buttons that were English, specifically Oxford English," says Martin Lyster, who joined the club later and wrote the book *The Strange Adventures of the Dangerous Sports Club.* "If you're photographed with a bottle of champagne in your hand, it's not entirely an accident."

Burly, bearded, a decade older than most of the others, and with grand appetites for fine food, wine, and literature, Kirke played his Falstaff role to a T. That he was a bit of a rogue—particularly when given access to others' expense accounts—only added to the romantic image. His nickname was Uncle Dodge. "Wives, girlfriends, mothers loathe David," says Rufus-Isaacs. "They see this creature dragging off their little loved ones and putting them in places where they can get seriously hurt."

Maternal types were right to fret over one of the more spectacular away days: a cocktail party held on Rockall, a fleck of stormy granite more than 300 miles off the coast of Scotland. "What do people do in London? They have drinks parties in Chelsea or wherever," says Kirke. "So we would have a drinks party as far away as possible." Engraved invitations were sent out, requesting black-tie. "We invited all sorts of women who, curiously enough, suddenly developed prior engagements," Kirke says, sighing merrily.

On the way to the port, the gang stopped to lift a sign reading INVALID TOILET from a restroom. They sailed for five days through Force 9 gales. ("At first, it was so awful, it was kind of entertaining," says Alan Weston. "Then we all started getting sick.") At one point, they narrowly avoided sinking by plugging a leak in the hull with a champagne cork. Finally, the sailors clambered up one of the island's 70-foot cliffs and spent the night drinking champagne and dancing to the Beach Boys. When it was time to go, Kirke and Chris Baker leapt off a cliff into the ocean. The INVALID TOILET sign was left behind, affixed to a plaque that claimed the rock for England.

'Oxford is like a fabulously interesting railway station," David Kirke tells me over lunch, "with fascinating people coming and going all the time." We had met at a pub across the street from the city's famous Blackwell's Bookstore where Kirke was holding court with a group that included a Jamaican Ph.D. candidate, a silent, mustachioed ex-officer of the Royal Air Force, and Shakespeare scholar Anthony Nuttall. After a few drinks, we headed to lunch nearby. Since I was paying, Kirke brought one of his friends—a septuagenarian banker named Ronnie who was leaving the next day for a windsurfing expedition in Sweden.

Nobody who has ever lunched with David Kirke is likely to forget the experience. Throughout the meal, he keeps up an intoxicating and baffling monologue—a running patchwork of erudition, circumlocution, conspiracy theories, shameless name-dropping (with particular attention to family lineage and whose father flew which aircraft in the

war), lapses into French and Latin, aphorism upon aphorism and anecdote upon anecdote, related with the gusto of a man who has dined out
on them for years. Except for a spell as drinks columnist for the laddie
magazine *Men Only*, Kirke hasn't held anything as bourgeois as a day job
in decades, relying instead on the kindness of friends and sponsors. The
bearlike bulk of Kirke's younger days is gone, but the beard remains. At
58, he looks at least 10 years older.

Alone among its members, Kirke has devoted his life to the D.S.C.
To him, the club was always about more than a mere adrenaline fix.
It was a political, philosophical, and artistic enterprise. Kirke's heroes
include Rimbaud, T. E. Lawrence, and Antoine de Saint-Exupéry, the
early aviator and author of *The Little Prince,* who disappeared over the
Sahara at age 44. "The D.S.C. was never a thrill-seeking organization,"
he says. "We're interested in new things. You make a fool of yourself,
your girlfriend leaves you, you lose money, but you may have advanced
things a tiny little half-inch. It's a vocation, strangely enough, not that
different from a Catholic priest."

Kirke was in Indonesia, thousands of miles from Somerset, when
Dino Yankov was killed, and neither he nor the D.S.C. has been legally
implicated in the death. Nevertheless, he is intent on participating in
Aitkenhead and Wicks's defense. "This is an extraordinary test case, about
the right to experiment, at personal risk, versus social responsibility," he
says, pointing out that an average of nine people are killed each year
playing cricket.

Yankov had signed a release concerning the dangers involved with
the trebuchet. But if it can be shown that the trebuchet's operators were
negligent (owing to Britain's strict contempt-of-court laws, the prosecution won't release any details of its investigation before the trial), the two
may face an uphill battle.

According to barrister Graham Blower, who handles many leading
criminal cases in London, the argument that Yankov was a consenting
adult will be of little use to the defendants. English law going back as far
as 1846—in a case involving the trampling of an allegedly drunk man

by a speeding horse and carriage—holds that a victim's own recklessness does not excuse the actions of the accused. "You can't say, 'He's a grown adult. He should have known better,'" says Blower. The releases and club membership forms, he says, are often "literally not worth the paper they're printed on."

"Look," says Kirke, "if Lindbergh had crashed into the Atlantic, he would have been flown right back to the U.S. and thrown in jail for multiple fraud and massive debt. Like all pioneers, he took huge risks."

But doesn't the equation change when those risks are being marketed to others? Kirke won't answer directly.

"I don't want to see these guys go to prison," he says with a sigh. "In part because, having done their catapult jump . . . it's an extraordinary sensation."

Two events in the Dangerous Sports Club's history magnificently crystallized the group's multi-pronged mandate for thrills, art, anti-authoritarian symbolism, and creative transport. In the process, they made the club internationally famous.

Clifton Suspension Bridge is a masterpiece of Victorian engineering—a delicate filament strung 245 feet above the river Avon, between the cities of Bristol and Clifton. As the plaques on either end advertising the Good Samaritans' suicide-hotline number attest, it's a structure that fairly demands to be jumped off of.

In 1979, Chris Baker was living in an apartment 200 yards from the bridge. At the time, he was using bungee cords to tie his hang gliders to the roof of his car. "It was my turn to provide some entertainment for the club," remembers Baker, who now owns and runs a bucolic cemetery not far from Bristol. "I remembered that, at school, we were shown a film of New Guinea vine jumpers who would build these bamboo towers, tie one end of the vine to the tower, the other to their ankle, and dive off," he says. "The idea of getting rolls of bungee cord and jumping off the bridge came up. And I thought, Yes. Why not?"

Baker says he brought the idea to the club (Kirke disputes the account slightly, saying the conception was more of a group effort), and Alan Weston and fellow engineering student Simon Keeling had friends run some computer simulations. The idea of testing the principle with weights was a nonstarter. "We couldn't very well call ourselves the Dangerous Sports Club and attach weights and see what happened," says Baker. Invitations were sent out for April Fools' Day 1979.

An enormous party was held at Baker's house on the night before the jump. Baker's girlfriend had stopped speaking to him on the grounds that he was about to kill himself, but midway through the party she called and said she had changed her mind. "So I left them all destroying my apartment and went to London to collect her," Baker remembers. "I got back at half past six in the morning and they were all in a horrible state. I said, 'Right, I'm just going to change into tails.' 'Ready for the undertaker' was the joke."

In the meantime, two of Weston's sisters had independently called the police, imploring them to stop their brother from committing suicide. The bridge had been staked out since dawn. While Baker was changing, the cops finally gave up, leaving a precious window of opportunity.

"It never crossed my mind that they would jump without me," Baker says, still a touch rueful. "It was my idea, my ropes, my *bridge*, as far as I was concerned. So I was walking back from the apartment and there are the bastards, jumping off the bridge."

Baker at least had the consolation of watching his idea succeed mightily. Kirke went first, clutching a bottle of champagne that unfortunately tumbled from his hand on the way down. Weston, Keeling, and Tim Hunt followed. Kirke had alerted the *Daily Mail*, and photos were quickly beamed around the world. "We want to trigger a worldwide craze," he told the paper. "That's our master plan."

For a while, at least, the craze remained a club affair. History's second bungee jump was off the Golden Gate Bridge, which brought Kirke and company even more attention. Next was a jump off Colorado's

Royal Gorge Bridge, filmed for the television program *That's Incredible!* Soon the club began staging bungee exhibitions around England, leaping from cranes at county fairs, store openings, and other gatherings. In 1981, a short film, *The History of the Dangerous Sports Club*, combining footage from the Kilimanjaro expedition and the Clifton-bridge jump, was released. The club even received the imprimatur of a high priest of subversive British silliness, Monty Python's Graham Chapman, who would go on to participate in several group activities. Kirke calls Chapman, who died in 1989, "the mischievous older brother I never had."

In 1983, Hugo Spowers had the idea for a bike race down the Matterhorn mountain in the Alps. The cyclists naturally would have parachutes to help them navigate the terrain. From there, it was a small step to sending all kinds of strange objects down the slopes, leading to the D.S.C.'s second great legacy: the surreal ski races.

"Think Fellini" was Kirke's instruction, and indeed the collection of vehicles that arrived in Saint-Moritz that winter would have pleased the director. They ranged from an ironing board, a baby carriage, and a tandem bicycle to a grand piano, a Louis XIV dining set, and a full crew boat, seating eight people. All were mounted on skis, and all provided magnificent crashes. "Kirke knocked himself unconscious by taking a C5 [electric scooter] down the slope," says Mark Chamberlain, who—improbably, considering the company—had earned the nickname Mad Child for his willingness to try anything. "He must have been clocking about 95 m.p.h. They were quite suicidal machines, really."

The accompanying parties were equally wild, even by club standards. In attendance was the club's mascot, Eric, a life-size mannequin in a full-body cast with an impressive hard-on. "It was incredibly hedonistic," says Chamberlain. "I remember Hugo Spowers swinging on a chandelier at the Park Hotel in Saint-Moritz and it coming crashing down. We were setting off C1 explosive charges everywhere. It got to the point where we were jumping off the bar, trying to get into a cart filled with ice."

The race was repeated in 1984 and 1985 with ever more elaborate devices, culminating in an aborted attempt to send a London double-decker bus down the slopes. Rufus-Isaacs had purchased the bus, and the group drove it to Saint-Moritz with great fanfare, attracting gawkers all along the way. Echoes of Ken Kesey and the Merry Pranksters were entirely apt; with the psychedelic revolution spent, the D.S.C. had taken the same impulse and found a way to turn it outward, pushing the boundaries of experience with their bodies rather than their minds, while tweaking authority and having a grand time doing it. It was perhaps their last truly great moment.

"I am absolutely hopeless at business," David Kirke says. By all accounts, this is a vast understatement. As the 80s rolled on, the question of making some sort of living inevitably began to plague the D.S.C. The bungee-jumping exhibitions—organized by Chamberlain and Martin Lyster—were bringing in some money, but the club was also searching for alternative sources of income. One plan involved branding a vintage of D.S.C. wine, complete with a label depicting a ski-jumping waiter. This scheme ended with predictable results once the crates of wine arrived at club headquarters.

Another idea was to open club membership to the public. "We'd get these people who were willing to pay 50 quid a year so they could have a card that said, 'I'm a member of the D.S.C.,'" says Lyster. "We were grateful for their money. They came to the parties. And a few even got involved and became active members." David Aitkenhead was among them.

Aitkenhead had left school at 15 and ended up working in a Harley-Davidson dealership in Somerset, selling spare parts. In 1984 he happened to catch a screening of *The History of the Dangerous Sports Club* and was entranced. A year later he sent in his £50 and began tagging along on bungee jumps.

Even as a newcomer, Aitkenhead sensed that the original club was unraveling. "By the time I came along," he says, "a lot of the early members had gone. They were getting married, getting good jobs."

One by one, Kirke's Prince Hals were returning to the straight world. "David used to say that the one thing that united us all was a fear of a regular job," says Rufus-Isaacs. "It's a nice student ideal, but you can't fucking live like that."

Those who remained were finding the relationship with Kirke increasingly strained. "Martin and I would go all over the place doing these shows and we would see fuck-all of the money," says Chamberlain, now a cinematographer who works with Aardman Animation, in Bristol. (Kirke responds, "Every single penny we made with the D.S.C. would go out to every member of the D.S.C.")

There were bigger projects—a helium-filled kangaroo floating across the Channel, a hang-gliding expedition to Ecuador, a doomed effort to send a giant inflatable "melon ball" (courtesy of Midori) across the Thames—but these all required well-heeled sponsors, a class of people Kirke was almost pathologically adept at pissing off. "I think he had a fear of success," says Chamberlain. "Whenever things looked like they were going properly, he'd panic and make sure there was a complication."

Hugo Spowers went as far as to begin organizing his own group, the Alternative Sports Club. "I got very frustrated with his spectacular ability to bugger things up all the time," says Spowers. "You won't see a sponsor who's dealt with the D.S.C. twice." Kirke responded with an angry volley of legal threats, and Spowers backed down. "He's fantastically creative, particularly when he's trying to destroy something," Spowers says.

Kirke's fierce sense of proprietorship continues to this day. When he discovered that Lyster was publishing a book that would pre-empt his own, unfinished account of the club's history (for which Kirke had received an advance from Penguin Putnam in 1989), he responded with the fury of a stung bear. His enemies "suspect I'm walking wounded and, like hyenas, they can bite pieces off me and slink away," he wrote to Hubert Gibbs, a longtime D.S.C. member unlucky enough to have assumed the role of club "arbiter of fair play." To Chris Baker he wrote, "To draw an analogy, anyone who volunteers for the British army who then volunteers for the I.R.A. knows it's within the terms of the game that he will be hunted down for treason and killed on sight by former colleagues." Later in that letter, Kirke got more to the point: "But then you see that (despite all my efforts to spread the load) it has been one man's story throughout, even if it has been a memorable chapter or two in over 40 people's lives."

"When you get on David's shit list," says Lyster, "you get shit by the truckload."

But above and beyond personal and financial difficulties, the Dangerous Sports Club's biggest problem in the late 80s was simply that it was losing creative steam.

"There's a huge difference between being a group of friends having a laugh and then basically having to perform at given times," says Chris Baker. "Risking my life for my own entertainment was fair enough, but being a badly paid stuntman struck me as the worst of both worlds."

When Kirke struck a deal with a Japanese TV company in 1988 to produce a movie that would combine several new stunts with old footage, one of the few people left for him to turn to was David Aitkenhead. Aitkenhead quit his job and moved into a rented hangar in Shropshire to construct machines for the new stunts. One of these was a human catapult.

The Japanese film was eventually completed, but it was not without its costs. One ill-conceived segment involved rolling the now repurposed Midori melon ball down a mountain in Scotland. With a 20-knot wind blowing upward, the sphere quickly pulled loose of its moorings and ripped itself to shreds. More seriously, another stunt called for Kirke to be shot off a cliff in Ireland by a device used to launch drones from aircraft carriers. The team had ordered a specially molded seat to protect Kirke's back from the fearsome g-forces, but when it didn't arrive in time, Kirke went ahead with an improvised seat of foam and duct tape. Slow-motion footage of the shot shows Kirke nearly flattened as he's thrust forward, and the stunt left him with serious back injuries.

As if to underline the end of an era, Kirke's past sins also began catching up with him. After an incident involving a borrowed American Express card (Kirke claims it had more to do with some political intrigue involving Dick Cheney), he was charged with fraud and, several months later, fled to France. Spowers and Rufus-Isaacs tracked him down there, where he was sleeping on the floor of an unheated farmhouse. Eventually, Kirke served four and a half months of a nine-month sentence. "I had a sabbatical," he says, "much enjoyed and appreciated."

Meanwhile, two New Zealand entrepreneurs had begun offering bungee jumping to the paying public. Soon Aitkenhead had started one of the first commercial bungee operations in the U.K. In Oxford, Ding Boston, who had been peripherally involved with the D.S.C. until falling out with Kirke, created the Oxford Stunt Factory, which marketed alternative sports to students and staged bungee stunts for TV and film. What had been the D.S.C.'s ultimate anarchic expression was well on its way to becoming the thrill of choice for a generation of midlife-crisis sufferers—organized, bureaucratic, and very profitable.

Aitkenhead rode the boom for several years—at one point jumping as many as 400 people per weekend. Under the D.S.C. flag, he and a partner also found time to sail a modified septic tank across the Channel—a stunt that lacked something of the panache of classic D.S.C. events, though Kirke still showed up in France to buy a round of drinks. As the bungee market grew saturated, Aitkenhead got out and opened a scrapyard in Somerset.

Visions of a human catapult, however, stuck with him. The device in the Japanese film had been a Roman-style catapult, with a seat on the beam. Aitkenhead himself, looking somewhat awkward in the requisite top hat and tails, had been thrown off it into an Irish river. But a Roman catapult, Aitkenhead and Richard Wicks quickly determined, would not be sufficient to send customers the desired distance: 100 feet. For that, they would need a trebuchet, a far more powerful machine that uses a sling to transfer more energy to its missile.

In the early 1990s, an eccentric Englishman named Hew Kennedy had built an enormous trebuchet on his Shropshire estate. He was making news by flinging old cars, dead cows, and burning pianos into an empty field. Aitkenhead visited several times, at first to see whether the huge machine could be used to fire humans (the g-forces, Kennedy told him, would kill a person) and then to gather tips for his own, smaller version.

Construction began on weekends in the front yard of Aitkenhead's countryside home. After several months, the men had created a machine capable of throwing a 100-kilogram test weight 100 feet. "We thought, Right, that's the difficult bit done. But little did we realize that what we'd done was the easy bit," says Aitkenhead. A year passed, spent experimenting with nets. Finally, the two decided that it was time for a test run. "I was happy for Richard to be the first man to do it, and it worked beautifully. Then, the next day, I did it and it worked beautifully again."

In 2000, Richard Wicks's girlfriend, Stella Young, was thrown. The throw itself was perfect, but Young bounced out of the net and broke her pelvis, making nationwide headlines. With help from Kirke, the men negotiated with MTV, which wanted to film the trebuchet, to fund a larger net. On his 55th birthday, Kirke himself had a go, with local TV crews in attendance.

"My cousin Tony had the imprint of a net on his forehead. Someone twisted their foot. David Kirke pulled a muscle in his neck. Richard landed on his head and it went numb for half an hour on one side. I twisted my ankle. But it was all part and parcel of what was going on," Aitkenhead says. "It was quite obviously dangerous and that's all there was to it. There were no complaints."

In 2001, Aitkenhead gave away the scrapyard, sold his house, and devoted himself to building an improved trebuchet at Middlemoor Water Park. The "Mark II" was ready six months later. "All the while, I was in touch with Ding Boston," Aitkenhead says. "He said, 'Look, if you do anything with this, let us know. We'll come down and we're happy to help, get involved. Or if you just want to throw us, great.'"

Boston—whose Stunt Factory has been banned from setting up

at Oxford's annual Fresher's Fair, where clubs recruit newly arrived freshmen—offers a more passive account of his involvement. Stunt Factory members, he maintains, had already heard about the trebuchet and were intent on giving it a try. "I ask anybody what they would do in a situation like this. You can either say 'No,' which in my experience with intelligent 18-year-olds goes nowhere. Or, if you care for people who are obviously going to go anyway, you accompany them and hope the collective experience will help [keep them safe]." Nevertheless, a link on the Stunt Factory's Web site, later removed, listed human catapulting as one of the club's activities, showed pictures of the trebuchet in action, and promised, "That could be you. No, really."

In any event, Stunt Factory members attended three separate events with the trebuchet. By the time Dino Yankov fell to his death, the machine had been fired successfully at least 40 times.

Since investigators are staying mum until the trial, what exactly went wrong remains a mystery. "Trebuchets were known to be extremely accurate. That's why they were still used for 100 or so years after cannons came in," says Colonel Wayne Neel, a professor of mechanical engineering at the Virginia Military Institute who was one of five experts called in to examine the trebuchet. "You could pretty much put a shot in a bushel basket at a couple of hundred yards."

There are a limited number of easily changed variables determining the shot's distance, says Neel: the length of the sling used; the angle of the peg on top of the trebuchet's beam, off which the sling flies; the amount of counterweight on the beam. "The things that can go wrong did go wrong," Neel says. "The things that can be adjusted, they just didn't have them adjusted right." He pauses. "But, of course, basically the thing that went wrong was doing it in the first place."

For what it's worth, D.S.C. alumni, almost to a man, say that they would never have taken a ride on the trebuchet themselves. When they discuss the accident, it's not long before old-fashioned Oxford snobbery peeks through. Nearly all offer up some pointed variation on the construction "David Aitkenhead is a nice guy, but . . ."

Kirke shakes his head sadly, saying, "This never would have happened if they were Oxford boys."

Some say that the tragedy was the inevitable result of marketing thrills to the public—a significant departure from the D.S.C. of old. "We were gentlemen adventurers who respected other people, did things themselves. We never, ever harmed anybody apart from ourselves," says Mark Chamberlain. "When that happens, something is missing. And it has to do with the reasons why people are doing it."

In a larger way, the tragedy may simply be the product of hanging on too long. "The D.S.C., in my view, stopped functioning around 1986. David Aitkenhead just came along when Kirke needed new playmates," says Rufus-Isaacs.

"I've had some of the most fantastic times, with some of the most extraordinary people, doing the most unusual things, all over the world. And I only have one person to thank, and that's David Kirke," Chamberlain says. "He's living 20 years ago. Dave Aitkenhead is a nice enough guy, but . . . the people who made up the D.S.C. were all real geniuses, in their own way. The thing is, you don't come up with things on your own. We bounced ideas off each other. I don't think there will ever be a group of people like the D.S.C. again, and why should there be?"

So, is there still a Dangerous Sports Club? Kirke bristles at the question. "There's no way that I can take on Xan, because he's bourgeois. I can't take on Alan Weston, because he's under U.S. Air Force regulations. I can't take on Martin, because he's been 'corrupted.' But we've got people in 50 countries. There are Jesuit missionaries in the western part of China who directly relate. I have a guy in Algeria who's very good. David Aitkenhead is still there. We're also political. It's an incredibly movable feast. And I'm an odd little cocked-up, goof-up, walkabout spider in the middle of the web."

With the trial approaching, David Aitkenhead has moved in with his parents, picking up construction work to make ends meet. His trebuchet still stands in the clearing at Middlemoor Water Park, rust creeping across its base and weeds sprouting up through the holes in the net and over the spot where Dino Yankov came to rest.

David Kirke says that it's finally time to complete his own book about the D.S.C. "Cervantes didn't begin *Don Quixote* until he was 58," he says. "[T. E. Lawrence's] *Seven Pillars of Wisdom* was printed in a private edition of 150 books. If you're going for literature, you're in for the long haul."

For the past several years, the chairman of the D.S.C. has also been trying to get a new project off the ground: a 25-foot-tall inflatable replica of a winged horse that Kirke hopes to fly 500 miles, from Mount Olympus into Libya. The 11-page pitch for the Pegasus Project asks for £100,000 and promises "a totally original, world first project."

"I would like to have one more flying machine," Kirke says wistfully, looking very tired. "I feel if I can get Pegasus off the ground I just might find myself in conversational distance from Saint-Exupéry in the next life."

After our lunch, I return from the bathroom to find Kirke talking with three nervous-looking undergrads. "Are you a don?" one asks him. "Be irreverent. Ask questions," Kirke signs off before adjusting his beret and disappearing out the door and down the streets of Oxford.

Earlier, he had outlined one other dream project. This one involved a return to Rockall: "What I really want to do is go back there again with two Wagnerian tenors and a Yamaha Clavinova and have a concert on that rock. And somehow or other we record it so that, long after we're all dead, people will be enjoying the sounds of Wagner floating over the sea."

It's a lovely idea, with all the grace and wit and imagination worthy of the Dangerous Sports Club. The only question is whether anybody will be listening.

[Aitkenhead and Wicks were acquitted of manslaughter charges in 2004.]

MORALITY TALES

"DEADLY DEVOTION"

By Sam Tanenhaus

MARCH 2000

One of the last happy nights in Lissa Roche's strange, tragic life came on a weekend last August, when she joined some 200 others at a picnic ushering in the new academic year at Hillsdale College. Faculty, staff, friends, and trustees gathered in the Slayton Arboretum, the most beautiful site on the southern Michigan campus, with its pond and groves and lovingly tended plantings. It was a perfect evening and the event had a touch of elegance. The tables, arranged in a clearing, had linen cloths and bottles of wine and candles that flickered in the soft breeze.

Everyone present knew this corner of the "arb" well, but few knew it as intimately as Lissa (pronounced Lisa), who had recommended it as the setting for the picnic. For longer than a decade, she and her husband, George C. Roche IV, a lecturer in history at Hillsdale, had lived with their son just up the incline, in a small stone cottage owned by the college. Often, when the pressures of her many professional duties at Hillsdale grew too intense, Lissa would slip out the back door, unlatch the wooden gate behind her house, and descend the stone steps to the fieldstone gazebo, her favorite spot—a sanctuary—to read or think.

That was before Lissa's family had changed residences. In August 1998 her father-in-law, George C. Roche III, the president of Hillsdale College, had suddenly separated from his wife of 44 years, June Roche, expelling her from Broadlawn, the pillared presidential mansion. Since he liked being surrounded by kin, and also needed help because of his health—he suffered from advanced diabetes and often had strong insulin reactions—Roche had invited his firstborn son and his family to share the 28 rooms with him. Lissa was elated. Moving into Broadlawn signaled her arrival at the pinnacle of "the Hillsdale family."

Now, a year later, as she circulated among the guests in the arboretum, fragrant with Norway pines and juniper, Lissa seemed not simply at ease but in command. When she excused herself to huddle with her tall, distinguished father-in-law, the pair formed a tableau that could have served as a heraldic image of Hillsdale: the college's two most visible public faces, both members of America's right-wing elite. George Roche, 63, was a peerless fund-raiser and riveting speaker who in 1998 alone had brought in donations totaling $45 million. Lissa was his indispensable partner. They occupied offices 30 feet apart on the third floor of Central Hall, the administration building whose clock tower dominates the small campus and its grouping of plain brick buildings. They appeared at high-powered lectures and gatherings of the faithful and collaborated on books that spread the Hillsdale gospel of free markets and family values and railed against the evils of the welfare state. George was listed as the author, but, according to a colleague, it was Lissa who did much of the research, drafted the text, and shepherded the result into print; she was, among other things, managing editor of the Hillsdale College Press. It is the rare conservative who didn't meet or speak with Lissa Roche at some point over the past 15 years. "She was familiar with the whole conservative movement," says Mickey Craig, a professor of political science at the college. "She knew it really well, all the players."

George Roche, as everyone on campus was aware, demanded loyalty, and no one exhibited it more fiercely than his daughter-in-law. While Roche's son struggled to find a useful, rewarding place in the Hillsdale firmament—many suspected he would have been far happier elsewhere, out from under his father's long shadow—Lissa and George shared a consuming passion for the college and its ideological mission. Others might complain of Roche's autocratic ways, marked by capriciousness and overweening ego. But Lissa brooked no criticism of him and interpreted any skeptical remark as a breach of faith. "Lissa thought, This is the man who's going to save the West," says Craig. In her eyes Roche was "the second Reagan, at least."

And with the move to Broadlawn her position was reified. The big house symbolized what Hillsdale had become under the leadership of George Roche, the site of lavish dinners and exciting cocktail parties. Ronald Reagan, Margaret Thatcher, and the elder George Bush, among others, had been entertained there. At age 40, Lissa had become its mistress, slipping comfortably into the role of "the First Lady of Hillsdale," radiating purpose. In a typically forceful territorial claim, she began a major renovation of the mansion.

Her triumph was plain to the 200 guests gathered in the arboretum last summer. "She was floating around, queen-bee-like," says a friend who sat near Lissa that evening. This friend also remembers a moment when Lissa gazed pensively at the gazebo. It had been made into a bar for the picnic, and the late-August light brought out the subtle hues of its large stones, extracted from Michigan farmland. It was lovely, wasn't it?, Lissa asked. She added, "I wish I'd been married there." But that wouldn't have been practical. Lissa and her husband, called IV (pronounced eye-vee), had been married in the winter—in fact, their wedding took place the day after they both graduated from Hillsdale, in December 1977. The ceremony was held at an Episcopal church in Hillsdale, with a reception at the Dow Center, the drab building where the college holds conferences and puts up overnight visitors. Lissa was only 19 at the time, a young woman in a hurry. She had arrived on campus at age 17 and completed her coursework in only two and a half years.

It was poignant, but a little jarring, that Lissa should recall an ancient disappointment at this moment of exultation. But sudden mood shifts of this kind weren't surprising to those who knew Lissa well. Often her bantering manner would fall away, and it was possible to glimpse hidden depths of sorrow and regret, as if the path she had trod so purposefully had been far more taxing than anyone guessed. Caught between vulnerability and tough-minded disdain, "she was unhappy in general," says a friend. "She would always have biting remarks to say to people, but she would do it with her arm around you." And yet, says another, "she had a side to herself that could move you to tears."

The climax of the evening came when Violetta Shtromas stood before the gathering and sang a song—she had a lovely voice—in memory of her husband, Alex, a professor of Eastern European studies who had recently died. She introduced the song with some tender remarks about Alex that she delivered unself-consciously, as if to a small gathering. It was easy to mock the phrase "Hillsdale family," but at times it really did seem that every member of the community was tightly linked to everyone else. As is so often the case at small colleges in rural settings, Hillsdale's faculty, educated and sophisticated but thrown back on its own resources—the nearest cultural center, Ann Arbor, is an hour and a half away—forms a densely layered society, as interrelated as the world of a 19th-century novel, in which friendships and enmities reach over generations, entangling lives in surprising ways.

As Violetta spoke about life and love, one colleague listened raptly. "I had lost a friend earlier that year, and Violetta's speech moved me to tears," she later recalled. Then she heard a voice, Lissa's, break in harshly. "Christ, you didn't know Alex." The colleague was taken aback. Lissa's contempt was so raw, the lack of sympathy so palpable. It was all the stranger since Lissa was a professed Christian who had edited an anthology of religious stories, songs, and prayers. What the colleague didn't know, though she would learn soon enough, was that a battle was raging inside Lissa Roche.

Those who witnessed Lissa's curious behavior leading up to that August evening are haunted by it today, because six weeks later Lissa made a final visit to her beloved gazebo and never returned. Shortly after the faculty picnic Lissa's life was overturned. In mid-September her father-in-law abruptly remarried. His 56-year-old bride, Dean Hagan, reportedly a nurse from Louisville whom he had met two years before at one of the many lectures he gave, became the new mistress of Broadlawn, and Lissa was banished once again to the stone cottage, a block away, with IV and their 20-year-old son, George V. (Discussions of the Roches can resemble dissertations on the British monarchy.) It all happened without warning and with startling rapidity. "She was shattered when Dean came on the scene," says a friend who saw Lissa in late September.

Plunged into depression, Lissa briefly quit her important job at the college and, abandoning her husband and son, fled to Los Angeles, where her twin sister, Laura, lived. But after two days she came back, resuming her life and her professional obligations. Still, it was a struggle. Sunday, October 17, was a particularly difficult day. Lissa and IV were up before dawn, tending to his father, who had suffered another of his frequent insulin reactions. The couple visited him at the hospital and then returned home, exhausted and emotionally depleted. At about 12:30 P.M., Lissa sent IV out of the house to look in on his 92-year-old grandmother, Margaret, who was visiting Broadlawn. With her husband gone, Lissa took a stainless-steel Ruger .357-magnum revolver—part of the gun collection IV, an avid outdoorsman, kept in a locked cabinet—and exited the house.

Five minutes later, when IV returned, he saw the back door ajar and the gate unlatched. Worried about Lissa's state of mind, he scrambled down the slope to the clearing, saw that the pine needles on the path had been disturbed, and found his wife on the gazebo's fieldstone floor in a bright pool of blood. He touched Lissa's neck, feeling for the carotid pulse. There was none. He ran back to the house and dialed 911. "Hello, I'd like to report a suicide," he said. "My wife shot herself." He was standing at the street corner outside his house, holding a portable phone, when the police arrived. IV climbed into their car and pointed the way to the arboretum. There was an entrance near the gazebo. The body, still warm, was clad in navy shorts that bore the words "Hillsdale College," a white T-shirt, and white L.L. Bean tennis shoes. A Saint Christopher medal hung from her neck on a gold chain. There was a pillow nearby: possibly Lissa had used it to conceal the handgun on her brief walk to the gazebo.

According to the police report, the officers on the scene were taken aback by IV's lack of emotion. On the way to the police station, he asked them to stop at Burger King. He had "stomach problems," he explained, and food helped him in moments of stress. At the station he calmly described his own movements and Lissa's that day and earlier. In the eyes of the police, his detachment raised questions. The brutality of the act was shocking—a single bullet had been fired into the head—yet "never once did George IV cry, even while making numerous phone calls from the station," one of the patrolmen noted in his report. One call was to Robert Blackstock, the college provost and an attorney, who counseled IV to tell the police all he knew and to let them search the stone cottage. Another was to Mickey Craig, IV's racquetball partner. Craig remembers IV's exact words as they came over the telephone line, chilling in their finality. "Lissa shot herself. She has died."

Three weeks passed before the police learned the whole story, first from George C. Roche III and then from his son. Lissa Roche's death, it emerged, had not come as a complete surprise to her family—rather, it was the culmination of a 10-hour nightmare. According to the police report, just two hours before her death Lissa had told her husband that for 19 years she had been conducting a clandestine affair with his father. She made this astonishing allegation in the hospital room where her father-in-law was recuperating. His new wife, of barely five weeks, was at his side.

In the days that followed, a despondent and confused IV waited for an apology or explanation from his father. None came. In fact, shortly after the funeral, George Roche III departed to Hawaii for a delayed honeymoon with his bride. On October 21, IV frantically unburdened himself to a friend and on the 27th repeated Lissa's allegation to Ronald Trowbridge, the college's vice president for external communications. Trowbridge acted swiftly. On November 1, Hillsdale's trustees announced that Roche was being suspended, and on November 10 he resigned, though he had reportedly denied Lissa's allegation. As quickly as that Roche, the man who since 1971 had been synonymous with Hillsdale, was gone.

By now rumors had engulfed the campus and were spreading far beyond. While George Roche III, back from Hawaii, remained inside Broadlawn, hints of Lissa's claim appeared in the Toledo *Blade* and *The Detroit News*. In its on-line edition, *National Review*, the conservative fortnightly that had long championed Roche and Hillsdale, published an account of the burgeoning scandal based on a lengthy interview with IV in which he described Lissa's tale of adultery. (In a brief phone call with *Vanity Fair*, IV stood by the *National Review* article as a "verbatim" account from "my perspective.") Reporters from *The New York Times*, *Time*, *Newsweek*, and *U.S. News & World Report* descended on the campus. Meanwhile, college officials, trapped inside a conflagration, were desperately battling the flames, even as they reminded the world that only two people knew the truth about the alleged affair, and that one of them was dead, while the other had dropped from sight. As of January, George Roche's whereabouts were a mystery. His ex-wife, June, believes he may be in Colorado. A college spokesman thinks he is in Michigan. "I haven't spoken with him in some time" is all IV will say. The office of the lawyer who represented Roche in his divorce told *Vanity Fair* he does not know his client's whereabouts and so could not relay questions to him about the events discussed in this article. The lawyer had no comment himself.

F̲ew in "the Hillsdale family" have trouble believing Lissa Roche's claims. Why, they ask themselves, would she kill herself with a monstrous lie on her lips? They had noticed for years that the relationship between George and Lissa Roche seemed unnaturally intense. The two were bound, it was clear, by more than ideology. Their personalities, both so large, both compounded of romantic idealism and hard-minded practicality, seemed perfectly meshed. Those who observed the two over the years, even from a casual distance, have no trouble imagining that Lissa's worship, simultaneously abject and aggressive, could have been taken by George as his seigneurial reward, like the silver Porsche he had received from Hillsdale's trustees soon after his arrival in 1971 and the compensation package that *Forbes* estimated at $524,000 for 1998 (placing him among the five highest-paid college presidents in the land).

Colleagues also noticed a kind of complicity between Lissa and George. Lissa, for example, did not hide her scorn for her mother-in-law, an attitude that mirrored what some observers say was George's mistreatment of June. IV too served as the butt of Lissa's cruel wit. She belittled him constantly. He was "worthless," a "loser" whose career had never amounted to much—when it seemed plain to some that he was suffocating under the control of his father. All this had simmered for years, felt but unspoken, like so much else at Hillsdale, where silence had become a reflex, for in truth the Hillsdale family was a repressive unit whose patriarch ruled with an iron fist. No one questioned George Roche's authority: the fate met by campus dissidents was well known. Some were hounded from their jobs, made so miserable they quit, on occasion abandoning tenured positions, or leaving academia altogether.

And so, when Lissa's corpse was found, grief mingled with shock and a collective sense of guilt. Something had been badly amiss but no one had dared acknowledge it, let alone try to stop it. That feeling persists today, along with the suspicion that Lissa Roche meant to send a message with her death. In some way she was inviting the world to look past Hillsdale's picture-perfect façade.

It's an intriguing idea, since Lissa wasn't just George Roche's most ardent defender and idolater. She was also a vital cog in Hillsdale's imagemaking machine, its relentless public-relations office and colossal fund-raising apparatus. She organized the college's Center for Constructive Alternatives (C.C.A.)—a program that brought public figures such as Tom Wolfe and Malcolm Muggeridge to the campus for lectures. She orchestrated the lavish off-campus seminars held in various plush locations as far away as the California coast. She was also managing editor of *Imprimis* (pronounced im-PRY-mus), a monthly newsletter whose circulation soared from 250,000 in 1990 to nearly a million today, a staggering number for so small an institution, even if, as in this case, the publication was sent to subscribers free of charge.

If Lissa's thoughts were clear at all on that Sunday in October, when the campus was slowly rousing itself after the hiatus of fall break, she understood that her act would have major repercussions. "When Lissa Roche killed herself I said to a colleague, 'This will topple the king,'" recalls Melinda von Sydow, whose husband, Ralph, retired in 1997 after teaching music at Hillsdale for 35 years. "Her suicide was a revenge suicide, violent and in a public place, in a 'temple-like' structure and in broad daylight. She designed her death to destroy George Roche." And, perhaps, to desecrate the most hallowed site on campus.

Whatever her intentions, Lissa succeeded in shining a powerful beam on Hillsdale. Its administration and trustees are now absorbing harsh criticism, much of it coming from the conservative press, which has lately been losing patience with movement leaders from Henry Hyde to Newt Gingrich who have been exposed as hypocrites and dissemblers. "Roche is not only a creator but also a creature of the conservative counterculture," wrote *The Weekly Standard*, protected far too long by trustees who overlooked persistent rumors of his extramarital affairs rather than offend a matinee idol of the right gifted with prodigious fund-raising skills.

Why, many were asking, was Roche's resignation announced in a bland letter that gave no hint of wrongdoing on his part, accompanied by a self-serving statement from Roche himself? Why was Ronald Trowbridge, a college spokesman who had believed IV's account sufficiently to report it to the trustees, now hinting that Lissa had told many lies over the years and that her husband was lost in a pill-induced fog? And why did officials seem intent more on parrying the press than on getting to the bottom of Lissa Roche's allegations?

These questions disturbed one prominent Hillsdale supporter, former education secretary William Bennett, who resigned, very publicly, from the search committee formed to find a new president. Bennett issued a stinging indictment of the college and complained to reporters: "This poor woman is dead and the turn here [at Hillsdale] is, 'She's a pathological liar.' The whole thing just reeks." Barrett Kalellis, the school's current spokesman, says that Trowbridge's remarks "did not represent a strategic public-relations attack" but were instead an "avuncular" attempt, however "fumbling," to defend a despairing IV. As to Trowbridge's specific comments about Lissa's history of telling untruths, Kalellis says there is no official explanation, although the "general word on campus is *de mortuis nil nisi bonum*." Translation: If you can't say anything nice about the dead, say nothing at all.

Meanwhile, various names have been floated as candidates for a presidency no one seems to want. By mid-December former Indiana senator Dan Coats had said no, and the list had been whittled so small that Kenneth Starr's name surfaced in news reports. [Larry P. Arnn has served as president since 2000.]

Few dispute that George Roche III made Hillsdale a showcase of modern conservatism—"one of the 10 most important institutions in the conservative movement," according to John Fund, who sits on the editorial board of *The Wall Street Journal* and has often lectured at the campus. The transformation happened hard upon Roche's arrival at the school in 1971. A promising but minor member of the conservative establishment, he had been the director of seminars at the Foundation for Economic Education, or FEE, a libertarian think tank located in Irvington, New York, near the bank of the Hudson River. That job was a networking bonanza, especially for one bent on accruing power. Six feet two, rangy and athletic, raised in the Rocky Mountains, he was a "Louis L'Amour conservative" with a quick, retentive mind and a smile worthy of Jay Gatsby. "He was always very genial and friendly and diplomatic," says Bettina Greaves, a FEE colleague from that time. "He was an apple-polisher, and buttered people up." He also had remarkable energy, finding the time to write several books.

Roche had been at FEE five years when he learned Hillsdale College was looking for a new president. At the time it was one of several relatively obscure institutions (another is Grove City College, outside Pittsburgh) that had withstood the campus upheavals of the 60s, becoming havens for economic and political conservatives who felt marginalized in an academic world increasingly dominated by doctrinaire liberalism. Hillsdale was not a distinguished school, but not a bad one, either. Its chief merits were its age—founded in 1844, it is one of the oldest colleges in the Midwest—and its honorable history of having admitted women and blacks even before the Civil War. But the quality of its faculty was spotty, and its admission standards were low. Even today it accepts a generous 84 percent of its applicants, despite its high profile and stiffened curriculum. Mean S.A.T. scores of incoming students recently reached 1,220—very respectable but markedly lower than at Amherst, Swarthmore, Carleton, and other truly elite small colleges.

Roche was only 35 when, after he dazzled the board of trustees in an interview, he was awarded Hillsdale's presidency over 130 other candidates. His experience as an educator at that point was slight: some teaching at the University of Colorado, where he earned a Ph.D. in history, and two years at the Colorado School of Mines. But his impact on Hillsdale was immediate. His youth and vigor, and his erect military bearing (he had served in the Marines after receiving his undergraduate degree from Denver's Regis College), made a difference. So did the gleaming Porsche. But he owed much of his success to, of all things, the federal government. Under affirmative-action policies, Hillsdale, like every other institution whose students received federal aid, was required to fill out compliance forms which asked for data on students, including their ethnicity. Roche, citing the college's tradition of nondiscrimination, refused to go along and instead launched a private fund-raising campaign whose goal was to amass enough capital to loose Hillsdale from its federal tether. Hillsdale was now more than a struggling small college. It was a cause, a free-market David standing up to the statist Goliath. Roche went further, declaring that in its long history the college had never accepted "one cent" of federal aid. This was patently untrue. In fact, as late as 1974, three years into Roche's tenure, the college received a grant from the Department of Health, Education and Welfare. But Roche was on his way to becoming the single most effective fund-raiser in the entire conservative movement, and his falsifications were ignored.

A vast roll of donors—ranging from Jeffrey Coors of the beer dynasty to Florida drugstore tycoon Jack Eckerd to a widow who contributed a portion of her monthly Social Security check—would eventually pour some $325 million into Hillsdale's coffers. All were spellbound by Roche and his vision. He depicted the college as a shining city on a hill, a model not only for other schools but for the republic itself.

By her own account, Lissa Roche's infatuation with the man who became her father-in-law began even before she met him. It appears to date from 1974 or '75, when she was aboard a sailing ship operated by the Flint School, a unique experiment in education devised by a Florida couple, George and Betty Stoll. The school was run "like a big Outward Bound program," says a former classmate of Lissa's who later went on to Hillsdale.

Like most Flint School students, Lissa came from the educated middle class. She was born Lissa Jackson in California; she later gave Lancaster, a small city in the Mojave Desert near Edwards Air Force Base, as her hometown, her father having uprooted the family several times. He was a surgeon, while Lissa's mother, with cruel asymmetry, was afflicted with a severe arthritic condition that affected her hands. Eventually she would suffer a series of heart attacks. The strain of raising Lissa, her twin sister, Laura, and a younger daughter, Linda, was more than she could withstand. When Lissa was in her teens, the couple divorced and sent their daughters to private schools. Lissa chose the Flint School and never regretted it.

The idea of the "floating school" was to combine a physical adventure in self-reliance and self-discipline with the rigors of formal learning. Instead of studying in classrooms, pupils bunked in cabins aboard one of two vessels and toiled as crew members on long ocean voyages. Lissa's ship, the *Te Vega*, crossed the Atlantic and then explored the Mediterranean. It was not a vacation. The day began at 6:45 A.M. and sometimes ended with a shivering night watch on the open deck. Students could go ashore only in groups strictly organized by rank. Some rebelled, but others, including Lissa Jackson, said it changed their lives.

The curriculum could be life-transforming too. In addition to the three R's, Flint emphasized a fourth, "Reason," which drew deeply on the objectivist philosophy of Ayn Rand, with its heady mix of aggressiveness, egoism, and unrestrained capitalism. At Flint the main text was Rand's novel *Atlas Shrugged*. Its hero, John Galt, organizes a strike of the world's geniuses to protest the global triumph of conformism. "We read it every night," says Spring Wright, who attended the Flint School a year after Lissa. "We would gather with [the captain] and read it out loud and discuss it. Like we were having a Bible meeting." *Atlas Shrugged* is an immense text—more than 1,000 closely printed pages. Reading it aloud, and dissecting its fine points, took six months. By the end the teenagers were not simply well versed in the novel's apocalyptic events and passionately drawn characters—they had been indoctrinated in the whole of Rand's will-to-power philosophy. They also read widely in her other works and performed Rand's play *The Night of January 16th*, whose protagonist is a woman accused of murdering the lover she once worshiped. Confined to a ship, with as many as seven to a cabin, "Flinties" developed intense camaraderie. George Stoll, the headmaster, moved among them like a demigod. The female students were especially in awe, according to one alumna; this too was part of the Randian package. "An ideal woman is a man-worshipper," Rand once wrote, "and an ideal man is the highest symbol of mankind." Young women exposed to this doctrine sometimes spend years in search of a John Galt to worship and serve.

Lissa Jackson found hers early—in the person, or rather the image, of George Roche III. As a teenager, she saw his photo, possibly in a magazine or on a book jacket, and was instantly smitten. Roche was then 40, tall and rugged, with a captivating smile. Lissa already knew about Hillsdale; its free-market ideology attracted a number of Flint graduates in the 70s. Lissa became one of them, though few others can have swept onto the campus with so clearly formulated a plan. Years later, she would matter-of-factly describe how as a teenager she had been attracted to its president, but "knowing he was married I came to Hillsdale and settled for his son." A friend of Lissa's remembers her telling this story on two separate occasions. Her tone was flippant but the effect was chilling. "IV was there both times she said it," the friend recalls. "He didn't crack a smile, just sat there and took it." To be a witness to such a scene was embarrassing, even painful, "one of those moments when you look at your shoes."

Though only 17 when she entered Hillsdale, Lissa was more mature than most of her classmates and far more ambitious. She and her fellow Flinties formed a distinct subgroup, "highly intellectual and very set in their view of the world," says Cheryl Lieblang, who graduated with Lissa Roche. Lissa was particularly standoffish, says Debbie Hazen, who was in her class and saw her often at Broadlawn, where Hazen babysat Roche's two young daughters, Muriel and Margaret. (A second son, Jacob, was born in 1983.) Lissa, Hazen thinks, had "a superiority complex."

At Hillsdale Lissa found one figure whom she not only respected but worshiped: the dynamic young president, George Roche, Hillsdale's master builder. Lissa Jackson also belonged to a crowd that was very involved in the Center for Constructive Alternatives, the campus lecture series. "They were like C.C.A. groupies," says Lieblang. "George III would bring some heavy hitters to campus to participate in C.C.A., and then throw cocktail receptions and dinner parties for them at Broad-lawn."

But Lissa had already selected another route to the pillared mansion. Soon after arriving at Hillsdale, she had "latched onto IV," says Arlan Gilbert, a retired history professor. After meeting at the local Big Boy, the couple became inseparable. They were an unlikely pair. George IV was, in most respects, the opposite of his father, quiet and shy with no apparent ideological zeal. A superb carpenter, he painstakingly built a deck for a neighbor's home. He also liked to fish and hunt. Still, by all accounts, the couple was well matched, Lissa's domineering personality finding a submissive complement in IV's gentler one. They seldom quarreled and were united in their admiration for George Roche III. IV was deferential and timid, Lissa craved the great man's attention. The first summer of their courtship she vacationed with the family and thereafter was folded into the clan, a virtual Roche, plainly exulting in the place she had won.

Brilliant and focused, Lissa plowed through the Hillsdale curriculum in five semesters, catching up to her fiancé in time to graduate with him in December 1977 and be married a day later. IV was 22. Lissa was 19. The next few years the couple was on the move. There was a brief stay in Lake Tahoe, where IV worked in construction and Lissa had a job in a gift shop. Then came a longer stay in Indiana: IV taught at a military academy while Lissa got her master's degree in history from Notre Dame. There was also an interval when the couple and their infant son (George V, born in June 1979) were back at Hillsdale. It was during this period, if Lissa's story is true, that she began a sexual relationship with her father-in-law. In any event, friends believe that it was Lissa's idea to return to Hillsdale for good in 1985.

The college now stood on the verge of its golden age. The election of Ronald Reagan in 1980 had catapulted Roche to prominence. He was named to the president's Education Task Force, and in 1982 was confirmed by the Senate as the chairman of the National Council on Educational Research. Hillsdale students, afire with missionary zeal, began filling internships at Washington think tanks such as the Heritage Foundation and the National Center for Policy Analysis; the school's graduates found positions on the staffs of Republican congressmen. Then, in 1984, the Supreme Court ruled that even if Hillsdale and like-minded colleges accept no direct federal aid, they still must comply with government guidelines if individual students were recipients of federal grants or loans. Roche immediately declared Hillsdale's total independence, barring students from taking government money. (Hillsdale then privately raised replacement funds.) He also resigned his position on the National Council. Hillsdale, in effect, broke off from the rest of the academic world. Its reputation, and Roche's, attained new heights among conservatives.

Always alert to political trends, George Roche, the longtime libertarian, played up his image as a Christian moralist, a champion of "Judeo-Christian and Greco-Roman heritage." He teamed with Lissa to build up Hillsdale's fund-raising road show under the umbrella of the Shavano Institute for National Leadership. These were costly off-campus galas, sometimes held in deluxe hotels (such as the old Santa Barbara Biltmore at Montecito) and featuring top-dollar speakers such as William F. Buckley Jr. and Colin Powell. Though billed as seminars they were closer in spirit to revival meetings. Audiences sometimes reached 1,000. The highlight came when Roche materialized in a corona of soft lighting and delivered homilies about "ethics." "Radical academics," as Roche said in 1989, had "pulled off one of the greatest hoaxes of all time," and it was Hillsdale's mission to counteract it. He spoke movingly of his own early education, which had taken place in a one-room schoolhouse in the Rockies. Transfixed donors opened their wallets and wrote large checks. Some placed entire trusts in the hands of Hillsdale College.

But from the outset the conservative Utopia functioned like the extension of a single man's ego and appetites. According to two sources, Roche, the distinguished educator, lifted entire paragraphs from a sermon by a clerical colleague, then brazenly delivered it as a lecture in Chicago. No one held him accountable for fear "the movement" would be jeopardized. "So we became enablers," says Robert Anderson, a former professor who helped bring Roche to Hillsdale and who has documents supporting the plagiarism charge. Inside the Hillsdale fortress, Roche consolidated his reign and used tactics of intimidation to enforce it. Before long, the word "Stalinist" crept into discussions, particularly among disgruntled faculty.

"For at least the last 10 years there seemed to be a paranoia that tended to emanate from Roche," says Charles Van Eaton, who left Hillsdale in 1998 after 20 years as chairman of its Economics Department, and who is now at the School of Public Policy at Pepperdine University. When faculty members tried to get a seat on the board of trustees, Roche punished the leaders by freezing their salaries. More often he left the dirty work to others. "He was away often but always present," says Bill Koshelnyk, a public-relations officer who ghostwrote Roche's various op-ed pieces. "I used to say, 'A sparrow doesn't fall from the sky without George Roche knowing about it.'" The greater world—at least of the conservative titans who lauded Roche and the Hillsdale experiment—had no clue, Koshelnyk says, about "all the bloodletting [that] was going on."

Not only the faculty was scared. Dissident students—and even mildly skeptical ones—were dealt strong penalties: the sudden loss of a campus job, bullying sessions with administrators, even expulsion, as happened in the case of Mark Nehls, who started his own newspaper, *The Hillsdale Spectator*, financed by ads he sold to local merchants. After clashing with the administration over censorship and other issues, Nehls was thrown out of Hillsdale on charges, which he strongly denies, of having defrauded local businesses by misrepresenting himself as an official of the college. Several years later, when pranksters tarred and feathered the large bronze eagle affixed to the campus's entrance, the school launched a "gestapo-like" investigation, literally "dragging people out of bed at night," says Jonathan Ellis, one of the accused. A Hillsdale spokesman says there is "no truth" to this allegation. But Melinda von Sydow, an instructor at the time, says one of her students, a prime suspect, told her "about being dragged out of bed in the wee hours."

All the while, Roche and Hillsdale were collecting accolades. In 1998, *U.S. News & World Report* ranked Hillsdale first among midwestern liberal-arts colleges. The Stanford economist Thomas Sowell extolled Hillsdale's open-mindedness in importing the occasional liberal guest speaker, such as George McGovern or Pat Schroeder, to challenge the college's orthodoxies. These presentations were carefully stage-managed by Lissa Roche. As students filed into Phillips Auditorium, the 170-seat hall where some of the lectures were held, Lissa stood at the door, quietly pulling students aside and feeding them intelligent questions so the guests would leave properly impressed.

A great deal rode on Hillsdale. It had become the flagship campus of an entire political movement. Conservatives who had never heard of Grove City or of Calvin College in Michigan were aware of "the little Harvard of the Midwest" and the new mandarinate being groomed there, foot soldiers of the Reagan-Gingrich revolution.

The symbol of Hillsdale's pre-eminence was *Imprimis*, the monthly "speech digest" whose main feature was usually remarks by the latest luminary who had made the pilgrimage to the college. Lissa Roche edited each issue, which often meant condensing or, as she complained, rewriting the threadbare ramblings of business leaders and politicians. It was a high-pressure grind that had burned out many an editor before Lissa joined the staff in 1990. Amazingly, she soldiered on until her death.

There was a greater purpose to her labors than just burnishing the Hillsdale myth: after so many years her idolatry of Roche was undimmed. For all her brusque professionalism—a trait many noted—she remained at heart the 17-year-old Flintie. "I always suspected she identified herself with the figure of Ayn Rand," says Bill Koshelnyk, who worked with Lissa for eight years. Like Rand, Lissa was hard-shelled, "rough and tumble," but her devotion to her father-in-law and his infallible vision was absolute. "She was one of the biggest defenders of the status quo at Hillsdale," says a friend, "and that was a line that was not to be crossed."

To what extent that devotion was rewarded is impossible to say. As some observers hasten to point out, there is no concrete evidence that an affair took place, despite Lissa's claim that it lasted 19 years. While Lissa's adoration of her father-in-law was apparent to all, his feelings toward her remain a mystery. But then George C. Roche's true feelings toward anyone were not easily discerned.

So much in Roche's thrall, Lissa failed to grasp an essential fact about him, one understood by George Roche's first wife, June. "George loves secrets," she says today, reflecting on her 44 years as his spouse. "He loves to keep secrets from people—from everybody." In the middle of a cocktail party, she says, he would often seize a guest by the elbow and whisper something to him, making sure his wife saw.

On this day in early December, June's voice is nearly inaudible: she is back from an exhausting day of chemotherapy treatment in Ann Arbor. Two months after her divorce she was diagnosed with Hodgkin's lymphoma. We are seated in the living room of her handsome home in Hillsdale, five minutes from the campus. A grand piano faces a bay window. There are elegant furnishings, a festive Christmas tree, and a feeling of unquenchable sadness. The heady days of dining at the Reagan White House or watching *Paint Your Wagon* on television with George Bush at Broadlawn belong to the distant past.

"There are two Georges," June says. "There's the good George and the mean George." The good George nightly read his children Tolkien and C. S. Lewis, and took his son sledding on the slopes of the Ardsley Country Club—this was 30 years ago, back in the FEE days, which June remembers nostalgically. The mean George, she says, more visible at Hillsdale, berated his wife for serving the wrong cut of meat, even as she carefully measured out to the last digit the 600 calories he was permitted on the diet required by his diabetic neuropathy. The mean George also occasionally drank, June says, sending his blood sugar to dangerous levels. Hillsdale faculty members recall Roche's relentless verbal assaults on his wife, unbearable in their cruelty. After enduring one such performance at a college event, recalls a professor, "I finally went to the proper person and said, 'Please don't seat my wife and me next to them again.'"

June admits that friends had been warning her for years about Lissa, but it was hard to take the allegations seriously. Of course Lissa worshiped George—"a long time ago, I thought of her as a groupie"—but it seemed a daughterly fixation. There was no outward indication that he reciprocated. There was also Lissa's weight. The slender coed ballooned in later years, packing as many as 170 pounds on her five-five frame and joking that her designer was "Omar the tentmaker."

But June suspects Lissa had something to do with her divorce. "I felt like there was something really off center, both with George and Lissa," she says of that period. In August 1998, George burst into a luncheon June was holding at Broadlawn. "He said, 'I need to talk to you upstairs,'" June remembers. "It was very cut and dried. He said, 'I've taken all the money out of the bank and canceled all the credit cards. Here's a check for $1,000 to tide you over. Don't worry. You'll be well taken care of. There'll be somebody here to serve you papers.'" It was the only warning she received—he had not previously hinted that anything was amiss, nor did he give her any real reason as to why he wanted the divorce, she says. Ten minutes later June was holding the documents that ended her marriage.

This happened on Saturday—the classic tactic. It meant June could do nothing over the weekend, not even put in calls to lawyers. She could only panic. Thus ended a relationship that had begun in the 1950s, when the two were teenage sweethearts in Denver. June gathered up some of her belongings in one sweep through Broadlawn. The rest of her things were placed in storage, she says, save for those stuffed in trash bins in the driveway of the mansion. The discarded items included a dollhouse used by one of George and June's daughters. A settlement was reached last April. She will say only that she's satisfied with the terms.

Lissa was now installed at Broadlawn. But even she was not privy, it appears, to all of George's secrets. For years there had been rumors about his alleged philandering, but college trustees "looked the other way because of that great god we all worship: money," says one school official.

In early September of last year, Roche introduced Dean as his fiancée. They would be married on September 13. Dean, too, belonged to the extended Hillsdale family, though distantly. She had reportedly attended Shavano lectures in Colorado. There was another connection: according to June Roche, Dean's first husband "had been a good friend of Lissa's father. He worked in the same hospital in Louisville where Lissa's father was a surgeon."

"**W**ho is John Galt?" is the famous question that reverberates throughout *Atlas Shrugged*. Lissa, perhaps, had never learned who George Roche really was. She was sent back to the stone cottage, her domestic duties no longer required. She began to work at home rather than on campus, setting up an office in her son's room. (George V, who had recently turned 20, was a student at Hillsdale and belonged to a fraternity where he spent much of his time.) But cutting back her time at Central Hall was no solution. Five days before the wedding, Lissa wrote a long memo to her colleagues, informing them of her intention to break away and start her life anew. "I am seeking a divorce from George IV for reasons I can't go into, and it seems best to get out of town immediately. . . . I will not be reachable by phone or mail." She left the address of her sister Laura Jackson in Los Angeles. "I will not be staying with her, but I will be in touch with her periodically." The letter concludes: "Will miss you, dearest friends."

But her escape was pathetically short-lived. After only two days, she came back; the pull of Hillsdale was too strong. Lissa even attended George and Dean's wedding, a very private event with a small guest list, then slouched back obediently to her official duties. When John Fund, the *Wall Street Journal* editorial-board member, lectured at Hillsdale in mid-September he was struck by Lissa's manner—"distraught and subdued, almost fatalistic" is how he puts it. "She was clearly in pain and had this scrunched-up look on her face. I tried to make conversation, but she was distracted." Lissa confided that she had hit hard times. "'There have been a lot of problems,'" Fund recalls her saying. "'I need to rethink my whole life. It got to the point where my marriage descended into a crisis [but] I decided I had to make the best of it.'" Fund says she looked as if she had been crying.

And then, as so often happens just before a suicide, hope flickered. On Friday, October 15, IV, Mickey Craig, and another friend were playing racquetball at the college's multimillion-dollar athletic complex (named for George Roche). Lissa suddenly appeared courtside, utterly transformed. "She'd been despondent, distraught, the previous three weeks," says Craig. "She looked awful." But now she looked happy, buoyant, serene. "Something's come up, IV," she announced gaily. "You've got to come home." After Lissa's death, IV gave Craig an explanation: George had asked Lissa for help on one last writing project—a letter to Dean terminating his new marriage.

But Dean was still at Broadlawn at one on Sunday morning, when she phoned IV to tell him George had had an insulin reaction and needed help. (This had become an almost weekly occurrence in recent years. June Roche thinks they exacerbated the irrational conduct in which "the mean George" prevailed over "the good George.") IV phoned 911, had an ambulance sent to Broadlawn, and, letting Lissa sleep, accompanied his father and Dean to the hospital. When he got back to the house at three, Lissa was awake. IV reported on his father's condition and said, "By the way, it looks like Dad and [his new wife] have reconciled."

The impact was tidal, according to the account IV gave *National Review*. "Oh shit, oh no," said Lissa. Now it was her turn to rush to the hospital, where she quarreled with George as he lay on his sickbed. She became loud and strident, and was asked to leave. Hours later Lissa phoned George, threatening suicide. Alarmed, George called his secretary, who located IV in neighboring Jonesville, where he was teaching a gun class. He interrupted it and went to Broadlawn. Lissa was there, looking in on George's mother. She seemed to have regained her composure but insisted they go to the hospital at once. It was about 11 o'clock in the morning when they entered the sickroom, and it was there that Lissa told the new Mrs. Roche she had been sleeping with George for years. "Is she telling the truth or is she having some sort of breakdown?," IV asked his father. George III said nothing, but his son was sure he read an answer in his stricken face. "I saw the look in his eyes. He was caught," IV told *National Review.*

The couple returned to the cottage. Lissa took charge as usual, weaving plans. The only solution, she said, was for all of them to leave Hillsdale. She told IV to go back to the hospital and speak with his father. He agreed, and while at the hospital called someone he thought could help Lissa. When IV got back, he and Lissa talked more, struggling to make sense of the horrific accusation now out in the open. Then Lissa sent IV on another errand, this time to check on his grandmother at Broadlawn. He was reluctant to leave Lissa alone, but he did as she said. When he got to the mansion, he saw that his father and Dean were back from the hospital; there was no need for him, so he returned to the cottage. By his own calculation, he was gone no more than five minutes—long enough for Lissa to unlock the gun cabinet and put a speed loader into the .357 magnum. Long enough to commit one final act of destruction conceived on a Randian scale.

An hour later, after the police had come and driven IV to the station, George III and June Roche stood outside the stone cottage. June was not yet aware of Lissa's allegation—her children would keep it from her for days—but she says she knew her ex-husband's remarriage had driven Lissa to suicide. She turned to him and said, "You have taken our family as though it were a sheet of glass and smashed it on the pavement."

To visit the Hillsdale campus is to discover how closely bunched the principal sites of this terrible story are: Broadlawn, the stone cottage, the arboretum, Central Hall. The complete walking tour takes perhaps 20 minutes. It is one more reminder of the perilous intimacy of small-town life. But something of value remains at Hillsdale. You can still sit in a classroom and hear a professor such as Mickey Craig quietly elucidate Tocqueville's *Democracy in America* and thus realize that teaching, an art little honored in our culture, means something here. Perhaps only on tiny, isolated campuses like Hillsdale do professors develop, over many years, a perfect pitch for the student mind, for what it can grasp, for what can light the fires of imagination or nurture an evolving worldview. The Ivy League schools and the great research universities don't ask this of faculty, who in any case are much too busy competing for grants and book contracts to think about the yearning hopes of eager freshmen. But at Hillsdale that transaction between professor and pupil, which is the essence of a liberal-arts education, still thrives. This is the college's strength, not the gaudy fund-raising, not the canned sermons by visiting bigwigs, not the junkets to Santa Barbara, not the bloated circulation list and Rotarian pieties of *Imprimis.*

It's a short walk from Kresge, the main classroom building, to the arboretum, where the gazebo sits, tranquil in its clearing. One can see why Lissa Roche would have sought peace here. In the late-autumn light the earth colors still hold their glow, and the skirt of lawn, hemmed with junipers, spruces, and catalpas, remains a lustrous green. The tall, sheltering Norway pines have shed some of their needles, which now form a spongy path. A plaque affixed to the gazebo explains that a biology professor, helped by his father and brother, both stonemasons, built the arboretum over the course of 27 years, from 1929 to 1956. Successive generations of students also lent a hand. Together they constructed an authentic shrine—a harmonious conjunction of human design and natural splendor that took one year less to build than George Roche's empire and will long outlive it. Lissa Roche made sure of that, though in doing so she has left a stain that will never be cleansed. "If George and Lissa walked on the wild side, they reaped a whirlwind," says June Roche. "I think Lissa's death was an act of rage and revenge. She brought him down." There is no triumph in her words.

[George Roche died in 2006 in Louisville, Kentucky, survived by his second wife, Dean. June Roche died in 2015 in Hillsdale.]

ST. PAUL'S SCHOOL

ST. PAUL'S SCHOOL

"DANGEROUS PRIVILEGE"

By Todd S. Purdum

MARCH 2016

Grant, O Lord,
That in all the joys of life we may never forget to be kind.
Help us to be unselfish in friendship,
Thoughtful of those less happy than ourselves.
And eager to bear the burdens of others
Through Jesus Christ our Savior.
Amen.

—St. Paul's School Prayer

I. ONE NIGHT IN MAY

He was 18, a scholarship boy from a bitterly broken home, a star scholar-athlete—captain of the varsity soccer team—who had won full-ride admission to Harvard, Princeton, Yale, Dartmouth, Brown, Duke, Stanford, Middlebury, and the University of Virginia, and two days later would be the winner of the headmaster's award for "selfless devotion to School activities."

She was 15, a privileged second-generation preppy who had been raised in Asia and whose older sister had briefly dated the boy and advised her to steer clear of him; by all accounts a naïve and impression-able freshman both flattered and flummoxed by the insistent e-mail en-treaties of one of the most popular boys at St. Paul's School, in Concord, New Hampshire.

On the evening of Friday, May 30, 2014, Owen Labrie, carrying a backpack, a blanket, and a key that he himself acknowledged was stolen, took the girl to a dark attic mechanical room, in the $50 million math-and-science building named for the old New York family that produced Mayor John V. Lindsay, for an encounter that turned sexual.

This is the beginning—and virtually the end—of agreement about what happened between two young people that night. Like a Rashomon episode of Showtime's *The Affair*, almost everything else depends on the protagonists' divergent perspectives, dueling recollections, and dia-metrically opposed interpretations of intent.

He says her underwear never came off. She says she held her under-wear up tightly with both hands but that he moved the front aside. He says they never had sex. She says he raped her, with both of his hands visible above her waist. He says she giggled and seemed to enjoy their kissing, caressing, and rolling around—an assessment she does not dis-pute. She says she said "no" three times. He says he got up to retrieve a condom from his shorts and suddenly realized that "it wouldn't have been a good move to—it wouldn't have been a good move to have sex with this girl." DNA from his skin cells was found in the inside panel of her underwear, as was semen that could not be definitely linked to him.

In the aftermath of their encounter, they exchanged tender e-mails referring to each other as angels—and anxious Facebook messages about her lost earring, and whether he'd used a condom. When the girl's older sister learned of the encounter, she smacked the boy in the face, giving him a shiner for his graduation that Sunday. In the small hours of the following Tuesday morning, the girl finally telephoned her mother. The school then reported the case to the local authorities as required by law. The resulting whirlwind has consumed the rarefied world of St. Paul's, made front-page news across the country, inspired an episode of *Law &*

Order: Special Victims Unit, and sparked fresh debate about the meaning of sexual consent and about teenage hook-up culture in the age of social media.

At his trial, last summer, the prosecution alleged, and the available evidence strongly suggests, that Labrie seduced the girl as part of an organized ritual—a competition with other boys to see who could "slay" the greatest number of younger girls in the weeks leading to graduation.

In August, a jury acquitted Labrie on the charge of forcible felony rape but convicted him on three misdemeanor counts of statutory rape—penetration of his under-age victim with his hands, tongue, and penis—and on a felony charge of using a computer to lure a minor for sex, an offense that requires him to register as a sex offender for life. In October, he was sentenced to a year in jail, five years of probation, and lifetime registry. He remains free while he appeals the convictions, with a legal team led by the former president of the New Hampshire Bar Association and with a likely assist from Alan Dershowitz, who is himself in the midst of vigorously disputing allegations that he had sex with an under-age girl. [The allegations against Dershowitz have been from the court record.] In the meantime, the victim's family has said it may sue St. Paul's in an effort to force changes in discipline and governance and ensure greater supervision of the 541 students who now have wide run of the bucolic 2,000-acre campus. [The victim's parents filed a civil suit against St. Paul's in U.S. District Court in Concord in June 2016. That August, she appeared on the *Today* show, publicly revealing her identity for the first time.]

II. "STATCH"

Disclosure: I am an alumnus of St. Paul's, from the class, or "form," of 1978. The school transformed the life of the small-town midwestern boy I was. At my graduation, I won the same prize that Labrie won at his—the Rector's Award, given by the headmaster to one who has "enhanced our lives and improved the community." Four years ago, when Labrie was a student, I was a visiting lecturer. Over the years, I have been active as a representative of my class and as a member of the alumni magazine's advisory board, and have edited a book of writings by a former rector, as St. Paul's headmasters are known. My classmates include parents of current and recent students, some of whom knew Labrie well.

Before receiving this assignment, I had corresponded with the rector, Michael Hirschfeld—himself from the St. Paul's form of 1985—expressing misgivings about the school's public statements and its handling of the case. When I began my reporting, Hirschfeld expressed a willingness to talk, but he and the school's lawyer and the president of the board of trustees repeatedly deferred or delayed requests for interviews before finally issuing a formal statement and answering some written questions. The account that follows is based on that information and on interviews with faculty, staff, parents, alumni, and students (all of whom consider themselves friends of the school); with a senior law-enforcement official involved in the case; with representatives of the families of Owen Labrie and the victim (whose identity *Vanity Fair* is shielding in conformity with standard practice in cases of sexual crimes involving under-age persons); and with the father of the victim. I have also spoken with Owen Labrie and his father. What I've learned has made me as sorry as if I were covering a crisis in my own family—which, in a sense, I am.

In public statements, St. Paul's and many of its students, alumni, and friends have insisted that what happened in this case was not representative of the broader culture of an institution that, since its founding, in 1856, has educated the cream of the American aristocracy. Its distinguished alumni include the novelists Owen Wister and Rick Moody; the diplomats John Gilbert Winant and John F. Kerry; Senator Sheldon Whitehouse; the actors Judd Nelson (my classmate) and Catherine Oxenberg; plus Garry Trudeau and a passel of Pillsburys, Chubbs, Reids, Rutherfurds, and Wilmerdings, along with the worthy heirs of clergymen, diplomats, teachers, and other promising scholarship kids like Labrie.

The school's lush grounds—a wonderland in winter; a lilac-scented Arden in the spring—are the envy of many a small college. All students and faculty are required to live "on grounds." The master plan for its interlocking network of ponds, waterfalls, and pathways was laid out by the firm of Frederick Law Olmsted, the designer of New York's Central Park. Watergate special prosecutor Archibald Cox, class of 1930, took a head-clearing walk around the Lower School Pond during the crisis over his subpoena of Richard Nixon's White House tapes.

Defenders of St. Paul's point to its curriculum on "Living in Community." In line with its tenets, students are taught "self-awareness, self-management, social awareness, relationship building and positive decision-making." As a prefect, or dorm leader, Labrie had received explicit training in the definition of statutory rape—"statch," as students call it—and responsible sexual conduct, and signed a statement affirming his special obligation to follow the rules. The school prayer beseeches God to "grant that in all the joys of life, we may never forget to be kind." The school's secular credo—coined by Hirschfeld when he was director of admissions—is "Freedom with Responsibility," a concept now under debate.

Yet it is hard to avoid the conclusion that something has gone badly awry at the school. About every 10 years since the mid-1990s, St. Paul's has been consumed by scandal: one rector resigned after a no-confidence vote by the faculty; a second was forced to resign after a state investigation into his compensation; and now there is the Labrie affair. The common thread? A rotating cadre of circle-the-wagons trustees and administrators who would defend the school's reputation in the face of damning facts and obvious misconduct.

While evidence suggests that the term "senior salute"—in which 12th-grade students of either gender in their last months at school reached out to younger students of the opposite sex—had not existed for more than two or three years, the practice of "scoring," or "secret scoring," in which students kept track of their romantic or sexual conquests, had existed for much longer, as had the ritual of upper-class boys' "ranking" younger girls' attractiveness as the boys sat in a common room outside the main dining hall after meals. In a 2013 essay in the school newspaper, *The Pelican*, Labrie himself had written about the practice. "Is secret scoring in dirty Schoolhouse closets the key to happiness?" he asked. "Anyone who has a sweet relationship can tell you it is not." In a speech to the student body last spring, Hirschfeld recalled having heard both male and female students use the words "slay" and "slayer" in references to sexual relationships. "These words made me uncomfortable, as I suspect they did many other people," the rector said. "While these words made me uneasy, I did nothing as the head of the School to address their use nor, to my knowledge, did anyone else. Why was that? Are these words and what they suggest a part of our air? We should be asking these questions." Hirschfeld's remarks have since been removed from the school Web site.

Faculty, alumni, and parents with whom I have talked reported that the ritual of "senior salute" could involve everything from holding hands to a walk to the school boat docks to sexual intercourse, while the definition of "scoring" was said to be similarly vague. But there is no disputing that school officials were aware of a "scoring wall" behind a washing machine in an upper-class dormitory, where an interlocking diagram of hookups had been logged for years. The school kept painting over it, only to have the list repeatedly reappear. The rise of social media has exacerbated the situation and driven such behavior underground to adult-free cyberspace.

According to one former longtime faculty member, Hirschfeld himself first heard the term "senior salute" in the spring of 2013—a full year before the Labrie case—when a student in Labrie's dormitory accidentally left his computer logged on and a dorm-mate punked him by sending a message to the rector's wife, Liesbeth, asking "Senior salute?" But the school year was ending and no one seems to have run the meaning of the term to ground, or ascertained the prevalence of the practice.

"I don't understand the culture of some of the adults there," another longtime former faculty member told me. "Somebody should have said, 'Senior salute? Not in our school.'"

In the spring of 2014, one faculty member, a housemaster in a girls' dorm, complained in an e-mail to senior administrators about senior boys trolling for under-age girls. The teacher involved declined to comment, citing school policy, but others with knowledge of the situation told me that the boys were given a talking-to by their faculty advisers and made to apologize to the housemaster but were not otherwise disciplined. (Labrie was not one of the boys.)

What is perhaps most depressing from the trial testimony, and documents submitted by the prosecution at the time of Labrie's sentencing, is that the rite in which Labrie participated was not the province of disaffected or marginalized students who were known rule breakers. Instead it involved some acknowledged leaders of the school: the captain of the soccer team; editors of the newspaper; a class officer of the grade behind Labrie. They shared stolen keys not just to the science-building mechanical room but to other private spaces on the grounds. They shared e-mail templates for inviting girls to a salute and passed around a papiermâché "slay" mask that amounted to a kind of trophy. This all apparently came as a shock to faculty and administrators—including Hirschfeld, a onetime scholarship kid and athlete, who is said to have seen in Labrie something of himself, the very model of a St. Paul's student, the kind of person that the school's diploma would have called in my day a "*juvenis optimae spei*," a youth of brightest hope.

III. BUCKET LIST

Owen Labrie (pronounced Luh-*bree*) lives in rural Vermont, in the town of Tunbridge. His parents are Cannon Labrie and Denise Holland. They divorced when Owen was two—in a bitter custody and child-support battle that, court records show, included his mother's accusing his father of sexually abusing the boy, an accusation that Cannon Labrie denied and Vermont authorities could not substantiate.

Cannon Labrie is a graduate of Andover with a Ph.D. from Brown, a onetime college instructor, an editor at Chelsea Green Publishing, and a sometime amateur musician. He now works mostly as a landscaper. Denise Holland is a public-school teacher in Vermont. In a letter submitted to the trial judge at the time of Owen's sentencing, she claims to have raised Owen mostly as a single parent, often with child-support payments in arrears—a contention that Cannon Labrie disputes.

In that letter, Denise Holland said that she runs a rescue shelter for Labrador retrievers in her home and that Owen sometimes falls asleep on the floor comforting the dogs. She described Owen's construction of a small wooden chapel on his father's property last year as a "service project." On her advice, after being questioned by police, Owen deleted some 119 Facebook messages relating to the senior salute and his interaction with girls at school. The prosecution was able to recover these messages but could not ascertain the date of their deletion, and is thus undecided about whether to file a destruction-of-evidence charge against Labrie.

Labrie was recruited by St. Paul's as a 10th-grader to play soccer, and a condition of his full-scholarship admission was that he repeat the grade. While St. Paul's has long prided itself on not accepting so-called postgraduate students—at other, less posh prep schools, typically fifth-year high-school jocks brought in to round out varsity teams—it has in recent years increasingly accepted promising athletes in 9th, 10th, and even 11th grade, and then made them repeat a year, as Labrie did, so that some seniors wind up being a year older than the normal age of their classmates. The result is that 18- and 19-year-olds are on the same campus with students as young as 14.

Hardly alone among teenagers, Labrie presented a radically different persona to adults than he did to his fellow students. A father of a recent graduate, who questioned his son about the prosecution's evidence that Labrie had kept a list of girls he wanted to "slay," told me that his son had reported, "Dad, if this guy was going to do it, he was the type that would make a list." By all accounts, Labrie was super-competitive, always eager to prove his worth among the group of mostly wealthy, well-connected kids who were his best friends.

Social-media and yearbook photos of Labrie often show a handsome, suntanned, windblown frat-boy-in-training—a marked contrast to the horn-rimmed Harry Potter persona he presented at trial. Labrie's documented statements about women and sex have a dark undertone. In a poem he published in the school literary magazine in the fall of 2013, Labrie wrote of a "lonely gynecologist" sitting in a greasy-spoon diner in Michigan, "mulling over the undeniably miserable and miserably undeniable fact that his vast knowledge of the vagina had never, not even once, been of practical use."

Some of the most damning evidence against Labrie was not introduced at trial. New Hampshire state-superior-court judge Larry Smukler ruled that nothing prejudicial to the defendant could be admitted. But in its sentencing memo after Labrie's conviction, the prosecution cited various electronic communications revealing Labrie's unvarnished views. After one girl had rejected his advances, for example, Labrie variously wrote: "she turned me down . . . fucking hate forbidden fruit . . . fuckin girls so much." He quotes from a comedian's routine: "another dumb cum-bucket struck from my nut sucking, suck it slut, slut fucking bucket list." Writing to friends, Labrie said his style with women was to "feign intimacy . . . then stab them in the back. throw em in the dumpster. . . . I lie in bed with them . . . and pretend like I'm in love."

IV. SHUNNED

Labrie's victim is the middle daughter of a 1980s-era graduate of St. Paul's. He attended the school with the help of scholarship aid and went on to a successful career in international finance, based for many years in Tokyo, where the victim attended Catholic elementary school. Her older sister enrolled at St. Paul's in Labrie's class in the fall of 2011, and the victim herself joined her at St. Paul's in the fall of 2013.

By all accounts, the sisters are extremely close, with the younger all but idolizing the older. But the father of one of the victim's contemporaries at St. Paul's told me that the younger girl also struggled at times "with her identity in competition with her sister." The victim testified at trial that she took daily medication for anxiety and depression, and the evidence shows that from the outset she was ambivalent—alternately curious and wary—about a potential encounter with Labrie, whom she had known only casually through her sister, who had broken off a brief relationship with him.

The victim initially rejected Labrie's flirtatious invitation to climb "hidden steps" to a door whose hinges had suddenly "swung open in my hands." But after the intercession of a fellow ninth-grader—a dormmate of Labrie's, now a varsity hockey player, still at the school—she relented. "He's the big man on campus, and he asked her," the contemporary's father said. "'Nuff said? That's not enough. There's a complex set of human things going on." The girl was particularly intent that the encounter remain a secret, though she would later tell Labrie that he could count it toward "the numbers" of the senior salute. Just what the victim expected of the rendezvous is unclear. She acknowledged at trial that she had shaved her pubic hair in advance, and her closest friend told the police that the girl had said she was probably willing to let Labrie finger her vagina, and to fellate him, though she herself testified that she did not recall saying this.

What she got was something else: a physical encounter that, she testified, quickly escalated beyond her comfort. She acknowledged being excited as she and Labrie kissed in the dark against a wall, then sank to the floor. She lifted her hips to help him slip off her shorts. But when he tried to remove her bra and underwear, she testified, she stopped him and said "no" three times. She said he bit her breasts through the bra, hard enough to hurt her. And when she felt something inside her that she knew could not be his hands—since she could see them above her waist—she froze.

Labrie told the police that in a moment of "divine inspiration" he had stopped short of intercourse. At the trial—after he knew that his

DNA had been found in the victim's underwear—he was more specific, recounting for the first time how he might have prematurely ejaculated during "dry humping" in a way that left semen on his boxer shorts or her underwear. As he finally moved to put on a condom, he said, he had begun to lose his erection, was embarrassed, and brought the encounter to an awkward end. The pair left the Lindsay building separately. The first person the victim saw was a classmate, who happened to be the son of the rector. "I think," she told him, "I just had sex with Owen Labrie."

When Labrie returned to his dorm, he told dorm-mates, who proffered high-fives—and friends with whom he later exchanged electronic messages—that he had, in fact, had sex with the girl. At trial, he insisted he had done so only to avoid confessing the fumbling details of a make-out session gone sour.

The victim testified that she returned to her own dorm in a state of confusion, offering the same half-giddy, half-stunned confession—"I think I just had sex with Owen Labrie"—to her friends. When Labrie soon e-mailed her, "You're an angel," she replied—with the help of her friends—"You're quite an angel yourself, but would you mind keeping the sequence of events to yourself for now?" As the night wore on, the exchange of electronic messages continued, punctuated on the victim's end by repeated "ha-ha-ha"s and light badinage.

Labrie's lawyer offered these messages as proof that the victim had not just undergone a traumatic experience—and perhaps had not even had sex at all—while the prosecution explained them as the reverse: a textbook example of a date-rape victim's efforts to placate and pacify her assailant. Her sister's graduation was looming, her parents were in town, and the last thing she wanted, she testified, was to make any trouble or have the word get out. By Sunday morning, again at the urging of her friends, she was worried enough about a possible pregnancy that she went to the infirmary and asked for a "Plan B" contraception pill, but told the nurse on duty that she'd had consensual sex. Late Monday night, when a dorm master found her in tears, the teacher told her to call her mother, who drove to school the next morning.

It is, of course, impossible to reconstruct the girl's precise state of mind in the aftermath of these events, but her family and law-enforcement officials say that the more she thought about the encounter the surer she became that she had been the victim of a crime. This, too, is far from unusual for victims of acquaintance rape. "I don't think she saw this coming," one law-enforcement official involved in the case told me. "She did say no. She held on to her underpants with both hands. She didn't know how hard to press. Compliance began to look like consent." As Judge Smukler noted at Labrie's sentencing hearing, compliance and consent are not the same thing. Because the jury acquitted Labrie of forcible rape, Smukler said, "does not mean the victim consented to the sexual penetration, and indeed it is clear from the impact of this crime that she did not."

In the fall 2014, the victim returned to school, after assurances from Hirschfeld that she would be safe. She re-entered the same dorm, with the same group of friends, most of whom now shunned her, according to her family. They say some of her volleyball teammates declined to eat with her the first night back and that members of the men's hockey team stood up and pointed at her as she walked down the street. Finally, that December, she gave up and asked to go home. She is now in a private day school in the distant state where the family lives.

But the reverberations continue. At one point in the trial, the girl's name was inadvertently broadcast, subjecting her and her family to Internet harassment and a smear campaign of the most vicious sort. In all these months, the victim's father told me, the family has not received a single supportive phone call from another St. Paul's parent.

The girl's family is wealthy. Money is not the principal object of its potential lawsuit against the school, which has brought on Michael Delaney, a former New Hampshire attorney general, as its lawyer. The family has hired Steven Kelly, of Baltimore, a nationally known lawyer in sexual-assault and -abuse cases, to use the leverage of a suit to force the school to adopt changes in training and discipline for students and faculty. "This is going to be a soapbox issue for the rest of my life," the father says.

V. ANOTHER SHOE

Owen Labrie's life is also in shambles. His offer of admission to Harvard—and his full scholarship—was withdrawn in the wake of his arrest. He hired and fired three lawyers and, whether out of ignorance or arrogance or wishful thinking, rejected more than one proposed plea bargain that would have involved minimal jail time and no registration as a sex offender. He finally settled on J. W. Carney, a prominent Boston defense lawyer who has also represented the mobster Whitey Bulger, retaining his services with $100,000 raised from several St. Paul's families. Labrie had solicited the defense fund in a letter that the prosecution contended violated the terms of his pre-trial release, which barred him from contacting the victim or her family or anyone associated with St. Paul's, but since he was in the process of firing his lawyer at the time, prosecutors conceded he might not have been aware of the conditions.

There has been much hand-wringing about whether Labrie's felony conviction for using a computer to lure a minor was warranted, since the impetus for the law under which he was charged was to stop adults from preying on under-age victims, not to police teenage behavior. Much less noticed is the fact that the trial judge's split-the-difference sentence of a year in jail was more lenient than the penalty recommended by the pre-sentencing investigation requested by Labrie's own defense counsel. This evaluation, conducted by a probation officer, concluded that Labrie had not been truthful about several matters—a contention Labrie's lawyers dispute. The report recommended that Labrie undergo a rigorous course of sex-offender treatment while confined to state prison—not jail—and should not be eligible for parole until he had completed that program. Judge Smukler did not adopt that recommendation but instead ordered a new "psycho-sexual evaluation" of Labrie to determine the appropriate course, and that evaluation—and any potential treatment—is on hold pending Labrie's appeal.

A senior law-enforcement official involved in the case told me that if at any point in the long investigation Labrie had acknowledged wrongdoing and expressed regret, the case could probably have been resolved without even a conviction, by sending Labrie to a sex-offender diversion program. Instead, Labrie has chosen to go for broke, filing a kitchen-sink notice of appeal, preserving his options for contesting the guilty verdicts on multiple grounds. His appeals lawyer, Jaye Rancourt, has said the ultimate goal is to overturn the felony conviction or get a new trial on all the charges, in which he might yet be acquitted. At this point, Dershowitz's involvement is more theoretical than practical, but Rancourt told me that Dershowitz has, in fact, offered his services in drafting the appeal. Labrie is now back in Vermont with his mother and spending time with his father, who lives about 10 miles away. He has given one on-the-record interview, to *Newsweek*, which portrayed him sympathetically as a young man whose ambitions to join the ministry have been derailed by a youthful indiscretion and a murkiness in the law. The article left the victim's family angry and distraught, they say.

The one sentiment that unites the families of Labrie and the victim is outrage at St. Paul's. Labrie's camp complains that the school named and shamed him in public letters to parents and alumni, revoked his Rector's Award, and banned him from campus even before the trial, much less the verdict. The victim's family says the school betrayed its promises to guarantee her safe and successful return to campus, and allowed a student culture to flourish in which teachers and administrators—cowed by rich and powerful parents—allowed the inmates to run the asylum.

For its part, the school has been hamstrung by legal constraints and fears of the victim's lawsuit. Its statements about the case have been so heavily lawyered as to lack proper nouns, action verbs, even palpable sadness.

In his statement to *V.F.*, Hirschfeld acknowledged that "the last 19 months have been heartbreaking for the School community, no more so than for the survivor and her family," and outlined various initiatives that St. Paul's has undertaken, including a comprehensive review of the school's safety and reporting procedures; the creation of the new post of vice-rector for school life to oversee the health center and chaplaincy;

the clarification of school rules to make "participation in games or competitions of a sexual nature" grounds for expulsion; enhanced training in anti-bullying techniques; and creation of a "bystander intervention program" in which students are taught not to remain passive in the face of misbehavior by their peers.

As for Labrie himself, Hirschfeld says, he was "profoundly disappointed to learn of his participation in such contemptible behaviors," and like others "felt betrayed by the duality of his life here and disheartened by his continued failure to own any part of his behavior."

Meantime, some prominent alumni and parents have rallied around the school, or around Labrie, or both. A group of recent graduates wrote a letter to *The Boston Globe* last September, insisting that the case was not representative of student life at St. Paul's. Their message was somewhat undercut by the fact that one of the signers, now a freshman at Princeton, is identified in court documents as having received stolen keys from Labrie. (He declined a request for comment from *V.F.*)

At a weekend symposium for alumni volunteers last fall, attendees told me, a student panel explained that, in recent years, traditional dating relationships had become the exception at St. Paul's. Short-term sexual encounters were the norm. The students said this seems to be changing in the aftermath of the Labrie case. Hypersexualized behavior among teenagers is not unique to St. Paul's. But the Labrie case shows that there may be aspects of life in the privileged—and highly independent—atmosphere of an elite boarding school that allowed an Owen Labrie to flourish undetected. Parents paying $54,290 a year in tuition to get their children into top colleges don't like hearing news of misbehavior by their kids—and so misbehavior is sometimes overlooked. And students, frantic to get into the best colleges themselves, can't stand the prospect of making the kinds of mistakes they might actually learn from.

There is at least one more very heavy shoe to drop. Last fall, the authorities in New Hampshire charged Donald Levesque, a former teacher's assistant at a nearby day school, with luring two of his former students—an 18-year-old girl and an under-age boy—in December

2013 for a mutual sexual encounter in his home, and with repeatedly abusing the boy over several months. Public records and local media reports in Concord have identified the girl as a St. Paul's senior at the time; the boy is understood to be the son of a St. Paul's staff member. A date has not yet been set for trial, but a public airing of the sordid details of the case would only bring more scrutiny to the school and raise new questions about Hirschfeld's leadership.

In its most recent accreditation of St. Paul's, in 2007, the New England Association of Schools and Colleges recommended that the school "review the balance between student freedom and institutional responsibility," particularly "with respect to safety and supervision in the evening hours." In 2010, the school responded in a self-evaluation, noting that dorm check-in hours had been moved up half an hour in the fall and winter to 10 P.M.; school buildings were locked at 10 P.M.; faculty were encouraged to walk around the dorms after hours; theater practices were moved from evening hours to afternoons. It would not be unreasonable to imagine that much more could be done.

All of this makes me sad. Forty years ago, when I arrived at the school, co-education was still a novelty. St. Paul's certainly had its problems. There was serious drug and alcohol abuse by students (and, in the case of alcohol, by some teachers), and these issues were dealt with inconsistently. There were sexual predators among the faculty, and they were allowed to skate by. But there were no locks on doors, and there was a pervasive attitude of mutual trust. Every other Saturday night, my friends and I were quietly allowed to stay in the school newspaper's basement offices until one or two A.M. in order to work on it, creeping back to our dorm through the dew unafraid. Now key cards are required at all hours to gain entry even to classroom buildings, and a peaceable kingdom seems an impossible dream.

"Freedom with responsibility?" a recently retired faculty member said of Mike Hirschfeld's motto. "Completely asinine, and not in tune with any teenager's reality. Freedom with responsibility? How about accountability?" In its school prayer, St. Paul's asks divine help to "bear the burdens of others." Its own burdens are the ones that need attention now. [Labrie was back in court with his new defense attorney, Robin Melone, in February 2017. As of this writing, the decision to grant a new trial is with a judge.]

(See page 240 for Alex Shoumatoff's 2006 story on St. Paul's School.)

"THE CODE OF MISS PORTER'S"

By Evgenia Peretz

JULY 2009

It's the perfect Edith Wharton morning at Miss Porter's School, in Farmington, Connecticut—brisk and snow-covered, with icicles hanging from the porticoes of the white clapboard 19th-century dormitories. Freshly scrubbed teenagers, weighed down by backpacks, are rushing to morning meeting and just *counting* the days until spring vacation. With no boys around to look hot for, they're dressed in jeans—not the skinny kind, but ones that are comfortable—sweatshirts, and either high-tops or Uggs. They hug and link arms and no one's going to make fun of them for it. All is good with the world, and every facet of life at Miss Porter's a cause for celebration.

"Remember, we're going to Tanzania in June," announces one girl,

standing on the stage, kicking off assembly, "so please bring back sup-
plies from the break." Applause. Woo-hoo! Hooray!

Another girl stands to speak. "Don't forget about coffeehouse this
week. We'll even have a belly dancer!"

"Yeow!" calls out a male teacher, adding quickly, "That wasn't me."
More applause. Lots of giggles.

And, finally, it's time to hand out the awards to the "Girls of the
Week": Alana, who sacrificed so much time to help her classmates in
chemistry; Sam, for doing such a great job organizing senior kitchen;
and Lillian, for having such a positive attitude and cheering so much in
gym. The honored girls approach the stage to take their certificates. The
rafters are thundering. Meeting concludes with a small a cappella group
singing "Here Comes the Sun." You'd have to be Scrooge not to smile
a little. Or paranoid about cults.

But last fall at least one student, a senior named Tatum Bass, wasn't
feeling the love. Miss Porter's made her so unhappy, in fact, that her parents hit the school with a lawsuit, alleging that a group of girls had verbally
abused Tatum for weeks. The family claims that despite its efforts to stop
the abuse Kate Windsor, who'd been installed as the new headmistress
just weeks before, did nothing to intercede. Eventually, Tatum claims,
the harassment caused her so much emotional distress that she ended up
cheating on a test and missing some school, which resulted in her getting suspended and then expelled—something the family says was unfair
in light of the circumstances. The school informed her college of choice,
Vanderbilt, of the cheating and suspension, without, the family says, giving
her the proper opportunity to defend herself—and Tatum was rejected.

Ordinary "mean girl" accusations maybe, but Miss Porter's is no
ordinary school. It's where Jacqueline Kennedy Onassis went, in
addition to many other famous debutantes and beauties, such as Gloria
Vanderbilt, Lilly Pulitzer, Brenda Frazier, Barbara Hutton, Edith Beale
(the "Little Edie" of *Grey Gardens*), and actress Gene Tierney, as well

as numerous young ladies with the last names Rockefeller, Auchincloss, Bouvier, Biddle, Bush, Havemeyer, Forbes, and Van Rensselaer, not to mention heiresses to the fortunes generated by a supermarket-aisleful of iconic American products, including one brand of breakfast cereal (Kellogg's), three meats (the Raths of Iowa and the Swifts and Armours of Chicago), and the world's most famous dough (Pillsbury). (Full disclosure: my mother, Anne Peretz, was class of '56.) Now, all of a sudden, these Bass people—*not* the Basses of Texas—seemed to be turning Miss Porter's good name into something out of a Lindsay Lohan movie. The shell-shocked school discouraged students from discussing the matter with the press and announced that it was determined to fight the suit "vigorously." Students and loyal alums, who call themselves "Ancients," were beside themselves—not because they doubted Bass was hurt by her classmates but because she had the audacity to whine about it, and to use it as an excuse for cheating.

"I was outraged," says Lauren Goldfarb ('98). "Look, she cheated. She lied. And guess what? It's a top academic environment."

A source closely involved in the school, who does not know the Basses, explains, "If a kid has any disciplinary action and has applied early-decision to college, the colleges have to be notified. As soon as that happened, Mommy back in South Carolina said, 'Wait a minute—my darling isn't going to get into Vanderbilt!'"

Nina Auchincloss Straight, Jackie Kennedy's stepsister, whose family has produced several Miss Porter's girls, can only laugh at the girl's sensitivity. "In this day and age, someone claiming that would have to be a lobotomy [case]." (The Basses decline to comment.)

Bass cheated, which was bad enough, but in the eyes of the school community she was guilty of something worse: weakness. From its very start, in 1843, Miss Porter's has been committed not just to the old-fashioned values of charm, grace, and loyalty but to another, unspoken value as well: the ability to tough it out. Deeply ingrained in the school's DNA, it makes the school a kind of upper-class, social Outward Bound. Throughout its history, Miss Porter's has tested girls' personal fortitude in a variety of ways: through academic rigor, strict rules, and rituals designed to produce anxiety and intimidate. Whatever their problems, Miss Porter's girls were expected to buck up, not to go crying home to Daddy. Think Jackie—charming, poised, cultured, and able to smile through her husband's many infidelities. Much has changed. Farmington—anyone over 50 who went there calls it Farmington; today's girls say simply "Porter's"—has gone from a sheltered, almost entirely Wasp institution to one that's impressively diverse. But this connection to its past, this remarkable stoicism, is what makes Miss Porter's Miss Porter's in the eyes of students and alumnae, and they wear it as a badge of honor.

GOLDEN RULES

The school was founded by Sarah Porter, the daughter of a minister and the sister of Yale president Noah Porter, when young women had few educational opportunities. Though it would become known as a "finishing school," a term you might associate with wearing Mummy's pearls and knowing how to set a table, its roots were puritanical and morally rigorous. Porter's goal was to make her charges good Christians and good wives and mothers. There were only a handful of girls in those first years, most of them, like Sarah herself, the daughters of educators and religious leaders, who might go on to become missionaries. While they worked on their "accomplishments," such as embroidery and needlework, Porter read to them, schooling them in literature, fine arts, and history—topics that would make them more interesting people, and more pleasing to their husbands and the company he kept. In the process, she released the intellectual powers of some extraordinary women, including Edith Hamilton (1886), the classics scholar, and her sister Alice (1888), who would become the first female faculty member of Harvard University and who founded the field of industrial medicine.

With its success, the school was flooded with the daughters of the newly wealthy, such as railroad executives Perry Smith and James Walker. As Barbara Donahue and Nancy Davis explain in their 1992 book, *Miss*

Porter's School: A History, the new rich, unlike the earlier students, believed that the whole point of having money was not to work, and to exhibit their wealth, which meant wearing fancy clothes, such as dresses with long trains. Porter, still dreaming of educating missionaries, delicately expressed to parents her horror over this development in an 1873 bulletin: "I have . . . observed more spirit of display in dress. . . . Our simple mode of life makes no demands for any other than a simple toilet, and hardly furnishes occasion for any other."

Porter died in 1900, and the swells eventually won out. From the 1920s until midcentury, Farmington's reputation as a finishing school would become unparalleled. Its students came chiefly from New York, Connecticut, Massachusetts, and the Main Line, outside Philadelphia, and they were often called by such nicknames as Bunky, Flossie, Hiho, A-Bee, B-Zee, Wheezie, Tug, and Poo. Women's colleges were now available, but Farmington, according to Farmington, was all that a girl needed. Once the school had given her a good education in the liberal arts and smoothed out her rough edges and made her shine, she was "finished" and ready for the proper husband, ideally a Princeton or Yale investment banker or businessman from a "good" family. To this end RoseAnne and Robert Keep, who reigned as heads of the school from 1917 to 1943, imposed a strict routine.

Girls were awoken each day at the crack of dawn with a cheerful "Good morning" from maids, who would raise the shades. The girls would dress behind screens for the sake of modesty, be at breakfast by 7 and ready for morning prayers at 7:55. Naturally, there was no smoking or drinking. There was also no cardplaying, no gumchewing, no reading of the popular novels of the day, and, eventually, no smoothing of the hair during meals, and no crumbling of cookies into ice cream. Miss Porter's was an island of correctness, and human contact beyond the school gates was practically prohibited. During term time, girls could rarely leave the grounds. They could not walk into town without special permission, and they were discouraged from talking to anyone once there. They could not receive phone calls except in emergencies.

For the right kind of Wasp, this convent-like rigor was heaven. "I just loved it. Absolutely loved it," says fashion editor Polly Mellen, who attended Farmington from 1938 to 1942. The school required no uniform per se, but Farmington girls had a distinctive look. As Mellen recalls, "You wore the Brooks Brothers polo coat, and you wore black-and-white saddle shoes or the brown-and-white saddle shoes, and the Brooks Brothers shetland sweater in all those different wonderful colors, over a little perfect white shirt, and a gray flannel skirt. . . . And the pageboy was very much a part of it. My husband would say we were kind of snooty."

Mellen, the youngest of four sisters who went to Miss Porter's, hit the target perfectly; she even became a fashion trailblazer by wearing her cardigan backward. But for less assured girls it was easy to get the rules wrong in the watchful eyes of classmates and be punished for it—for instance, if any part of the wardrobe was from the wrong store. "There was the gold round pin," recalls Pema Chödrön, a Catholic from a middle-class family in rural New Jersey, who is now a well-known Buddhist nun. "Their gold pin was always just slightly—more than slightly—classier than mine. You were always aware of it." Alternatively, a girl could screw up by being too showy. According to C. David Heymann's 1983 biography of Woolworth heiress Barbara Hutton, *Poor Little Rich Girl,* to the displeasure of the school and the disdain of her classmates, Hutton, who inherited $26 million from her grandfather and had a $60,000 debutante ball, wore tweed skirts from Chanel, frilly jabot blouses, and angora sweaters with lynx collars and cuffs. "It was as though she wanted to show us up," one of her classmates recalled.

It didn't matter that the Miss Porter's outfit might be inappropriate for the weather. Discomfort was part of the point. As Nina Straight recalls, even in September, when the temperature could reach the 80s, girls had to keep their collars and sleeves buttoned and their wool socks on. And in the dead of winter, neither pants nor stockings were allowed unless the temperature dipped below 10 degrees.

In addition to being able to tolerate physical discomfort, Farmington girls were expected to tolerate loneliness and emotional distress. The actress Barbara Babcock, who attended Miss Porter's in the mid-50s and went on to star in television's *Hill Street Blues,* cried every night because she was homesick at first. Her housemother saw that she needed a talking-to and brought her into the office of the headmaster. "I still remember him saying to me in a very severe tone, 'You are the daughter of a general, now just snap to,' " recalls Babcock. "And I remember standing bolt upright, thinking that I've got to do what he said and behave like I was in the army." An army, that is, of Jackie Bouviers.

It was the school's prerogative to make girls aware of their shortcomings, be they related to background or appearance. Omaha-raised Letitia Baldrige (1943) recalls that she was the first student ever on scholarship, which she immediately learned was a dirty word: "Bob Keep called my father [an Air Corps major, who had gone to Andover with Keep] and said, 'Mac,' as he called him, 'I just want you to know we'll take care of Tish's tuition and we'll keep it a deep, dark secret, so she won't be discriminated against.' " Her teachers were determined to beat the Nebraska out of her. "My English teacher, Miss Watson, said to me, 'You come from the Middle West, and it's going to take you a year or two to get over that.' She really gave it to me." (Those with southern accents didn't fare much better.)

If a girl was too fat or too thin, that had to be fixed, too. As Babcock recalls, "I was supposedly 25 pounds underweight or 20 pounds underweight, which seemed horrendous, and they put all of us [skinny girls] at a table where we had to eat what was put in front of us." Of course, the thin table wasn't as mortifying as the fat table. No wonder the girls were obsessed with dieting tricks. Barbara Hutton subsisted on coffee and biscuits, and every morning lay on top of two wooden weight-reduction rollers, a popular fitness tool of the day. Brenda Frazier, the world's most famous debutante in the late 1930s, was considered one of the most beautiful girls in the country. Despite this, everyone focused on her thick legs.

OLD TRADITIONS DIE HARD

For teenage girls, feeling sorry for someone can be a pure joy. Nowadays, one hardly needs any more documentation that girls' social dynamics can be complicated and malicious, that fear goes hand in hand with admiration, and that with deftly delivered cruelty comes power. Rather than attempting to ameliorate such dynamics, Miss Porter's, like other boarding schools, to be sure, effectively institutionalized them. The starting point was to separate the Old Girls (who'd been at Farmington at least a year) from the New Girls (who'd just arrived). Though the Old Girls were supposed to serve as guides to the New Girls (and in many cases they did), the New Girls were constantly reminded that the Old Girls were better. New Girls were expected to rise whenever Old Girls came into the room, to hold the door open for them, to step aside when passing them on the walkways or sidewalk. New Girls weren't allowed to wear the school color combination of gray and yellow, weren't allowed to sing songs that the senior a cappella group, the Perilhettes, sang, and weren't allowed to step on one special patch of Old Girl grass.

The hierarchy devolved into ritual hazing over Thanksgiving week, when all the girls remained on campus because they were prohibited from returning home to their families. It started on Monday, when the Old Girls would suddenly stop talking to the unsuspecting New Girls, no explanation given. A few days later, the New Girls, studying in their dorm rooms, would hear Gestapo-like stomping of Old Girls marching up the stairs, coming to get them. The Old Girls would march them out of the dorms and line them up. Sometimes, the Old Girls might do this all while shouting at the New Girls to count to 100 in German or perform random chores. "It was like the Nazis," says an Ancient, who, in violation of Farmington spirit, warned the next class of New Girls what they were in for.

It was hugely intimidating, says Straight, and some people cracked. "There was a girl from Chicago. She became anorexic and just got thinner and thinner. That kind of thing put pressure on you: 'I'm away from my mother. This person has just threatened me with a hockey stick and says I'm going to have to go out and stand until sunset!' " Some Ancients, on the other hand, claim it was all in good fun. Lest anyone balk at the status quo or question one of the rules, a group of tradition keepers, calling themselves "the Oprichniki," eventually sprang up. They named themselves after Ivan the Terrible's secret police, who destroyed anyone disloyal to him, something the girls learned about in a course called "Communist Societies." At the end of each school year, the departing Oprichniki would tap next year's Oprichniki. It became Miss Porter's very own Skull and Bones.

But in the spring all the intimidation was theoretically washed away with the Wishing on the Rings ritual, in which each New Girl would ask a senior Old Girl to wish on her new school ring. "My God! It was a tidal wave of emotions and romance," says Straight. " 'Where will so-and-so wish on your ring?' . . . And 'Who will I ask that won't have hysterics behind some bush to wish on my ring and could I do it in the middle of the highway?' There were tears and presents and people were madly in love with each other." (According to her biographer Sarah Bradford, Jackie, poking fun at this tradition, "vowed to find the ugliest girl in the school, who would know that Jackie couldn't possibly have a crush on her.") The Old Girls' approval of the New Girls eventually made up for the suffering they had endured. "Those who put up with being put down got to be the ones who put down the next year," says one of the more skeptical Ancients. By commencement, younger girls would sob as they watched the Old Girls perform the parting Daisy Chain ritual while singing, "Farmington, Farmington . . . / There my heart will turn forever, / Be the friendships broken never, / that so lightly were begun."

The system worked for many. Having to tough it out at Farmington prepared them for the world they were entering, both academically— after Farmington, many Ancients found college to be a breeze—and on a more personal level. An Ancient from one of the country's most famous families says, "I hate to think of who I would have become if I hadn't gone there. . . . I had an image of [myself as] being stupid, lazy, and trouble. I shed that pretty rapidly. By the time I went home the first year I had lost weight, my rash was gone, I was getting A's." The school changed Polly Mellen in a similar manner—from a poor student who was plump to a svelte and exacting tastemaker. "It made you feel like you were somebody," says Mellen. She went on to thrive as a fashion editor at *Vogue*—an arena not unlike Miss Porter's in its female rigor and hierarchies. For Letitia Baldrige, suffering through Miss Watson equipped her to become nothing less than Jackie Kennedy's premier handmaiden. She handled all the First Lady's social affairs and eventually became an etiquette expert. As for Jackie herself, the perfect Miss Porter's student in every way, she managed to achieve what she had vowed on her yearbook page: "Never to be a housewife."

While its star Ancient was helping her husband, President Jack Kennedy, usher in a new world, Miss Porter's was in many ways stuck in the old one. "They were very much, in the early 60s, preparing us for life in the 1930s," says Beth Gutcheon, who wrote the 1979 novel *The New Girls*, based on her time at Miss Porter's, in the early 60s. "It was a man's world. And Farmington was making it clear to us that we should learn to survive and learn to be our best selves within those strictures." Jackie was constantly being held up by teachers and the headmaster, Hollis French, as the Female Ideal. "Miss Watson never ceased rubbing our noses in the fact that Jackie would have gotten it right, that Jackie would have said that correctly," recalls Victoria Mudd, who attended in the early 60s and went on to make socially conscious documentaries.

As in the early days, Miss Porter's—thanks to impassioned teachers such as Miss Smedley, who taught European history—was turning out minds whose ambitions and interests were surpassing the gentler expectations the administration had set for them. When Gutcheon decided she wanted to go to Radcliffe, for example, the school discouraged her: "They really wanted us to go to the colleges that were more like finishing schools." The brightest girls often ended up in high-profile art-world careers, such as Agnes Gund, president of the Museum of Modern Art until 2002; Eliza Rathbone, chief curator of the Phillips Collection, in Washington, D.C.; Jennifer Russell, a director of exhibitions at the Museum of Modern Art; and Dede Brooks, chief executive of Sotheby's until 2000, when she resigned amid a price-fixing scandal.

While the country's top colleges and prep schools were opening themselves up to women and minorities, Miss Porter's clung to its ancient attitudes about blacks, Irish, and Jews. According to Gutcheon, a student in her time asked the headmistress, Mary Norris French, why there were no Jews at Farmington, to which she replied, "How do you know there are not?" Whoever they were, says Gutcheon, "they all had to pretend they were Episcopalian."

"The level of political awareness at that time was pretty much zero," Mudd says. By the time she got to Stanford, in 1964, she had learned from a senior who had been involved in the Mississippi Freedom Summer, registering voters, about what was going on in the world, with the war in Vietnam and the civil-rights movement. "She had pictures and stories, and I'm like, 'What? There's racism? There's poverty?' "

SEEDS OF CHANGE

In 1968, under the leadership of Richard Davis, the school dipped its toe into diversity by inviting its first black student, Glenda Newell, to attend. Davis made it clear that she was an experiment. "They told me that they were going to take a chance on me," recalls Newell, now Glenda Newell-Harris, a doctor in the San Francisco Bay Area, "and that if I did well they would then believe what they had heard, which was that many people of color may not be good test takers but could be good students. . . . And so, therefore, I had that burden." For the most part, her classmates were ready for Newell and to learn about something new. They got into the Motown she was listening to; she started liking James Taylor. The parents were trickier. She and a fellow student wanted to become roommates their junior year, but the girl's parents initially objected. She was continually reminded of the disparity in wealth. At the mail table, she watched other girls opening typed notes from their fathers' secretaries along with a $300 check, while she got two or three dollars to buy some toothpaste. "People had homes in Eleuthera. I didn't even know where Eleuthera was."

But Newell-Harris, the Jackie Robinson of Farmington, toughed it out, eventually serving on the board of trustees. She saw that others were toughing it out in different ways, by quietly enduring troubles back home. A number of Farmington girls had divorced parents, alcoholism in their families, or mothers they weren't speaking to. But it was not the Farmington way to talk about it or let it send you off course.

Still, stoicism could go too far. In 1976, three years after *Roe* v. *Wade,* one girl suffered alone through the most unimaginable horror. A rather stout, seemingly overweight New Girl from the Midwest entered Miss Porter's several months pregnant, unbeknownst to anyone at the school, her physician father having apparently signed off on her health form. In mid-November, as a former teacher tells it, the girl went to her classes, played soccer, skipped dinner, returned to her dorm, and gave birth to a boy by herself in the bathroom. She cleaned up the mess, wrapped the baby up, stashed him under her bed, and went to study hall. She began to bleed ferociously and was taken to the infirmary. "Dear, you have something you must tell us," the nurse said. By the time they got to the baby, he had suffocated. Miss Porter's was left with a sudden shock to the system.

"I think there was sort of a collective sense that we had betrayed her in some way," says Avery Rimer, who, like her classmates, missed the signs. "That we hadn't been able to be there for her and help her through something that lonely and scary. In a way, you feel like you've borne witness to a murder that you could have helped prevent."

But the trauma was also a wake-up call. In response to the obvious fact that girls might need help more than they let on, the adviser and counseling systems were ratcheted up. At the same time, the school felt the pressures of the outside world. Rules for dressing were loosened.

Now girls could wear the hip fashions of the day: long, wraparound skirts, puffy blouses, and clogs. Church was no longer a requirement, a nod to the fact that some people weren't Christian. Acknowledging that school should have a real-world component, Miss Porter's began sending girls off in January for various work projects. One of the most popular, of all things, was interning with Ralph Nader.

Just as Miss Porter's began catching up with the outside world, the outside world took one more big step forward. All-male schools such as Hotchkiss, Choate, Taft, and Exeter became coed, which meant that fathers who had attended them could now send their daughters to their alma maters. Miss Porter's turned down offers to join up with nearby all-boys schools. But in doing so it struggled to attract the same caliber of girl. Something had to change. To dispel the notion that Miss Porter's was only creating future society ladies, it redoubled its efforts to focus on science, math, and technology. Starting slowly, it broadened the diversity of its student body, accepting more people of color and more scholarship students. Today, Miss Porter's college placement is respectable, given the increasing toughness of the admissions game, but it still lags behind such prep schools as Exeter and Andover, and other top-notch all-girls schools such as Brearley.

With its modernization, many Miss Porter's traditions had to be re-examined. "Times were changing," says Burch Ford, Miss Porter's exceptionally well-regarded headmistress from 1993 until 2008, who brought the school's endowment up to $104 million, "and so behaviors that were either overlooked or not looked at could no longer be acceptable for any number of reasons." Some students balked at the hazing of New Girls in the fall. "It was something that no longer could really be defensible," says Ford. "Theoretically, it was a welcoming tradition. Well, it wasn't very welcoming." The word "Oprichniki" came to be associated with traditions that were inappropriate. The school tried to soften the rituals by helping to make sure that the girls tapped were among the nicest in the class, and it attempted to change the name to "the Keepers of Traditions."

But Miss Porter's traditions die hard. According to a source long involved in the school, "Children of Ancients would go home and say, Well, we can't do this, we can't do that anymore. And the mothers, if not egged them on, said, 'I think that's terrible. Without the traditions, it won't be Miss Porter's School.' . . . The Oprichniki would be squashed, and then four or five years would go by, and then there'd be a critical mass of Ancients' daughters again, and it would bubble up." And so, in certain years, if a New Girl wore the forbidden gray-and-yellow combination, for example, she might be forced by an Old Girl to get on all fours and start doing push-ups, or other tasks, says an Ancient from the mid-80s, that would "make you feel like shit."

ANCIENT REGIME

Visiting Miss Porter's today, you'd be hard-pressed to spot the Oprichniki in the crowd. The girls seem friendly, curious about the world, and intellectually fired up. Those I am allowed to meet on my visit there—the school handpicked five of them—bang the drum of sisterhood in a genuine and endearing way. Maggie, a junior from Ohio with adorable ringlets, says that when she arrived at Miss Porter's she had low self-esteem and was constantly putting herself down, focusing on her bad hair. "The other girls would say, 'No! How can you say that?'" Many young Ancients recall Miss Porter's as a bastion of warmth—especially when they were in the most desperate state of need. Imani Brown (2000), who was diagnosed with terminal brain cancer six weeks before commencement, recalls, "I didn't know that there was that much love in the world. I felt that maybe this was a parting gift." Brown not only survived but is thriving, and works as an administrator in a San Francisco high school.

In spite of the warmth that permeates the community today, it seems being a member of the Oprichniki has remained for some a badge of honor. Blair Clarke, who graduated in 2007 and who was an Oprichnik, recalls that after enduring the intimidation of the Oprichniki her freshman year—in which she and her classmates wore plastic on certain days for fear of getting pelted with tomatoes and crash-studied basic German just in case—she wanted to become one. "I decided, 'This is kind of cool.' A lot of my friends were like, 'We want to be Oprichniki when we're seniors.' And some people were upset if they didn't get it, so they would make it seem like, 'Oh, they're so bad, they're so bad.' " She maintains that the Oprichniki don't inflict real pain, just the anticipatory fear of pain.

But Tatum Bass, in her lawsuit, claims they are more powerful than that. An honor student from Beaufort, South Carolina, she loved the school under the leadership of Burch Ford, who was also her adviser. Bass was elected to the student-government position of student-activities coordinator. While planning the prom, she made the suggestion that Miss Porter's participate in a multi-school prom. According to her, this breach of tradition prompted an onslaught of cruelty, spearheaded by the Oprichniki. Classmates allegedly called her "retarded," referring to her attention-deficit disorder. The Basses claim a group of girls yelled "Fuck you" at her in front of hundreds of people during a school dance. They taunted her through mean text messages and on Facebook. Tatum's adviser was "fundamentally and functionally unavailable to offer support and guidance," according to the lawsuit. Despite the family's pleas to the administration to intervene, it did not. (Miss Porter's School has declined to comment on the suit.)

Bass began to fall apart. This led to the cheating, she claims, which she felt so awful about that she immediately confessed to Kate Windsor. After a three-day suspension, she stayed with her parents, Nina, a child psychiatrist, and William, the president of an insurance agency, at a local hotel. Days later, the suit claims, she returned to her dorm to find her belongings thrown into a pile in the corner with a sign that read, FOR RENT. Tatum became fearful of being on campus. Two doctors recommended that she take a medical leave, but the school allegedly denied those requests and instructed its medical director not to communicate with any of her physicians. On November 11, according to the suit, Miss Porter's disabled Tatum's school e-mail address and Internet access, and instructed her not to contact her teachers. A week later, the school informed the Basses that it was expelling their daughter, for alleged unexcused absences and violations of school rules. This was done, the family claims, without giving Tatum any opportunity to be heard.

In the opinion of some Ancients, Bass just couldn't hack it. Not every girl who gets taunted ends up cheating. "You can't sue a school for girl drama," says Clarke, the recent Oprichniki member. "She was very insecure. She was kind of, like, I wouldn't say timid, but she just reminded me of a little girl." She adds, "If such a place was so horrible to you, why do you still want to go back there?"

Perhaps because Bass, according to a source close to her, still loves the school and has faith that maybe the abuse she experienced was an aberration. The real issue, says this source, is that all of this—the cruelty, the cheating, the lawsuit—could have been prevented had the school's leadership stepped in. The family sued (for damages and to void the expulsion, among other things) because they believed they were given no other recourse. The clear implication is that Kate Windsor, the new headmistress, either was ill-equipped to handle the matter or believed that it didn't warrant her attention.

Windsor, 42, is a tall, rather glamorous-looking blonde who stands out from her somewhat earthier, New Englandy colleagues. Her last job was as head of the Sage School, a K–8 school in Foxboro, Massachusetts, for academically gifted children. Her very being exudes an obsession with excellence; you might say she is a modern-day Mrs. Keep. On the day we meet, she's wearing tan wool trousers, leopard-print pumps, a string of black pearls, and a black cape with a fur collar. Though she won't comment on the allegations in the suit, she makes her views on coddling perfectly clear. She believes, essentially, we've become a nation of politically correct softies, afraid of distinguishing anyone from anyone else lest anyone's feelings get hurt.

"This idea of a structure of hierarchy or power has been really dismissed in our culture as being not part of the American way or the American Dream: 'We can all do, we can all be, and we're all successful,' " says Windsor, who speaks in a matter-of-fact, rather formal manner. "If you have kids and they play soccer, everybody gets the banner. It doesn't matter if you lose—sometimes you think, Did we even win?"

In her position as headmistress of Miss Porter's, Windsor is determined to rectify this unfortunate development—at least for the 330 girls who are in her charge. That's where the traditions come in. "One of the things that is awesome about our traditions, about our Old Girl, New Girl tradition, is that we actually create these rites of passage where girls *get* anxious. The positive side is that it teaches girls to be prepared. How do you prepare for the unknown?" Windsor believes that, as long as the situation is supervised by adults and no one is doing anything physically harmful, it's a good thing—they'll be more prepared and confident when they get to the other side.

Bass feels she never had the chance to make it to the other side. She's slowly putting her life back together. She's now enrolled in another private school, in South Carolina, and has received offers with scholarships from two colleges for next year. But in her battle against Miss Porter's she finds herself alone. [Tatum Bass settled her lawsuit against Miss Porter's in early 2011.]

In Burch Ford's day, when a girl unleashed her meaner instinct, Ford attempted to rein it in. "One of the ways that you can establish you're cool is to put other people down," says Ford. "I'm thinking about one girl in particular. She was kind of a bombshell. She had learned one way to be popular, and it just wasn't working." Ford sat her down with a bunch of other students and explained, " 'You probably need to take a look at that because you may be coming across the way you didn't intend. . . . You don't have to like [people], but you have to be respect-ful.' . . . That was the end of anything we heard. She actually became a very nice girl."

Windsor, it seems, is reaching farther back into Miss Porter's 166-year history, to a time when girls stoically forged ahead through the social minefield of adolescence on their own. Perhaps her tradition-fortified, tough-it-out approach will create an armada of winners, perfectly poised to compete in our increasingly challenging world. Still, one can't help but wonder at what price this comes to the losers.

STANFORD GRADUATE SCHOOL OF BUSINESS

"CASE STUDY IN SCANDAL"

By David Margolick

DECEMBER 2015

When, in November 2013, Stanford University held one of its seminars on sexual harassment, the one its faculty and supervisors must take every two years, Professor James A. Phills, of the Graduate School of Business, heard a lawyer from the general counsel's office describe a romance gone sour at a primate-research center. A scientist ("Ed") kicked his former paramour ("Melissa") off a project involving monkeys, then slashed her bonus 80 percent, all because she refused to bleep him back at the hotel.

Such a problem, the lawyer declared, could *never* arise at Stanford. Had Ed worked there, she explained, he'd have had to cede all decisions regarding Melissa to a higher-up as soon as things turned sexual between them. But even before it was time for questions, Phills was sufficiently skeptical to butt in. "So the policy that Stanford has actually says that where such a recusal is required you must notify your supervisor, department chair, or dean," he said. "What if the person involved *is* the dean?"

"If the person who is involved is a dean, you should go straight to the provost," the lawyer replied. "And we will let the deans that are here know that," she added, prompting scattered laughs from the crowd. She resumed her talk, but before long Phills was at her again. "So suppose Ed were a dean and Melissa was a senior faculty member who was married to another senior faculty member," he began. "Ed was involved in a relationship with Melissa. Ed would have to recuse himself from making decisions about both Melissa *and* her husband?"

"That would probably pose a real problem," the lawyer replied. "Do you know something I don't know?" she asked playfully.

He might, Phills replied. "Don't out him or her here!" the lawyer exclaimed. There was more laughter.

"And your expectation would be that the provost or the general counsel, if something like this were to happen, Stanford would be concerned?" Phills pressed.

"Yes," the lawyer said. "And you and I need to talk outside!" More laughs still.

Phills assured the Stanford lawyer he was "speaking hypothetically." Only, he wasn't. By the time of the seminar, the dean of the business school, Garth Saloner, had been involved with Phills's estranged wife, Deborah Gruenfeld, a social psychologist and professor of organizational behavior there, for more than a year. And while Saloner had ostensibly removed himself from all decisions involving either Phills or Gruenfeld, Phills believed Saloner had remained enmeshed in his affairs, penalizing him professionally and injecting himself into his divorce and custody battles, all to drive him out of Stanford.

Some of this was not just conjecture. For three months in the summer and fall of 2012, as the incipient romance between Saloner and Gruenfeld developed, Phills, either sitting at his home computer or manning one of his other electronic devices—including, in one key instance, playing with the cell phone his wife had asked him to fix—had monitored and preserved the e-mails, text messages, and Facebook chats between the two. He'd followed their first walk together, and their first drinks, and their first date, and their first intimacies, real and cyber, fumbled and consummated. And all of this unfolded as he believed the Stanford Graduate School of Business (G.S.B.) was slowly squeezing him out, denying him crucial and lucrative teaching assignments and, by calling for a $250,000 loan to be repaid within less than a year, attempting to force him out of his house on the Stanford campus.

He knew that Saloner had disclosed the fledgling relationship to one of the main authors of the university's harassment policy, Provost John Etchemendy, as the regulations had required, but doubted whether the dean had done so in a timely fashion or had been fully candid with him when he did. And he knew, at least from what Saloner had had to say about it, how seemingly blasé Etchemendy had been about Saloner's disclosure. Phills had also come to believe that, with Saloner, the co-author of a textbook on strategy, now egging her on, the normally diffident and indecisive Gruenfeld had suddenly grown more aggressive, even ruthless, in their ongoing divorce and custody disputes.

"You are being too rational and generous," Saloner—sometimes posing as "Jeni Gee" on Facebook—had counseled her at one point. "Spewing the anger that you feel, even if it is unrelated to what you want, would make you a less predictable and rational adversary." Telling Phills what she *really* thought of him, he advised, would "push him back like a right to the jaw." At regular intervals, he bucked her up. "You are awesome," he told her. "You are the victim here. Roar!" Or "You're a star! Way to totally act w power. . . . Can you drive this process home now while you have momentum?"

Phills says that his monitoring wasn't hacking but simple self-protection. He had had to decide whether to stay at Apple University, the company's training school in Cupertino, where he'd been working while on a short leave from Stanford, or return to the G.S.B. And whether or just how much his boss, motivated by his ardor for Phills's wife, had it in for him surely mattered. Phills, in fact, denies he stole or hacked anything: he and his wife always shared equipment and passwords. Indeed, the technophobic Gruenfeld continued to use Phills as her personal Genius Bar even after she'd taken up with Saloner. (In her deposition, Gruenfeld denied sharing her passwords with Phills.) Only too late did she realize how much more difficult it has become these days to disentangle from someone electronically than emotionally. "I had e-mails to worry about," Gruenfeld testified this past June. "I had Facebook to worry about. I had Gchat to worry about. I had iMessages to worry about. And there were texts. I didn't know how to unhook myself." Earlier, in a text exchange later produced under court order, she and Saloner had chatted about the problem.

GRUENFELD: I am sorry I did not change my facebook [*sic*] password when we started dating. Never occurred to me that Jim would go there. . . . My denial was profound.

SALONER: Only a truly awful human being, the lowest of the low, would snoop on private conversations and then use them as blackmail. . . . The depravity and lack of conscience is [*sic*] unbelievable.

For Saloner, that was mild. At other times in his chats with Gruenfeld he referred to Phills as an "asshole," a "sociopath," and a "dick." To him and Gruenfeld and Stanford, Phills's monitoring was a gross and unjustified invasion of privacy. The dean and the university have filed a counterclaim against Phills over it, which has been appended to the lawsuit Phills filed against Saloner and Stanford for unspecified monetary damages for discrimination based on race, gender, and marital status, as well as for wrongful termination and intentional infliction of emotional distress, on April 2, 2014—the day before Stanford fired him.

MUTUALLY ASSURED DESTRUCTION

Phills's head, it has turned out, was not the biggest one to roll. This September, after Poets & Quants, a Web site specializing in business-school news and gossip, prepared to post a story on the case, Saloner abruptly announced his decision to step down as head of what *U.S. News & World Report* ranks as the top business school in the country.

The shocking move came only a year after Etchemendy had reappointed Saloner, who is 60 and has been the G.S.B.'s dean since 2009, to a second five-year term. (Gruenfeld, 53, had sat on the search committee that originally recommended him.) The provost re-upped him despite a petition signed by 46 former and current administrators and staffers at the school complaining that Saloner led by "personal agendas, favoritism and fear."

In his resignation statement, Saloner—who'd long coveted the business-school post, which might well have served him as a springboard to the soon-to-be-vacated Stanford presidency—insisted he'd done nothing wrong. Even so, he did not want "a baseless and protracted lawsuit related to a contentious divorce" to distract from the business school's business. (As things now stand, he will remain dean until the end of the school year.) [Saloner stayed on as dean until September 2016. He is now the John H. Scully Professor of Leadership, Management and International Business at the G.S.B.]

By any standards, *Phills* v. *The Board of Trustees of Leland Stanford Jr. University and Garth Saloner* is a colossal mismatch, pitting the infinite resources of a mighty institution against a lone individual who, though at the G.S.B. for 15 years, was never a tenured superstar with an endowed chair like his wife. Legally, his case seems tenuous—"a lawyer in search of a theory" is how one of Stanford's lawyers dismissively described it. Much of it is based on assumptions rather than facts. Saloner is a man who was known for playing rough and for playing favorites. ("He has a lot of the same qualities as [then presidential candidate] Carly Fiorina," one G.S.B. professor told me. "He loves you as long as you agree with him, and if you don't, you're toast.") Phills alleges in court papers that he has been "maligned and marginalized," and harmed "financially and emotionally" by Saloner. Still, anyone making more than a million dollars a year at Apple, as the 55-year-old Phills now does, will be hard-pressed to prove damages or elicit much sympathy from a jury. Phills's friends have implored him to drop the lawsuit and get on with his life. Though he's brought down a dean, his action could cost him his job at the famously press-shy Apple. Stanford will bleed him dry, they warn, then crush him.

But Phills, a former Harvard wrestler good enough to make the 1984 Canadian Olympic team as an alternate (he grew up in Montreal), says that winning, at least by conventional terms, is quite secondary to him. So is money: he already has had legal fees approaching half a million dollars. (His divorce and the case against Stanford have required the services of eight attorneys thus far.) His principal objective was never the dean's scalp, he says, but to expose the hypocrisy, dishonesty, cronyism, and bad character at a place charged with imparting ethical leadership to the next generation of moguls.

Thanks in large part to its proximity to Silicon Valley, the G.S.B. has become the most selective, prestigious, and sexy business school in the U.S. Its only real rival is stolid Harvard (which has nearly twice as many students). But no school, even one admitting a tiny percentage of its applicants, is untouchable. More than some of its competitors, the G.S.B. depends on donations from alums, who can always deposit their dollars elsewhere. And like any elite institution, it is particularly susceptible to embarrassment, especially to charges of poor leadership and mismanagement of its own affairs, which could jeopardize its ranking. Saloner won the deanship in part by revamping the G.S.B.'s curriculum, but the revised course offerings clearly did not include Judgment 101 or Introduction to Crisis Management.

Yet Stanford says it's serious about discouraging sexual harassment—

its regulations on the subject fill seven single-spaced pages—and Saloner himself said it would not be tolerated on his watch. "Are we doing everything we can to build a culture of mutual respect, a culture in which we behave in private in such a way that we will not be ashamed if our actions come into the public eye?" he has asked. "That training [on sexual harassment] is crystal-clear about our obligations," says Charles O'Reilly III, who teaches leadership and organizational behavior at the business school. "And if the dean doesn't comply, what's the signal to the rest of us?" Some of Saloner's faculty colleagues predict that, given the likely emergence of additional embarrassments, he won't survive the academic year as dean.

Further fueling Phills, a polite yet physically imposing man (an Ivy League wrestling opponent, who also boxed, once told him that, of all his adversaries, only Mike Tyson had intimidated him as much), is skin color. For the first time in his life, says Phills, who was one of the rare black professors at the business school when he arrived (and still rare, plus two or three, including Condoleezza Rice, when he left), he has felt the sting of racism, and at allegedly liberal Stanford, where bigotry seems bleached away by the perpetual California sunshine. At various points in their chats, Saloner—a Jew who fled apartheid South Africa rather than serve in its military—and Gruenfeld spoke of putting Phills in a cage and castrating him in public. Saloner relished seeing him in an orange jumpsuit in prison, and compared him to an elephant seal and a tarantula. To punish him and gain custody of their two mixed-race children, Phills charges, Gruenfeld reduced him—a man with three Harvard degrees, including a Ph.D. in organizational behavior—to the quintessential "angry black man." He calls the experience his "O.J.-ification."

Phills is obsessed with the lawsuit, he admits, and paranoid too. But he maintains he has a case if only 30 percent of what he believes happened actually did. He is clearly not the textbook "rational actor" they study in business schools. As such, he is easily misunderestimated.

"I don't back down," he says. "I don't like bullies. It's not about money; they could offer to write me a big check right now and I would say no. I'll be able to look myself in the mirror and have my kids look at me."

For Gruenfeld—who has been cited by Malcolm Gladwell; who tutored Sheryl Sandberg on gender issues (and sits on the board of Lean In, the nonprofit foundation connected to Sandberg's best-selling book of the same name); and who sold her own book, *Acting with Power*, at auction last fall for nearly a million dollars—questions of credibility are equally crucial. How does it look for someone who built her career analyzing the abusiveness (she dubbed it "disinhibition") of the powerful, and who, until a month before she became romantically entangled with the dean, was the G.S.B.'s sexual-harassment adviser, and who, as co-director of Stanford's Executive Program for Women Leaders, counsels high-powered women on how to overcome gender stereotypes, to wind up secretly sleeping with her boss?

Once, Phills says, he'd have happily settled the case: all he'd have wanted would be to stay in the house in which his two children were raised and teach at Stanford for a few more years before becoming emeritus, and for the university to pay his then modest legal fees. But as Stanford dug in, the costs, and the bitterness, and the indignities, have escalated. Phills assumes that Stanford has gone through all of his university e-mail for the past several years. (Stanford says it has reviewed only those e-mails produced in litigation.) Gruenfeld has seen an investigator for Stanford probe her love life, including whether she ever had affairs with her Stanford students. (She did not.) Gruenfeld has accused Phills of drinking excessively. Phills says that Gruenfeld confessed to him that she fudged research on the paper that launched her career, and charges that, in the two years since learning about it, Stanford has looked the other way. At a certain point, Gruenfeld, fearful that Phills would shoot her, had an armed guard stationed outside her classroom.

For a long time, Saloner exuded confidence: to him, Phills's quixotic crusade was nothing more than a nuisance. "Everything [is] going to go your/our way because we are on the right side and hold all the cards that count," he reassured Gruenfeld in one of their chats. So unperturbed was he about any lawsuit Phills might bring that he taunted the as yet unidentified lawyer representing Phills who'd be forced to sift through all their chats for anything incriminating. "Well, whoever you are, I apologize in advance :)," he wrote in one exchange. (Not everyone thought it such a sure thing. Shortly after Phills filed his case, in 2014, he says two Stanford professors who have taught leadership, Jeffrey Pfeffer and Robert Sutton, made a small wager—the stakes: dinner at a fancy San Francisco restaurant—over whether Saloner would last another year in his post.)

Now the case has tarnished everyone involved, including Stanford itself. The money-raisers, one former administrator told me, are in "panic mode."

"What a mess," one G.S.B. professor lamented to me. "You know the phrase 'mutually assured destruction'?" asked another. "This is what we got."

STAR AND SPOUSE

But juicy as the case is, for more than two years most professors, and staffers, and alumni, and trustees, and students, knew next to nothing about it.

Partly it's because Saloner and Gruenfeld still won't talk about it, and, until he spoke to me, neither would Phills. Partly it's because the G.S.B. is an astonishingly atomized, antisocial place, more a loose confederation of independent contractors than a community. As long as he or she funds their projects and leaves them alone, the dean is quite immaterial to them. (Since Saloner took the job, the G.S.B. has raised more than $500 million.) Saloner clearly knew as much; recounting to Gruenfeld how he'd just asked Phil Knight—the Nike co-founder and a G.S.B. alum, who helped bankroll its new campus with a $105 million gift—to speak at commencement, he texted, "We r developing a great relationship. So so good. That's my job really."

Partly it's because the students, their futures guaranteed simply by having gotten into the place, aren't engaged enough even to gossip. Their seeming insouciance may account for the intermittent scandals, such as the Stanford business student charged with vehicular manslaughter and felony drunk driving after crashing into a taxi and killing a passenger not long ago, or regular weekend bacchanals in Las Vegas. Partly it's the press. There's not much left of it in the Bay Area, and *The Stanford Daily* has proved supine: "Not quite the [*Harvard*] *Crimson,* which would have printed this story gleefully years ago," a former business-school student, one of the few to learn about and follow the Phills case, complained on her blog. Partly it's the reluctance to challenge conventional wisdom: since everyone connected to so hot a place looks good, no one wants to take it down. And partly it's fear. Everyone wants to work at Stanford, or to keep working there, or to send a child there, or to find a job in a place run by its ubiquitous alums, who include Mary Barra, the C.E.O. of General Motors, Jeff Skoll and John Donahoe, of eBay, and Laurene Powell Jobs, widow of Steve and a powerhouse in the world of philanthropy.

In court papers, Stanford argues that it bent over backward to keep Phills, extending his leave multiple times (asked in his deposition to explain one such extension, Etchemendy said, "I'm just a nice guy. What can I say?"), and that, "annoying" as Gruenfeld's romance with the dean may have been to him, it did not create a "hostile work environment." In fact, the university contends that Phills never really wanted to return to campus and is simply out for revenge and money. "At its core, this is an angry husband who is angry at his estranged wife, in a messy divorce that's gone on and on, and he seems intent upon using whatever he can to hurt her and now Garth," said Michael T. Lucey, of Gordon & Rees, the San Francisco law firm representing Stanford and Saloner in the case. (Gruenfeld is a party only in the separate divorce action.)

Stanford's lawyers say the dean excused himself from any decisions involving Phills before he and Gruenfeld shared their first kiss. And that the decision to recall the loan on the house the couple shared prior to their separation was a "no-brainer" made by apparatchiks in Stanford's housing office rather than Saloner's nefarious attempt at eviction. Such loans, they say, are made only to entice or retain elite professors such as Gruenfeld, who might otherwise be put off by insane real-estate prices in the area, and were never intended for add-ons such as Phills— "trailing spouses," in academic lingo, meaning the satellites of the university's stars.

And Gruenfeld is a star. At a G.S.B. road show in New York last December, I got to see the professor give her "Acting with Power" speech—the same kind of speech for which she earns, at Facebook or Genentech or eBay or PayPal, $25,000 a pop, according to Phills, who handled the family finances. It distills her two decades' worth of research on power—an interest, as she explains in her presentation, sparked by her own lifelong feelings of powerlessness—along with her more recent collaboration with actors in Stanford's drama department.

People assess trustworthiness, she'll tell you, in a tenth of a second. What they decide depends far less on what you say (7 percent) than on how you carry yourself (the other 93). At times one must be consciously contemptuous of others—i.e., reach for your cell phone while someone's talking—just to show who's boss. Lifting your chin and looking out of the bottom of your eyes (which also "pulls down the corners of the mouth, effectively removing the smile") can have "amazing" results. If substance is overrated, so is authenticity: "Just be yourself" is "terrible advice."

It's simple: lots of it you already know, or would if you thought very much about it. And unthreatening, requiring no great psychic overhauls. Last year Crown Business, part of Penguin Random House, agreed to pay Gruenfeld $900,000 to turn it into a book, slated to be published in the fall of 2017. [At the time of this volume's publication, the contract still stands, though the book does not yet have a scheduled on-sale date.] She will earn an additional $198,000 from foreign sales: readers in the Netherlands, Japan, Korea, China, and Taiwan, eager to imbibe state-of-the-art American self-salesmanship, will get editions of their own.

G ruenfeld earned her doctorate in psychology at the University of Illinois in 1993. Her dissertation, on decision-making in the United States Supreme Court, won all sorts of prestigious awards and helped land her a teaching job at Northwestern. That same year, she met Phills, then teaching at Yale, but the two did not start dating for several years, and, fearful it might cloud her prospects, she refused to make their engagement public until, as she put it, a tenured post was "in the bag." (According to Phills, she would remove her engagement ring every morning before going to work.) They married in September 1999. The next year the two officially joined the Stanford faculty. While Gruenfeld was tenured, Phills was imprisoned between a pair of parentheses: his job description—"professor (teaching)"—meant he would never get tenure, though he says that with continuing appointments he felt he had almost the same thing.

With the help of supplementary loans, the two gutted and rebuilt a home on the Stanford campus. By the time they'd moved back into it, in 2005, Phills was an associate professor (teaching)—capable, he contends, of assuming the extraordinary loans himself if Gruenfeld were ever to move out. Courting the pair, Yale invited Gruenfeld and Phills to visit for a year in New Haven. But before that could happen, the younger of their two daughters, not yet two, was diagnosed with cancer. Her treatment, which was ultimately successful, kept the couple at Stanford.

But it put further strains on what was becoming a shaky marriage, which they discussed in 2010 in workshops run by the Handel Group, an executive- and life-coaching company. Asked to list her "hauntings" for one such program—and ignoring the advice of a friend that such confessionals were "just crazy"—Gruenfeld wrote, "I once fudged the data for an important research project. The paper is published. I will go to my grave with that one." Phills says Gruenfeld told him shortly afterward that the paper in question was her award-winning dissertation. Gruenfeld says in her deposition that she does not remember writing or saying any such thing, and that in any case it's not true. Margaret Neale, a G.S.B. professor who has co-authored articles with Gruenfeld and had been a mentor to her at both Northwestern and Stanford, said "her scholarly integrity and courage are unassailable" and called any suggestions of data manipulation "impossible."

By early 2012, after two years of counseling, Phills and Gruenfeld—he feeling unsupported and neglected professionally, she feeling unsupported and neglected in child rearing—were heading toward divorce. In June, Gruenfeld moved out. Phills was now teaching at Apple University. Thanks to prior leaves, he had until the end of November to decide whether to stay there or return to Stanford. He says it posed a tough choice: Apple paid far better and was more exciting, while Stanford was more secure and cushy. And then there was the house, in which he could remain, he hoped, as long as he was affiliated with the university and had that crucial loan.

"WE R NUTS"

Gruenfeld and Saloner, whose wife had long suffered from cancer, had bonded several years earlier over the illnesses in their respective families. At one point in 2008 or 2009, according to Phills, they'd shared a "moment" in Saloner's office emotionally intimate enough for Gruenfeld to have told him about it afterward. (Phills acknowledges having had a brief affair early in their marriage.) At an engagement party for one of Saloner's daughters in March 2012, Phills thought Gruenfeld and the dean had spent an awfully long time talking. That June, Saloner's wife died. Two weeks later the dean, who'd learned that Gruenfeld and Phills had separated, e-mailed her, he later said, to congratulate her on her wildly popular "Acting with Power" class. "It is so wonderful to see you find your thing and blossom," he told her in one of the first e-mails Phills intercepted. "I hope you are doing OK—I am thinking of you." (It wasn't flirting, Saloner later testified; he regularly reached out to faculty members in distress. He was asked if he had also comforted

Phills. "I did not," he replied.) Gruenfeld thanked him, and invited him to her yoga class. "Absolutely!" he replied.

In August, Saloner invited Gruenfeld for a walk in a nearby nature preserve, one, coincidentally or not, further removed from the Stanford campus than the more popular hiking paths around the satellite dish in the Stanford foothills. "9AM Hike Arastradero," she wrote on the Google calendar she and Phills still shared. "PS because I'm now curious, who did you go hiking with?" Phills wrote her that night. She did not reply. He did not yet suspect Saloner, but would not have approved: he did not like the man—he didn't think he was "nice"—and, besides, Saloner had eviscerated the social-innovation center, a do-good place with scant constituency in a school dedicated to bottom lines, which had grown substantially under Phills's leadership, and had canceled two very popular executive-education programs he'd designed and run. Two years later, both programs were reinstated, without Phills. Some of his friends speculate that Phills's growing marginality at the G.S.B. made him less appealing to Gruenfeld and Saloner both. For obvious reasons, Saloner—who once told Gruenfeld he was a "possessive type"—was uncomfortable having Phills around.

Sometime that summer, Phills's younger daughter, now eight, told her father how "Garth" had just visited with her mother, and how friendly he had been. That fall, in the ongoing pre-divorce mediation, Gruenfeld seemed to be digging in. Phills, suspecting that Saloner was doing some coaching, and that his wife was bad-mouthing him to his boss (and that some of his colleagues had become standoffish), began his surveillance. Technically it was easy, Phills says—Gruenfeld's passwords were stored in his computer and iPad—but morally it was more dicey, and he sought out advice from both the university "ombuds" and its dean for religious life. As relevant tidbits turned up, and he grew more alarmed, the frequency of his reconnaissance increased. Though Saloner and Gruenfeld vowed to each other to delete their conversations immediately, in some instances Phills was too quick for them, capturing the exchanges with screen shots.

In mid- to late October, Saloner and Gruenfeld saw each other several times. What ensued would normally be of only voyeuristic interest but for the issue of recusal, which became obligatory at Stanford once a "consensual sexual or romantic" relationship begins. So it matters that, in the space of 10 days or so, the two scuttled dinner plans upon spotting some G.S.B. colleagues in a Palo Alto restaurant, and ended up at Saloner's house; that Saloner proposed going to a movie in another county, where they could hold hands undetected; that Saloner grew "dizzy" while embracing Gruenfeld in his kitchen; that, before reluctantly parting ways one evening, they groped each other at her house. (Despite all these facts, contained in intercepted chats, Stanford insists they had yet to kiss—that, defying the rules of both flirtation and baseball, the dean had somehow approached second base, and maybe even third, without ever touching first.)

That his estranged wife was seeing someone didn't much concern him, Phills says; he'd begun dating an environmental biologist. But decisions on the loans and his teaching load were pending, and though he assumed Saloner would be too smart—too *strategic*—to leave any traces, he suspected the dean was weighing in. Finally, on October 28, 2012, Phills wrote Etchemendy, Stanford's longest-serving provost, to express his concerns. He explained that further complicating the difficult career choice he now faced was what he called "some very sensitive personal issues" involving "the dean's office at the GSB." Etchemendy, with whom Phills had always enjoyed a cordial relationship, agreed to see Phills the following Friday, November 2.

But before that could happen, on Halloween morning, Saloner also wrote Etchemendy, to say that Gruenfeld and Phills had separated and that he'd "seen Deb a few times socially." Though it was unclear where things were heading, he went on, he was letting the provost know about it, both out of "an abundance of caution" and because the situation was "so fraught." No decisions regarding Gruenfeld loomed, he explained, but questions concerning Phills did; could Saloner still weigh in on them? "Obviously we are being as discreet as we can," he added. "I'd like to spare her the rumor mill if I can."

In fact, as their chats make clear, that very secrecy had become an aphrodisiac. When would someone looking up at the windows of the G.S.B. figure out they were texting each other? What would her colleagues on the deanship search committee make of how things had turned out, and whether she had had a personal interest in the outcome? Could they look at each other during meetings and keep a straight face? And when should they go public? Attending a Springsteen concert together in Oakland might be "too dangerous," but could they go out in New York "without being scared shitless?" (Once, he typed her texts from Etchemendy's waiting room. "We r nuts," he admitted.)

"I had heard some noise about this," Etchemendy replied to Saloner, referring to Phills's cryptic message. "I'm absolutely supportive of anything you decide wrt [with regard to] Jim. I'd be very sorry to lose Deb." Etchemendy concedes it was a "non-sequitur"; Gruenfeld wasn't going anywhere. And if Saloner's continued desire to "weigh in" on matters regarding Phills didn't sound much like recusal, neither did Etchemendy's support for "anything you decide." Etchemendy seems to have taken Saloner at his word: the relationship remained, as the provost noted, "fairly cursory" and "nascent." Had they entered the realm of the romantic or the sexual, Etchemendy added, everything would be very different.

The dean quickly shared the good news with Gruenfeld. The provost, he told her, was "totally cool."

SALONER: He basically ignored what I said about the two of us and, not in these words, that he trusts me to make any decisions regarding Jim. That is his style. It is almost as though he pretends he hasn't heard, although of course he has. I think it is his way of saying "you have done what the policy says you have to do, I appreciate it, but the policy wasn't written with you/this in mind and so I'm respecting your privacy and ignoring it."

GRUENFELD: Love that. So discreet and respectful.

SALONER: It is a non-issue for him.

That Saloner may not have leveled with the provost, and had understated the relationship, was further apparent from fragments of their conversation that same day. "You make me feel safe and it is such a gift," she told him in the morning. That night, he urged caution when she proposed "sneaking out": they probably could not limit themselves to a hug, he warned. "I want to hold you," Saloner told her a few minutes later. "I want you to hold me," she replied.

Phills says he had already concluded that telling the provost what was going on would only inflame things, and had canceled his appointment. Now, from reading the exchange between the dean and his wife, he says he believed that Saloner and Etchemendy were in league, making any meeting with the provost pointless. Replying by e-mail, Etchemendy wished Phills well and said nothing of what Saloner had told him.

During one of their periodic family dinners, a couple of weeks later, Phills says, Gruenfeld asked him to clean up her sluggish cell phone. Buried in its trash bin he found a 17-page marathon chat between his wife in Palo Alto and Saloner in Dubai from November 4, five days after Saloner's note to Etchemendy, one so graphic and salacious that before producing it in court Phills's own lawyers redacted it. Of far greater relevance to Phills than what the two imagined doing to each other was what they had actually done on the eve of Saloner's departure two nights earlier. "What an amazing night. What an incredible gift," Saloner wrote, in an exchange that also had them discussing what kind of birth control to use going forward. Clearly, the relationship had gone beyond "nascent," but Saloner never said so to the provost. "It would have been better had Garth let me know that the relationship had progressed to the next stage when it did," Etchemendy says.

SCHOOL FOR SCANDAL

Four days after that long chat, senior associate dean for academic affairs Madhav V. Rajan, who like everyone else in the G.S.B. brass still knew nothing about the dean's romance, contacted Saloner in India about Phills's request to assume the loans. The "unanimous sentiment," Rajan wrote, was to turn Phills down, but did Saloner concur? "I agree with the view of the SADs on this," replied Saloner, who, whether or not he had weighed in earlier, would normally have had the final word at the G.S.B. on such a question. He blind-copied the provost. Rajan gave Phills the bad news. The decision represented "the collective opinion of everyone in the dean's office," Rajan told Phills. "Everyone" included Saloner.

Phills's November 30 deadline for deciding whether to return from Apple approached. The day before, Gruenfeld and Saloner chatted about it.

GRUENFELD: Maybe he's staying at apple.

SALONER: Let's hope. We deserve something good tomorrow.
We've earned it. . . . the universe owes us. Big time.

But Phills decided not to decide. In a letter to Etchemendy, copied to Stanford general counsel Debra Zumwalt, he said he would neither resign nor return. (A few months later he laid out his terms: the loans had to be extended and guarantees be provided that he would report to someone beyond Saloner's control.) He then called Gruenfeld to tell her he knew about the affair. Only then, she later testified, did she realize he'd been "spying" on her. Later that day, he texted her to say he was "not feeling anything big emotionally" and that he hoped "we can work things out so that nobody gets harmed more than has already happened . . . That includes Garth and his family as well as ours." He added, "So I am hoping you don't do anything rash that would escalate the situation." With litigation looming, he asked Etchemendy that all relevant records—i.e., communications between his wife and the dean—be preserved. But word reached Saloner only after he'd destroyed at least the Facebook postings.

Etchemendy was puzzled by Phills's concerns; in incestuous academia, estranged spouses co-existed all the time. But henceforth, Etchemendy told Saloner, he'd officially handle everything involving Phills, effectively recusing the dean. He directed Saloner to tell Rajan to lengthen Phills's leave by four months to help the university "sort things out," the first of several such extensions spanning more than a year, during which Phills continued to teach at Stanford, sometimes without pay. Shortly before they were to go to the 2013 Rose Bowl together, Saloner and Gruenfeld went public.

Meanwhile, according to her deposition, Gruenfeld had construed some of Phills's statements, like about being careful or not escalating things, not as pleas but as threats. His prodding her to fill out certain life-insurance forms—he was replacing the Stanford policy with one from Apple—seemed menacing to her, in a *Double Indemnity* kind of way.

In early March 2013, three months after Phills had filed for divorce, he and Gruenfeld had an argument in the driveway of his home. Gruenfeld promptly drove off to Saloner's house, and the two then went to the Stanford police, where Gruenfeld asked for an emergency protective order. It was denied, but a couple of days later, she asked for a restraining order. To stress the peril she was in, she noted that Phills had been a wrestler; that he had been arrested as a teenager; that he owned three guns; and that, during another driveway altercation, he had "reeked of alcohol." Phills was not informed of the restraining-order request, and was given no chance to respond. She got the order, effective for six months. Henceforth, Phills had to stay 50 yards away from her (tricky, because they worked in the same building) and notify her a day in advance when planning to be on campus (less tricky, because they shared an assistant). Since the original version of the restraining order forbade

Phills from being on campus without such notice, and his house was on campus, he arguably violated it even when he was at home. Gruenfeld was also awarded primary custody: aside from Tuesday nights, Phills could now see his daughters only every other weekend.

Though one of Gruenfeld's friends told me Phills was "an extremely scary person," this is very much a minority view. If he resembles a Tyson, it's far more Neil deGrasse (a friend and teammate with whom he periodically wrestled at Harvard) than Mike. Questioned by the police, neither Gruenfeld nor her daughters could cite any time he had ever lifted a hand against her; in fact, what the younger daughter told the police had most frightened her that day in the driveway was that her mother might "roll over my dad's toes." Yes, Phills had been arrested once as a minor, in the course of rescuing his younger sister from a sexual assault, but he'd never been charged with anything. Yes, he had guns, but he'd used them only four or five times—for skeet shooting. Yes, he drank, but he was "vigilant": his father had died of liver disease. His championship wrestling days were long over, and, as he told the family-court judge, he'd become "a largely sedentary and overweight academic."

Desperate to regain co-custody of his children—and to dent Gruenfeld's credibility—Phills pulled out her apparent admission about fudging research and gave it to both the G.S.B. and the court-appointed custody evaluator. He says he remained convinced that without Saloner's encouragement—"poke a stick at him every day," the dean had advised Gruenfeld at one point—none of this would be happening. Though it took a year, co-custody was eventually restored.

Shortly after Saloner's resignation in September, one of his loyalists at the G.S.B. expressed fear to me about the dean's well-being. Long ago, he explained, Saloner had opted for administration over scholarship, and now all that was gone. "This is going to destroy him," he warned. "I don't quite know how he recovers from this."

Since then, though, Saloner appears to have regrouped, and, like Phills, has even hired his own publicist and may soon hire a lawyer. Yet with the heat from the case now likely to shift to Etchemendy, the question is whether the provost, too, might turn on Saloner. [Etchemendy stepped down as provost in January 2017.] Some of the dean's colleagues believe his insistence on staying at the school, and Stanford's willingness to let him, is but the latest in a long list of maladroit moves and miscalculations. One G.S.B. professor predicted that, among students, Saloner will become an object of ridicule, and that the castration he spoke of in one chat—"Knife. Penis. Public Square," he'd texted Gruenfeld, apparently referencing the erotic Japanese art film *In the Realm of the Senses*—will surely be reprised as a campus catchphrase. He also predicted that Saloner will be tapping into his extensive Silicon Valley ties to find himself a job there.

As for Phills, he says Saloner's resignation surprised and saddened him: "It was completely avoidable, if the university had done the right thing." Meanwhile, his lawsuit plods on. Phills says he remains convinced that, if they can be retrieved, whether from their equipment or from the servers, the lost electronic exchanges between Saloner and Gruenfeld (which the court has ordered that they produce) will finally reveal the extent of Saloner's inappropriate involvement in his professional and personal affairs. Settlement talks have gotten nowhere. If the case does get to trial, it probably won't be before next April or May. [The lawsuit is still pending.] Noting the complicated financial issues (including the status of the house), Phills put the chances that he and Gruenfeld will still be officially married a year from now at 90 percent.

When Phills packed up his Stanford office, this past July, some colleagues were surprised: they hadn't even known he'd been sacked. For now, he is a nonperson at Stanford, still in the house (the university is no longer pressing him to repay the loans) but required to sell it by June 2017, and so unsure whether he'd be admitted to the school's libraries and gyms that he hasn't even tried. (Stanford says he is entitled to a "courtesy" ID card, but he would have to apply for one through Gruenfeld.)

Recently, though, there was a friendly communiqué from the university. That academic ritual at Stanford had come back around: time, once again, for sexual-harassment training.

PHANTOM
CHARGES

DUKE LACROSSE CASE

"THAT CHAMPIONSHIP SCANDAL"

By Buzz Bissinger

JULY 2006

*We have only one rule here: Don't do anything that's detrimental to
yourself. Because if it's detrimental to you, it'll be detrimental to our
program and to Duke University.*

—Mike Krzyzewski, Duke University basketball coach,

from his book *Leading with the Heart.*

The series of photographs depicting the inside of the
house at 610 North Buchanan Boulevard around midnight on March
13 were by all available accounts taken before the alleged gang rape of
a 27-year-old black woman by three members of the Duke University
lacrosse team. They were taken before the almost surreal legal chaos
that unfolded in coming weeks, during which a phalanx of seasoned
defense attorneys gathered on the steps of the county courthouse passionately insisting that no sexual assault ever took place that night,
and before a neophyte district attorney in the midst of an election
campaign insisted with equal passion that a brutal rape did occur.
They were taken before the lacrosse team, ranked second in the country, had the rest of its season canceled, and before the coach of the

team, Mike Pressler, resigned following the revelation of a shocking e-mail sent by one of his players.

They were taken before hundreds of reporters descended on the campus of Duke and the North Carolina city of Durham and pumped out quick and mostly facile stories on race and gender and privilege. They were taken before the results of a crucial DNA test on 46 Duke lacrosse players found no match with the accuser, making her allegations, that she was choked and raped and sodomized for about 30 minutes, even more uncertain. They were taken before two sophomore lacrosse players, one of them dressed in a coat and tie, as if he might score points for decorum, arrived at the Durham County magistrate's office in handcuffs in the early-morning hours of April 18 charged with first-degree forcible rape, first-degree sexual offense, and kidnapping. They were taken before a third player was indicted nearly a month later on the same charges.

The pictures reveal nothing about the alleged crime beyond possible circumstantial evidence. They do little to clarify whether the alleged horror took place, or whether something equally horrible occurred—a false accusation. The only certainty in this case is that, no matter what happens at trial, lives and reputations have already been ruined. But the photos do reveal the atmosphere of that night, a side of major college athletics at one of the finest universities in the country.

They show the living area of 610 North Buchanan Boulevard, just off Duke's East Campus, in a lovely residential section known as Trinity Park. A banner on one wall reads, TAILGATE PARTY. Over a doorway on another wall is a poster with the slogan IT'S HARD TO BEAT A TEAM THAT NEVER GIVES UP! and an insignia of the Duke lacrosse team. The boys— 41 of the 47 members were there that night for a party, according to an application for court-ordered DNA testing that was later filed—ring the living room like spectators at a cockfight. They are watching the escort-service dancers who have been hired for what a defense attorney describes as "the entertainment for the evening." Several of the boys sit with their backs pushed against the white walls. Several more sit on a patterned couch. Most are in shorts. There is a smattering of short-sleeved shirts, yellow and green and red, with one that says, "I ♥ Girl Scouts."

There is clearly under-age drinking going on—it's one of the few points of the case that no one disputes—and many of the boys have the evidence in their hands, cans of Natural Light and red cups, apparently filled with Jack Daniel's and Coke. There has been drinking going on for much of the day, according to neighbor Jason Bissey, who remembers one young man in the backyard wearing suspenders with built-in beer holders.

A few of the boys are smiling as they watch the two dancers gyrate in various states of undress. It's spring break at Duke, and since the team is stuck on campus for practice, watching these women perform is apparently a way of team bonding and having fun. One of the boys is looking away, and one is looking down at his cell phone, as if to suggest that the evening's entertainment, which they reportedly paid $800 for, isn't turning out to be very entertaining at all.

A documented legacy of boorish, we-can-do-whatever-we-please behavior by the Duke lacrosse team over the past five years, during which various university administrators have talked and pondered but failed to curb the activity, is catching up with the team now, no longer containable in the guise of a boys-will-be-boys attitude. The team's collective acts have built up toward the night of March 13, but unlike all the others, this one will have consequences beyond all imagination.

Whether what happened inside the house on Buchanan Boulevard amounted to something as horrible as a gang rape is a question that won't be answered until trial, presumably next spring, if it is ever definitively answered at all. The case is already awash in controversy, the veracity of the accuser's claim clouded by everything from when she first reported a rape to police, approximately two hours after it allegedly occurred, to her own past, which includes a criminal conviction and reported treatment for a nervous breakdown, to the fact that 10 years earlier she made a similar allegation, telling the police in Creedmoor, North

Carolina, that she had been raped by three men three years earlier—an allegation that resulted in no charges. According to one of a series of reports issued by Duke in the aftermath of the March 14 rape allegation, part of the reason for Duke's initially muted response to the incident (incredibly, the president of the university, Richard Brodhead, did not know there had been an allegation of rape until he read about it in the student newspaper on March 20, and did not know the accuser was black until March 24) was that members of the Durham police did not at first believe the accuser to be credible.

Already in the Duke case, one of the suspects, Reade Seligmann, according to motions filed by his lawyer, has attempted to establish what appears to be a convincing alibi to show that he was not even in the house when the alleged rape took place. Seligmann called taxi driver Moezeldin Elmostafa at 12:14 A.M. and was picked up at roughly 12:19 A.M., according to an affidavit from Elmostafa that was part of the court filing. Those same motions also raise legitimate legal questions about the identification procedure police used with the accuser, in which she was shown only photos of members of the lacrosse team, as opposed to authorities' interspersing them with so-called fillers—pictures of nonsuspects—to ensure the fairness of the process. There is also the fact that the accuser did not identify the subjects until April 4, three weeks after the alleged incident.

If the three suspects have been charged with a rape they did not commit, it's a hideous tragedy. If the accuser's claims are in fact true, it's a hideous tragedy. The damage done to Duke, which in roughly three decades has transformed itself from a finishing school for the southern elite into a world-class university, is incalculable. The damage done to the lacrosse team at Duke, which was in the N.C.A.A. championship last year and which, many felt, would win it all this year, has been incalculable.

It's really fun to go to Duke. It's really fun socially. There's that little thing in the middle called classes.

—A Duke professor.

U p until the night of March 13, Duke's rapid rise to prominence over the past several decades was perhaps without precedent in academia. Under the guidance of former presidents Terry Sanford, H. Keith Brodie, and Nannerl Keohane, the school transformed from a regional institution competing with such southern counterparts as Vanderbilt University and Emory University into a national institution competing with the Ivy League and Stanford University.

The marketing of the school was aggressive, and so were efforts to lure high-profile professors from other universities in what was likened to a professional-sports bidding war. In the early 1970s, the school took out a 16-page advertising supplement in *The New York Times* extolling its virtues. Beginning in the 1980s, the school, in an effort to make its field of humanities perhaps the best in the country, enticed such scholars as Frank Lentricchia from Rice University and Stanley Fish from Johns Hopkins University and Henry Louis Gates Jr. from Cornell University into its fold. By the late 1990s, Duke had risen to third, behind only Harvard and Princeton, in the vaunted rankings of universities by *U.S. News & World Report*.

This year, the school offered acceptances to only 19 percent of the 19,358 seniors who applied, the lowest admissions rate in the school's history. Of the applicants, 1,548 were class valedictorians and more than 1,300 had combined SAT scores of 1,550 on the math and verbal sections of the test. Tuition at the school, including room and board, is $44,000 a year, and roughly 40 percent of Duke's 6,244 students receive some type of financial aid or grants.

But in spite of the transformation, the sense of immense wealth and privilege lingered. There was a sense that the school was still a kind of plantation on the hill built by the tobacco fortunes of the Duke family in a city that was still rediscovering itself after the closure of the factories that had once produced such iconic brands as Chesterfield and Lucky Strike. There was also the lingering sense of a school where students, regardless of their academic credentials, still considered partying as something of a Duke birthright, what one professor dubbed "Cruiseship Duke."

The allegations of rape were called a perfect storm by many, as they brought issues of race and gender and town-gown friction and the role of athletics into glaring view. "This is like Katrina in your own backyard," said history professor Peter Wood, and resentment of Duke as a perceived place of white privilege was particularly acute at North Carolina Central University, the mostly black institution in Durham attended by the accuser. "It's the same old story. Duke up, Central down," said a Central student in an interview with a reporter, a refrain that was echoed repeatedly.

Relations between Duke and the neighborhood of Trinity Park, where the rape allegedly occurred, had been horrific for years. According to numerous interviews with residents, Duke students, in a partying cycle that began on Thursday, routinely roamed the tree-lined streets of the neighborhood in the wee hours of the morning drunk and unruly, lying in their own vomit, urinating on cars, smashing beer bottles, calling residents who asked them to keep the noise down "bitches."

The night of March 13 also unleashed questions about the role of athletics at Duke, which, unlike its Ivy League counterparts, plays in the highly competitive Atlantic Coast Conference and offers athletic scholarships. Without a doubt, the greatest public face of Duke is its vaunted basketball team, among the top-ranked teams in the country year in and year out. The most visible person on campus is basketball coach Mike Krzyzewski, and he may be the most powerful.

When Richard Brodhead left Yale to become the president of Duke in July of 2004, one of his first acts, literally within days of his arrival, was to help keep Krzyzewski from leaving the university for the Los Angeles Lakers. At one pep rally, Brodhead reportedly took a megaphone and yelled for "Coach K" to stay.

"I like Dick. I know him," said Orin Starn, a professor of cultural anthropology. "I thought it was humiliating that the president of the university, when we should be celebrating, thinking about plans for the university, is forced to play the role of supplicant begging the basketball coach to stay."

"It revealed the lay of the land, that athletics is oversized at the university," said Starn, who noted that in a class of 125 students he taught one semester on cultural anthropology, roughly 15 came up to him at the beginning with a list of eight to nine classes they would have to miss because of their participation in sports. "The fact is, you can't be a real college student if you're missing a lot of class and too tired to do the work."

Within the culture of sports at Duke was the subculture of the men's lacrosse team, described in interviews and documents as almost sect-like in the way members tended to live together and take the same classes together and go out together and party together. That did not necessarily make them different from other sports teams at Duke, where, as Starn put it, "athletes are isolated from broader student life." But unlike college basketball and football, where student-athletes routinely come from inner-city settings and small rural settings and play on teams in which African-Americans have a dominant presence, lacrosse offered no diversity.

The 2006 team, with the exception of one player, was exclusively white. Only 2 players were from west of the Mississippi, while 33 were from New York, Maryland, or New Jersey. The background of the team was rooted in East Coast suburbia, with a sizable percentage coming from private schools. (Twelve players came from the exclusive private schools the three rape suspects attended.)

Sometime around seven P.M. on March 13, 31-year-old Kim Roberts got a call from the escort service she worked for saying there was going to be a bachelor party at a private residence with about 15 men. Roberts had been working for the service for about six months. "It was what was available," she said in an interview with *Vanity Fair*, in which she openly acknowledged a conviction in Durham County for embezzling from an employer and going to California in violation of the terms of her probation. Upon her return to Durham, she said, she knew there was a warrant for her arrest for a missed appointment with her probation officer. The mother of a young daughter, unable to find a regular job, she said, she had turned to the escort service for work.

Roberts said all of her escort experience up to that point had been confined to small parties of two or three at local hotels, so the number of men she was told would be at this event did give her pause. It was "something to think about," she said, but such concerns were alleviated when the escort agency told her that a woman with "more experience" in such settings would also be there. In addition, as it was going to be a bachelor party, she assumed the men there would be close to 30 or perhaps a little older—in other words, like the men she had danced for before, only more of them. "I guess the biggest thing I was expecting was the guys to be more mature. To me, when a man is more mature he understands that you might not get what you think you're gonna get, so they're more apt to be O.K. with that."

She drove to 610 North Buchanan Boulevard, arriving at about 11. She wasn't familiar with the address, and as she approached she realized that the house might be some type of off-campus student residence. Initially, she did not stop, as it was clear to her that this wasn't a bachelor party but a party with students. "At first I didn't want to stay, because I saw all these young guys," she said. So she drove around the block before deciding to stop.

She was met at the car by someone she called "Dan F." during the evening. According to the application for DNA testing, he was Dan Flannery, one of the team's co-captains and a resident of the house, and he had made the arrangements for the party. Flannery's role was also confirmed by his lawyer.

He was "very respectful," Roberts said. But she still wasn't sure she wanted to stay, because it wasn't the setting she had expected. She talked to Flannery for several minutes, then to another person, whom she believed was also a resident of the house. As she was doing so, other members of the Duke lacrosse team started coming out the front door. She saw them urinating in front of her off the front porch. "There was plenty of pissing off the porch outside," she said, and in the course of waiting for the second dancer to arrive, roughly half an hour, she saw at least five players relieve themselves in this manner.

As Roberts was waiting, a Durham police car drove by twice. Because of the warrant for her arrest, she said, she became nervous and asked to move behind the house.

At first, she said, she had been told that the boys inside were members of the Duke track and baseball teams. Once she got to the rear of the house, she said, she was told that in fact they were members of the lacrosse team. It was in this conversation, Roberts said, that she learned that a specific request had been made for a white woman and a Hispanic woman. She said she was asked about her nationality at one point—she was born to a Korean mother and an African-American father, but in the past she had been taken for Hispanic. "I fit the bill of the Hispanic, so of course they were assuming the next girl would be white," she said. "And then here she comes, walking around the corner."

The second dancer to arrive was black. Roberts said she could sense the hesitation in those milling outside as the second dancer arrived. According to Roberts, the person who had told her that a white dancer had been asked for "expressed in some way that they might not be happy" with the second dancer. "I can't remember how he put it or what way he said it, but I said to him, 'Well, they're going to have to make a decision and make it now.' "

The decision was made to go forward. Roberts told the boys to go inside the house so she could talk to the other dancer for a few minutes and try to get to know her. Defense attorneys have vigorously asserted that she was highly impaired when she arrived. Unlike Roberts, she arrived already in costume, and based on the pictures that were taken that night, there also appeared to be open cuts both on her knee and on her foot.

On the basis of a private conversation Roberts had with one of the defense attorneys in the case, statements were attributed to her publicly that said she had found the other woman "loopy" from the very outset.

In the interview with *Vanity Fair,* Roberts said that characterization was incorrect. She said that, when they had been behind the house initially, the other dancer was "absolutely fine," in stark contrast to the end of the evening, when Roberts found her completely incoherent. "We talked. We joked a little bit," said Roberts. "I told her I was new to this and didn't really know what I was doing. [She] told me that she danced at a club and was a little more experienced. She told me about her kids." She had two children and was a student at North Carolina Central University, in Durham.

"It was a regular, normal conversation," Roberts said, "nothing that set off any alarm bells in my head."

Before Roberts went inside, she spoke to several players about the need for the respect shown her outside to continue inside once the performing started. " 'O.K., you guys seem very respectful,' " she said she told them. " 'If everybody acts as you are acting, I'm sure we'll have a fun time. I'm sure we'll have a good time.' They completely assured me that everybody in there were good guys—'Everybody in there is respectful, and you will be fine and safe.' [I was] completely assured of that."

But from the outset, when she and the other dancer began to perform in the living room, Roberts said, she felt overwhelmed. "They definitely were drunk and drinking," she said, and it wasn't simply beer but hard alcohol, as she saw a large bottle of Jack Daniel's. As soon as Roberts got her first look at the boys in the room, she could see that some of them were very young. In hindsight, she also thinks there was an expectation that she and the other dancer would fully degrade each other during the course of the performance.

"As soon as we showed ourselves in our costumes, it was on," she said. "They were ready to see whatever they were going to see, and so it got loud from there and there was no time. There was no time. There was no wait. It was just a go from there.

"You have to think of two little girls among how many big boys? That in and of itself is intimidating if they are not being respectful of my feelings, my space.

"How is someone supposed to perform a show if they're wondering, O.K., what's this guy talking about over here? Am I going to have to worry about my safety? Things were said that made me concerned for my safety."

Because she is certain to be called as a witness at trial, she was reluctant to provide full details of all that happened inside the house when she and the other dancer were performing. According to defense attorney William Thomas, representing one of the team captains, it was shortly after the performance had begun that one of the players asked the dancers if they had brought "any toys," an apparent reference to sexual toys. Thomas said Roberts responded by saying something to the effect of "What's wrong, white boy, is your dick too small?" (Roberts refused to comment on Thomas's claim. A source, however, readily conceded that she did make a comment similar to the one described by Thomas, but only at the end of the evening, after one of the players had called her a "nigger.")

Thomas said that the same player who made the reference to "toys" subsequently lifted up a broomstick and said words to the effect of "Here, you can use this." This version is also borne out by the application filed by the district attorney's office for court-ordered DNA testing, but with words far more graphic. According to the application, the player said to the women, "I'm gonna shove this up you." It was after the reference to the broomstick, according to both Thomas and the application, that the dancing ended.

According to the application, Roberts and the other dancer went outside. It was upon the other dancer's return to the house, after having been talked back inside, that she was pulled into a bathroom, held down, and sexually assaulted anally, vaginally, and orally by three males over an approximate 30-minute time frame. Roberts has said in previous interviews that she did not witness the alleged rape and has no knowledge of whether it took place.

It wasn't until the end of the evening, sometime around 12:50 A.M., that an already unsettling night grew even more unsettling for Roberts. She and the other dancer were near Roberts's navy-blue Honda getting ready to go. Many of the boys were milling around at that point, she said, some on the front lawn, some in a field across the street. They were angry, said Roberts. According to defense attorneys and previous media accounts, they felt cheated because the performance they paid $800 for had lasted only several minutes. But Roberts said she found the anger hard to fathom, given the way the boys had behaved. "Any human should understand they were acting idiotically," she said. "There was only one person who said to me, 'I understand that you might feel intimidated.' He at least made it seem like he understood where I was coming from, why I stopped [dancing]." It was when she was in the car with the other dancer, getting ready to drive off, she said, that she heard one of the boys in the field yell the word "nigger," followed by several other boys shouting the racial epithet.

Roberts was not the only person who heard a racist comment. Jason Bissey, the next-door neighbor, said in an interview he heard one of the players say, "Hey, bitch, thank your grandpa for your nice cotton shirt!" as the Honda was driving off.

"They just hollered it out, 'Nigger,' 'Nigger,' 'Nigger,' " said Roberts. "They were hollering it for all to hear. They didn't care who heard it."

Roberts said she immediately got on her cell phone and called the police and told them what had occurred. She did not give her name, she said, because of her arrest warrant, and because she didn't want them to know she was an escort-service worker coming out of a party.

Then she tried to figure out what to do with the other dancer in the passenger seat next to her, who, she said, was completely unresponsive. Roberts did not know where she lived. She did not know her real name, only her dancing name. She did not know if someone was supposed to pick her up. She did not know where to take her, so she drove to a Kroger grocery store on Hillsborough Road, since it was open 24 hours and fairly close.

Once there, Roberts approached a security guard, who called 911 at 1:22 A.M. and described the second dancer as "like intoxicated, drunk, or something . . . she's barely talking," and refusing to get out of the car. When police responded, at approximately 1:51 A.M., an officer on the scene reported to a dispatcher that she was "breathing, appears to be fine. She's not in distress. She's just passed out, drunk."

Police took her to a mental-health and drug-treatment facility because of her apparent inebriation, according to the motion papers filed by the defense counsel for one of the accused. At about 2:31 A.M., she was transported to the Duke University Medical Center and checked in at 2:45 A.M., the court papers state. It was five minutes later, at approximately 2:50 A.M., the papers say, that the report on the woman was "changed from passed out drunk to alleged rape." She was then taken to the emergency room of the hospital, where a university policewoman trying to reassure her reportedly saw her "crying uncontrollably and visibly shaken, shaking, crying, and upset." A forensic sexual-assault nurse and a physician examined the woman. According to the application for DNA testing, "Medical records and interviews that were obtained by a subpoena revealed the victim had signs, symptoms, and injuries consistent with being raped and sexually assaulted vaginally and anally. Furthermore, the [forensic sexual-assault] nurse stated the injuries and her behavior were consistent with a traumatic experience."

At some point that night, the alleged victim reportedly told police that she had been raped and sexually assaulted by approximately 20 members of a Duke sports team, before modifying the number of assailants to 3.

As Roberts made her way home, she had no idea what was unfolding with the other dancer. All she knew was that a night that had started out respectfully had ended with her being called a "nigger." And in between she had felt overwhelmed and intimidated and ultimately scared.

When she left the house that night, trying to process the racial epithet, trying to figure out what to do with the woman next to her, "it was almost unbelievable," she said. "All I kept going back to was 'I can't believe these are Duke students.' "

Within roughly an hour of when Roberts left, one of the players identified in a police application for a search warrant as having been a guest at the party that night, sophomore Ryan McFadyen, sent an e-mail from his dormitory room that said the following:

To whom it may concern

Tommorow night, after tonights show, ive decided to have some strippers over to edens 2c. all are welcome . . however there will be no nudity. I plan on killing the bitches as soon as the[y] walk in and proceding to cut their skin off while cumming in my duke issue spandex . . all in besides arch and tack please respond

Bill Thomas knew it was a last-ditch effort, this meeting in the middle of April, in all probability futile. He could see the way the wind was blowing in this case, that virtually from the beginning, once it had gone public, Durham County district attorney Michael Nifong had fanned fires of guilt despite the fact that there had been no arrests and no charges.

Nifong, in the course of more than 50 interviews he gave to the news media before he abruptly stopped talking, said on MSNBC's *Abrams Report,* "I am convinced that there was a rape, yes, sir." He said on Fox's *The O'Reilly Factor,* "There's no doubt in my mind that she was raped and assaulted at this location." On ABC News, he said that 46 members of the team were united in silence and refusing to talk with investigators probing the rape case, despite the fact that the three captains who lived at 610 North Buchanan Boulevard—Flannery, David Evans, and Matt

Zash—had voluntarily given statements to the police, provided DNA samples, and also offered to take polygraph exams.

Thomas had been a defense attorney for 26 years. He worked in a city of roughly 200,000 that was almost equally divided between black and white. From previous experience he knew the way in which issues of race could take hold in Durham. He had represented a white defendant named Michael Seagroves in the early 1990s against a voluntary manslaughter charge in the killing of a 15-year-old black youth who had broken into Seagroves's house during an attempted robbery. He had received death threats during the case, which ended in a hung jury. The racial tension had been so palpable, there was concern there might be riots. But the attention given the Seagroves case paled in comparison with what was happening here, fueled, Thomas believed, by Nifong's interaction with the media.

Such conduct was uncharacteristic of Nifong. In his 27 years as a prosecutor in the Durham County District Attorney's Office, the 55-year-old had been known to be fair-minded and not publicity-hungry. But the circumstances here were different. Appointed district attorney in April 2005 after his predecessor became a superior-court judge, Nifong now found himself in his first election—a heated three-way race against a high-profile white opponent and a black opponent in the May 2 primary. Given the racial characteristics of the electorate, Nifong's ability to capture black votes was considered by some to be crucial, and it was hard not to wonder if his statements were a thinly disguised ploy to get votes. "It's all about tactics and motives," Nifong's black challenger, Keith Bishop, said before the election. "He wants to win so badly that he will do anything and say anything. It reflects political immaturity. He thinks that simply pandering to race will give him the breakout he needs."

Whatever Nifong's motives, Bill Thomas felt that a grave mistake would be made in indicting any of the Duke lacrosse players for a rape that in his estimation, and the estimation of defense attorneys representing other players, had not happened. "It took me 48 hours before I knew this was a false allegation, without question."

Thomas had at his disposal not simply the statement his own client had given him—that no sexual assault had taken place—but also the statements of all the other players who had been at the party. What struck him was not simply the denials but also the way, he says, the players' stories all matched up.

In those 26 years as a defense attorney, Thomas had rarely made information available to a prosecutor in an ongoing proceeding. But on April 13, he and two other defense attorneys involved in the case, Wade Smith and James Williams, met privately with Nifong to try to convince him that he was making a mistake. According to Thomas, they were willing to share the statements that had been gathered by defense attorneys. They were also willing to share the time-stamped photos taken that night that, they believed, proved the alleged rape couldn't have occurred as described by the victim in the application for DNA testing. One of the pictures, thought to have been taken after a rape could have occurred, showed the victim on the back porch with what appeared to be a smile on her face, an incongruous expression for someone who had allegedly just been sexually assaulted.

"Our goal was not to attack him but [to show] that this thing is heading the wrong direction," said Thomas in recounting the meeting. "The question we were addressing was to let Mike effectively know that this indictment is a mistake." The meeting was cordial, said Thomas, but tense, and it became clear to him that Nifong had no interest in the defense attorneys' offer. "He wasn't interested in any dialogue about the evidence," said Thomas, and that puzzled him, given his own sentiment that there was nothing to lose and a tremendous amount to gain.

"As much as you're convinced that these boys did not do this, I'm convinced that they did," Thomas says Nifong told the three lawyers. And he would not consider any slowdown of the process.

The list of disciplinary incidents involving the Duke lacrosse team over roughly the past five years, as compiled by the university's Office of Judicial Affairs, amounted not to a single sheet or two but to eight full pages of small type. There were dozens upon dozens of confirmed and suspected incidents, involving not just a handful of players but 48 of them. The list, read in any context, was alarming, depicting a team headed toward what one Duke official described in 2005 as a "train wreck."

"Over the last five years . . . many lacrosse players increasingly have been socially irresponsible consumers of alcohol," concluded the committee's exhaustive report.

"They have repeatedly violated the law against underage drinking. They have drunk alcohol excessively," the report said. "They have disturbed their neighbors with loud music and noise, both on-campus and off-campus. They have publicly urinated both on-campus and off. They have shown disrespect for property."

With the exception of that of the men's golf team (which has only nine members), the disciplinary record of the lacrosse team was by far the worst of the 26 men's and women's teams that Duke maintained. On the Duke football team, 15 of 103 members had disciplinary histories, or nearly 15 percent. On the men's indoor-track team, which had 50 members, 9 had disciplinary histories, or 18 percent. On the Duke basketball team, which had only 11 members, 4 had disciplinary histories, or just over 36 percent. But on the lacrosse team, which had 48 members at the time of the examination, 50 percent of the team had disciplinary histories.

Many of the incidents cited in the eight-page list were drinking offenses. Such offenses were not uncommon at Duke, or on any college campus. There were no incidents involving sexual assault or harassment, or racist behavior, or academic misconduct. And Duke lacrosse players were found to do well in the classroom, have a 100 percent graduation rate, and, perhaps indicative of the tight network of lacrosse players, benefit from a steady pipeline of jobs after graduation as analysts at such prestigious investment houses as Goldman Sachs, Morgan Stanley, and UBS.

In many ways the players embodied the very best of the student-athlete model, able to juggle the rigorous demands of academics at a place such as Duke along with the rigorous demands of competing at the Division One level in intercollegiate athletics. Lacrosse is taken seriously at Duke. Those familiar with the program describe it as a full-time job. On the field, the team had a 17-and-2 record last season. Off the field, between 2001 and 2005, 146 lacrosse-team members had been named to the Atlantic Coast Conference Honor Roll, more than twice as many as the next-closest team.

In its report, the committee did recommend the return of the lacrosse program next year, but with strict monitoring because of past misconduct. The list of incidents is long and excessive, and provides a telling portrait of a team that at the very least was behaving in a boorish and potentially reckless manner. And in 2005, after lacrosse players damaged the Southgate residential hall, Eddie Hull, the dean for residential life and housing at Duke, at one point banned the team from further use of housing on the East Campus, according to the report.

If problems were occurring on campus with Duke lacrosse players, they were occurring off-campus as well, in the Trinity Park neighborhood. The behavior of the players who rented houses there over the years was not as problematic as at some other student rentals, but it was not without incident. In general, 90 percent of the students who lived in Trinity Park were welcome additions, according to city councilman Eugene Brown. The remaining 10 percent, whose houses could easily be spotted in the otherwise pristine neighborhood, with their bald front yards, were "hard-core," as Brown put it.

"Anybody that could see what was going on knew these kids were abusing alcohol, [were] remarkably insensitive to anyone else, and seemed to experience no consequences for their behavior," said Wilkie Wilson, a Duke neuropharmacologist who had moved into Trinity Park in 1975 with his wife, Linda, and had seen out-of-control behavior by students in the neighborhood year after year.

"This was a train that was moving, and I'm not surprised at all where it ended up," he said of the events of March 13. "It was obvious to anyone looking at it that it was going to result in tragedy."

The Duke committee's report concluded that not enough was done to effectively clamp down on the lacrosse team's behavior. In the fall of 2004, according to the report, there was "no question" that the "extensive disciplinary record" of the team had come to the attention of administrators. Among those aware of it were dean of students Suzanne Wasiolek, executive vice president Tallman Trask III, and athletics director Joseph Alleva. Wasiolek, according to the report, thought the conduct of the players was an "irritant." Trask did not think the conduct was "particularly serious," according to the report, although in 2004 he did speak with Alleva about the team's conduct. Wasiolek said in an interview that she in fact felt "a very obvious, high level of frustration" with the conduct of the lacrosse team and with the response of the coach and the athletic department. But apparently no sense that the problem might be urgent was ever conveyed to lacrosse head coach Mike Pressler by the athletic department. Pressler took the responsibility of disciplining lacrosse players seriously, the report concluded, but without any formal system of monitoring and notification in place, there were many incidents he simply knew nothing about.

On the current team, 15 players had misdemeanor citations, all but two of which were for drinking-related offenses. According to Pressler's own handwritten notes, he was not aware of 11 of those citations.

At the end of February, after years of putting up with raucous parties, residents of Trinity Park received what for many was blessed news: Duke had purchased 12 properties in the neighborhood, historically student rentals, with the intent of selling them as owner-occupied residences. Among the houses was 610 North Buchanan Boulevard.

"I felt this enormous sense of relief," said Wilkie Wilson.

But before that happened, there was still time for one more party at 610 North Buchanan Boulevard.

On April 17, the Monday after Bill Thomas's private meeting with Michael Nifong, on the basis of evidence presented by the district attorney's office to the grand jury, two Duke lacrosse players were indicted on charges of first-degree forcible rape, first-degree sexual offense, and first-degree kidnapping. Sophomores Collin Finnerty and Reade Seligmann both came from well-to-do suburban settings around New York. Both had attended all-boys Catholic schools. Finnerty, from Garden City, Long Island, attended Chaminade. When he graduated, in 2004, the 389 members of the senior class had been accepted to such schools as Cornell, Duke, Harvard, Yale, Boston College, and Villanova. His father, Kevin J. Finnerty, is an investment banker, and the Finnerty home in Garden City is valued at $2.4 million, according to tax records.

In November of 2005, Finnerty and two other individuals were arrested outside a bar in Washington, D.C., after a man told the police that they had punched him in the face when he asked them to stop calling him gay. Finnerty entered a diversion program in which the charge of simple assault against him would be dismissed upon completion of 25 hours of community service and no arrests for six months. Because of his indictment in the rape case, that deal has been revoked and he is scheduled to stand trial in July.

Seligmann had attended the Delbarton School, known in northern New Jersey for its high-caliber mix of athletics and academics and its tuition costs of $22,500 a year. He was from the small town of Essex Fells, in New Jersey, about 17 miles west of Manhattan, with a median household income of $148,000 a year.

Both men, through their attorneys, vigorously assert their innocence.

Fifteen days after the indictments were issued, Nifong was successful in his election bid to remain the district attorney of Durham County.

And 13 days later, on May 15, a third player, 23-year-old David Evans, was indicted by the grand jury on the basis of evidence presented by Nifong's office. Like Finnerty and Seligmann, Evans was charged with first-degree forcible rape, first-degree sexual offense, and first-degree kidnapping. His father, David Evans, is a Washington, D.C., lawyer and a partner in the law firm of Reed Smith. His mother, Rae Evans, is the chairwoman of the board of the Ladies Professional Golf Association. Evans had attended the prestigious Landon School, in Bethesda, Maryland.

He appeared with his lawyer, Joseph B. Cheshire, to issue a statement before voluntarily turning himself in and being released on a $400,000 bond. He became the first player to publicly comment about the rape allegations.

"These allegations are lies, fabricated, fabricated, and they will be proven wrong," Evans said.

He said that when police came to 610 North Buchanan Boulevard to search the premises, he and his two roommates assisted them in finding evidence. He said that repeated attempts to contact Nifong through his attorney had been refused. He also said that he had voluntarily taken a polygraph test, administered by a former F.B.I. examiner with nearly 30 years of experience, and had passed.

Cheshire reiterated Nifong's refusal to speak with either him or his client. He reiterated the questionable legality of the identification procedure, noting that the accuser had told police that Evans had worn a mustache the night of the alleged rape when, according to Cheshire, his client had never worn one. He pointed to a new round of DNA testing, released three days before the indictment, reportedly indicating that the only male the accuser was shown to have had sex with was not a Duke lacrosse player.

(Following Cheshire's assertions, three defense sources told the Durham *Herald-Sun* that, based on nearly 1,300 pages of documents handed over by Nifong's office, the forensic examination on the alleged victim showed no tearing, bleeding, or other injury associated with a sexual assault. The newspaper also reported that defense sources said that the accuser had told police she had had sex with her boyfriend and two escort-service drivers around the time of the alleged rape.)

As Cheshire vigorously defended his client, a mother and father in Durham were vigorously defending their daughter against what they believed had been relentless attacks on her character. "She's a good girl," the mother told a television interviewer.

With each peeling-away in the case, perhaps the only certainty that emerges, as Cheshire said, is this:

"This is one of the saddest days for justice in the state of North Carolina."

[In April 2007, the North Carolina attorney general announced that Reade Seligmann, David Evans, and Collin Finnerty were exonerated of all charges. In June of that year, Michael Nifong was disbarred. In the wake of the case, Duke convened several committees to examine the lacrosse team, the university's response to the incident, and campus culture in general, and later revised certain aspects of its sexual misconduct policy.]

"SHADOWS ON THE LAWN"

By Sarah Ellison

OCTOBER 2015

I like the dreams of the future better than the history of the past.

—Thomas Jefferson

I. THE FIRST LAYER

Any story about the University of Virginia must begin with its founder, Thomas Jefferson, who is often referred to locally as "Mr. Jefferson"; with an invocation of the Rotunda and the surrounding "academical village"; and with a discussion of the venerable Honor Code and the exclusive secret societies. There must be a reference to the university as a "Public Ivy" or perhaps a "Southern Ivy," and to the act of being physically on campus as being "on grounds." There must be a nod to "girls in pearls and guys in ties" attending football games and horse races but paying attention to neither.

More recently, there's another thing that any story about the University of Virginia must mention: the horrific period the institution has just come through. The school year started in September 2014 with the disappearance and murder of Hannah Graham, an undergraduate in her second year. Then came the publication, in November 2014, of an explosive *Rolling Stone* story about the alleged gang rape of a young woman named Jackie at a U.Va. fraternity—an investigative report that was quickly discredited and has now been retracted but that has left lasting divisions. In late November, a second-year U.Va. student and heir to the D'Agostino supermarket chain committed suicide, one of three students to do so last fall. The following March there occurred an incident involving a 20-year-old African-American honor student, Martese Johnson, who presented his driver's license at a bar near the school and was turned away. Shortly afterward, after questioning the validity of his ID, two white state Alcoholic Beverage Control (A.B.C.) agents had him pinned to the ground. With rivulets of blood lining his face, he was heard to scream, "I go to U.Va.! I go to U.Va., you fucking racists!" Any one of these events would have been enough to puncture the idyllic façade of Mr. Jefferson's university. Taken together, the impact has been profound. The entire school seems to be suffering an institutional form of PTSD.

I recently returned to my alma mater on a glorious day in May. Final exams were under way, amid radiant bursts of azaleas, tulips, and dogwoods. I walked the serpentine gardens that surround the Lawn with an old friend who has settled in Charlottesville, and we talked about how hard and strange the year had been. I felt the familiar pull of the loveliness of the place—eliciting a desire, built into the mortar of the undulating brick walls, not to dwell too much on the negative.

When I arrived at U.Va., in 1992, Bill Clinton was on the presidential campaign trail for the first time. We were already hearing stories about his alleged longtime mistress, Gennifer Flowers. We took it for granted that Clinton was the Horndog President. He was a recognizable archetype—the roguish, charming, bad-boy southerner, though far too plebeian for the University of Virginia's tastes, which run to a

Regency-rake version of the same basic character. But Clinton's election spurred a revived discussion of a New South, one that was modern and attractive to the rest of the country. It was this part of Clinton that appealed to students at U.Va., who are always engaged in an exercise of trying on the variety of southern raiment that the university has to offer.

Many people love their alma mater, but the University of Virginia invites a special loyalty. Part of this, I think, has to do with the care Jefferson took when he conceived the place. He designed the campus personally and regarded the creation of the university as more significant than his presidency. U.Va. has been at the forefront of defining what an American university should be ever since its founding, in 1819. The ranks of its alumni range from Edgar Allan Poe and Woodrow Wilson to Tina Fey and Katie Couric to Tiki Barber and Ralph Sampson. This year, *U.S. News & World Report* ranked it as the second-best public university in the country (behind Berkeley and tied with U.C.L.A.). About 70 percent of the school's 16,000 undergraduates come from Virginia and pay $13,000 a year to attend, one of the great bargains in higher education; the 30 percent from out of state pay $42,000, still a relative bargain. Poet laureate Rita Dove, civil-rights leader Julian Bond, and philosopher Richard Rorty have all taught at U.Va. William Faulkner was a writer-in-residence. Graduates of U.Va. see the place as particularly distinctive. Whenever my husband wants to get a rise out of me, he tells me that U.Va. is a great school, just like Michigan or Wisconsin. And like any place that is particularly distinctive, the flaws are distinctive as well.

If the Deep South is determined to position itself deliberately as "Other," something that is separate and apart from the rest of the country, U.Va. provides a southern buffet, a place where one can dabble as a Virginia gentleman or a southern belle—trying on a lifestyle if not fully committing to a life. In her book, *Bossypants,* alumna Tina Fey wrote, "At the University of Virginia in 1990, I was Mexican. I looked Mexican, that is, next to my fifteen thousand blond and blue-eyed classmates, most of whom owned horses, or at least resembled them." One friend recently described U.Va. to me as the "first layer" of the South—the safe version. U.Va. sets itself apart from its coarser cousins in the Deep South, the region that elites up North reject and that revels in this rejection. Even so, it embodies the South in all its inconsistencies and contradictions. The university is a defining institution in a state that, perhaps more than any other, has a rooted aristocracy. Wealthy donors, many of whom sit on the university's Board of Visitors, are hugely influential. In the past, U.Va. students looked at Ole Miss, with its Confederate flags hanging in fraternity-house windows, and felt superior. Sure, you might have come across the occasional Confederate flag at U.Va. too, but they were hardly ubiquitous and were usually met with a roll of the eyes. In the Deep South, the shadowy side is actually out in the sunlight. Thomas Jefferson's U.Va. prefers the shadows to be in the shadows.

Over the past few months, I've spoken to students and administrators at U.Va., and to many of the school's alumni. They described a feeling of deep exhaustion. I have also spoken to people who were close to Jackie, the woman at the heart of the *Rolling Stone* story, and who were willing to address on the record for the first time how the story came together, now that the official police investigation has concluded. These young women are exhausted, too, as well as confused and angry. Visiting U.Va., you can't escape a beleaguered defensiveness. When I walked onto the front porch of Phi Kappa Psi, the fraternity at the heart of the *Rolling Stone* story, one of the brothers politely gave me the name of the fraternity's public-relations representative and said that he and others had been instructed not to talk to anyone. The notion of college kids' being fluent in the art of public-relations deflection saddened me. But it seemed fitting, given the horrors of the year that had just ended.

II. JACKIE'S STORY

At the end of the third week of classes, in the early-morning hours of Saturday, September 13, 2014, an 18-year-old student at the university, Hannah Graham, texted her friends: "I'm coming to a party . . . but I'm lost." It was the last anyone heard from her that night, or the next day—or ever. On Sunday, the police were notified. On Monday, the university's president, Teresa Sullivan, issued a statement expressing "deep concern." On Thursday, the police released a surveillance video of Graham and a black man walking separately on Charlottesville's downtown pedestrian mall, and that night students held a vigil. Graham was freckled and blue-eyed. She had studied abroad and was on U.Va.'s alpine-ski and snowboard team. Many people I spoke to about the episode followed it like a grim soap opera, relating emotionally to Hannah and her parents.

Students felt unsafe. No one wanted to walk alone from the libraries. The case became even more emotionally charged when, on September 23, an African-American man who worked at the U.Va. medical center, Jesse Matthew Jr., 32, was identified as a suspect in Graham's disappearance. The next day, Matthew was arrested and charged with abduction with "intent to defile" in the Graham case. In early October, with Hannah still missing, Hannah's parents delivered a tearful, televised plea for her safe return. The divide between Jefferson's privileged university and the neighborhoods that surround it moved from the back of students' minds to the front. "We saw Charlottesville breaking into the world of U.Va.," one student told me.

On October 18, five weeks after Graham had disappeared, Kevin Spacey was in Charlottesville to give a speech on the arts, the second in a series inaugurated a year earlier by Tina Fey. The much-anticipated Spacey event was to start at six P.M., in the John Paul Jones Arena, named for the father of hedge-fund manager and U.Va. alumnus Paul Tudor Jones II. Spacey took the stage, but members of the audience were distracted by something else: the police had found remains that would turn out to be those of Hannah Graham. Jesse Matthew Jr. was charged with her murder and will face the death penalty when he goes on trial next July. (In June of this year, Matthew was found guilty of attempted murder and sexual assault of a young woman in Fairfax, Virginia, in 2005. He faces up to three life sentences. And forensic evidence links him to the 2009 slaying of 20-year-old Virginia Tech student Morgan

Harrington.) [Matthew struck a plea deal with prosecutors in March 2016, admitting to killing both Graham and Harrington, and was sentenced to life in prison without the possibility of parole.]

The search for Hannah Graham was still in full swing when another series of events began to roil the campus. Emily Renda, who had graduated from U.Va. in the spring of 2014 and taken a job at the university as the project coordinator for sexual-misconduct prevention, would find herself in the middle of them. Renda had arrived at U.Va. in August 2010, planning to major in religious or environmental studies. "I thought I was going to be a pastor or a park ranger," she recalls. Her path was deflected by a sexual assault six weeks into her first year. Those first three months of college are a period that some experts refer to as the Red Zone, when new students are most vulnerable to sexual assault as well as accidents due to alcohol abuse. Renda told me she had let her perpetrator walk her home after a party, and he suggested they go back to his room until she sobered up. She agreed, and what happened next shaped the rest of her college experience.

Renda's assault involved "pushing, hitting, and punching," elements that, she explained, later helped her realize that the incident was not her fault. She didn't report the assault initially, and listed for me the reasons why not: "I didn't want to ruin someone else's life. It was a mistake. This person had parents, too. It wasn't worth it." She became an intern at the university Women's Center and an advocate for sexual-assault survivors. She also became involved in the school's annual Take Back the Night events, whose centerpiece is a candlelight vigil during which sexual-assault survivors can speak out about their experiences. By the time Renda was ready to report to the university what had happened, her alleged attacker had transferred to a different school and the issue was moot. Under federal Title IX legislation, colleges and universities are required to have procedures in place to adjudicate all such complaints. According to the U.S. Department of Education's Office of Civil Rights, in

2015 U.Va. was one of 106 colleges and universities across the country with open Title IX sexual-violence investigations. Renda never considered going to the police or the courts, believing that she didn't have the kind of evidence she needed for a successful prosecution.

In the spring of her final year, 2014, Renda was nearly finished with her major in sociology and had been accepted to a joint law-school and master's-in-public-health program at the University of Maryland and Johns Hopkins. That was when, through her work with the sexual-assault-prevention community, she met a young woman at the university named Jackie. It was a fateful encounter. Jackie told Renda that she had been raped during her first year at U.Va., in 2012, by multiple assailants. Renda says that the conversation between the two women focused primarily on the unsupportive reactions that Jackie said she had received from friends and family, not on the alleged assault itself. Renda elected to stay at U.Va. as an intern in the Office of Student Affairs. In June 2014, Renda testified before a hearing of the Senate Health, Education, Labor, and Pensions Committee, and used Jackie's story to underscore the need for increased reporting of sexual assault. She referred to Jackie anonymously and told lawmakers that Jackie didn't report her assault until almost a year after it happened "because immediately after the attack she confided in peers who did not believe her," a reaction that meant that the young men she claimed had attacked her "went unpunished and remained a threat to the other students throughout that year."

Another young woman drawn into Jackie's orbit was Alex Pinkleton, who had come to the university in 2012. Pinkleton sailed through the Red Zone with no problem, but in November of her second year, she says, she was sexually assaulted at a party. She had been drinking, and all she remembers is eventually coming to, naked, with a friend's friend on top of her, and asking him what had happened. She put on her clothes and walked out. Afterward, she tried to joke about it but grew increasingly uncomfortable. She says the young man she had had sex with later told her, via a private Facebook message, that she had been so drunk she had forgotten his name four times in the course of the evening. The two ran into each other at parties and were, in Pinkleton's telling, hostile to each other. Eventually, she says, she talked about the incident with Nicole Eramo, U.Va.'s associate dean of students and the school administrator responsible for handling sexual-assault complaints. Eramo asked Pinkleton if she felt safe, how she was doing emotionally, and if she wanted to pursue a formal or informal complaint through the university system, or instead wished to report the incident to the police. Pinkleton told Eramo she didn't know what she wanted to do and deferred any decision.

In February 2014, as Pinkleton was walking out of the bathroom in New Cabell Hall, a 1950s-era brick building with classrooms and faculty offices, a young woman stopped her. It was Jackie. Because of her role in One Less, a student sexual-assault-education group, Pinkleton was well known as a victims' advocate. Jackie told Pinkleton her story—which allegedly involved being raped by multiple perpetrators—and asked Pinkleton about her own history. The discussion, again, focused not on the details of any assault on Jackie but on the reaction from friends and family afterward; on how to feel safe; and on what action she might take to help the healing process, such as an adjudication through U.Va. The two women ultimately agreed to make their accounts public at the next Take Back the Night rally. "We decided, 'If you do it, I'll do it,' " Pinkleton remembers. They did speak at the event, but Pinkleton says Jackie offered few details about the assault itself—it was very much in the background.

That was the state of affairs when, on July 8, 2014, after most of her fellow class-of-2014 graduates had left Charlottesville, Emily Renda received a phone call from a woman named Sabrina Rubin Erdely, a writer for *Rolling Stone* magazine. According to her notes—as laid out in a report by the Columbia University Graduate School of Journalism, which *Rolling Stone* asked to investigate its article after serious questions about it arose—Erdely was intending to write about rape at colleges and universities and was looking for an emblematic case that would show what it is like to be on a college campus today—where, in her view, sexual harassment and assault were so prevalent as to constitute a "rape culture." Renda was soon to begin a new job at the university. "She was talking broadly about rape culture, and we talked about whether it was even an appropriate term," Renda recalled, adding, "I think it is divisive"—her argument being that it makes the conversation immediately contentious when it doesn't need to be, and therefore makes finding a response all the harder. The conversation ranged from psychology and advocacy to policy and law. Renda remembers speaking to Erdely for "four very unpleasant hours about my own experience." In the end, Renda directed Erdely to five women, all of whom had very different stories to tell. Jackie's was meant to represent the invalidating responses women often get from their friends and family. Another woman had successfully prosecuted her rapist through the criminal-justice system. Yet another had received protective orders through the school. She also put Erdely in touch with another woman, who had gone through the school process.

Erdely contacted multiple women but evidently came to view Jackie's story as the most dramatic. (Erdely, through a *Rolling Stone* spokeswoman, has declined to comment for this story.) The next time Renda spoke with Erdely, in August, Renda learned that the writer was focusing her article narrowly on the alleged gang rape of Jackie. Renda says she regarded Erdely's journalistic focus on a single extreme episode as misleading—an outlier, even if true. She told Erdely that Jackie's story "wasn't representative of campus rape as a whole." Much of Renda's work involved speaking to students whose cases do not include explicit violence, that occur in the context of a lot of drinking and between people who already know each other. Even though Renda didn't have the details of Jackie's story, she was aware that it allegedly included multiple assailants, and she worried that it could make the experience of other victims, whose stories weren't nearly as dramatic and yet were personally devastating, seem almost trivial by comparison.

Erdely, meanwhile, had been in touch with Jackie by e-mail, and on July 14 they spoke on the phone. According to Erdely's notes, Jackie seems to have shared her rape story with Erdely in a way she never had with Renda or Pinkleton. A fellow lifeguard, given the name "Drew," had invited her to her first fraternity party, and after midnight he led her upstairs. As reported in *Rolling Stone:*

> "My eyes were adjusting to the dark. And I said his name and turned
> around. . . . I heard voices and I started to scream and someone pum-
> meled into me and told me to shut up. And that's when I tripped and
> fell against the coffee table and it smashed underneath me and this
> other boy, who was throwing his weight on top of me. Then one of
> them grabbed my shoulders. . . . One of them put his hand over my
> mouth and I bit him—and he straight-up punched me in the face. . . .
> One of them said, 'Grab its motherfucking leg.' As soon as they said it,
> I knew they were going to rape me."

Jackie's account was graphic. She described the lifeguard's coaching seven other young men as they raped her, seemingly as part of a fraternity pledge ritual. "Don't you want to be a brother?" one of the young men asked another who had hesitated. Erdely told the Columbia investigators that she had been "sickened and shaken" after the call, even though she was also "a bit incredulous" about some of the details, such as a glass table shattering under Jackie as the first rapist assaulted her. The article, published in the fall, described U.Va. as an institution so defined by rape culture that women had taken to calling it "UVrApe." Erdely portrayed U.Va. as a place that discouraged the reporting of sexual assault and infantilized survivors by telling them to focus on healing rather than justice. In the article, Nicole Eramo, the associate dean of students who served as a counselor to sexual-assault survivors, was quoted as responding this way to a question posed by Jackie about why U.Va. statistics on rape were hard to find: "Because nobody wants to send their daughter to the rape school."

In the fall of 2014, Pinkleton felt she had somehow become a main pillar of support for Jackie as she navigated the process of telling her story publicly to a reporter for a national magazine. In Pinkleton's recollection, Jackie appeared increasingly distressed. "She would message me at four A.M.," Pinkleton told me. To give Jackie someone else to talk to, Pinkleton introduced her to Sara Surface, a fellow U.Va. student and a co–selection chair for One Less. The three women met in September at Para Coffee, on the Corner, the commercial strip of shops and bars where U.Va. students regularly socialize. They sat outside, and, Pinkleton says, Jackie shared certain general elements of her story with Surface, though not in anything like as much detail as she had with Sabrina Rubin Erdely. Jackie was talkative and friendly but appeared anxious about the upcoming *Rolling Stone* article. "I don't think she fully grasped how big the article would become, but she was worried about it," Pinkleton recalled. Pinkleton was worried, too. "The extra stress on someone who had been gang-raped by tons of people would be a reason someone might do something dramatic," Pinkleton told me. "I was worried she would kill herself."

Erdely arrived in Charlottesville for interviews two days before Hannah Graham went missing. Pinkleton told me Jackie met with Erdely alone, and then the three of them had dinner the night Graham disappeared. By that time Erdely had been reaching out to various administrators and students at U.Va. but making little headway. The administration seemed to be media-shy—a consequence, possibly, of ugly events in 2012, when some high-profile members of the Board of Visitors had led a failed coup against the university's president, Teresa Sullivan. But it was also preoccupied: Around this time, Erdely "called to complain that no one was talking to her," Renda told me. President Sullivan had postponed phone interviews with Erdely. Renda thought at the time, Do you know we have a student missing and an all-out manhunt for her?

There was another reason the U.Va. administration may have seemed guarded. Word was getting around—based on the nature of Erdely's questioning and her apparent disdain for university officials—that the article was likely to be deeply critical of the administration's handling of sexual-assault cases. "People thought it was best not to talk to her, because anything you told her was not going to be fairly represented," Renda told me. This made Erdely's reporting all the more difficult. At that point, Renda felt hesitant about continuing to speak to Erdely, and told me she emphasized to the reporter that anything she said reflected nothing more than her own personal experience—that she didn't have access to case files from Jackie's discussions with Dean Eramo or any other U.Va. administrators, could not have shared them even if she did, and knew only what Jackie was telling her. "I knew so little about the actual story," Renda explained—meaning the specific details of the alleged gang rape.

Skeptical of U.Va. officials, Erdely appears to have relied increasingly on Jackie and her circle of supporters, but her friends knew only what they had been told, which was relatively little and not always the same thing. Although Jackie had told Erdely her story in graphic detail, she wasn't always eager to maintain contact with the reporter. Jackie seems to have cut off contact with Erdely, or tried to. At one point, Renda says, she received an e-mail from Erdely asking if she had heard from Jackie lately, because Erdely hadn't. After getting Erdely's message, Renda contacted Jackie directly and told her that if the story was becoming too much she could drop out of participation at any time. Jackie told Renda that she was fine—just stressed out by school. Jackie wavered on whether she should name the fraternity explicitly. Pinkleton felt that Erdely was trying to manipulate Jackie into cooperating, though Pinkleton's view of the dynamics would gradually become more complicated. Pinkleton remembers contacting Erdely on one occasion to tell her that Jackie didn't want her name in the story. Erdely called back, confused, saying she had just spoken to Jackie, who *did* want her name in the story. "At first I thought Sabrina [Erdely] was manipulating us,"

Pinkleton told me. Later, after everything unraveled, she came to a different conclusion: "Jackie was manipulating us as well."

In October, according to Pinkleton, arguments and tensions mounted among Jackie, Surface, Pinkleton, and Erdely. Surface and Pinkleton were trying to shield Jackie, or help Jackie shield herself. For her part, Jackie seemed uncertain about how she wanted to be represented in the story. She went from not wanting to be named at all to agreeing to the use of just her first name. Pinkleton said, "She started evading questions from us and confessing more to Sabrina." And Pinkleton went on: "I just feel like she really started telling us things that didn't make sense. We offered her help in standing up to Sabrina, but she didn't want it." Pinkleton noted a few worrying signs as the story was closing and *Rolling Stone* was calling to confirm various pieces of information: "I remember telling the fact-checkers that 'UVrApe' was nothing I had ever heard of." Other rape-prevention advocates at the school had never heard the term, either.

III. THE UNRAVELING

The week the *Rolling Stone* story came out, the four women—Renda, Surface, Pinkleton, and Jackie—were scrambling to prepare for what they suspected would be a bombshell. On Tuesday, November 18, a friend of Sara Surface's found a copy of the magazine on a newsstand. The friend took pictures of the pages with her cell phone and sent them to Surface, who downloaded them onto a laptop. All four women had been anticipating the story for months. Some of them had come to distrust Erdely. Nobody wanted to read it alone. They wanted to see one another's reactions and talk about it afterward. "Everybody come to my apartment now," texted Renda. She lived off campus, far enough away from most student housing to feel truly removed. Everyone arrived right away. "We were really nervous, and we knew it was going to be really bad," Pinkleton told me. Bad for U.Va. and bad for Dean Eramo, whom the women, save perhaps Jackie, regarded as a mentor.

Once the women had gathered, Renda read the story aloud, detail by harrowing detail. Jackie was identified by her first name only, and the leader of her alleged rapists, as noted, was given the pseudonym "Drew." Three allegedly unsympathetic friends whom Jackie had sought out in the aftermath of the attack were also given pseudonyms—"Cindy," "Randall," and "Andy." Renda read aloud the story of Jackie's brutal gang rape at the hands of seven men at the Phi Kappa Psi fraternity house. She read aloud how, after the attack, her friends and U.Va. officials had discouraged Jackie from reporting the incident to the police or the university. As some of the women had feared, Dean Eramo became the face of an administration that was depicted as unsympathetic and indifferent to a pervasive rape culture.

As Pinkleton listened to the horrific details, she said, she thought, Oh, I didn't hear that, and Oh, I didn't know that. While they were aware of the outlines of the story, much of the specific information was being imparted to them for the first time. Looking back on it now, Pinkleton remembers that Jackie seemed upset as Renda read the story but did not break down. At one point, Pinkleton reached over to pat Jackie's back to comfort her. Renda told me that hearing the story read aloud was "like being hit over the head with a baseball bat," because the details of Jackie's rape were so shocking and because the dean had been treated so unfairly. After Renda finished reading, Jackie's boyfriend, who had driven her to Renda's apartment, took her home. Once Jackie had departed, the three women left behind looked at one another, realizing that there was a lot they didn't know about what had happened to Jackie. And maybe a lot they didn't know about Jackie.

The next day, "A Rape on Campus" was on nearly every laptop before, during, and after classes at U.Va. There were countless "I stand with Jackie" messages on Facebook, Yik Yak, and other social media. There was a lot of anger at Jackie's friends—"Cindy," "Randall," and "Andy"—who were portrayed as unsupportive in *Rolling Stone*. Renda described to me the protests that followed the story. Vandals painted UVA CENTER FOR RAPE STUDIES on the side of the Phi Kappa Psi fraternity house. They threw rocks through the windows. The Phi Kappa Psi brothers moved out. Especially distressing to Renda was a sign she saw at a protest march: PROTECT OUR WOMEN. The sign seemed to epitomize all the "damsel in distress" tropes that women like Renda had been trying to dispel—a difficult task anywhere but particularly at a place like U.Va., with its ethic, in some quarters, of chivalrous paternalism. "I remember feeling really overwhelmed and like this was going to set back all the positive work that had been done," Renda told me. There were only two types of women in Erdely's story, she explained: bimbos and victims. "There were no women of agency," she said. One key issue from Renda's perspective was that much of her work had been trying to help women who had suffered a much less violent, much less dramatic version of Jackie's story—the so-called gray area of rape, one that, Renda says, is all too common at U.Va. and other college campuses. For her part, Pinkleton was annoyed that she and Surface weren't identified as working to prevent sexual assault at U.Va., nor was anyone else. Erdely "acted like there were no feminists or anyone supporting survivors," Pinkleton told me. Pinkleton was also upset that Erdely "had destroyed the administration's credibility and said"—falsely—"that there is no one at this school who will listen to your story and believe you."

Jackie's circle of supporters were in an unenviable situation. They ostensibly knew more than anyone about what had happened to Jackie—but began to appreciate that they really didn't know what they knew, or whether what they thought they knew was true. At some point during the two weeks that followed the story's publication, Jackie told Pinkleton and Surface what she claimed to be the real name of "Drew," the alleged ringleader of her rape. Pinkleton says that, when she and Surface looked him up, they realized he didn't fit the story. There was no one by his name who was a member of the Phi Kappa Psi fraternity. Then it began to get worse: a *Washington Post* reporter, T. Rees Shapiro—one of the many reporters who had descended on U.Va.—was attempting to speak to the student Jackie identified as "Drew." "We realized the chances of it happening at Phi Kappa Psi at that point were slim to none," said Pinkleton. And they realized that they had, in Pinkleton's words, a "moral obligation" to tell Shapiro about discrepancies in Jackie's story. Sara Surface added, "At a certain point Alex and I had to start making decisions about Jackie versus every other survivor in our cause. It wasn't a distinction that we as advocates ever thought we would need to make."

On Tuesday, December 2, two weeks after the *Rolling Stone* story's release, Surface and Pinkleton had dinner with Jackie and told her they were concerned that the person Jackie had identified to them didn't match the description of the Drew character named in the story. Pinkleton says that Jackie avoided answering their questions. She began to cry and told them she was stressed and tired and overwhelmed. On Thursday, December 4, Surface and Pinkleton met with Shapiro, the *Post* reporter, and essentially compared notes. They had all identified what seemed like discrepancies in Jackie's story. "We just sat there, like, 'Holy shit—what is going on?,' " Pinkleton told me. "Meanwhile, Sara and I are, minds blown, but we also felt like we had betrayed her. Did we just have it wrong?"

Later that Thursday was the traditional "Lighting of the Lawn," when students string lights, sing, play music, and have a party. Pinkleton, Surface, and Renda missed the lighting and instead met with Jackie at her apartment. "We needed to tell her that the *Washington Post* article was coming out and destroying her story the very next day, because we didn't want mental-breakdown suicide going on," Pinkleton told me. The meeting included a university-affiliated counselor in the event some sort of emergency arose.

"We all got together to say, 'Jackie, this is what's coming. How are you going to prepare for this?,' " Renda told me. What was coming, they feared, was a virulent backlash against a false accusation—and an onslaught of victim blaming. The women wanted to support Jackie, because they sensed that what was about to follow would be difficult.

They also, gingerly, wanted to get some explanations for the inconsistencies in her story. They told her that the *Post* story would be out soon, and she said she knew. Pinkleton lost her temper. She told Jackie she should stop thinking about herself and start thinking about the damage a discredited story would do to the movement against sexual assault. Pinkleton told me that the conversation was heated and that she doesn't remember what everyone said, but she does remember that at one point Jackie, frustrated, told them: "I don't even know why I talk to you guys anymore. Sara and Alex, you all have been such shitty friends lately." The women told Jackie that Shapiro had offered her one last chance to tell him what really happened.

Later that night they met with Shapiro in an academic building, where Jackie repeated her story again, including details such as the color of the alarm clock. To Pinkleton, the level of detail about the room seemed unusually vivid. Jackie was adamant: what she had told Erdely was what really happened. "That is my story," Jackie said.

That night, Sabrina Rubin Erdely, who had been engaged in her own effort to find Drew and who had just spoken to Jackie, called Pinkleton at one A.M. "I need to hear from you if her story was true," she said, in Pinkleton's recollection. "And I just said, 'I don't think you should have written the article.' " The following morning, December 5, Pinkleton said, she received another call from Erdely. " 'I'm writing the retraction right now. I just need to hear one more time what you think,' " Pinkleton told me. "She started bawling and said, 'I am going to lose my job.' " That same day, *The Washington Post* wrote that Phi Kappa Psi said that it had not held an event the night of Jackie's alleged rape, and that the "friends" who had spoken to Jackie then had heard details of her attack that differed from what was in the *Rolling Stone* article. *Rolling Stone*'s managing editor, Will Dana, issued a statement later that day in which the magazine admitted to mistakes in the story and apologized to readers. Dana would leave the magazine in August.

In the next week, the *Post* identified further holes in the story. The friends of Jackie's provided Shapiro with text messages from Jackie that made it seem that she may have simply invented the Drew character in the *Rolling Stone* article. Some speculated about another source for certain details in Jackie's account: in 2011, a U.Va. alumna named Liz Seccuro published a book in which she described how, as a student in 1984, in the midst of a date function at Phi Kappa Psi, she had ventured upstairs, been drugged, dragged into a room, and raped repeatedly.

Eramo has sued Erdely and *Rolling Stone* for nearly $8 million for the way she is described and quoted in the story, which she has claimed is false and defamatory. Three Phi Kappa Psi brothers, one of whom lived in a second-floor bedroom of the fraternity house, have sued *Rolling Stone* and Erdely for causing them "mental anguish and severe emotional distress," even though none were named in Erdely's story. Renda and Pinkleton, not to mention Jackie, have all been personally attacked by media outlets for their role in the article. [*Rolling Stone* filed a motion to vacate the judgment, but Eramo dropped the suit and settled with Erdely and the magazine in April 2017. The terms of the settlement were not disclosed. The three Phi Kappa Psi brothers' lawsuit was thrown out in June 2016. The fraternity also filed its own lawsuit against *Rolling Stone* and was granted $1.65 million in June 2017. Jackie's identity has not been publicly revealed.]

Shortly after the publication of *Rolling Stone*'s statement, Jackie vanished. Renda, Surface, and Pinkleton have not heard from her in the nine months since her story fell apart. Approached through her attorney, Jackie has declined to answer questions. For Renda, the rest of the year has been "all hell and hopelessness." The experience has made her abandon the idea of working with sexual-assault survivors, she told me. She is headed to law school—electing to go to Berkeley, as far away from U.Va. as she can get. "I don't want to say it's been the worst year of my life, but it has been the worst year of my life."

IV. "FARM EQUIPMENT"

When the *Rolling Stone* story appeared, my U.Va. friends and I were transfixed by it—and took the account at face value. There was a reason for that. Extreme as Jackie's story was, it touched on something recognizable about U.Va. While a fraternity pledging ritual that involved gang rape was shocking, there were certain aspects of U.Va.— in its history and its rituals—that could be characterized as debauched, dehumanizing, or just plain bizarre.

When I was applying to college, my brother, who had gone to Princeton, was in his first year at U.Va. law school. My mother told me she thought I'd like the young women better at U.Va. than at Princeton, and I applied early and was accepted. I arrived with a flowered bedspread and a curling iron. I dressed up for football games and, in the spring of my first year, pledged a sorority. We attended fraternity mixers where we drank "grain punch" scooped from a garbage can. I heard stories of fraternity hazing and secret societies. On the night I was inducted into Tri Delt, we drank a lot and wore blindfolds, and I think we may have had to wear our bras outside our blouses, but only for a short time, and only in the company of our sorority sisters. Any hazing was halfhearted. There was no forced vomiting or the occasional simulated fellatio on bottles—as there was, however, for the women's society at U.Va. known as Thursdays, a "secret" society that was essentially a drinking club. There was no staged fighting or bodily penetration with fruit—as I had heard about, however, from friends in the male drinking society known as Eli Banana, which at one point in the late 19th century was disbanded for its behavior (but then allowed to re-materialize). On bid night—when secret societies tap their initiates—some of the drinking societies have been known to gather privately in a basement for a cockfight. This is the kind of atmosphere where someone could be forgiven for thinking that misogynistic or violent episodes might occur.

"Pimps and Hos" mixers between fraternities and sororities were still pretty common when I was a student, and when I started reporting this story I was certain that I didn't know anyone who had been sexually assaulted at U.Va. That changed within hours of calling friends, and I came to understand that what passed for a "bad hookup" when I was in college is today what we would rightly call rape—which was precisely Renda's point. We just weren't talking much about any of it. When we did talk about it, we tried to laugh it off. I'm sure this is true at most colleges. But U.Va. has a particularly challenging past. It was among the last of the flagship state universities in the country to become coeducational (in 1970), and did so even then under the threat of a federal lawsuit. When women were first admitted, U.Va. men referred to female classmates as "U-bags."

An act of violence was responsible for the creation of the vaunted Honor System in the first place. During a disturbance in 1840, a masked student shot and killed a professor who had tried to restore order. The Honor System at U.Va., today overseen by a 27-student Honor Committee, grew out of that incident: students agreed to "vouch" for one another and to voluntarily report episodes of misbehavior. Since 1998, U.Va. has expelled 187 students for lying, cheating, or stealing, but not a single person has been kicked out for sexual assault. The deliberations are confidential, and there have been allegations both of vigilante justice and of a double standard at play. In 1990, *The Washington Post,* in an article exploring the Honor System, reported that in 1988 J. Brady Lum, the Honor Committee chair at the time, was accused of plagiarism in a letter he wrote to incoming students introducing them, ironically, to the Honor System. He was cleared by an investigation. Lum's successor, Lonnie Chafin, had been convicted of an assault involving the Charlottesville police. He was voted off the Honor Committee but not expelled from the university.

The Columbia report on the *Rolling Stone* article, which found failures at all levels of the magazine's editorial process, was made public in early April. By then the university was caught up in yet another controversy. The day after Saint Patrick's Day, U.Va. students started seeing a cell-phone video from the night before pop up in their social-media feeds. It showed a fellow U.Va. student, Martese Johnson, who is black, lying on the pavement outside a bar on the Corner, his face bloodied, with two white A.B.C. agents on his back. He kept yelling, "I go to U.Va.!" It was a linguistic amulet that was both heartbreaking and ineffective.

The issue of race has never been faced squarely by the university, just as Jefferson never faced it squarely. Johnson is an honor student, heavily involved in extra-curricular activities, and one of only two African-Americans on the Honor Committee. Virginia's population is 20 percent black, but the percentage of African-American students at U.Va. has dropped from 12 percent in the 1990s to around 6 percent today.

Most black U.Va. students I spoke to told me that they face a choice when they arrive in Charlottesville. They have to decide whether they want to be part of the black culture of U.Va.—which has its own so-rorities and fraternities, its own clubs, and, effectively, because of self-segregation, historically, even its own bus stop—or be part of the white culture, which entails joining predominantly white organizations such as the predominantly white fraternities and sororities and the predomi-nantly white debating societies and other clubs. U.Va. throws a "spring fling" for incoming black students, hosted by the office of admissions. "A lot of African-Americans come with a bit of apprehension as to whether there is a place for them" at an institution with "a southern, white, aris-tocratic history," Vendarryl Jenkins, an African-American second-year student, told me. The spring fling is designed to show "there is a com-munity here for you."

The white and black communities don't mix much. Memories of those "Pimps and Hos" mixers can't help. Jenkins told me of the night last fall when Martese Johnson, who happened to be a friend of his, was tapped to be a member of the secret society IMP. Not many African-Americans are tapped for secret societies, but Johnson brought Jenkins and a few other black friends to the party for new members. At first, everyone, black and white, was in the main room of the house hosting the party, listening to music together and dancing. "As the party continued, a slow separation began to take form," Jenkins later wrote in an unpublished account of that night, which he shared with me. "Black students remained in the main room, lights off, blasting hip-hop, and dancing jovially in celebration." The white students migrated into a separate room, brought up the lights, and turned on Bon Jovi's "Livin' on a Prayer" "with the door shut."

Last December, black students at U.Va. protested the decision not to indict a police officer involved in the death of Eric Garner, an African-American who died on Staten Island after police arrested him for selling loose cigarettes and the officer held him in a choke hold. Among other things, the black students marched through the university's libraries. Virulently racist messages soon appeared on Yik Yak. "I hope the people who protested ride back home on the back of the bus," one commenter wrote. Another, referring to the protesters as if they were field slaves on a plantation, wrote, "Did anyone just see all that farm equipment walk through Clemons?" Jenkins told me, "That is what people are saying in private. It's not what you see on a tour of grounds." All this occurred before Martese Johnson was turned away from a bar on the Corner and found himself set upon by law-enforcement officers. Johnson spent several hours in jail and was released that morning. All charges against him have since been dropped. No charges were lodged against the A.B.C. agents. A crucial six-minute segment of a police surveillance video had apparently gone missing.

There is a temptation among many in Charlottesville to blame the national media for the sheer intensity of this year's events, and it's certainly true that the continual presence of camera crews has not been a positive inducement. Others voice what I think of as the Pantene theory of U.Va.'s situation: some people dislike the school in part because it's beautiful. If nothing else, the year has been hard to explain and translate to outsiders. One student told me about a conversation she had had with a former high-school teacher. "How's U.Va.?" he asked her. The student replied, "What do you want to talk about—murder, rape, or beating?" For all that, students I spoke to said time and again that they loved U.Va. I can understand why. Though fraternities and sororities dominate the popular image of the school, only 30 percent of students participate in Greek life. Two of the most prestigious and secret of the secret societies, the Sevens and the Z's, are primarily philanthropic in nature, not sowers of drunken discord. An active minority, a layer of elites within the university's elite clubs and other institutions, sets an inescapable schoolwide tone, but a great variety of experiences are available to students at U.Va., and there are many communities to join. The people I met there remain some of my dearest friends today.

But the university is also a petri dish of issues facing society at large, and a little more intensely so, given its location and its special history. The events of the past year forced a reckoning of sorts, and some students and professors I spoke to said they were optimistic that the trauma would bring positive changes: it's an example of that Cavalier instinct to look for solutions. But the feeling was by no means universal. In one dialogue group that Jenkins moderated last semester, a young woman said to him, "I just want everything to go back to normal." A return to normal is not what U.Va. needs. Normal is part of the problem. It was Jefferson himself who said that he liked the dreams of the future better than the history of the past. If there's anything U.Va. should be able to get behind, it's a directive from Mr. Jefferson.

CAMPUS
CONTROVERSIAL

"THE KENT SCHOOL MYSTERY"

By Michael Shnayerson

OCTOBER 1999

It would have made a perfect story line for his show, both diabolical and hilarious, but not even Seth MacFarlane, the talented 26-year-old creator of Fox's animated sitcom *Family Guy*, could have imagined it before it occurred.

First came the press hype last winter for a show judged promising enough to debut after the Super Bowl. Like *The Simpsons* but raunchier, *Family Guy* featured a household of dysfunctional characters, including baby Stewie, who, in a Rex Harrison–inspired British accent, conjured plots to kill his mother. Along with drawing the characters and writing the first episode, MacFarlane did many of the voice-overs. The *Washington Post* television critic, Tom Shales, called it "utterly excremental . . . another tiny drop of toxic waste in the festering Love Canal of the Air," but *Family Guy* immediately became Fox's most popular program among teenage viewers and fourth most popular among adults aged 18–49, with an average 7.7 rating that translated into 12.8 million viewers a week. The show's sponsors seemed happy, too, before the start of a curious letter-writing campaign to 20 advertisers by a group called ProudSponsorsUSA.

The letters alluded to some of the show's more flagrant exercises in gleefully offensive humor, such as the episode in which a boy shoots the head off a "John F. Kennedy Pez dispenser," then remarks, "At least I have my Bobby Kennedy Pez dispenser to back him up." Along with gibes at blacks, Jews, women, the handicapped, the deaf, and other politically incorrect targets, *Family Guy* had its share of mere gross-out jokes about flatulence and urination, which ProudSponsorsUSA also deplored. No fewer than 14 sponsors were reported to be unhappy with the content of the mid-season replacement show, which some claim not to have seen before they bought advertising time, and chose not to back the show. (Among them: Coca-Cola, Sprint, and Philip Morris USA, which decided that *Family Guy* was "not consistent with our values.")

When MacFarlane learned of the campaign, he was disconcerted. Especially so when it turned out that ProudSponsorsUSA was not a group but a single irate viewer. And that viewer was MacFarlane's old headmaster, 48-year-old Father Richardson (Dick) W. Schell, at the Kent School in Kent, Connecticut.

The story was bizarre enough, when it broke last summer, to stir a wave of national interest. As MacFarlane's 52-year-old mother, Perry, remarked dryly, "I've never heard of a headmaster who would make it a mission to bring down one of his alumni." But when Schell did little more to explain himself than reiterate in print his ProudSponsorsUSA stance, and MacFarlane kept mum, the feud vanished from the news as a mystery.

There was, in fact, more to it. What lies beneath is a complex story of small-town passions and prep-school politics, as resonant as a Hawthorne novel, with a woman's honor at its core.

Despite Schell's best efforts, *Family Guy* has survived into the fall season, and Fox is bullish enough about it to be expanding the staff, refurbishing the show's North Hollywood offices, and even adding a state-of-the-art digital recording studio. Amid the hubbub, MacFarlane looks more like a lost intern than a serious young executive producer and creator who has a $2–2.5 million three-year deal from Fox Television to do *Family Guy* and develop new series. Rangy and handsome, he's also a bit of a geek, with thick round glasses, a perpetual blink, and a shy, expectant grin. But at a run-through of the latest episode's script, he's the obvious star, reading half the parts with an outsize gift for mimicry, getting laughs from dubious lines that do poke fun at every minority group imaginable, even singing his own new, loopy lyrics to an old Hope-Crosby *On the Road* number as the episode's finale.

Throughout, a network "suit" from the "standards and practices" department makes notes in the margin of her copy of the script whenever a joke or obscenity seems too crass. At a writers' meeting later that day, the other executive producer, David Zuckerman, 37, reports gloomily that there seem to be more notes requesting changes than there were for previous episodes. "A chilling effect?" MacFarlane says, trying to joke about it.

Stewie the baby, Zuckerman reports, can't say "whore" or "bitch" anymore. MacFarlane slouches lower in his chair, doodling the show's characters on his notepad. Brian, the alcoholic dog, can't indicate intercourse with a to-and-fro motion. "Can we have a pelvic thrust at least?" MacFarlane asks. Then there's the takeoff on *This Old House*, called *This Old Woman*, which features the old woman nailed to two-by-fours. "Maybe if she's not strapped to two-by-fours?" MacFarlane ventures sweetly. And the gag where Peter, the dopey father, brings home a short, fat black man and announces, "Look who I found at the train station! Will Smith!," may have to be omitted. "It's funny," MacFarlane says to his writers—mostly young, male, and white—"but is it racist?" MacFarlane wants to get away with as much as he can: "For me," he says, "it's always 'How can this gag be funnier, and fuck everything else.'" To the writers assigned to revise the script, he has only one edict of his own. "Just be sure there's nothing in these episodes about Kent!"

Over dinner at a nearby Italian restaurant, MacFarlane explains that the first he heard of his former headmaster's ire was the call he got from him, out of the blue, a week before the show's debut. Having grown up in the town of Kent and attended the boarding school as one of a handful of day students, MacFarlane was better known to Schell than many of his peers. His mother had worked at the school for 22 years. "There was that familiarity, in that he knew my parents," MacFarlane says. "We would occasionally exchange a few words. But I never had any extensive dealings with him."

If Schell had found no fault in young Seth as a student, he felt no less indignant for that at learning MacFarlane planned to name his animated family "the Griffins." Schell's secretary is named Elaine Griffin. Surely, Schell insisted over the phone, Seth could see that that was unacceptable: Elaine Griffin was devastated by the prospect. In fact, the whole Griffin family—Elaine, James, and their children, Lauren and Jamie— were baffled and hurt.

Surprised, MacFarlane told Schell he'd had no intention of parodying the Griffins of Kent. He'd chosen Griffin because it was a common Irish name: he might as well have picked O'Leary or Callahan. "I said I wasn't going to change the name," MacFarlane recalls. "It was a civil conversation.

"What I had expected," he adds, "was that after they called me . . . that [would] be the end of it. Because they'd see [the show is] too out there for these characters to resemble anyone. It's so removed from the real world." Nor did he have any desire to upset the Griffins. "I know them well; they were friends of the family: it wouldn't make any sense to bash them. I don't know what motive they think I'd have for this. It just doesn't make any sense."

MacFarlane says he didn't hear from Schell again until he read in the newspaper of the headmaster's campaign. But his mother did.

When Perry MacFarlane learned from a faculty member that Schell was upset, she called him. She says he declared, to her astonishment, that she and her husband, Ron, a history and English teacher at another private school, were irresponsible parents. "I said to Ron, 'I work in the admissions office judging character, and here he was questioning mine?' So I wrote him to resign. He called me to say, 'This is ridiculous; I've washed my hands of it.'" MacFarlane resigned anyway. "Then I began hearing rumors: he was doing a lot of xeroxing."

The Kent School, with its campus of Georgian red-brick buildings backed by the forested green hills of northwestern Connecticut, lies along the Housatonic River. Founded in 1906 by Father Frederick Herbert Sill, an Episcopal monk, as a haven for boys of moderate means to study and spend their free hours doing farm chores, it evolved into one of the pack of New England prep schools that draw most of their students from more moneyed circles and graduate them into Ivy League colleges. Currently, it counts among its alumni trustees a partner at Goldman Sachs and one at J. H. Whitney, though its best-known alums of recent times are, as it happens, actors Ted Danson and Treat Williams. If not quite in the top tier with Groton, St. Paul's, and Exeter, Kent occupies a secure niche just below, and many in its extended community like it just as it is: more modest than those others, perhaps more nurturing and more intimate and, until recently, more private.

On a midsummer day with school out of session, the campus lies somnolent, deserted but for a crew team practicing on the river: students row in one boat as their coach calls out pointers through a megaphone in a small outboard beside them. In the weeks since the story broke, Schell has gone from boasting of his success in the press—even reporting a new letter to Pottery Barn, chiding the company for a catalogue cover showing the American flag draped carelessly over a dock—to ducking all inquiries. Accordingly, I bypass the front office, park by the river, and stroll directly into the headmaster's lair. The secretary's post, where Elaine Griffin usually sits, is, by chance, vacant, and Schell is at his desk doing paperwork.

A tall, heavyset man with longish sandy hair and a round freckled face,

Schell greets me with a headmaster's practiced charm but also, clearly, the desire to usher me immediately out of his office. "I just don't want to talk about this anymore," he says. Behind us appears Elaine Griffin, an attractive woman with straight brown hair, who looks alarmed. "You're late for your meeting," she tells her boss a bit desperately. "They're waiting for you . . ."

Yet when he walks me outside, Schell seems driven to clarify a version of events that almost no one, to his surprise and hurt, has chosen to accept. "It started out as an objection to the use of a name, in this small town, of some family friends," he says, standing under a covered walkway that looks across a green to a white-columned building and the river beyond. "We're talking about a town with 2,500, 3,000 people. After 25 years, these families have all been friends together." Was there no doubt in Schell's mind, I ask, that Seth MacFarlane chose that name to parody the Griffins he knew? Schell rolls his eyes at the thought. "I don't even want to get into that."

In response to the notion that only one call was made to Seth MacFarlane to get the name changed, Schell gives me another look. "I don't want to make them out to be telling you things that aren't so," he confides, "but numerous efforts were made to get them to change the name. That's a serious problem." Later, Perry MacFarlane insists that "Dick only did make that one call; there weren't other efforts."

Because of the name dispute, Schell says, he watched the show when it aired, and realized it had a bigger problem. "I saw the content! I said to myself, The corporations, if they knew what they were sponsoring, they would be concerned." In his letters of complaint, Schell chose not to mention that he knew the show's creator, or to make any reference to the local family whose name he felt had been impugned. The show's content, he suggests, now outweighed those factors. "The show is so bad," he says, "that I can't [see any] correlation between the family on that show and the wonderful family I'm talking about."

Schell says he created the ProudSponsorsUSA letterhead not to misrepresent himself or to foster the appearance of a large, established lobbying group, but rather to avoid associating the Kent School with his campaign. "I didn't want to use Kent School," he says. "I wanted to convey a clear message: this is about being a proud sponsor. "I don't wish anyone ill," Schell adds as he sends me on my way. "I don't even know what the implications of [this] are for this show. I was just pointing out to the sponsors that they should look at what they're responsible for."

To the Kent faculty, Schell's campaign embodies a number of dizzying contradictions. For one, he's a proud liberal on most social and political issues—proud enough to have written letters to the editors of newspapers over the last four or five years taking strong stands on, for example, President Clinton's right to prevaricate about his affair with Monica Lewinsky. "Most Americans have no doubt the President lied," Schell wrote to *The Lakeville Journal*. "But they also know he was responding to a crisis, protecting his family and friends, answering questions that were an affront to his personal dignity." The letters, which Schell took to pinning proudly on the school's bulletin boards, hardly square with his moral stance on crass television humor, free speech, and the role of commercial sponsors in determining the content of shows they buy into. Curiously, too, earlier letters to newspapers were signed by Schell as a rector and headmaster of the Kent School.

As roughly a dozen current and former faculty members and close observers see it, Schell's campaign is not so much a moral stand as an inexplicable act of revenge against MacFarlane for using the Griffin name. "He finds high moral justification for immoral acts," scoffs one. Morality is simply a cloak, they feel, for his vindictiveness. But on a deeper level, suggest his colleagues, Schell's campaign is the misjudgment of a man whose 18-year rule at Kent has been marked by growing isolation and authoritarianism, to the point where he seems cut off, his instincts blunted. They say he has one confidante, and that her own judgment sometimes seems marred by volatile emotion: his secretary, Elaine Griffin.

As the teachers observe, a New England prep school is, in a sense, like a feudal fiefdom, with the headmaster its duke. Because the institution is private, he has the power to expel students and dismiss faculty virtually as he pleases. The trustees are, in theory, his overseers, but they're busy people who live elsewhere; complaints, if they arise at all, tend to be given short shrift if the headmaster is doing his most important job well—fund-raising. And, again like dukes, the longer headmasters rule, the more unassailable they become.

Schell first came to Kent as a student in the mid-1960s. "He was the golden boy," recalls one disenchanted observer. "He was brilliant, he was an athlete, and he was senior prefect, which means he was the No. 1 boy as a senior." In his last year at Harvard, he was made Kent's youngest-ever trustee—a sop to student protesters demanding more of a say in how Kent was run. After Yale Divinity School, he took a job as a cleric at a church in Lake Forest, Illinois, where he had been raised as an upper-middle-class son of a Quaker Oats executive—and where, along with his Episcopal duties, he played a minister in a walk-on part in the movie *Ordinary People*. Soon, though, he was brought back to Kent as its chaplain and heir apparent. When the then headmaster succumbed prematurely to a brain tumor, Schell was given the job. He was 30 years old. By then he had married Jennifer Almquist and had twin daughters.

For more than a decade, Schell impressed most of his colleagues as an administrator, charmed wealthy alumni into making generous gifts, and did a particularly good job expanding the campus in 1992 to fully integrate Kent's girls' school, which had begun in 1960 on separate grounds four and a half miles away. By this time, however, more than a few observers had begun to feel that Schell was getting heavy-handed in his dealings with the faculty, and increasingly remote.

"He has talked at great length to me personally about his management beliefs," says one insider. "He's used the word 'Machiavellian': keep your groups separate, pit them against each other. As far back as 1986, I remember saying, 'Dick, that's so old-fashioned!' To him, it has no negative connotation."

More than one faculty member believes that Schell's manner began to change after his divorce in the mid-80s from Almquist. In an insular world of faculty couples, they suggest, a divorced headmaster has a harder time being the host he needs to be. And emotionally, without a partner's judgment, Schell seemed to suffer, in the eyes of one faculty member, "a steady deterioration."

"He started using people he could control," says another faculty member, "rather than people who could give him sound advice." Says another observer, more bluntly, "Anyone who may question his actions or motives is categorically and irredeemably an enemy."

Originally, Schell convened faculty meetings twice a month. But when faculty began posing serious policy questions, the meetings stopped, says one observer. Last year, there were just two such meetings, the first of which was the inevitable opening day introduction of new faculty members, without any give-and-take. "He even discouraged the faculty from going into the dining room for coffee," the observer adds. "It allowed for faculty to say hello to each other. He no longer allows this."

Over time, older faculty found themselves eased out, their places taken by teachers half their age—or just out of college. The older faculty were more likely to challenge their headmaster, the young replacements to be compliant. Also, as one close source says, the young ones were cheaper. "That makes it easier for him to contain the budget [and] impress the trustees." But something was lost. "Some of them are oddballs," says one observer of the older teachers, "but the unusual one may be the one that inspires your child." The young ones, less idiosyncratic, also tend to leave more quickly, having sacrificed a year or two to put Kent on their résumés. A decade ago, one faculty member recalls, two or three teachers left each year. "Now it's 16 or 18. And they're all under 30 or 31."

Almquist takes issue with all this. "The school was in dire financial straits," she says. "What they needed was a masterful fund-raiser, and that's what they got. Dick was also instrumental in getting the school to return to its roots as a church school. It's been said of prep-school faculties that individually they are fine, but as a group they would eat their headmasters alive if they could."

Paradoxically, as older faculty came to feel restricted, they saw Schell grow more lenient with students. "The things he attacks in *Family Guy* he allows in the school," exclaims one. "There is no code of morality on paper. If someone is caught cheating, the attitude is: 'We don't know if they actually read the notes on their arm or not.'" The school has a tough drug policy. Yet, as the mother of one former student observes, "They didn't want anyone to investigate where the kids were getting those drugs. I thought it would have made more sense to do that." More important, the policy may not be effective. "If my daughter's stories are true," says the mother of another former student, "virtually everyone in the dorms was on drugs. They were doing angel dust, cocaine, and grinding up Adderall, a prescription drug for attention deficit disorder, in order to snort it." In fairness, one of Schell's faculty critics thinks that may be overstating the case. "I'm not sure Kent has more drugs than any other prep school," he says.

In light of his moral stance on *Family Guy*, Schell took a surprisingly lax position when it came to social issues for the faculty as well. Last year a messy extramarital affair involving three faculty members shocked the entire school but drew no public censure from the headmaster.

And Schell's unwanted romantic interest in at least one unmarried female faculty member created another problem. After she rebuffed him, she felt a chill descend on her professional prospects at the school. "It became extremely clear that there was no room for advancement with him being in charge after [that]," she says. She has since left the school.

As for Schell's relationship with Elaine Griffin, it too has stirred debate—if for no other reason than that the defender of her honor and good name might more logically be her husband.

In a small town like Kent, people often work in the same job a long, long time. Elaine Griffin has sat outside the headmaster's office nearly as long as Schell has been there. He brought her over from the admissions office, where she had found her first job at the school with the help of her best friend, Perry MacFarlane. Ever since, the lives of both families, and of the headmaster, have been closely linked.

"The MacFarlanes were the Griffins' only friends [in Kent], to my knowledge," says one rather biased observer. "Jimmy Griffin, who works for Metro-North [the commuter rail line], plays guitar, as does Ron. They could hack around and sing folk songs. Elaine was in the same workplace with Perry. And the two Griffin children, Lauren and Jamie, were around the same age as Seth and Rachael."

If the Griffins were not quite typical of Kent, which consists mostly of writers, artists, and weekend people from Manhattan, the MacFarlanes, says this same observer, "were the most popular people in town." Though hardly wealthy—for a while, Ron supplemented his teacher's income as a butcher—they were charming and funny and enormously talented. Both Seth and Rachael inherited fine singing voices, and from an early age Seth's artistic talent was unmistakable. "He was brilliantly creative," says one of his former teachers, who, like every faculty member interviewed for this story, is reluctant to speak on the record. "Good in the theater department, contributed cartoons to the newspaper, and was generally seen as the kid who was going places." In his most memorable cartoon, a boy kneeling at the Communion rail says to his priest, "Can I get some fries with that?" A local Catholic priest was scandalized.

The two families vacationed together more than once on Cape Cod, and, while over time the children were less willing to be thrown together, Elaine Griffin seemed to become more and more dependent on Perry as a confidante. "Elaine is very good at playing the victim, and Perry was endlessly sympathetic," says a MacFarlane friend. At one point in the last few years, Elaine came to live with the MacFarlanes for three months, staying in a basement apartment of the house. While she was there, Schell often came to take her to school concerts and plays and do what he could to cheer her up.

As an Episcopal minister, Schell had officiated at the 1997 wedding of Lauren Griffin, now a schoolteacher. Schell seems to have become

Elaine's other confidant. More and more, the two seemed to protect each other. As Schell grew more withdrawn from the faculty, Elaine became a stricter gatekeeper. "She controls access," says one former employee. "It's a bunkerlike situation," says a faculty member. "She's very careful about whom she allows in." At the same time, says the former employee, "he will protect her. If she reacts emotionally, he will weigh in on her behalf. She has her little blowups; we keep our heads down. Most of us have learned to keep our distance from her."

In the small, insular world of a New England prep school, such closeness stirred inevitable gossip. "Elaine does show up at receptions, not exactly on his arm," adds the former employee. "But she's at dinner parties at his home, often checking up in the kitchen. She's not a surrogate spouse [however]."

Clearly, Schell reacted to *Family Guy* as a deeply personal affront to his closest ally. Along with preparing his ProudSponsorsUSA campaign, he combed the Internet in search of negative reviews of the show and put copies of them in faculty mailboxes. At least one packet was mailed anonymously: "A colleague in the town of Kent received one of these xeroxed things, mailed anonymously from Chicago," Perry MacFarlane recalls. "It was when Dick was in Chicago. We recognized the handwriting!"

To one faculty member, says Perry, Schell described his campaign as a war with the odds in his favor. "My aim is to get this show pulled off the air," he allegedly told another faculty member in a restaurant. To yet another he declared he had a "mole" at Fox television, and warned that Seth MacFarlane was preparing a character based on that teacher. Still another teacher came in for a formal review, only to be subjected to 20 minutes of fevered talk from Schell on the horrors of *Family Guy*.

Elaine Griffin was striking back, too. On the MacFarlanes' answering machine, she left a long rant so bitter it led the MacFarlanes to call the police. "I feel like I never knew any of you, that you have absolutely no morals. . . . You have absolutely destroyed me, and I can't believe you have connected our names to such a horrible cartoon that belittles everything. . . . Enjoy your fame! I am so ashamed I have such poor judgment on choosing you to be my friend. . . . I think you are the most horrible people I have ever met. And I just hope you enjoy Hollywood, because you belong there because you are garbage."

By summer, the MacFarlanes had moved to Southern California, partly to be closer to Seth and Rachael, a singer and songwriter who also lives on the West Coast, partly to get away from Kent's headmaster and his secretary. "The whole town," says one friend of the MacFarlanes', "is devastated that they're gone."

Jennifer Almquist is sorry the MacFarlanes left, too. "I've known [Seth] since he was a small boy, and the whole town, including Dick, has admired him and cheered his success." But she feels Schell's campaign was justified. "Dick is getting a lot of punishment for being able to stand up and take a high moral ground. In his job as a headmaster and Episcopal priest, it's essential that he be willing to take a moral stand. I'm sure that most Episcopal priests would back him up."

Finding a faculty member to defend the headmaster's campaign is somewhat more difficult. Finally, one senior faculty member close to the headmaster and his secretary volunteers. "We all love Elaine," says this teacher, "so I can see why he felt obligated to intervene by talking to the MacFarlanes, then picking up the spear."

As for the form Schell's campaign took, this faculty member views it as merely the most recent example of Schell's long-standing interest in public issues. "Clearly, though opinions can vary, it is a legitimate issue to talk about—the politics and ethics of broadcasting 'edgy' material, especially on open-air television. I think it's also a legitimate issue to talk about the possible linkage between the characters and the person of [Schell's] secretary." The sympathizer pauses. "I'm actually not in agreement with him on either one, but I think they're both legitimate."

The sympathizer, however, declines to go on the record.

As angry mutterings have spread among faculty and alumni, the Kent administration has clamped down. Word has gone out to the faculty ordering them to say "No comment" to any and all press queries. And when one influential alum strode into the development office to demand a list of the trustees and their addresses in order to write them a letter decrying Schell's campaign, he claims he was told by a female staff member to wait. Upon his return an hour later, the request was denied. "Who told you you couldn't give it to me?" the alum demanded. The headmaster, admitted the woman. "But I guess I have to give it to you," she went on, "because under the bylaws it's public."

In Burbank, Seth MacFarlane has just moved to a new house—a sign of his growing success. He has stopped worrying about his old head-master; the greater threat now is that Fox has moved *Family Guy* from Sunday to Thursday nights. "They said it was strong enough to anchor a new night for them, that it could launch a couple of new shows," he says with a sigh. "I wish I had the same confidence—that after only six episodes we can carry new shows. It seems to me that it's too soon."

Schell, meanwhile, repaired to Nova Scotia for the end of the sum-mer, possibly hoping that the storm would blow over. Several calls to Schell and Elaine Griffin at the headmaster's office went unreturned. At least there will be no more letters to sponsors of *Family Guy*. "I could, if I wanted to, become . . . I could go on talk shows, I could talk to magazines, I could be out there hammering this program," Schell told me from his doorway during our truncated visit. But he's not going to, because "I have a job to do, which is running this school." Which means that a powerful top job at ProudSponsorsUSA is available even now. No pay, no benefits, but lots of publicity, and influence over dozens of major U.S. corporations.

Any takers?

[Schell remains the school's headmaster and rector. *Family Guy* has been broadcast for 15 seasons—nearly 300 episodes—and is currently in syndication.]

"MAJORING IN CRIME"

By *John Falk*

DECEMBER 2007

On the morning of December 17, 2004, Betty Jean Gooch, a librarian in the Special Collections Library at Transylvania University, in Lexington, Kentucky, was preparing for her 11 o'clock appointment with Walter Beckman, a man she had never met. Over the phone and by e-mail, Beckman had asked to view, among other items, a first edition of Charles Darwin's *On the Origin of Species* and four double-size folios of John James Audubon's *Birds of America*.

Wearing a heavy coat, gloves, and a wool cap, Beckman signed the visitors' log. With a long, thin face and bleached-blond hair and sideburns, he appeared younger than Gooch had expected. He was also less cordial and more agitated in person, asking Gooch soon after arriving if he could invite a friend along to see the books. She agreed. A few minutes later, a short, dark-haired young man, also dressed in a winter coat, cap, and gloves, entered the library. He said his name was John.

The two men followed the librarian into the Rare Book Room, and John closed the door behind them. As she was heading toward a display case, Gooch felt a tingling on her right arm and collapsed to the floor.

By one o'clock that afternoon, the 227-year-old liberal-arts college was swarming with campus police, uniformed Lexington Police, plain-clothes detectives, and forensic teams, as well as local news crews cover-ing the developing "Transy Book Heist," a crime that would one day be listed among the F.B.I.'s all-time most significant art-theft cases.

From the facts that were available, it appeared that a team of four men, described as Caucasian, in their 20s, had stolen some of the most prized books and manuscripts in the university's collection, and attacked a librarian in the process. The take could be more than $5 million. The thieves left no fingerprints behind, and there were almost no witnesses.

The Lexington Police Department's commercial-burglary squad was assigned to the case. In terms of the dollar amount involved and the extraordinary circumstances, the theft was one of the most significant in its history. The first call went out to the National Crime Information Center, alerting law enforcement to be on the lookout for a gray mini-van with temporary plates, the description of a vehicle seen screeching away from the library. The L.P.D. notified all the airports in the area, dispatched officers to surrounding neighborhoods, and called the F.B.I.

Still shaken from her ordeal, Gooch, in her 50s, told police that shortly after entering the Rare Book Room with the two men she had been struck on the arm with a Taserlike weapon, her hands and feet were bound with zip ties, and a wool cap was pulled over her eyes. Though she couldn't recall much else about her assailants, one odd detail stood out.

"[Beckman] said, 'B.J.,'" a nickname her friends and colleagues used for her, she told officers. "'Quit struggling, B.J., or do you want to feel more pain?'" she remembered the man saying.

GOOD BOYS, GOOD FAMILIES

The minimum-security Federal Correctional Institution in Ashland, Kentucky, 125 miles from Lexington, houses approximately 1,200 inmates in multi-story cellblocks encircled by concentric layers of razor-topped fencing and fortified guard towers. Among the prisoners are three of the four unlikely masterminds behind the Transy Book Heist: Warren Lipka, Spencer Reinhard, and Eric Borsuk. (The fourth, Charles "Chas" Allen II, was transferred to a federal medical center in Lexington.) All four, now 22, children of privilege, products of elite Lexington high schools, are serving seven-year sentences for their parts in the crime.

Behind the main building and through three blastproof security doors is the prison visitors' room, where I meet separately with Lipka, Reinhard, and Borsuk for a series of interviews almost a year into their sentence. (Through his attorney, Allen declined to be interviewed.) Because the boys pleaded guilty, many of the case's crucial details remain unknown even to law enforcement. What they would tell me, then, is their version of events—and the only complete account of the planning, execution, and aftermath of the heist.

They're all slim and dressed identically in cheap sneakers and khaki uniforms emblazoned with their incarceration numbers, and all have hair down to their shoulders. Each has a different style of facial hair—muttonchops (Lipka), a Fu Manchu (Borsuk), a Tom Selleck (Reinhard)—which Lipka informs me they had carefully trimmed for my visit.

When the four boys were arrested the news was met with disbelief, as none of them had been in any serious trouble before. Far from being social outcasts, they had been popular athletes, and two were on some form of college scholarship. The press invariably described them as "good boys" from "good families"—upper-middle-class kids afforded every opportunity, the ones with the most to lose.

There were all sorts of theories as to why they had done it: they were drug addicts; they had amassed large gambling debts—or Lipka's father had, and the boys did it to save the family's honor (the variant most popular with the local papers). By far the most common theory around town was that the heist had been just a frat prank that spun way out of control.

A painting by Reinhard, a gifted artist, may offer some clues. Titled *A Plan to Fail*, it was part of a series he had done on the crime for a local art gallery while out on bond. The painting is a kaleidoscope of images, including what appears to be a computer, a cell phone, a bong, the Transylvania library, and loose sheets of notepaper, floating above a desiccated one-eyed young man in a watch cap, kicking back on a beat-up couch with a blue dog on his lap. Opposite him there is another young man, fully fleshed and with a neat haircut, resting in a chair, staring into space. The painting, in digital form, would become a popular screen saver on the F.B.I. computers in the Lexington field office.

FRESHMAN FUNK

Spencer Reinhard and Warren Lipka had grown up together in adjacent subdivisions on Lexington's south side—fully planned residential tracts wedged in between the city and the gradually receding horse country that rings it. Built over old tobacco fields in the 80s, they feature ponds with fountains, cookie-cutter brick Colonial houses, street names like Ironbridge Drive and Turnberry Lane, and regulations authorizing penalties for unkempt yards and tacky lawn Santas. In high school, Warren, a lanky six-footer with a mop of brown hair, was a popular jock and a class clown who delighted his classmates by bear-hugging his nemesis, the dean of students, at graduation. Spencer, meanwhile, was short, wiry, distant, and in many ways Warren's opposite: an over-scheduled, over-achieving, diamond-tipped drill of a kid who excelled at whatever he set himself to. He focused above all on painting, gaining admission into a prestigious Lexington arts program.

Despite the differing temperaments—and the disapproval of Spencer's parents—the two were best friends from the age of eight, a friendship that revolved largely around soccer. Though they attended different high schools, both were varsity captains, and both made all-state. In their senior year the two became local celebrities after a dramatic photo appeared in the *Lexington Herald-Leader* showing Lexington Catholic star goalkeeper Lipka and Tates Creek forward Reinhard battling midair during a playoff game.

In the fall of 2003, Warren left for the University of Kentucky on a full athletic scholarship, eager to take his game to the next level, and with vague plans of getting into politics. Spencer, meanwhile, was accepted to Transylvania on an arts scholarship, his sights firmly set on a career in graphic design. Because their campuses were only a mile apart, they assumed they would stay close, but as with most freshmen, their assured identities and easy expectations muddied once they hit campus. For Spencer it all started with a series of mild disappointments. "I was expecting to play soccer quite a lot, but the coach was a completely different person once I got on the team," he tells me. "And I pledged a fraternity, but I really didn't get into that too much. In all my art classes I was the only guy—in with a bunch of girls who didn't have any idea what they wanted to do. All these girls I could draw better than when I was in sixth grade."

Across town at U.K., in a towering cinder-block dorm, Warren's world was spinning apart at a much faster clip. His malaise was likely exacerbated by his parents' impending divorce amid his mother's allegations that his father, Big Warren, the celebrated coach of the university's women's soccer team, had gambled the family into bankruptcy. (Big Warren declined to comment on the gambling accusations at the time.) When not at practice, Warren spent his time smoking pot, watching Comedy Central, and reading German philosophy.

"It was very punishing, that first couple of months in college. Not what I expected, not what I wanted it to be," Warren says. "I want to say living that kind of life—the country clubs, sitting in a classroom and listening to two girls argue about turning down a BMW S.U.V. because she wanted a new Range Rover, like, *what?* These people's perspectives, because they have money, they're tweaked."

In October of his freshman year, Warren quit the U.K. soccer team, forfeiting his scholarship. He was still enrolled, but only nominally, and remained on the fringes of campus life. Shortly thereafter he was introduced to a Lexington Catholic alumnus who was making an easy living in identity theft. Seeing something in the wayward Warren, the preppy grifter pitched him the idea of selling fake Kentucky driver's licenses in the U.K. dorms. Warren jumped at the opportunity and recruited another adrift freshman, his old high-school soccer teammate Eric Borsuk, as a partner. By early November the boys were selling fake IDs at a hundred dollars apiece, and had apparently branched out into more lucrative identity manipulations. "I can't really get into too much specifics," Eric says, "but we were doing all kinds of little scams: making fake IDs, making little things here and there. That's what we were doing, kind of living this little *Matchstick Men,* college kind of life."

The partnership flourished, with Warren as the face of the operation and Eric in charge of ID production, until the two had an argument over $2,000 that went missing from Eric's drawer. They stopped talking entirely and disbanded. Suddenly without Eric's mock-ups, software, and equipment, Warren thought of Spencer. Although the two hadn't really been in contact in the first few months of school, Warren knew that Spencer's artistic talents would be an asset. Spencer, feeling increasingly disaffected with school life himself, readily accepted the offer.

PLANTING THE SEED

Several weeks before Spencer was approached by Warren about the fake-ID business, he had been on a freshman-orientation tour of Transy, including the library and its exceptional collection of rare books and manuscripts.

"They take you in the Special Collections and show you these books," Spencer remembers, including Transy's prized *Birds of America,* by John James Audubon, a four-volume set of life-size engravings the pioneer wildlife artist completed in London in 1838. The set was one of fewer than 200 produced. "I'd heard about them before, but I didn't know anything about them. And the woman there says, 'We had a set just like this that we sold four years ago for like $12 million.' It could have been eight. I'm not sure, but it was a lot. It immediately had kind of sparked my imagination, like a fantasy."

"O.K., so we're sitting in the car, smoking weed," Warren recalls, "and then Spencer said, 'I just took a tour in that library, and there's shit sitting there you wouldn't believe. They said that this set, *Birds of America,* sold for $12 million.' I said, 'Twelve million dollars, just sitting there? They got security around that?' Nonchalantly, very nonchalantly, I mean, just kind of shooting it between us. So I kind of go, 'That would be pretty crazy, wouldn't it?' He said, 'Yeah, that would be kind of crazy.' I then said, 'You know, why don't you look into it more and we'll go from there?' Just like . . . very unofficial."

Between studying for his first semester's finals, working out, and painting, Spencer made time to scope out the Special Collections section of the Transy library, reporting back to Warren weeks later that there was zero security other than an old lady librarian named B.J. and having to "sign a fucking book." By hitting the ball back into Warren's court, Spencer thought he would keep that thrilling flicker of criminality burning for a bit longer, while fully expecting there to be an insurmountable obstacle somewhere down the road. Even if they did steal the books, for example, how would they ever sell them?

Spencer had underestimated his friend's resolve. Warren was already busily working out the problem, returning for advice to his underworld contact: " 'What if we had some artwork that we wanted to sell?' " Warren remembers asking him. " 'How the hell would we do this?' And he said, 'I know a guy in New York.' "

After several phone calls Warren managed to arrange a meeting in New York. The contact, who identified himself only as Barry, stipulated that Warren had to bring $500 in good-faith money. Late one Thursday afternoon in mid-February, the two friends bought a bag of weed and drove the 700 miles to Manhattan in Spencer's Acura Legend. They checked into the Hilton Hotel in Midtown, Warren signing in under the nom de guerre Harry Ballsani—a name backed up with one of their fake Kentucky driver's licenses—and paying in cash. (Having seen their fair share of heist movies, they knew how dangerous it was to leave a paper trail.) The meeting was scheduled for the next morning on the southern edge of Central Park near the Plaza Hotel. Barry described himself as an older man with a long ponytail and said he'd be wearing a green scarf.

The meeting initially hit a snag when Barry was put off by the boys' youth. "He was visibly unnerved," Warren remembers. "It was hard for us. We weren't, like, hardened criminals, so we kind of had to really put up a front." Warren deepens his voice: " 'How ya doing?' That kind of stuff." After an awkward back-and-forth, Warren finally handed the man the $500. In exchange, Barry slipped him an e-mail address with instructions to sign off any communication with the name Terry.

Once safely back in Lexington, the two created a Yahoo account and sent off the e-mail in which they claimed to have unspecified rare books in their possession, using the name Terry, as instructed. A week later came a terse reply, telling Terry that, if he wanted to sell something, he was going to have to come in person to Amsterdam, "as that is where I do business." Both Spencer and Warren were thrilled—until they realized it would require traveling with a passport. Spencer believed it was an insurmountable problem. Again, Warren thought otherwise.

"So we go back to the guy in Lexington and we say, 'Listen, we want to go somewhere, we want to go out of the country, and we need documentation,' " Warren explains. " 'We can do a license, but now we need a passport.' So he says, 'Come see me in a couple of days or a week, but I need money, $2,500.' All right, you know, just another thing, O.K., 2,500 bucks. Bam. Bam. So we get the passport from the dude, plane tickets. Boom. Spencer drives me out to Lexington [Blue Grass Airport] on a Friday. Spencer gives me 500 bucks, in my pocket. Can't have any of this documented. Like if we ever get caught, we're talking about international issues, way past interstate commerce or whatever the hell it is."

Because of the expense, only Warren made the trip, touching down at Amsterdam's Schiphol Airport on a Saturday morning in early March 2004. He took a cab to Dam Square, an old hippie hangout in the center of the city he had read about on the Internet. He scored a joint before checking into "a hole-in-the-wall" and falling asleep.

The next morning, all nerves, he left for the meeting site, a café within walking distance. He was told to look for a bearded, heavyset man in a solid-blue sweater. When Warren arrived, he saw a man fitting that description seated with three other men. Undeterred, Warren introduced himself as Terry, firmly shaking hands before sitting down. Like Barry, the men were immediately put off by Warren's youth, and even more so by the fact that he hadn't brought any of the books with him to Amsterdam. He also didn't have photos, photocopies, documentation, or even the slightest ability to intelligently discuss the books. The meeting lasted no more than 15 minutes, but still, it was a turning point because the men explained to Warren a crucial step of selling rare books, stolen or otherwise: appraisal by a legitimate auction house.

"They were skeptical," Warren recalls. "And then they came up with the issue of getting these appraised. He said, 'You do that and you are free then to give them to us when you can.' O.K., great. So I walk off happy, come back to the States, and blow Spencer's mind."

"We figured, All right, well, now we just got what we thought would be impossible . . . possibly taken care of," Spencer tells me. After researching auction houses online, Warren singled out Christie's in New York.

"I was kind of skeptical," continues Spencer, "but the way I rationalized it was: it's the biggest auction house. If we go in there they're not going to suspect that we stole these. Because no one would go to

Christie's with stolen books to get them appraised—that's how we did a lot of stuff, like, we would smoke weed directly under the [security] camera on the Transy campus, park a car right underneath it and then smoke for like an hour. We figured the more obvious [we were], the less likely [we would be suspected]."

As it was already nearing the end of the school year, and there was a lot of planning yet to be done, they agreed to postpone the theft until at least the fall. But even at that point, it became apparent that Warren and Spencer wouldn't be able to pull it off alone. "We're going to need more people," Warren remembers thinking. "Who do we trust?"

"Warren called me one night and he's like, 'We need to get together. We need to just get over this stuff,' " Eric tells me, explaining how Warren re-entered his life after their falling-out the previous semester. "So we ate at Pazzo's pizza pub. We had a few pitchers, feeling each other out. He's probably thinking I blamed him for [stealing] the money, which I never really did. And one thing led to another and we were just like, 'Let's put this behind us.' And once we get past all of that, we started talking about this plan that he and Spencer have.

"Warren was like, 'I've talked to these guys. I've met with them,' " Eric continues. " 'They think we have [the books]. Now the hard part— we have to steal them.' I was nervous. I'm not going to lie. Because this is so much bigger than anything we've done before."

When summer break began, the three returned home to the subdivisions of South Lexington. Spencer received a commission to paint murals at a local school and kept up his soccer training, Eric started a lawn-care business with his friend Chas Allen, and Warren landed a job at a local day camp. The guys hung out together when they could, with Warren frequently conjuring up fantasies—through billowing clouds of marijuana smoke—of post-heist life for them in the Mediterranean, complete with sleek catamarans and topless women.

A WORKING PLAN

Wedged in among the other houses on Beaumont Avenue, a quiet residential street near the U.K. campus, is a beaten-down yellow cinder-block bungalow, with two bedrooms on the second floor and two on the first. In the fall of 2004, Warren Lipka moved into the unfinished basement. At only $200 a month, the price was right, as Warren was broke after having shut down his and Spencer's fake-ID business and dropping out of U.K. for the semester to focus full-time on the heist. More important, the basement was secluded. Warren sectioned off a bedroom by hanging bedsheets from the rafters and furnished it with an old mattress and a tangerine easy chair he had picked up from Goodwill. Near the boiler he also jerry-rigged a greenhouse for growing marijuana. He topped off his new living quarters with the last of his worldly belongings: a large-screen television, a DVD player, and a Sony PlayStation. Eric rented a proper bedroom upstairs, while Spencer moved back into the dorms at Transylvania.

During a meeting in the basement, Warren convinced the other two that they were going to need a fourth, principally to help haul the nearly 250 pounds in Audubon folios out of the library. After a brief discussion they chose Chas Allen, a handsome, clean-cut U.K. business major who had started the lawn-care company with Eric the previous summer. Chas not only lived in the yellow bungalow but also was a part owner of it with his father, a prominent Lexington real-estate investor.

When Eric let him in on the plan, Chas mocked the three as deluded potheads, he recalls. But after stewing in the magnitude of the potential dollar amount involved, and once convinced of the ease of the heist, the logic of the appraisal, and the legitimacy of Warren's Amsterdam connections, they say, he threw his lot in with the others.

In between soccer practice, classes, painting, and studying, Spencer drew detailed sketches of the inside of the Special Collections Library and the adjacent Rare Book Room, making several appointments with the Special Collections librarian, Betty Jean Gooch, to scout the premises. The others spent time in the library, too, taking notes on staff routines and viable escape routes. They surveyed the offices of the campus police. They climbed onto dorm roofs, where they'd stake out the library for hours at a time, marking down the comings and goings of teachers, students, and security personnel. They also did considerable research on the Internet, using such key terms as "auction house appraisals," "stun guns," and "Swiss bank accounts." For inspiration, they watched heist movies like *Ocean's 11* and *Snatch*.

Around Halloween, Warren drafted a working plan, which he presented to the other three in the basement. The day of the heist was to be Thursday, December 16, one of the last days of final exams—the library would be nearly empty. Warren, under an alias, would make an appointment with Gooch for that afternoon to view the books they wanted to steal.

The plan for the actual robbery sets out three distinct phases. Phase 1 begins at the bungalow when all four get into what Warren designated the G.T.A.V., or the "Go-to-and-Away-Vehicle," all disguised as old men. Phase 1 ends when the G.T.A.V. is parked in front of the library and the four "are in 1st Position at bottom of stairs of library."

Phase 2 involves the actual theft, and begins when Spencer takes his position at an upper-floor window of the nearby athletic center, where he will be on lookout. (Because Spencer was a Transy student, he risked being recognized in the library.) Warren and Chas go up to the Rare Book Room, on the third floor, and Warren "brings Gooch down hard and fast" with a stun gun, making her "a non-factor throughout the operation." Warren and Chas then let Eric in and they begin wrapping the Audubons in bedsheets and put any smaller books in backpacks. The three then take the staff-only elevator down to the bottom floor and escape out the west fire exit. Phase 2 ends when the "loot" is loaded into the G.T.A.V.

Phase 3 is the escape, which involves switching the G.T.A.V. for a second vehicle at a secret location, which, according to Warren's plan, "is used to transport team and loot to temporary resting place." After the heist, since it is certain that the stolen books will be entered into art-theft databases within a week, they have to get the books appraised at Christie's in New York immediately.

Lifting a technique straight from the film *Reservoir Dogs*, Warren assigned code names based on color: Mr. Green (Spencer), Mr. Yellow (Warren), and Mr. Black (Eric)—as in the film, emotions turned testy when he assigned Mr. Pink, in this case to Chas.

The reaction to the plan was generally positive—shortly after Thanksgiving, they moved forward.

Warren made an appraisal appointment at Christie's in New York for Walter Beckman, a pseudonym inspired by the soccer star David Beckham. He covered his tracks by using public phones and campus comput-ers. Writing from walter.beckman@yahoo.com, Warren sent B. J. Gooch an e-mail confirming Beckman's December 16 appointment at the Rare Book Room to view the Audubons and a few other items.

"I know the collection is extensive and anything you think I might be interested in seeing, by all means, share," he wrote. Warren also or-dered four stun guns over the Internet. Meanwhile, Eric lined up the G.T.A.V. from an unsuspecting friend and got his hands on zip ties, a wool cap, electrician's tape, and bedsheets. Spencer assembled a small wardrobe of fake beards, gray wigs, and costume glue. To have time to properly apply the disguises, he tried to reschedule his art-history final for later in the day on the 16th, but was unsuccessful. Warren called Gooch back to change Walter Beckman's appointment to three P.M.

On the morning of December 16, Warren's carefully scripted plan began to unravel almost immediately. Eric couldn't get hold of his friend's car, leaving Chas to borrow a Dodge Caravan his mother was fortuitously selling the next day, the boys say. The stun guns Warren had ordered never arrived, so he drove around town and returned with a Black Cobra Stun Pen, and had Spencer zap him and Eric to test its knockdown power. When they arrived on campus in the replacement

G.T.A.V., they couldn't find a parking space anywhere near the library. Once the boys were inside the library, students stared at the ridiculous old-man disguises. (Spencer had had to do a rush job on them because his art-history final had run long.) They also noticed a group of people lingering in the Rare Book Room. After a quick powwow in the stacks, the conspirators decided to abort the mission for the time being and retreated to the bungalow.

By five P.M., Warren—as Beckman—was back on the phone with Gooch explaining that he had missed his appointment because he had been out of town on business. Gooch agreed to reschedule for 11 the next morning. According to the revised plan, they would ditch the old-man disguises and only Warren and Eric would enter the library. Eric would stay on the main floor while Warren subdued Gooch in the Rare Book Room. Afterward, he was to call Eric up to haul the books in two trips to the G.T.A.V., which was to be driven by Chas.

Spencer would communicate with Warren from a cell phone, which Warren would steal from a student in the morning. The whole operation would have to be completed by 12:30 P.M., as the boys say Chas needed to return the Dodge Caravan to his mother in time for her to sell it, and Spencer and Eric had to get to their final exams in sociology and tennis, respectively. For added anonymity, Warren bleached his hair blond that night.

At 11 the next morning, Chas slipped the G.T.A.V. into a perfect parking space and watched as Eric and Warren entered the library. Warren went up to the third floor to meet Gooch, while Eric waited downstairs for him to call.

THE HEIST

6 I get the call on the cell phone. [Warren's] like, 'Come on up,' " Eric remembers. "I'm expecting when I get up there it's going to be taken care of and I'm just going to start lifting books. That was the plan. When I get up there, B.J. opens the door for me and I'm just like,

'*Holy shit.*' I quickly came up with some fake name and started walking in and I'm like, 'Oh, shit, this is gonna happen at any moment.' So while I'm shutting the doors I look back and Warren took her to the ground. And that's when I came up. . . . I took my zip ties and I put them around her feet and put them around her arms." It was about at that point that Gooch remembers Warren saying, "Quit struggling, B.J., or do you want to feel more pain?"

Once Warren had pulled the cap over Gooch's eyes, the two laid a bedsheet on the ground and began piling on the seven Audubon folios they intended to steal (the four-volume *Birds of America* plus three volumes from another Audubon series). The books were much heavier than the boys had projected, and the pair could handle only three at a time. They stuffed some of the smaller books Gooch had pulled out for them into their backpacks. With each taking one end of the Audubons, they made their way to the staff-only elevator.

"We told B.J. as we left we were going to make an anonymous phone call so they knew she was up here," Eric continues. "We felt bad." Warren and Eric rode the elevator to the basement, but they couldn't find the fire exit. They went back up in the elevator, accidentally stopping on the main floor, where they were spotted by another librarian. "[This librarian] doesn't know what we're carrying, but she's like, 'Where did these kids come from?' " Eric says. "So we go back down to the bottom floor just to get away from her. I guess when we did that she went upstairs to check on B.J."

Realizing that the only way out was through the main floor, they took the elevator up once again and carried the books into a back stairwell that led to another exit. As they scooted down the stairs their arms gave out and they stopped to catch their breath. Eric had propped the folios on the steps with his foot when the librarian appeared at the top of the stairs, beside herself with rage after finding Gooch hog-tied in the Rare Book Room. Eric dropped the books, and he and Warren made a run for it.

"I see Warren and Eric bust out of the back door," Spencer says, describing what he saw unfold from his lookout position. "They were 20 steps ahead [of the librarian]. Chas backs up [the van] and almost hits the woman as Eric comes around to the door. Warren had run up the side of the hill and frantically ran off. And Eric calls to him. And so I see Warren go back. . . . They jump in the van and peel out around the loop."

Chas turned the G.T.A.V. onto nearby Fourth Street and careened through traffic before stopping a mile farther on, in front of a predominantly black housing project. Improvising on the plan, he kicked Eric and Warren out on the street, believing three men in a gray minivan would draw too much attention. Chas promised to return to pick them up in another car after dropping the minivan off at his mom's house.

Warren and Eric got out of the G.T.A.V. believing that they had escaped with next to nothing. In fact, wedged in their backpacks was nearly three-quarters of a million dollars' worth of books and manuscripts: an 1859 first edition of Charles Darwin's *On the Origin of Species by Means of Natural Selection* ($25,000), an illuminated manuscript from 1425 ($200,000), a set of the two-volume 15th-century horticultural masterpiece entitled *Hortus Sanitatis* ($450,000), 20 original Audubon pencil drawings ($50,000), and Audubon's *A Synopsis of the Birds of North America* ($10,000).

The two boys sought cover from the cops in the sprawling grounds of the housing projects. But before long they were put to chase once again, this time by two local thugs. Frightened and alone in an unfriendly neighborhood and weighed down with priceless books, Warren and Eric barreled down the street, frantically trying to hail a police cruiser to rescue them. As they ran, they stumbled again into Chas, who had returned in another car as promised, just in time to save them and drive Eric to U.K. for his tennis-class exam. "It was only a tennis final," Eric says, "but that final that day was actually harder than I thought it was going to be. It had some tennis trivia in there that I wasn't expecting."

Back at Warren's later that afternoon, the boys were transfixed by local coverage of the "Transy Book Heist." According to the news, it appeared that neither Gooch nor anyone else was able to provide the police with an accurate description of the boys. (The librarian who chased them out of the library did tell police the correct total of four thieves, even though she had seen only three.) A witness had written down a license-plate number, but it was way off. They tried to come up with some link the cops could make between them and the theft, but they couldn't. In the early evening, they say they smoked some celebratory "Kentucky Bluegrass" weed they had stashed away for the occasion.

Having told their parents that they were going on a ski trip to West Virginia, that weekend they loaded the loot into Eric's Ford Explorer and took off on the 12-hour drive to New York for their Christie's appointment. Along the way a stoned Spencer read aloud from the purloined first edition of *On the Origin of Species,* particularly fascinated by the section on how the ears of domesticated animals have drooped over generations "due to the disuse of the muscles of the ear from the animals not being much alarmed by danger."

ROAD TRIP

The crew arrived in New York City early Sunday morning. They had reserved a room in the same Midtown Hilton that Spencer and Warren had stayed in nearly a year earlier. That night they had dinner at a Japanese restaurant, followed by drinks at the hotel bar, where Warren chummed up to an Iraq veteran, Spencer almost started a brawl after knocking a table full of drinks over, and Eric picked up a middle-aged Brazilian tourist. Warren and Chas left the other two and staggered to the nearby China Club, a tacky West Side nightclub, which they knew about from the famous "Rick James" episode of *Chappelle's Show.*

The next day, they worked off their hangovers by checking out Ground Zero before strolling into the bustle of Chinatown for lunch. That afternoon they worked their way back uptown, to scope out Christie's steel-and-glass headquarters before their Tuesday appointment. Afterward, they returned to the Hilton for an early night.

It had been agreed that Warren, with his smooth talk, and Spencer, with his artistic knowledge, would go to the meeting. The other two would wait around the block in the S.U.V.

Warren and Spencer readied themselves early without waking the others, silently showering, shaving, and putting the finishing touches on their outfits. Dressed for success in a tailored dark-blue suit his parents had bought for special occasions and future job interviews, Warren cultivated the young-conservative look, using a Windsor knot on his red tie and giving his wing tips a last-minute buff. Spencer assembled his outfit with even greater care. Starting with a 1970s Pierre Cardin canary-yellow blazer that had belonged to his grandfather, he wore a dress shirt with an ostentatiously large collar and a gold silk scarf. For footwear he went with clean white sneakers.

Eric and Chas dropped Warren and Spencer off around the corner from Christie's. As a precautionary measure, they left the books in the car. A uniformed doorman cheerily welcomed both boys into the lobby, where they informed reception that they were there for Mr. Walter Beckman's appointment with Thomas Leckey, Christie's rare-book specialist. After a short wait, a young Christie's employee, Melanie Halloran, came out to apologize, as Mr. Leckey, due to an impending public auction, would be unable to see them. She offered to take his place. The boys readily agreed, and she escorted them through the offices to a small conference room.

Warren introduced himself as Mr. Williams. Spencer called himself Mr. Stephens. As they took their seats in the conference room, Warren explained that he and Mr. Stephens "are the sole representatives of Walter Beckman," whom he described as "a very private individual from Boston" who had recently inherited several valuable rare books and manuscripts. Mr. Beckman now wanted these books appraised. When Halloran inquired about them, Spencer spoke up and offered to fetch them from the car. Returning five minutes later with a rolling red suitcase in tow, Spencer opened it on the conference table. Inside were the books, wrapped in sheets and pillowcases. As she inspected the items,

Halloran dutifully took notes, then asked a few questions regarding their provenance, which Spencer answered as best he could under the circumstances. The meeting ended after 30 minutes, and Ms. Halloran escorted the two out, assuring them that she'd be in touch after conferring with her superiors on the best way forward. When she asked for contact information, Spencer gave her his cell-phone number.

Afterward, Warren and Spencer briefed the others, and the four went to lunch, where, the boys say, Chas insisted they spend another night in New York and attempt to see Mr. Leckey the next day.

In the morning, Warren says, he left two messages with Leckey's secretary and two more that afternoon. No response. That night Chas snapped, they say, fearing the Christie's book appraisal—the Jesus bolt holding Warren's entire heist plan together—was in danger of falling through. Chas cursed Warren as an incompetent, and condemned the other two as burnouts, demanding that the three figure out a way to get the books appraised so they could move on to the next phase of the plan. They simply ignored him, and the four returned to Lexington. (Throughout the interviews with the three, it became clear that Chas was the odd man out among the group. During our interview Eric told me, "He was like just a weight on us. He was just so unbearable. He thought he was much better than everybody else, and he got to the point where he wasn't like us. Us three, we were much thicker than he was.") And what Chas likely didn't know was that, for Warren, Eric, and Spencer, the actual appraisal and sale of the stolen books had become irrelevant to the mission.

ENDGAME

In the weeks following the book heist, law enforcement followed leads at Transy and reviewed countless hours of security footage from the U.K. computer lab, to which a police technician had traced the e-mail from Walter Beckman to Gooch. Nothing panned out until mid-January, when, following a federal subpoena, Yahoo delivered all the data on its servers related to the walter.beckman@yahoo.com address. Buried in the files was a series of e-mails to Christie's in New York. The F.B.I. sent a team to interview Melanie Halloran, who told the agents about her meeting with Mr. Stephens and Mr. Williams.

She described one of the young men as about six feet tall, with bleached-blond hair, well dressed in a nice suit, and very talkative. The other was short and quiet, wearing a yellow jacket two sizes too large and a matching scarf. "He looked like he was dressed from a thrift store," Halloran told the agents. She also said that she was so suspicious and put off by the young men's youth and demeanor that she had recommended to her boss that they not pursue the business.

After the Halloran interview the F.B.I. received two additional pieces of evidence from Christie's: security-camera footage of the meeting and a cell-phone number the men had left behind. The phone number was registered to a Gary Reinhard of Lexington, Kentucky. When an agent called, he got a voice-mail recording, "This is Spence. Leave a message." A Google search of Spencer Reinhard brought up numerous hits for soccer in the Lexington area. Among them was the 2002 photo from the *Lexington Herald-Leader* of Spencer and Warren playing soccer. Both boys were spitting images of Mr. Stephens and Mr. Williams.

In early February 2005, the F.B.I. and Lexington police put the pair under surveillance. A female detective went undercover as a Transy student, tailing Spencer while a team staked out the yellow bungalow. It didn't take long to tie in Eric and Chas.

By that point Warren, Eric, and Spencer knew for certain they were going down. Warren had been convinced after spotting a suspicious man loitering near the yellow bungalow—when he stepped outside, the man disappeared into an unmarked white van with tinted windows and sped off. One evening it occurred to Spencer that they had used the Walter Beckman Yahoo account to contact both Christie's and Gooch.

Waiting for the law to snatch them was nerve-racking, but they went on with their lives as if nothing had been amiss. Spencer continued with his heavy schedule of classes, studying, painting, and working out, while Warren returned full-time to U.K. With the pressure mounting, however, Warren was caught shoplifting a TV dinner from a local supermarket, Eric was arrested and charged with D.U.I.—police pulled him over not only for running red lights but also because Warren was on top of the car, hanging on to the roof rack—and Spencer crashed his Acura Legend. Just days before their arrests the three even took in a movie: *Ocean's 12*.

"It was just funny because we've been in a lot of places that they've been," Eric says. "Like, they were doing something serious, talking about the heist, going over the plan, and somebody would make a joke. So we would see parts like that and we would be 'Oh, this is just like us.' " Little did the three know that F.B.I. agents were sitting behind them the whole time, listening to their every word.

The investigation of the Transy Book Heist came to an explosive end on the morning of February 11, 2005, as a SWAT unit broke down the front door of the yellow bungalow with a battering ram, blasting stun grenades throughout the building. A 20-man task force of Lexington police and F.B.I. agents poured in over the wreckage. The ground floor quickly filled with shouting cops, screaming young women, and a few dazed men in boxer shorts. On the second-floor landing, Chas, in high-end flannel pajamas and thinking they were being robbed, pulled out a derringer, only to drop the weapon at the last moment.

"Oh, yeah, he almost got shot," says Eric, laughing. "I was surprised he didn't."

Cops entered the basement, a dank pit reeking of marijuana, and found Warren sprawled out on a mattress. He was whisked into a squad car. In a duffel bag by his bed an F.B.I. agent discovered the stolen books, all undamaged, as well as the five-page typed plan for the heist, an accounting ledger, wigs, instructions for opening a Swiss bank account, and stun guns, which had apparently arrived after the robbery.

Spencer was arrested in a simultaneous raid on his dorm room at Transy. All four were brought to Lexington police headquarters and individually interrogated by F.B.I. and local detectives. Faced with overwhelming evidence, they all eventually confessed.

Two months later, amid a local media frenzy, the four formally pleaded guilty to all six federal charges, including theft of cultural artifacts from a public museum and interstate transportation of stolen property. During their sentencing hearing, in December 2005, the federal prosecutor asked for 11 to 14 years each for Eric, Chas, and Spencer, and 14 to 17 years for Warren, deeming him the leader, organizer, and recruiter. The severity of the requested sentences was predicated on the dual propositions that, although the Audubon volumes had never been physically removed from the library, according to the letter of the law they were nonetheless *stolen*—increasing the monetary value of the crime—and that the Black Cobra Stun Pen used to subdue B. J. Gooch not only inflicted "physical harm" but was in actuality "a dangerous weapon." Worse still for the defendants, B. J. Gooch's ordeal had become a cause célèbre among librarians, many of whom wrote letters to the judge arguing against leniency.

Before rendering her decision, the judge made preliminary findings that each of the boys was equally culpable, that the value of the books stolen would include only those physically removed from the building, and although Gooch suffered no "bodily injury," the stun pen was in fact a dangerous weapon. Because the boys made the highly unusual decision not to accept the prosecutor's offer to testify against one another during sentencing in exchange for leniency, they were each sentenced to identical seven-year terms. In early 2006, they began serving their sentences in federal prison, with no possibility for parole.

"The truth is, but for one obvious, big mistake"—the trip to Christie's—"they probably would have gotten away with it," a Lexington police detective told me.

ESCAPE PLAN

Aside from harming B. J. Gooch, Spencer, Warren, and Eric maintain that they have no regrets. In fact, they all tell me that as the planning picked up in the months before the heist, the three of them came to believe that it was their best and perhaps last chance to create a viable life for themselves after college. Only by committing a felony could they ensure that they would never end up living back in the sterile, suburban world of the subdivisions. As far as they could see, there were only two ways out: either getting away with the crime or getting arrested for it.

"We did the robbery as a way to escape," Eric says. "I think we all knew that we wanted something different, and we had to break away from where we were living. If we got away with it, we'd be in Europe living this crazy life thinking we were *Ocean's 11* types. If not, we were going to get caught and it was going to be a crazy story."

"And now that we've diverted from that path, we feel liberated," Warren tells me, waving his arms around the room. "We can never go back if we wanted to—I would rather have not been busted, but all I can say is it feels right in here, and before, in college, it just never did."

"I remember talking to Eric and Warren one day and I was like, 'So what, they're going to put us in jail,' " says Spencer. We spoke about his paintings, especially *A Plan to Fail*. He loved that it had been made the screen saver on the F.B.I.'s computers. "You know, most people look at that painting as if it was a plan *destined* to fail, but at the same time, we were *planning to fail*."

"In a few years we'll be released. We'll all be . . . still young," Warren says. "We will be stronger, better, wiser for going through this together, the three of us. Before, in college, growing up, we were being funneled into this mundane, nickel-and-dime existence. Now we can't ever go back there. Even if we wanted to, they won't let us. That was the point all along. See, we have no choice now but to create something new, someplace else. Believe me, you haven't heard the last of us yet."

PERILOUS
PATTERNS

"EXETER'S PASSION PLAY"

By Jesse Kornbluth

DECEMBER 1992

'**E**verything your life has been about is over." If one of his students had written that, Lane Bateman would have reached for his red pencil. But last July, Bateman wasn't in any position to play drama teacher—the local policeman who delivered some version of this line carried a search warrant and was accompanied by half a dozen other lawmen. Shocked, Bateman opened his front door wider. Melodrama entered.

According to Bateman, the policeman said, "Let's have a look at your film collection."

"I have *hundreds*," he replied. "I've collected movies for years. I'm like the school librarian—kids borrow tapes on weekends."

"We know that buried deep inside *It's a Wonderful Life*, we'll find you having sex with students."

The police had some reason to think this. A "confidential informant" had told them that the 51-year-old Bateman, chairman of the drama department at New Hampshire's Phillips Exeter Academy, owned a world-class pornography collection featuring boys as young as 7. They believed that he bought and sold these videos, and they sought the computers that contained the names of his customers. "The I.R.S. will be brought in," they reportedly warned him. "We're sure you haven't paid taxes on what you made."

"Look outside," pleaded Bateman, whose salary had never topped $40,000. "I drive a seven-year-old Ford Escort."

His protest was dismissed. Soon Bateman was leading the police through his apartment, and, depending upon whom you believe, he either insisted that although he owned some child pornography he had never shipped any to anyone, or admitted that he both possessed and shipped it. Whatever he told the police, it was less eloquent than what they found: enough videotapes to fill eight footlockers ("No normal person would have so many," a policeman said, according to Bateman), a 100-foot rope with a hot-water bottle tied to one end and boxer shorts tied to the other ("A trick from my magic act," Bateman swore), a case of Albolene makeup remover (Bateman had told the informant it was "my fave" lubricant), video cameras and editing decks the authorities valued at $200,000 ("You only have this equipment if you're producing and selling," Bateman says one of the officers noted), and, in a hidden compartment beneath Bateman's bed, videos labeled *Ballin' Boys Duo*, *Young Mouthful*, and *Now, Boys!*

That afternoon, the police arrested Bateman. That evening, as Bateman waited in jail for his lover of 17 years to bail him out, he had a revelation: "I thought, By midnight, I can be dead. The idea was like a warm bath. This solves everything." But when he returned home, his lover threw his arms around him. "With that, I knew I didn't have to die," Bateman says.

From Exeter's point of view, it would have been more convenient if he had killed himself. The following morning, as police were telling reporters that many of the 800 videotapes they had confiscated contained footage depicting sex acts "involving boys under 10," an academy security guard delivered a brief note to Bateman's home. In 79 words, Exeter principal Kendra Stearns O'Donnell fired him, ordered him out of his apartment within two weeks, and barred him from school property.

But no summary judgment on Exeter's part could keep its name from being dragged through the mud with Bateman's. Teachers get arrested for sex-related offenses all the time—but never at venerable, highly respected Exeter. If ever a school had an unblemished reputation, it was this New Hampshire powerhouse. Set in the state's third-oldest town, Exeter's ivy-clad buildings give it the appearance of a geographically displaced Harvard. It is. Only slightly smaller than arch-rival Andover, Exeter turns out students who are verbally acute, organized, and programmed to achieve; its graduates include Daniel Webster, Jay Rockefeller, and John Irving. While this factory for academic excellence doesn't feed its fair-haired elite products into Ivy League colleges as it once did (of its 992 students, 5.2 percent are African-American, and 31 percent are on scholarship; of its 326 graduates last year, only 39 went to Harvard or Yale), Exeter is still the model of the American prep school, what the novelist John Marquand once called "the most beautiful and aesthetically satisfying of all New England schools."

So the New England press fanned the story of the "Academy porn bust" and the suspect who "lived 10 years with male students." Early in August, *The New York Times* took the story to a new level of scandal—it reported that in the raid on Bateman's house police found videotapes showing 10 former Exeter boys nude or involved in sex acts. Although this charge was apparently untrue, all ambiguity vanished after that, and Exeter, like Bateman, was convicted in the press of every possible charge.

The media orgy was unsurprising—this was a subject with broad appeal. For those who couldn't pay $17,000 a year to send a child to

Exeter, Bateman represented an opportunity to throw rocks through elitist windows. For preppies and their parents, the idea that a well-disguised pedophile could gain access to even the most exclusive chicken coop was fresh reason to worry about the boarding-school experience. And for defenders of tradition, Bateman's downfall was proof that Exeter's principal—the first female to head the school in its 211-year history—had been wrong to champion "tolerance" and "diversity."

Within Exeter, the Bateman story provoked a very different reaction: shock that one of the school's most admired teachers could have done anything wrong. It usually takes four years for instructors to get tenure at Exeter. Bateman was tenured after just two; in his third year, he was named department chairman. In 1990 he won a prestigious faculty award that honors excellence in both classroom instruction and dormitory supervision. And each year there were students who told him, "If it hadn't been for you, I wouldn't have survived here." So when Kendra O'Donnell claimed that Bateman was no longer "an appropriate role model," there were many who disagreed.

In October, Bateman was convicted in Federal District Court in Concord, New Hampshire, of one count of possessing and two counts of transporting child pornography, as well as one count of forfeiture; slated to be sentenced by year's end, he faces a possible 10 years in jail and a $250,000 fine. But while outsiders may be satisfied with the official resolution of the Bateman drama, questions still linger at Exeter. Who was Lane Bateman, really? Was he an obsessive sex offender, star of a secret production: Master Bateman and the Boys? Or was this *The Children's Hour*: a case of a young informant with a grudge turning a private matter into a public scandal? In either event, how did this gifted drama teacher forget the Chekhovian adage that a gun displayed early in a drama will be fired at its climax—why did he keep that time bomb of kiddie porn ticking under his bed?

Lane Bateman was raised by devout Mormon parents in Idaho Falls, Idaho, where a great many of his fellow citizens shared the Mormon belief that homosexual behavior was a sin. In this prim, self-contained community, Bateman's most unusual childhood activity was directing his four younger siblings in beauty pageants and spooky dramas. "I grew up not watching TV," says his sister, Judy, "because Lane was so much more interesting." At 12, inspired by his drama instructor, he decided he wanted to dedicate his life to teaching theater. In Idaho Falls, this wasn't a common male ambition; from then on, some schoolmates called him "Batwoman."

"I met Lane when he was 17. . . . I knew he was gay the minute I met him," says Sylvia Harman, one of his first drama coaches. "He didn't. I remember him coming back from an acting seminar in Texas. The costumer there was gay, and Lane made fun of him. We all laughed, but I thought, Poor Lane, he still doesn't know."

Bateman was such a faithful Mormon that he dutifully enrolled at Brigham Young University. At 21 he finally had his recognition scene: "I was traveling with a group from school, and my girlfriend had our itinerary. Every place we stopped, there was a thick letter from her waiting for me. It got to the point I couldn't stand to open my mail. Then, alone in a shower, I suddenly understood: I was homosexual. . . . I felt my psyche change. I *wasn't* sick—I saw myself as an oppressed minority, and my feelings were valid."

He came out to his girlfriend, took a year off to work in his father's construction business, pulled himself together, graduated from college—and, he says, insisted on being "excommunicated" from the Mormon Church. Three years later, at 26, he became head of the drama department at the Interlochen Arts Academy in Michigan. He was, by all accounts, an inspiring teacher: supportive yet objective, artistic but businesslike. And he was aggressively "normal"—when boys visited, his copy of *Playboy* just happened to be on display. "It was unnecessary camouflage," a male student recalls. "I didn't have a clue he was homosexual, and almost all the women were in love with him."

"I told a friend I was mad for Lane," says Gay Marshall, an Interlochen student who went on to sing "What I Did for Love" as Cassie in *A Chorus Line* on Broadway. "She told me he was gay. I was so relieved. I thought, Now we can be friends. But when I told Lane, he looked *destroyed*—he didn't want anyone to know. He loved what he did so much he'd overcompensate to protect it."

In 1969, New York police and homosexuals battled in what has come to be known as the Stonewall riot. Although reports of that event radicalized Bateman, he wasn't ready to take more than what appeared to be a small, personal risk: when he was a drama teacher at Augustana College in Illinois, he fell in love with a 21-year-old student. But the young man's mother complained to the school, and rather than risk publicity that might have ended his teaching career, Bateman resigned.

As a doctoral candidate at Southern Illinois University, Bateman was finally free to become what he describes as "militantly gay." His Ph.D. thesis more than confirms this. Entitled "Three Proud Plays," it consisted of three dramatic works, two of which celebrate the strengths of professor-student relationships, chronicle the threat to these affairs when the younger man's parents show up, and are obviously inspired by his truncated romance at Augustana College. One of them, *Lying in State*, was a winner at the American College Theatre Festival. It was performed at the Kennedy Center in Washington, D.C., in 1974, and got the author an agent at William Morris.

But Bateman had no desire to be recognized as a playwright. He wanted only to teach. His early mentor, Sylvia Harman, who had taught at Exeter off and on for a decade, knew of his dedication, and in 1980, when the school asked her to recommend a candidate for a job as drama teacher, she could think only of Lane Bateman. Before she endorsed him, though, she had a question: Would he have problems living with all those boys? "I have someone with whom I'm very much in love," Bateman told her. "The problem is that I won't be seeing him enough."

"Where do you picture yourself in 10 years?" the chairman of Exeter's drama department asked Bateman at his interview. "Right here," Bateman replied. "I can't imagine anything more satisfying than teaching at Exeter." He had, without knowing it, paraphrased the school motto: *Non sibi*—Not for oneself. Two days later, he was offered the job.

At Exeter, he was a compulsive dramaturge: "Like Streisand getting hold of something, he'd learn everything about the sets and costumes of a play," a former colleague notes. But he never tried to surround himself with kids who would make a similar commitment to the theater. He scheduled auditions for an entire season's plays at the same time, so the bigger talents couldn't snare all the good roles; when a colleague suggested that they put on *The Normal Heart*, the landmark Larry Kramer play about AIDS, he vetoed it less for political reasons than because there weren't enough female roles. And he encouraged "fac brats"—teachers' children, who are sometimes regarded as charity cases—to join the choruses of *Godspell* and *Nicholas Nickleby*.

Bateman had an acute understanding of the school and its clientele. Exeter is famous for its work load—students average three to four hours of homework a night—and he made it clear that he expected even the most dedicated of his drama wonks to get it done. "Face it, kids at Exeter aren't going on to Broadway," he told me. So he was blunt with them: Theater at Exeter isn't a place to indulge specialness; it's a place to explore your creativity, a safety valve for your frustrations. Your academic work comes first.

And he led by example. After a long day of teaching, an evening of rehearsals, and hours of dormitory supervision, he was still available for academic consultation. Even with all that, his batteries were still charged. "I was having trouble writing a script about Edith Piaf, so I descended on Lane," Gay Marshall recalls. "The term was in full swing, but night after night he'd stay up and work with me until three A.M."

On one visit to Exeter, Marshall saw a locked box in Bateman's apartment. She asked him what it contained. "Nasty movies," he said. She was about to urge him to jettison them when she reminded herself that this was Bateman's well-contained private business.

Very private. Exeter is a school that now has a Gay/Straight Alliance—but only for students. Homosexual teachers don't acknowledge their sexuality even to their colleagues; on a faculty that may be 10 percent gay, only one instructor has come out. Still, Bateman wouldn't have shocked anybody if he'd announced that he was something other than a bachelor. But he never did. Few of his students knew he was gay; even fewer were aware that he was partnered with another instructor.

"It's not healthy to be so secretive, but Lane never felt secure enough at Exeter to come out," explains a friend who has long known of Bateman's interest in pornography. "He lived in a dorm for 10 years, and there were kids walking in and out of his room late at night in their underwear. If he ever had a chance to do something with a kid, Exeter was it. But that's not Lane—if the most gorgeous kid in the world had presented himself to him, he would have said, 'Go take a shower.' . . . He's heavy into fantasy. These sex movies are the legacy of the closet."

Bateman says he purchased the material that ultimately brought him down several years before he started teaching at Exeter, when he was coming out of the closet and wanted to make up for lost time. "For a few years, you could buy anything, and I bought some films and books that featured young boys," he says. "For me, these pictures were aesthetic, not pornography. I know people say, 'These images are *despicable*—how can you think that?' But the key point is that I identified with the boys, not the men. If someone young had grabbed me when I was that age and said, 'Let me teach you something,' I would have said, 'Sure.' . . . That's what I see in those images—the most secret part of my being."

But did he really "identify" only with the boys? Michael Caven, the "confidential informant" in this case, was only a boy when he met Lane Bateman in 1979. And Caven says that Bateman abused him sexually.

Bateman was then 38; Caven was 16. Bateman was head of the drama department at North Shore High School in Glen Head, Long Island, 20 miles from New York City, and Michael Pappas, as Caven was then known, was his student.

During free periods at school, Michael took his problems to his drama teacher. And then, early in 1980, according to Caven's testimony, Bateman suggested that they work on a video project, and invited him to his house. There, Caven says, Bateman outlined the plot: a boy returns home from his first homosexual encounter, is overcome by shame, and kills himself in the bathtub. Although he'd never taken his clothes off for another man, Caven claims that marijuana and wine and the admiration he had for Bateman overrode his nervousness—he did what Bateman asked.

A few days later, Caven says, he returned to Bateman's house to watch the edited video. Bateman again offered him marijuana and wine. And then, Caven insists, Bateman propositioned him. Although he didn't give this testimony at the trial—it would have been too incendiary—Caven told me that "Bateman said, 'I want to be the first man to make love to you.' But that wasn't sex. It was me and a current teacher in bed, with Bateman having given me wine and pot and having put poppers under my nose, putting Vaseline on his penis and sticking it in me—and he wanted me to believe he was doing me a favor! I had no erection, no orgasm. The experience was about pleasing my teacher, my friend, my father figure. My feeling was that I'd make him happy, and he'd love me."

To keep Bateman interested in him, Caven says, he posed naked for some Polaroids on his third visit. Then Bateman announced that his roommate, who was out of the country, was returning, and that they weren't just friends, they were lovers. This affair, he said, would have to end.

Lane Bateman says that none of this happened.

Michael Pappas, he agrees, often talked to him at school about the verbal and emotional abuse the boy said he experienced at home. But Bateman insists that talking never led to a video project and that it couldn't have—in 1980, neither he nor the school owned a video camera. What did happen, he says, is that Pappas discovered where he lived by following him home after school; when he next had difficulties with his mother and stepfather, he fled to his favorite teacher's house. Reluctantly, Bateman says, he let Pappas spend the night, but when Pappas crawled into bed with him, he rebuffed him. As for the Polaroids, Bateman insists that he took those pictures two years later, when Pappas was 18, at the young man's suggestion. At that time, he says, his former student told him he'd found a new way to make money: hustling in New York City. (Pappas says he never had sex for money alone.)

In the fall of 1980, Bateman and Pappas went their separate ways. The teacher took up his new post at Exeter, and his student slipped off into a quite different world.

One of Michael Pappas's schoolmates remembers him as "a tormented guy, a storyteller, people didn't take him seriously." Another classmate, now a prosecutor, says that "everything Michael said was a lie." A North Shore drama teacher describes him as "a triple threat— couldn't sing, couldn't dance, couldn't act"—whose greatest skill was "hiding the fact that he wasn't playing with a full deck."

For his high-school-yearbook caption, Pappas chose a Bernie Taupin lyric—"Life is short and the world is rough and if you're gonna boogie, boy, you gotta be tough"—and as the 1980s rolled in, he began to live that line. Asked at Bateman's trial if he had ever been a male prostitute, he had to admit that "there were times when I emotionally, physically, and mentally prostituted myself—not only for money, but for love, a father figure, and an education." Along the way, he noted, there were drugs: marijuana, poppers, cocaine, tranquilizers, and gallons of alcohol. Unsurprisingly, his 20s were marked by three arrests for drunkenness and as many as 10 suicide attempts.

In 1983, when he was 19, Michael Pappas met Frank Caven, the fabulously successful owner of gay bars in Texas and Florida. "Michael arrived with the shirt on his back," recalls a man who witnessed that meeting, "and once he got in, he wasn't leaving." Caven was generous and controlling; Pappas was attractive and charming. Mutual exploitation followed.

The capper came one drunken night when the 63-year-old Caven decided to adopt Pappas. This unlikely move, the younger man has come to feel, was the legacy of his education at the hands of his former teacher. "Lane Bateman taught me more about manipulation than anyone, except for my parents," he told me. "He taught me that if I want a sex connection, to do everything and anything to make it happen. He was clear with me that my looks—my beauty—would work well for me in the gay world."

Lane Bateman finds his former student's memory to be completely inaccurate. "I don't remember ever having a conversation with Michael about his looks and the gay world," Bateman says. "What I told him was 'You can find somebody out there and be happy. I did it. So can you.' As for being a manipulator, I've been very careful about that—as a stage director, you have great power to twist people and hurt them."

Whatever Bateman did or didn't teach Michael Pappas, the young man recognized one thing: Frank Caven was the ultimate score. "He was the omnipotent father who gave me what I wanted: travel, school, business. But the price was sex and undivided attention."

Michael Caven often accompanied his new father to the White House (Frank Caven was a Republican Eagle, and he gave more money so Michael could be a Young Eagle), where he met [Ronald] Reagan and [George H. W.] Bush any number of times. "I acted like an obnoxious Republican preppy," he now says. "When I lived in Dallas, I loved to go out for fancy dinners and play the big shot. There was a sober Michael who spent a summer at Oxford and traveled to the Soviet Union, and there was an alcoholic Michael who walked down the streets of Dallas as a drunken mess. I was a Dr. Jekyll and Mr. Hyde."

In 1986, Frank Caven sent him to Washington to help open J.R.'s, a sleek gay bar. "Michael seemed energetic, and because of the bar, he was immensely popular," a longtime J.R.'s employee recalls, "but he was a jerk and an egotist. He was media-crazy. He'd type out wacko press releases, and ride on a float in a gay parade dressed as the Church Lady—he loved to get his face in any rag in town."

Michael Caven disputes his co-workers' harsh assessment. Although several Caven associates claim he was relieved of duty in Washington because he couldn't get along with them, he insists that it was his decision to return to Dallas and finish his education. In this "he says"/"he says" contest, the only verifiable facts are that Frank Caven died in the spring of 1988 and that, of his $10 million estate, Michael was left just $25,000. "At the funeral, Michael sat with the public," a friend of Frank Caven's says. "He knew better than to talk to us."

Although their communication had been limited to a postcard every year or so, Michael Caven wrote Bateman a long letter four months after Frank Caven's death. And Bateman, unaware that he was the surviving father figure in his former student's life, responded—with a letter and, according to Caven, some child-pornography tapes. Caven says that he told Bateman he wasn't comfortable watching under-age boys, and that he smashed the tapes with a hammer. Still, he went to great lengths to arrange a weekend in January of 1989 with a wealthy older man in Boston, whose main attraction seems to have been that he could drive his guest to Exeter for a visit with Lane Bateman.

On this visit, Bateman says, he gave Michael Caven the Polaroids he'd taken of the younger man and all the child pornography he would share with him. If there was ever interstate transportation of illegal material, he insists, the only criminal was Michael Caven. "I'm not totally stupid," Bateman said at his trial.

But even if Bateman filled a heavy box for his young visitor that weekend and mailed only adult porn to him in the coming years—an assertion that didn't fly with a jury faced with a mountain of tapes—the choice of Caven as a recipient of any sexual material was fatally dumb. That season, Caven was bottoming out. And while he was then grateful for Bateman's attention, he would eventually come to see Bateman as his ultimate oppressor.

For his part, Bateman giddily imagined that he'd found the ultimate video-and-pen pal. "Been fun raiding my collection—haven't seen many of these in years," Bateman wrote. "Hope some sequences make you squeal and moan." He also sent Caven a video camera so the younger man could covertly tape his sex partners. "It could be put into, say, a gift box or store box—the type one might have sitting on a dresser in a bedroom," he advised. Soon, Bateman was asking Caven to put the camera on a tripod and send him the tapes he made so he could edit them and enhance their eroticism. "Word of honor—No one else shall ever see your work," Bateman wrote. "I have triple security (been at it long enough to know tricks and tricks and tricks and tricks)." Bateman liked what Caven sent: "HOT can't keep hands out of pants." And he knew what he liked. "Want to see you solo—featuring close-up of ass play," he wrote Caven. "Finger/dildo—open it wide, talk/moan."

In 1990, Bateman sent Caven more than a hundred pornographic videos—and Caven sent Bateman an early draft of an autobiographical play. "I said, 'Do you want to know what I really think or do you just want to feel good?'" Bateman recalls. "He asked for the truth, so I was very frank—I told him it was terrible. The play, told in endless monologues, was about an abused child who became a hustler. I said, 'I know it's your life, Michael, but that doesn't make it theatrical.'" Caven wrote back that he wasn't surprised by Bateman's reaction, but "it is difficult not to take it personally since I am so connected to the piece."

Was that critique the real reason Caven turned Bateman in to the authorities? Bateman thinks so. Caven denies it. A few months earlier, he says, Bateman mentioned that he'd found the Polaroids he'd taken a decade earlier. Caven claims he was curious about them, and that Bateman mailed them to him. "I looked at my eyes and thought, Who is this person?" Caven says. "My eyes seemed sad and lost. And I started writing the play."

As he wrote, he came to believe that his despair was the inevitable product of his refusal to admit that he'd been sexually abused. "Mr. Bateman was my teacher when he perped me, and from that time on, we were never peers, never adults," says Caven, who is now almost 30. "With me, Bateman had the perfect boy, someone he could control through technology. Even in my late 20s he could get into my bedroom."

"No!" exclaims Bateman. "I deny that. In every way. I deny it completely."

In the spring of 1991, when Bateman sent him more adult-porno tapes, Caven wrote "Enough" on a single sheet of paper and sent them back. Then he began to think about one of the tapes that Bateman had sent him. It featured a former Exeter student whom Caven had briefly met on his 1989 visit to Bateman, and it featured this young man—who was still at the school when the video was made—taking his clothes off for Bateman's camera. It seemed clear to Caven that when the video ended, sex began. (Bateman's lawyer acknowledges that there was a video, but won't comment further.) As he saw it, that meant there was another student, in another decade, whom Bateman had abused. If he failed to act, Caven thought, there might be more. And so, in consultation with his lawyer and his therapist, he wrote Bateman a letter that he intended to hold for a year.

That September, Bateman called Caven, who immediately hung up. Bateman called again. This time, he left a message on Caven's answering machine. "I know I'm on your shitlist," he said. "I don't know why." To make sure he would, Caven mailed the letter. In that two-page document, Caven retraced their relationship from the point of view of a victim of 13 years. He said he wanted to return the Exeter-owned video camera that Bateman had sent him. He didn't want Bateman to have the camera; he wanted to return it directly to the school so it couldn't be used in inappropriate ways on other boys. He noted that he was considering "legal actions available to me." He urged Bateman to "reflect upon the fact that what you did was abusive, manipulative, and a sexual molestation." He ordered Bateman never to contact him again and gave him the name of his attorney. And he taunted Bateman: "You never entertained the thought THAT I WOULD RECOVER, did you?"

"The thought of destroying Lane Bateman never entered my mind," Michael Caven insists. "My goal was for him to take responsibility. . . . I wanted to stop him from doing to others what he did to me."

According to Caven's lawyer, Rhonda Rivera, her client really didn't want to see Bateman arrested. Nor did he want to be paid off by Bateman. "It's hard to go back in time and determine what might have happened," she says, "but I think Michael would have been satisfied if Bateman had acknowledged the abuse, destroyed all his child pornography, and entered a treatment program."

Bateman never called Rivera. Because he regarded Caven's letter as a threat—he thought its message was "I'm going to ruin your life and you can't see it coming"—he discarded the pages.

Last spring, after six months of silence from Bateman, Rivera contacted County Attorney Carleton Eldredge in Exeter on Caven's behalf. Eldredge found Caven so impressive that he later decided to go public with his own story of childhood victimization: "I was abused by a neighbor when I was seven years old." And he is rhapsodic about Caven's influence on his life. "I'm almost twice his age, but I see him almost as a mentor," he told me. "If this were an A.A. situation, I'd ask him to be my sponsor. I have a deep respect for him."

In another prosecutor's office, there might have been questions raised about the motives of a young man with a history of drug and alcohol problems whose charges, if made public, would surely end the career of a respected teacher. In Eldredge's office, those questions never came up. "The victim's story has to be treated as credible, whatever it is," the 63-year-old Eldredge has said. "We go under the assumption that the allegations are true."

Bateman's employers operated under a similar credo. "There's an Exeter tradition of swift justice and the Star Chamber," Gore Vidal, class of 1943, told me. "They said, in effect, 'There are no rules here until you break one—and then you're on the morning train to Boston.' The place has always been brutal in that way." And the school wasn't defensive about that brutality. "Exeter is not a warm nest," the headmaster announced with pride on graduation day in 1973.

The admission of girls in 1970 and the appointment of Kendra O'Donnell as principal in 1987 are the high points of Exeter's belated effort to humanize its frosty environment. As a former assistant professor of English at Princeton and a key aide at the Rockefeller Brothers Fund, O'Donnell long ago acquired the executive skills necessary to run a 1,000-student institution with a $167 million endowment. But she is also a mother and a woman, and she hasn't forgotten it. In her first year at Exeter, she appeared at the faculty talent show—directed by

Lane Bateman—as Cyndi Lauper, lip-synching "Girls Just Want to Have Fun" in a costume so outrageous that it took 15 seconds for Exonians to recognize her. Last year, after a hastily called chapel service on the eve of the war with Iraq, a student stopped to thank her for bringing the school together. To his surprise, O'Donnell was weeping. "We've screwed up the world so badly for you kids," she said.

For all her strengths, O'Donnell was hamstrung by a hypocrisy that's as old as boarding schools—the presence of unacknowledged male homosexuals as teachers and dorm masters. In that situation, a principal can do nothing more than hope for the best, and, when the worst strikes, trust the authorities. Here, O'Donnell was operating under a disadvantage, for, in the hours following Bateman's arrest, she was barraged with information from the Exeter police, and some of it was highly exaggerated.

Had O'Donnell talked to Bateman before she terminated him, she would have come to the same decision—prep schools have no due process when the allegations concern sex—but the letter that she mailed to 25,000 Exeter students, parents, alumni, and friends of the school four days after Bateman's arrest might have been more reassuring. "The anxiety alone is hard to accept," she wrote, as if she feared that any minute the local authorities would present her with a list of students buggered by Bateman. In fact, the confidential help line she set up produced not a single new allegation that Bateman had made porno videos or had sex with Exeter boys.

Bateman did possess a tape, made by some Exeter girls from their dormitory windows, that shows male Exeter students wearing only their underwear. In this footage, the boys are standing in their dormitory windows, holding cafeteria trays over their Jockey shorts. On the trays, they've made shaving-cream arrows pointing to their crotches. It's not the raciest tape ever made.

Between the filming and the telling, there seems to have been some hallucinating. As Fox Butterfield of *The New York Times* heard it, Bateman had videos that showed as many as 10 Exonians in the act of oral and anal sex. And at the height of the school's nervous breakdown,

Butterfield wrote that the police had "identified" a tape with 10 former Exeter boys being compromised on it.

"We had a major source—a ranking law-enforcement official—tell us that Exeter students were involved in the videos," says Butterfield, who is perhaps best known for the 1991 front-page *Times* story that named William Kennedy Smith's accuser and a 1987 piece about the Iran-contra hearings that was so inaccurate he had to write an unprecedented front-page correction a few days later. "Our source told us not once but half a dozen times over nearly a week. The official specified what kinds of acts the students were performing in the videos, and he volunteered the number of students: 10. Other law-enforcement officials also said they had information that a number of Exeter students had shown up on the videos, and that they were continuing to investigate the situation."

The Exeter police and Carleton Eldredge denounced Butterfield's story and denied they were his source. O'Donnell, who had given Butterfield her only interview of the summer, was aghast. Not only had the *Times* printed a story apparently unsupported by fact, but Butterfield seemed to be putting some of the blame on the "socially progressive" aspects of O'Donnell's administration: homosexual teachers as dormitory supervisors, gay graduates speaking at school assemblies, an English teacher discussing her lesbianism at a student meeting.

Between the lines, the newspaper of record appeared to be suggesting that pedophilia and homosexuality are virtually indistinguishable.

In an unheated cabin on the shores of a New Hampshire lake, as he awaited his trial, Lane Bateman reached for another of the cigarettes he now chain-smokes. The price of his freedom was strapped to his ankle: a monitoring device that he had to press against the phone receiver three or four times a day. He wasn't allowed to leave the house without permission from his probation officer, and minors weren't allowed to visit him, even if they happened to be accompanied by their parents.

If the punishment phase had already begun for Bateman, acknowledgment that he had a problem hadn't. Like many defendants, Bateman saw himself as the victim, blamed his accuser, and looked forward to seeing Caven destroyed in court.

At Exeter, some were worried that Bateman's lawyer, a local attorney named Mark Sullivan, might succeed in doing just that—and then, on Bateman's behalf, file a massive civil lawsuit against the school. "Mark is a very nice guy," a school official told me. "On the other hand, I've watched him play basketball in our gym, and all he sees is the basket."

At the trial, however, there was little that Sullivan could do for his client. The only real mystery in the entire proceedings concerned Michael Caven—why had he come forward, and could he be believed? Frank Caven's friends said Michael was consistently untruthful; one even testified that when he first heard Michael was involved in a legal matter he assumed that the young man had at last been caught in some nefarious act. Other questions were never satisfactorily answered. In those 1980 encounters Michael Caven remembers so vividly, did he, as he testified, see tapes of two Bateman friends masturbating—or was he just discrediting men he knew were going to be testifying for the defense? (Both denied the allegation.) Was it really possible to be so "addicted to the perpetrator" that, after eight years of virtually no communication, he would suddenly contact Bateman and slavishly do his long-distance bidding? And why, if confronting Bateman was so important to his recovery, did the U.S. attorney ask the judge three different times to let Caven testify under the cloak of anonymity?

In the circumscribed version of events presented to the jury, however, those questions were mere quibbles. Ultimately, the physical evidence was all the jurors needed. One video alone could have persuaded them to convict Batemen—it featured prepubescent blond boys masturbating to a disco version of "Baby Face." And although Bateman sounded feisty, he couldn't deny that he had a long-standing interest in child pornography and kept a collection of it under his bed.

When the verdict came in, Bateman sounded almost relieved. "At least I don't have to sit there any longer and hear them say those awful things about me," he told me. His friends continue to be shocked at what they regard as a prosecution that got out of hand in large part because the defendant was a teacher at Exeter. And they loathe Michael Caven. "If he wanted to do Lane a favor, he could have said, 'Get help,'" one snapped. "Lane doesn't deserve to have his life ruined."

As for Michael Caven, he says he is healing, thanks to therapy and his newfound ability to confront the man he regards as a perpetrator. "The point was that I was no longer loyal to the secrecy of this relationship," he told me. "My life is good now. I'm healing. For 15 months, I've been in a serious, committed relationship. I'm now completely responsible for taking care of myself and for not letting myself be victimized. And in the future I see myself as a psychologist or counselor, working with victims of abuse."

Exeter, however, is having less success exorcising the ghost of one of its best and most dedicated teachers. At a faculty meeting shortly before school opened this fall, O'Donnell briefed teachers on the case, giving only the police version of the facts; when some spoke of Bateman's betrayal by the school, she asked why they didn't, instead, feel betrayed by their former colleague. She made a point of sitting in on meetings when the drama department was hiring Bateman's replacement—and, according to a teacher involved, blackballed one candidate simply because he had the unfortunate name of "Butt."

Student leaders, meanwhile, were asked to monitor campus opinion, but because O'Donnell pointedly said nothing about Bateman at the school's opening assembly, the biggest ongoing debate among Exonians concerned the dress code. By late September, students in the few classes that addressed the Bateman case were wondering why no one else talked about it. The silence was curious, for Exeter is hardly cloistered. At football games, students have been known to wear T-shirts that proclaim ST. PAUL'S SUCKS, BUT ANDOVER SWALLOWS. A recent campus notice advertising a girls' soccer game promised that "the bigger the balls, the better we head." The school health service provides advice on contraception.

And although gay students sometimes describe the school as homophobic, recent meetings of the Gay/Straight Alliance have drawn as many as 50 students.

So the idea that single male teachers might be homosexual and appreciate young men would not be a soul-shattering revelation to Exeter students. In the wake of the Bateman scandal, only one new student withdrew from the school, more as a result of his fear of the media than of a concern that he'd be exposed to unwanted sexual advances. And on campus this fall, the entire episode was reduced to a predictable joke: "Lane's World." But that's just the surface. Bateman's fall from grace, as one student has noted, became "like a secret in a dysfunctional family."

Dr. Fred S. Berlin, director of the National Institute for the Study, Prevention, and Treatment of Sexual Trauma, in Baltimore, worries about the implications of this silence. "What concerns me is that we've reached a point, in some circumstances, where we begin to respond more out of fears and prejudices than analysis and reason," he told me. "There are men who watch pictures of rape scenes and say it's a turn-on, but don't go out and commit rape. Heterosexual teachers often find 16-year-old students attractive and stimulating, and yet they control themselves without difficulty. . . . There's no reason to think that students are more at risk from a homosexual teacher than a heterosexual one."

That thought may be too complex for a school that has dealt with the Bateman situation only on the most pragmatic level—by hiring two married men to take his place. It's a thought that won't be germane for the federal judge who must, in a month or so, decide what to do with Bateman. But it's surely something for Lane Bateman to consider as he sits, his life in ruins, awaiting the ultimate review. A gifted teacher who wanted to inspire his students gravitated to an environment where his fatal weakness would pose a constant threat to his career. And, as a result, he became a living symbol of the fear that makes so many people equate homosexuality with pedophilia.

In the weeks before his trial, Bateman wrestled with that assumption, and found himself innocent. "When I was being questioned, the police brought in a pedophilia expert, and he said, 'This is what I deal with—if you have the pictures, you did the deed,'" he told me. "But I don't believe I'm capable of inflicting myself on someone who's unwilling, and I don't believe I'm capable of having sex with a minor even if he's willing. If you asked kids, 'How much sexual interest was aroused in you by Mr. Bateman?' they'd laugh."

[In January 1993, Bateman was sentenced five years in prison without parole and died in 2013.]

"A PRIVATE-SCHOOL AFFAIR"

By Alex Shoumatoff

JANUARY 2006

F or the past 150 years St. Paul's School, the "exclusive" (as it is invariably called) boarding school in Concord, New Hampshire, has been the Eton of America's upper crust. Or perhaps it is its Hogwarts, as Harry Potter's fictional academy is called, providing the country with many of its most accomplished wizards—not just at making money, although that is what its graduates have tended to do, but in practically every endeavor. Its main constituency has traditionally been the conservative old Wasp families of New York, Boston, and Philadelphia—the plutocracy that has been running the country for generations. But this is changing. Since the first black student was admitted—in my class, which graduated in 1964—the school's admissions policy has been progressively more meritocratic. The "natural aristocracy," based on virtue and talent, to use Thomas Jefferson's distinction, has been displacing the "artificial aristocracy," based on wealth and birth. Every year there are fewer "legacies," fewer fourth- or fifth-generation Paulies, among the 533 students, who now come from 37 states and 21 countries.

Despite its reputation for being a breeder of staunch, old-line Republicans, St. Paul's has also turned out a distinguished roster of liberals, including the cartoonist Garry Trudeau and Senator John Kerry. Kerry was in the class of '62, two years ahead of me, and even then he seemed to be plotting his run for the presidency. When he finally got his chance, many of us alumni were hoping he would win, not only because we felt the Bush administration was such a disaster but also because St. Paul's has yet to produce a president, whereas Groton prepped F.D.R., Choate J.F.K., and Andover both Bushes. But Kerry was a terrible disappointment. He simply lacked the common touch—which is not something you acquire at St. Paul's.

Last November, while Kerry was underperforming at the polls, a series of crises was rocking our alma mater. Elements of the trouble had been brewing for several years, but what busted the whole thing open was an article in the August 25, 2003, *Wall Street Journal* which revealed that the rector, as the headmaster of this venerable Episcopalian hall of learning is called, was being paid $524,000 a year in salary, pension, bonuses, and perks that included having his daughters' tuition at the University of Chicago picked up by the school. Parents, students, and alumni were stunned, and a rumor went around that the amount was more than the president of Harvard is paid. (It's actually a little less, and some prep-school headmasters get even more.)

The rector, as his name implies, is supposed to be a pillar of rectitude, especially if, as Craig Anderson was, he is also a bishop of the Episcopal Church. But "the Bish," as he was fondly called by students, had been accused of using the rector's discretionary fund—which is supposed to be reserved for school expenses—to pay for personal ones, including his membership in a yacht club in Maine. ("It was not a fancy yacht club," Anderson says from Minnesota, where he and his wife now live. "The dues were minimal—$1,000 to $1,200 a year. In my contract, there were certain provisions for memberships in clubs. One year, this was used for the yacht club, but when this was brought to light and felt to be inappropriate, I repaid it fully.") On top of this, the trustees who were managing the school's $364 million endowment were accused of having "cozy relationships" with some of the companies they had it invested in, although an investigation found nothing illegal.

All of this prompted an investigation by the New Hampshire attorney general's office, which put the school's finances under review through 2008, even though the rector and vice-rector had cut their own salaries by 10 percent. It also prompted an audit by the I.R.S., which has yet to be concluded. [The I.R.S. prohibits commenting on this or any specific audit.] Not one but two scathing articles about the school eventually appeared in *The New York Times*, the paper of record. Not good for the old image, especially when you are competing for top students against other well-endowed institutions such as New Hampshire's Phillips Exeter Academy, Connecticut's Choate Rosemary Hall, and Massachusetts's Groton School, Phillips Academy Andover, and Milton Academy, not to mention the excellent private day schools and public schools that are attracting a growing number of high-performing teenagers.

This embarrassing spot on the school tie was still painfully fresh when, a few days into the 2004–5 school year, 15 sixth-form (senior) girls were suspended for hazing some of the new girls. The worst thing that happened was that some of the younger students were forced to simulate fellatio on bananas. Not such a big deal, compared with the 15-year-old girl at Milton Academy who performed oral sex on five members of her school's hockey team in succession a few months later. (Not such a big deal either, apparently, judging from a recent S.P.S. graduate's response: "The question is: Did they win?") Or compared with the student at Northfield Mount Hermon School, in Massachusetts, who had the word

HOMO carved into his back by two jocks in 1999. Or with the freshman football player at McGill University, in Montreal, who was prodded in the rear with a broomstick during a hazing ceremony last August 27, prompting the school to cancel its entire 2005 football season. But the banana incident violated New Hampshire's hazing law and had to be reported to the police. Groton's trustees had gotten into hot water a few years earlier for trying to keep the lid on sexual-abuse allegations. So there was an investigation, and the papers got wind of it, and the school suffered a second public-relations disaster.

Then, on November 7, only five weeks after the school's monumental new, $24 million gym and fitness center opened, a boy in the fourth form (the 10th grade) drowned in its Olympic-size swimming pool. While this appeared to fall into the category of pure tragedy (although the parents have sued the school), it couldn't have happened at a worse moment. One couldn't help thinking that the Lord was not smiling on this devoutly Christian school, where attendance at chapel four times a week is still obligatory.

The fourth element of the St. Paul's calamity had been incubating for years: the allegations that, from the late 1940s through the early 90s, dozens of the school's masters (as the teachers were known until women joined the faculty, in 1972), including several revered ones, had sexually molested students. Perhaps this shouldn't have been surprising, given that molestation—or "inappropriate boundary-crossing by a teacher," as it was more delicately described by Dean of Faculty Candice Dale—is a problem in schools the world over. Some of the alumni of Selwyn House, a private all-boys day school in Montreal that has educated much of the city's Anglophone elite, for instance, have filed a class-action suit against the school for abuse they allegedly suffered from a teacher in the 70s and 80s. Both Andover and Exeter have also had sex-abuse incidents in the past 15 years.

My heart went out to the school. I had a great time there and learned so much that I entered Harvard as a sophomore. St. Paul's really gave me a leg up, as it did almost everyone who went there, including the ones who were kicked out or ran away and went on to have stellar careers. So it was distressing to see the treatment it was getting in the press. As one scandal followed another, none of the news articles that my classmates disseminated to one another in hundreds of mass e-mails conveyed what the school was actually like. Many of my media colleagues seemed to be taking relish in tearing down the reputation of one of the sanctums of American elitism. It was such a juicy target, how could you not go for the jugular? But anyone who has gone to St. Paul's knows what a magical, and surprisingly democratic, place it is.

My interest was piqued because I knew many of the players, including one of the most notorious of the accused masters, who is now living in disgrace in another state. At least I *thought* I knew him. (He had never come on to me.) I knew the new, interim rector, Bill Matthews, who had been an exemplary sixth-form supervisor in the Lower School when I was in the third form. And I knew the new head of the board of trustees, Jim Robbins, because we'd grown up together in Bedford, New York, in the 50s. Both of them had taken office after their predecessors resigned in June. We hadn't seen one another in years, but I remembered them as good men. I also knew one of the lifetime trustees who had been on the secretive, too powerful Executive Committee and had stepped down, and the investment adviser who had done the report on the school's governance for the state A.G.'s office. The New England prep-school world of 40 to 50 years ago is a small one.

I had also written the history of two other private schools, attended by my five sons over the years—St. George's School of Montreal, and Rippowam Cisqua School, in Bedford, New York—so I knew that schools are fascinating microcosms. They act out what is happening in the society at large. As the parent of a former student told me, after I started writing about the crises and their repercussions, "Everything that happened at St. Paul's is symptomatic of what our society has become."

The St. Paul's campus spreads over more than 2,000 acres of deep woods, spotted with dark ponds, on the outskirts of the state capital. On the largest pond, Turkey, the crews of the rival rowing teams, the Halcyons and the Shattucks (every student belongs to one of these, whether or not he or she goes out for crew), race each spring. When they are good enough, usually every other year, the best oarsmen go to Henley-on-Thames, in England, to compete in the Princess Elizabeth Challenge Cup against the crews of Eton, Harrow, and other British public schools. The Halcyon jacket is maroon, the Shattuck cerulean blue, and the lapels of both are fringed with white. Straw boaters, white ducks, white oxfords, and white shirts with the Halcyon or Shattuck tie complete the after-the-race outfit. Hogwarts has Quidditch; St. Paul's has crew, hockey, and squash.

The central part of campus is bisected by a broad, straight road which becomes a ceremonial way on Anniversary Weekend each June, when the alumni parade down it, class by class. It is the gratitude and the generosity of its 7,441 living graduates that keep the school going. But, as a classmate of mine who hails from one of the nation's oldest families told me, "Those who give like the idea of their kids and grandkids going there, but this has been a problem since the late 80s, when the school turned into some kind of a hothouse that only the crème de la crème can get into anymore."

My six-day visit to the school in October coincides with one of those glorious little windows known as Indian summer, a combination of Gershwin's "Summertime" and Johnny Mercer's "Autumn Leaves." Each morning the ponds are swathed in mist. I watch students running across the bridge from the Coit Upper dormitory, where they have just had breakfast, to chapel. If they aren't inside by the time its Westminster chimes toll eight times, their names will be taken and they will get a "bag," which was called a demerit in my day. Back then, enough demerits put you on a work crew, which was run by a little man who was known to us as "the Toad." The Toad used to take some of the boys from the best families on a tour of whorehouses in the summer. As far as I know, no one who participated in these outings has ever complained. "The Toad was not a pedophile," says an alumnus who has made it his mission to expose abusers among the faculty. "At worst he was a voyeur-facilitator."

By nine o'clock the mist has burned off, to reveal massive white pines, flecked with the flaming oranges and reds of turned hardwoods, leaning out over the ponds. One golden, sun-flooded day follows another. The campus is as idyllic as I remember it. On my first day there, a Friday afternoon, the form directors—who get their classmates to come to reunions, and shake them down for checks—and the trustees have gathered for a "volunteer leadership weekend." I find everybody in the Schoolhouse, wearing the school tie—black with red and white diagonal stripes. It's a very bright, high-powered group, like a meeting of the Templars. Marvelous-looking old Wasps, including one who could be the twin of Ben Bradlee, mingle with other distinguished men of less obvious provenance. (Bradlee himself went to St. Mark's School, in Massachusetts.) There are a few African-Americans and Asian-Americans, and a few women, but it still seems like an old boys' club.

A lot of the people in the room are very pissed off. The class of '55, which had its 50th reunion in June, deliberately failed to meet its $2 million goal as a protest against the board and administration that allowed all these things to happen. But the treasurer of the class of '56's upcoming 50th tells me, "We have a couple of million at least in the bag already. We've got a good momentum going." And after the Bish was sent packing, donations shot up dramatically. It has turned out to be a banner fund-raising year. "Our return is higher than any endowment out there," reports the new treasurer of the board, Bob Lindsay ('73), who is a nephew of former New York mayor John Lindsay ('40) and is also head of the search committee that will choose the next rector. By all the metrics—the number of applications, the percentage of students accepted, the proportion who get into the Ivies, the amount of money being raised—the school is in vibrant health.

Jim Robbins, the new president of the board of trustees, is at the lectern, fielding questions like a White House press secretary during a hurricane. Robbins runs his own media company in Atlanta. "Are you going to tell who did what, when, or is that protected?" asks one form director, and another says, "Let's cut to the chase. How much did the Bishop rip us off for?"

Robbins says coolly that what is released will be what is best for the school, and that Anderson is repaying every penny of his questionable expenses. Robbins would be happy to discuss the exact sum, he says, but he doesn't want to publicize it lest it trigger another article in *The New York Times*. I have heard that the dubious expenditures add up to around $300,000. Peanuts by Enron standards, but it's enough to pay for more than eight full scholarships for a year. (Annual tuition at St. Paul's is $35,000, plus fees.)

Anderson later tells me he is constrained by the I.R.S. audit from saying how much he is paying back. He says the $300,000 figure is wrong but won't say whether the actual number is more or less.

Robbins and I have known each other since we were kids. In the summer of 1963, my father and I took him and another boy to climb a small mountain called Les Diablerets—the Little Devils—near Villars, Switzerland. We ran into trouble, as can happen in the mountains. Robbins was very brave and really pulled his oar in this life-threatening situation, so I have faith that he is capable of "righting the good ship St. Paul's," as he puts it.

But not everyone is convinced that the housecleaning within the board has been thorough enough. One member of the class of '69 would later complain in a mass e-mail, "Much is being said lately by the board leadership about clearing the air and restoring trust. That's a difficult thing to accomplish when many are still on the board who signed 'unanimous' declarations of support for Anderson, and managed to heap praise on themselves at the same time. A boatload of trust would return quickly, and much air clear, if those board members would demonstrate their sincerity by resigning. There's really no other way to 'clean break' with the past; those are honoured who fall upon their swords."

Robbins apologizes to the form directors for the way all the trouble has made their jobs harder, and tells them, "The problem was that the board did not do due diligence in checking out Anderson before he was hired. They fell in love with the candidate and suspended disbelief, and that can't happen again." He cites other problems: concentrated power in the Executive Committee—the board's five-member administrative body, which has since been shaken up and expanded—and a lack of communication among the rector, the board, and everyone else. Then he adds, "The school is phenomenal, but this murmur—this noise at the top—we need to establish a disconnect with it. The students' experience is unencumbered by whatever noise there has been at the top of the organization. But it's going to take a while to get out of this ditch." [Robbins died in October 2007 while still serving as board president.]

There is a lot of talk about getting new blood on the 23-member board, but it already seems to be somewhat diverse. In addition to classic Wasps such as Robbins and Lindsay, there is an African-American judge who serves as the clerk and a Jewish New York investment banker who heads the audit committee. There are also Sabrina Fung and the Nigerian-born Dr. Olufunmilayo Falusi Olopade, as well as Trinka Taylor of Dallas, originally from Midland and a dear friend of the president's [George W. Bush]. And there is Julie Frist, a relative of Senate majority leader Bill Frist, who is under investigation for dumping his stock in HCA Inc., a company his father helped found, a few days before it tanked.

Lindsay tells the room that "the view that the trustees were enriching themselves is not true." This will be confirmed a few days later by Harold Janeway, the investment banker who did the report on the school's endowment management for the A.G.'s office. "There was nothing that was a chargeable offense or even close to it," Janeway says. According to the report, one trustee, George Baker, had been managing the endowment for more than 25 years, with very little oversight. He had invested it in more than 50 "instruments," many of them hedge funds and private venture-capital firms, so the money was very difficult to track. "It wasn't so much what they were doing, but the way they were doing it," Janeway says.

Reached at his investment firm in New York, Baker confirms that he ran the endowment committee almost single-handedly from the late 70s to 2005 and had "pretty much carte blanche" because "few trustees were trained in the business." He adds, "Those were simpler times." During this period, Baker says, he grew the endowment sixfold and shielded it from the dot-com bust that clobbered many other schools.

It is a relief to know that the alleged financial improprieties seem to have been limited to Anderson. Even he didn't think he was doing anything wrong—just getting what he was entitled to in his contract. "The current climate, with Sarbanes-Oxley [the federal regulations imposed on corporations in the wake of Enron's collapse, in 2001] migrating to the nonprofit sector, has brought schools like S.P.S. under a lot of scrutiny, which is probably good," he says. "But to judge the past in terms of the new government regulations, to suggest that people acted inappropriately, is insensitive. There is just a new way of operating."

W ondering how the whole thing got started, I began to piece together the bizarre and rather sordid chain of events that ended with Anderson's resignation and vice-rector Sharon Hennessy's indefinite sabbatical. Hennessy, whose salary also nearly doubled in the eight years she was there and whose perks included a membership at the Canyon Ranch spa—which reportedly cost between $20,000 and $30,000—and an annual trip to a pedagogical conference in Cannes, was not charged with any wrongdoing, but after she left, the position of vice-rector was abolished.

The chain begins in the fall of 1974, when a revered teacher named Lawrence Katzenbach (whose uncle Nicholas had been deputy attorney general under President Kennedy) allegedly dropped his trousers and exposed his erect penis to a senior girl who was babysitting his newborn baby. "His wife was in the hospital," says the victim, who asked not to be named. "He said, 'Come on, touch it,' and I ran out of the house and just kept running until I stopped somewhere in the woods, shaking." Deeply traumatized for years, the woman was unable to tell anyone what had happened until her 25th reunion, in 2000, when she decided to finally get it off her chest.

Ursula Holloman ('75), now a screenwriter in L.A., describes the scene to me: "I was sitting on the lawn with [the victim] and a couple of other women in my class when she started to tell us what Mr. Katzenbach did to her. I was stunned. I took Modern Novel with Mr. Katzenbach, and he was one of the best teachers I had at S.P.S. So we started talking and we remembered that another teacher had a bad reputation as an abuser, and there he was on prominent display right there at Anniversary."

The teacher in question, who has never been charged with any crime, had worked at the school for decades. By 2000, he was retired but still involved with the school, and was one of its best-regarded masters. "We decided, Something has to be done about this, so, using the e-mail chain for our 25th, in the fall of 2000 we started our *pro tempore* task force on student molestations." [The result was a school report on sexual misconduct released that same year, investigating claims against three staff members. A 2017 report revealed that as many as 23 former staff had been involved in a range of inappropriate behavior with students between 1948 and 1988, prompting wide criticism of the school's 2000 probe.]

Alexis Johnson ('76), a native-rights lawyer in Flagstaff, Arizona, who says he had been propositioned by this teacher, joined the task force, which collected eight reports on the retired master and nine on Katzenbach. The former was accused of forcibly holding hands and of physical assault, but not of any sex acts or fondling of private parts. "His victims ranged from some who felt slimed to others who felt completely destroyed," Holloman says.

Eventually the group gathered allegations of abuse by 29 masters over a 50-year period, including 5 who were active in the early 60s, when I was there. "Many who are abused have had their boundaries violated already," Holloman went on. "Predators can smell a victim."

In the fall of 2000, a delegation from the task force, consisting of some of the alumni who had been abused and some who had not, presented the rector and the board with numerous signed, firsthand accounts of abuse—"just to give them an idea of what had been going on," Holloman says. "They said, 'This is ancient history. It could never happen now.' They were concerned with, basically, covering their butts. They asked if any of the teachers were still at the school, and we said, 'Yes.' And it all became about [the unnamed teacher]. The dead and long-departed teachers they didn't care about. They never asked for the list. They were not interested. He was the only one they had to protect themselves from." Anderson disputes this, saying, "I complimented the work of the task force. . . . I never said the incidents were ancient history. I said, 'We want to do everything in our power to ensure that this never happens again.' . . . We were not interested in just [the one teacher]." (The school declined to answer a host of questions for this article.)

Even when the teacher cut his remaining ties with St. Paul's, no reason was given. The school's policy in such situations appeared to be absolute confidentiality, which deprived the victims of the closure they sought in all the other cases. "It was pretty similar to the Catholic Church," Holloman says. "All we got was lip service: 'We're formulating a new policy on this. It's under control.' We were accused by one trustee of plotting to sue the school, but we were just trying to bring this out into the light so people could talk, because we discovered a culture of secrecy among teachers and students that kept these things hidden and enabled the abusers to keep abusing—a whole repeating pattern."

Katzenbach's victim adds, "The thing that became really appalling is that the administration knew it had been happening over a very long time."

As its 25th-reunion gift, the class of 1975 gave a sizable amount of money for boundary training for the faculty and other measures to enhance the security of the students. These have been implemented, according to Dean Dale. But boarding schools attract sexually conflicted adults. Over the years, at least one staff member suspected to be preying on students at St. Paul's was dismissed, but the administration didn't implement a zero-tolerance policy until the early 90s.

Frustrated by what he saw as stonewalling, Johnson says, "I started to wonder: If there is a lack of candor on the crucial issue of the children's safety, what else aren't they being candid about? So I started to look into the financial operation." At the same time, Eleanor Shannon, a wealthy parent from Hanover, New Hampshire, who co-chaired the Parents' Committee with her husband, David Salem, was also looking into it. The couple had been on the verge of giving a six-figure gift to the school when a fellow parent familiar with fund-raising efforts told Shannon at a squash match that she had better take a look at the school's finances, starting with the rector's salary.

Shannon's husband is the founding C.E.O. of a big investment fund for nonprofit organizations, and she believed that, as head of the Parents' Committee, she could be legally liable under New Hampshire law if there were any financial impropriety. Using the Internet, she pulled up St. Paul's statements, as well as those of Andover and Exeter and Deerfield Academy, in Massachusetts, and noticed some unusual expenses in St. Paul's $30-million-plus annual budget that Shannon says were not in those of the other schools—such as $932,118 for legal fees and $3,909,861 for "other." The school explained that there had been an error in filling out the forms but that the problem had been subsequently addressed. According to an alum familiar with the situation, "Shannon asked for more detailed stuff than what was on the 990 [the statement the school, as a nonprofit institution, was obligated to file], which she was entitled to do."

A 30-page exchange detailing her frustrated attempt to get answers to her questions was posted on an alumni Web site, and she soon resigned from the Parents' Committee. Then she really started digging. Another alumnus started an online chat forum that detailed all sorts of damaging revelations and allegations, which sped around the alumni and ultimately reached the media.

At that point, the momentum leading to the downfall of Anderson and Hennessy and the Executive Committee was unstoppable. As my old blue-blooded classmate reflected, "A school administration used to be able to handle the news. But now there are blogs and cell phones that spread rumors, and the school has to react. The ability to keep information private is gone, and that is really hard for the administration of a school. Something happened at St. Paul's one night at 11 o'clock, I don't remember what it was, but there was an accurate account of it in the Andover student newspaper the next morning. God, I'd hate to be a headmaster and have to wake up every morning wondering, What have the little fuckers done now?"

The faculty was also at odds with the rector and the board. Partly it was because the teachers were liberals, and the trustees were for the most part stodgy conservatives "who have not crossed the postmodern line into the world with the rest of us," as one faculty member put it. And partly it was a class issue: the trustees acted as if the teachers were underlings, when in fact it is the teachers who dedicate their lives and careers to fulfilling the school's mission.

The questions about the school's financial operations were brought to the attention of *The Wall Street Journal,* possibly by an ex-teacher, and a three-inch-thick dossier entitled "St. Paul's School: Legally Actionable Acts of Commission and Omission" was sent to the New Hampshire attorney general's office. Some of the claims cited in the dossier have the whiff of shadiness, but few Paulies seem eager to go into it. As another classmate told me, "There's probably more bad stuff to be uncovered, but nothing really salacious." People would prefer to let sleeping dogs lie—as long as they don't become rabid again.

Hoping to gain some insight into how these events fit into the flow of the school's history, and that of the country at large, I spent every minute I could at the fabulous Ohrstrom Library, sampling its enormous collection of books. Designed by Robert A. M. Stern and finished in 1991, the library is one of the masterpieces of late-20th-century educational architecture. I didn't have the slightest interest in the school's history when I was a student there, but, as I now discovered, it is quite fascinating.

The school was founded in 1856 by a Boston doctor named George Shattuck, who hoped to implement the beliefs of an early-19th-century Swiss pioneer in progressive education named Johann Heinrich Pestalozzi. Pestalozzi espoused the Rousseauian idea that society was irredeemably compromised but that children were a fount of natural goodness. The only hope for reforming society, therefore, was to begin with children and give them a "natural" education.

This meant removing the sons of the Gilded Age's ruling class from their corrupting environs and building a school for them in some pristine place where they could experience the sublime directly through their senses. Green fields and trees, streams and ponds, beautiful scenery, flowers and minerals, are "educators," Shattuck wrote. Nature was character-forming, and so was what Groton's legendary headmaster Endicott Peabody called "corrective salutary deprivation." So the boys had to take cold showers and live in spartan alcoves and were completely cut off from the outside world and the opposite sex.

In 1911, Dr. Samuel Drury became the fourth rector and ushered in the school's golden age—the days most people would like to bring back—which lasted until his death 27 years later. Dr. Drury was a feared and revered, larger-than-life headmaster in the mold of Peabody. When

Gary W. Hill, president of the American Tobacco Company, visited his son at the school and lit up a Lucky Strike, Dr. Drury struck it out of his hand. Dr. Drury had been a missionary and had seen the misery that most of the world lives in; the main thing he tried to instill in his privileged charges was the notion of service. He was always reminding them, "From those to whom much is given, much is expected."

But already the campus was becoming quite grand. The chapel and the Gothic Upper Dining Room, with its high, vaulted ceiling, were positively Hogwartsian. Money was corrupting the mission, despite Dr. Drury's best efforts. "[The school] must not become a place of fashion, an exclusive retreat, where like-minded sons of like-minded parents disport themselves," he expostulated. "Our function is not to conform to the rich and prosperous world which surrounds us but, rather, through its children, to convert it." Nevertheless, St. Paul's was beginning to resemble the St. Midas's School—"the most expensive and the most exclusive boys' preparatory in the world"—of F. Scott Fitzgerald's 1922 short story "The Diamond As Big as the Ritz." Nelson W. Aldrich Jr. ('53), in his book, *Old Money: The Mythology of Wealth in America,* describes his time at the school as "the St. Midas Ordeal." One observer said of the recent scandals, "St. Paul's has always been a mélange of church and money, and money won out, because the church is dying."

In the 60s, the complexion of the school began to change. More scholarships were awarded, and the first minority students were admitted. A revolt of 162 sixth-formers along with a teacher named Gerry Studds, who later became a congressman, led to a relaxation of the dress code and the admission of girls in the early 70s. The new, secular rector, William Oates, espoused the prevailing educational and developmental thinking of the day, that schools should not be repressive and that adolescents should be free to experiment and try out different identities. In the 80s an impressive performing-arts center was built, and the school became more artsy.

Thanks to Manchester Airport and the improved interstate highway system, the school was no longer so remote and tucked away. And now that greed was good, some felt the notion of service barely received lip service. The school had an enormous ability to raise money and to scour the country and find the best and brightest kids. To keep up with rival prep schools, monumental building projects were undertaken, architecture that will one day be seen as late-imperial, climax-of-the-consumer-culture.

By the mid-80s, however, the board was getting alarmed that the students were out of control and the faculty had too much leeway, so they brought in David Hicks, the headmaster of a day school in Dallas called St. Mark's, to tighten things up. Hicks, who now lives in Montana, recalls, "One of the mandates I was given was to improve the quality of the school academically. Nobody had gone to Harvard in five years, except for legacies. I was also mandated to get control of student behavior. The students were polled and 80 percent of them said they were using drugs. It was very obvious to anyone who walked around the school on Saturday night that many of them were under the influence of something. . . . On my watch, some prospective parents from Philadelphia walked into the student center and found a boy and a girl having intercourse on a couch. I expelled them, which was not popular.

"The original parents of the Gilded Age, who knew what it was like out there, wanted their children to be hardened and not spoiled, but by the time I got there, silly faddistic ideas encouraged them to think they were something special, that the rules didn't apply to them, and that was not good. The kids would have been better off in a more meritocratic environment."

Hicks alienated the faculty by firing some of its most prominent members as part of a program to streamline the curriculum, and was so disliked by the students that the Christmas tree in front of the Rectory was torched and a steaming turd was left on the doorstep. When the faculty voted in favor of a no-confidence motion, Hicks left in the middle of the year.

In 1996, he published an article in *The American Scholar* called "The Strange Fate of the American Boarding School." It includes a thought-provoking passage: "Although the old-monied families still exert a considerable influence and control over their alma maters, they often do so in ways that reflect their own social and financial insecurities. . . . To some extent, the selfishness born of mounting social and financial anxiety among this class has caused the boarding school to do what it has often been accused of doing, but now with more reason—namely, to serve private rather than public interests. This may seem to increase its appeal, but it also undermines its integrity and contributes to its destruction."

Hicks was suggesting that the moral slippage at the school was related to the decadence of the old Wasp establishment. One can certainly draw a parallel with what was happening to the country as it entered the era of Enron, but it wasn't just the old money that was greedy, and the extent to which the old Wasp establishment is actually declining is also questionable.

The man who replaced Hicks couldn't have been more different. Bishop Anderson was ready to deal—with the parents and the board. Physically, he was the rector from central casting—an exceedingly handsome, square-jawed guy with a great smile who knew how to wear the miter and had a closetful of the most splendid vestments in the church. And he had a way with words. Even after he came under fire, he couldn't resist closing a sharply worded letter to Eleanor Shannon with a grand ecclesiastical flourish: "In the sure and certain hope of the Resurrection to eternal life, I wish you a blessed Eastertide."

"He was the most narcissistic man who ever came to the school," a teacher told me. The nurses in the infirmary, which is right next to the Rectory, used to watch him primping in the upstairs bathroom for a half-hour before morning chapel. ("Yes, I did shower and shave every morning, but I hope this could be seen as good hygiene," Anderson says. "And when we realized [the nurses could see us], we pulled the shade.") A parent of a former student found the Bish "very glossy, like a used-car salesman." Anderson, 63, had started out in marketing at Procter &

Gamble, and he had been an infantry officer in the army before entering the ministry. He had risen to be the bishop of South Dakota and then became the head of the General Theological Seminary, in New York City. There, he had performed expensive renovations on his residence, and that was one of the first things he did at St. Paul's after the school hired him away. "The Rectory was built in 1872," Anderson explains, and the renovation "was almost all structural, not cosmetic. . . . That's part of running an institution."

But Anderson's arrival coincided with the tanking of the dot-com boom, and money became harder to raise. In an effort to cut costs, the board let go longtime staff and adjusted benefits to the children of faculty. No one seemed to realize that implementing such measures when the rector and the vice-rector were still getting whopping salaries was bound to create resentment.

When the stories about the school's financial irregularities surfaced in the national press, the board rallied behind the Bishop. "I find it incredible that people who have affection for this school would go to these kinds of levels . . . to tear down its leadership," Jim Robbins, who was by then on the Executive Committee, protested to *The Wall Street Journal*. But two years later, with the A.G.'s investigation concluded and the I.R.S. audit in progress, the board felt compelled to demonstrate that it was taking steps to rectify the situation, and just two weeks before graduation and Anniversary, it announced that the Bishop had resigned.

A man who was there for the alumni procession that weekend recalls, "We all thought, How ghastly and embarrassing, and surely he'd be gone by the time we got there. But we show up and there's a cocktail party in the afternoon and there is Craig Anderson front and center, representing the institution. I've been married to a Wasp family for 25 years, and I've seen the power of politeness and repression, but for stiff upper lip this really took the cake. A lot of kids were wearing a T-shirt that said, 'I heart the Bish.' So the general sense I got was that, whatever Anderson's peccadilloes were, the kids really loved him and were in a rebellious mood that he had been shown the door."

————————

D r. Shattuck's ideal of keeping out the outside world has long since been abandoned. The Internet, cell phones, and the rules allowing DVD players in the dorms made sure of that. But Jim Robbins's wish to shield the students from the "noise at the top" is coming true. One night I went to the school's $2 million observatory to look at a few stars and get some perspective on the antics of us foolish mortals. The observatory has six telescopes in four domes. One of the school's two astronomy teachers, Dr. Tom McCarthy, took me into the Lowell Dome. Untold Lowells have gone to St. Paul's over the decades. I asked McCarthy if the dome was named for Percival Lowell, the eccentric 19th-century astronomer who moved to Flagstaff, Arizona, and from his observatory there claimed to have seen water-filled canals on Mars. McCarthy said it was named for Lowell Swift Reeve ('69), who had died tragically in his youth.

McCarthy is clearly passionate about the sky, the kind of teacher who is so enthusiastic that he can change a student's life. "With these telescopes we can find supernovas and extraterrestrial planets. We can spot near-earth asteroids, the ones we fear could slam into us one day," he said.

Two students arrived. McCarthy was taking one of them down to Harvard in the morning to receive some kind of award. McCarthy trained the telescope on Alpha Andromedae, the brightest star in its constellation. It looked like a dazzling rhinestone. The instrument, I noticed, was called the St. Paul's Alumni Telescope. "Just what we could use," I said to him, and he laughed. I asked him what he thought about all the recent goings-on, and he said, "That's administration. The school is rock-solid as far as its mission goes."

I sat in on a Greek class for second-year students. You don't find Greek being taught at too many high schools anymore. The students, who included one African-American boy and two Asian-American girls, were extremely bright, as were all the students I talked to. And so polite and welcoming. When I asked how they liked the school, they invariably said it was awesome. And who wouldn't feel the same way? How many high schools have a harpsichord and a corps de ballet?

I jammed with a "frelk," a new category of student since my time who might be described as a latter-day hippie or freak. Frelks (the word is derived from "frolic") are really into the Grateful Dead. This frelk had a head on his shoulders. He was an excellent musician and had already recorded a CD. His plan was to move to New York and get into the music business.

I had lunch with Ike Perkins, the son of some filmmaking friends of mine and the great-nephew of Maxwell Perkins, the fabled editor of Ernest Hemingway, F. Scott Fitzgerald, and Thomas Wolfe. Scads of Perkinses have gone to St. Paul's. Since arriving at the school, Ike had met eight cousins with other surnames whom he never even knew he had, and he was having the time of his life. A fifth-generation Paulie who graduated last year told me that "there is a lot of fucking, but it's all safe." Apparently, most students are wise enough to choose condoms over diseases and unwanted pregnancies.

There are still "preps," like the one in my class who used to turn over your tie and snicker if the label wasn't Brooks Brothers. Most of the preps live in Simpson House. "The preppiest ones are not the old-line kids, many of whom are not preppy at all," a student told me, "but the wannabes who have new money."

Chapel, which I attended twice, had become a totally different experience. It had become fun, an opportunity for the kids to express themselves rather than have the word of God stuffed down their throats. Both times, a conga line of girls started bumping and grinding in the center aisle. Dr. Drury would have rolled over in his grave if he had witnessed this sacrilege. But the old hymns whose words I knew by heart, though I hadn't sung them in years, were being sung, as was the school anthem, an overt paean to capitalism taken from Psalm 122:

O pray for the peace of Jerusalem;
they shall prosper that love thee.
Peace be within thy walls,
and plenteousness within thy palaces.

I found myself whispering the wonderfully consoling words of the closing blessing as they were delivered by the new, interim rector, Bill Matthews: "O Lord, support us all the day long, until the shadows lengthen and the evening comes, and the busy world is hushed, and the fever of life is over, and our work is done."

After chapel, Matthews met me at his office in the Old Schoolhouse. I had not laid eyes on him in 44 years, since his days of supervising my form-mates and me, but he was just as I had imagined he would be: a sweet and unassuming 62-year-old with a grizzled crew cut, dressed in a tweed jacket and a tie that he must have worn a thousand times before. This is the standard uniform of the New England prep-school teacher, like that of the masters in my day, and in sharp contrast to the Bish's spiffy attire.

Matthews went to Bowdoin, where he majored in Latin, and returned to St. Paul's in 1966. Except for a sabbatical year in Paris, he has been there ever since. He taught Latin and Greek, coached hockey and baseball, and served as the director of college placement, the director of admissions, the vice-rector of students, the executive director of the alumni association, and, for the last five years, the director of development (in which capacity he staved off Eleanor Shannon's request for clarification on the school's finances with a letter saying: "It would be simpler if you just trusted us; we're not perfect, but I do think that we are a place of integrity, and that does have a fair amount to do with Craig Anderson and our Board as its leaders"). Two of Matthews's children attended St. Paul's. He is of the school. He understands the values, the joy, and the tremendous responsibility of nurturing vibrant young minds. He is not a guy who is out for himself.

Nevertheless, the school has enlisted Wickenden Associates, an executive-search company that has installed headmasters at more than 200 independent schools, to find a permanent rector to replace Matthews next fall. [Bill Matthews ended up staying on as rector until 2011.] In October, the firm circulated an admirably frank 12-page job announcement that includes a section titled "Opportunities and Challenges Awaiting the Next Rector," warning prospective candidates that whoever gets hired will have to:

1. Lead the school with absolute integrity, humility, and transparency.

2. Make a concerted effort to rebuild bridges with disaffected alumni. . . .

3. Support the Board's continuing efforts to strengthen its own governance and communication practices. . . .

4. Counter the effects of negative publicity and restore the school's external reputation through a carefully considered communications and public relations plan.

In the meantime, Matthew's motto for the 2005–6 school year is "Do the right thing." "This is a school that has a soul," he told me, "and it always has."

I went for a walk in the woods, where I had spent so much time four decades ago. There hadn't been a course to teach me the names of the trees and birds back then, but there is one now. Some of the animals are even wired so that their movements can be radio-tracked. Sitting down, I soon attracted a half-dozen curious, nervously chirping chickadees.

I felt glad that the school had weathered its storm and that the kids had come through pretty much unscathed, although there are still plenty of issues that need to be addressed. The unifying thread among the various constituencies that are always doing a Darwinian dance in any school—the teachers, the students, the alumni, the trustees, the administration, the parents—is that all of them obviously care deeply about the place. And, in the words of John Buckston, a former vice-rector at St. Paul's, "Everybody is the hero of his own novel."

A number of alumni have characterized Anderson's regrettable tenure as a case of "hubris"—the tragic flaw of overreaching that has brought down mythical kings such as Oedipus and money kings of today. It seems to be the big word of the moment. The other day, a commentator on CNN was expounding on the "hubris" of the Republican Party.

Hubris seems to have affected not just the Bish but the board too. "They're an arrogant, snotty bunch, and not very smart," one teacher told me. Their fatal error was to blow off donors, alumni, and teachers who care about the school and were trying to raise important questions about its direction.

Some stodgy old Paulies think the school itself has a case of hubris. In their view, it was the extravagance of the new gym that brought about the drowning of a student in the swimming pool. The school had survived for almost 150 years without a pool. Now money is being raised for a multi-million-dollar boathouse. Where is it going to end?

Instead of building a new boathouse, why not use the money to make an inventory of all the products the school uses, and get the kids involved? It could even be a course. Maybe they would think twice before ripping off three feet of toilet paper once they found out that a million acres of old-growth boreal forest in northern Alberta are being ground up every year to make the stuff.

Why not have the kids follow the money trail—find out how the money coming into the school was made, and in exactly what sort of "instruments" the endowment is invested? Have them look into how much of the oblivious hyper-consumption taking place not just here but across America is made possible by the backbreaking labor of millions of Third World peasants. How many ecosystems are being degraded and destroyed by our way of life? Get the kids to print their homework on both sides of the page, case their dorms for energy leaks, and take quick showers—and be grateful that the water's hot.

A course like that would produce some responsible citizens, and it would save the school a lot of money. St. George's, the quirky little progressive school in Montreal that my three youngest sons attend, got the whole student body involved in a consumption-and-waste inventory of its physical plant, and has saved a bundle as a result. Once the St. Paul's inventory is done, the kids can go forth and get the whole country to do it. If the school could get that going, and implement a little "corrective salutary deprivation," then it would be a complete Utopia, and Drs. Shattuck and Drury would be proud of it once more.

The chickadees cheered.

(See page 71 for Todd S. Purdum's 2016 story on St. Paul's School.)

UNITED STATES AIR FORCE ACADEMY

"CODE OF DISHONOR"

By Clara Bingham

DECEMBER 2003

our young women dressed in civilian clothes entered an office conference room in Colorado Springs on July 10, 2003. They sat down and one by one told their stories of how, while attending the nearby United States Air Force Academy, they had been raped by fellow cadets and subsequently punished by the academy's administrators. The women were not addressing a judge or a jury. They spoke instead to seven people: a former congresswoman, two retired generals, a retired colonel, a military sociologist, a rape-victim advocate, and a psychiatrist, all of whom had been handpicked by Secretary of Defense Donald Rumsfeld to investigate the burgeoning scandal at the academy.

By the end of the private two-hour testimony, every member of the audience had tears in his or her eyes. "It was just devastating," retired lieutenant general Josiah Bunting III said later. "I couldn't get over it. Listening to their stories was harrowing. It was a moment of cataclysm for me."

Bunting knows military academies. As the former superintendent of the Virginia Military Institute, Bunting opposed allowing women to attend that school, which had been a southern male bastion since 1839. But in 1996, when the Supreme Court ordered the publicly funded military academy to admit women, it was up to Bunting to find a way to peacefully and safely matriculate female cadets. Recently retired from V.M.I. with his mission accomplished, Bunting was a particularly astute choice to serve on Rumsfeld's panel, which was headed by former Republican congresswoman Tillie Fowler. But even the reports Bunting had read on the academy scandal in the newspapers, and his own experience with the macho rigors of V.M.I.'s infamous "rat line," a hazing ritual, did not prepare him for what he heard in Colorado Springs on July 10. "It was much worse than what I had ever expected to find," he confessed.

W omen make up roughly 16 percent of the Air Force Academy's cadet wing (as the student body is referred to). Bunting's realization that life for them was nearly intolerable came six months after the first news of trouble exploded onto the nation's airwaves and front pages. It all started in January when a handful of female cadets broke the code of silence and began telling their stories to the media and a few members of Congress. In the following months, even as women were flying strike sorties in F-16s and B-2s in the skies over Iraq, more and more victims came out of the woodwork. Many had never made rape allegations to academy authorities, often out of fear that their claims would not be taken seriously, or that they themselves might end up being punished for minor transgressions of academy rules. Indeed, officials seemed to be dragging their feet, or worse, when an investigation led by the air-force general counsel concluded in June that there was "no systemic acceptance of sexual assault at the Academy [or] institutional avoidance of responsibility." But by September, 61 academy women had told Colorado senator Wayne Allard's office they had been raped or assaulted, four top academy administrators had been replaced, dozens of rules and regulations had been changed, and the Pentagon had launched three investigations, which in turn were being closely scrutinized by Congress. As revelations mushroomed, the Air Force Academy's problems began to make Tailhook—the 1991 navy pilots' and Marine Corps aviators' convention in Las Vegas where 83 women were groped—look like a case of mere high jinks.

The numbers are staggering. Over the past 10 years there have been 142 formal allegations of sexual assault at the academy. (Three of the victims were men.) But as high as this figure may seem, it reflects only a fraction of the truth. A recent Defense Department inspector general's draft survey revealed that 80 percent of all sexual assaults at the academy go unreported, meaning that the true 10-year casualty list could be as high as 700. The same survey indicated that 7.4 percent of last year's female student body at the academy were victims of rape or attempted rape, and 18.8 percent were victims of sexual assault. (By way of comparison, a 2000 Department of Justice study reported that nationwide 1.7 percent of female college students claimed to have been raped.) To this day, no cadet has been incarcerated for raping another cadet.

While the academy struggles to change its culture, the looming question is: Who will be held accountable? Members of the Senate Armed Services Committee, which has been holding hearings on the subject, are pointing fingers at air-force secretary James Roche for mishandling the scandal; his nomination to become secretary of the army is for the time being on hold. Meanwhile, the Fowler panel has singled out one current administrator, Brigadier General David Wagie, and two former academy officials, Brigadier General Taco Gilbert and Colonel Laurie Sue Slavec, for review by the Defense Department inspector general—a move that likely ensures the end of their military careers. Major General John Dallager, the academy's former superintendent—the school's equivalent of president—was reprimanded in July, and later forced to retire with two instead of three stars.

But the problems at the Air Force Academy go deeper than just an administration that has been ineffective at best: interviews with current and former cadets paint a portrait of an institutional culture steeped in hostility toward women, a hostility made even more dangerous by the school's sometimes brutal hazing of new cadets. And as students in the academy's newly entered class of 2007 finish their first semester of courses amid shifting rules and with their behavior being observed in microscopic detail, another question hangs over their heads: Will the military ever fully integrate women?

When Beth Davis joined the ranks of the United States Air Force Academy's cadets in 1999 with the class of 2003, it was high summer, and she thought the campus setting was awe-inspiring. At that time of year, the wind blows down from the Rockies, sweeping across the vast green acreage known as the Terrazzo, which, marbled by white, sunlit pathways, forms the heart of the 18,000-acre wooded campus, built in 1958. Its 7,258-foot altitude—"far, far above that of West Point or Annapolis," goes the academy boast—yields wind that can make a newcomer feel airborne. It whistles through the spires of the Cadet Chapel, a gigantic, white modernist structure whose 17 A-shaped peaks look like the teeth of a colossal government-issue paper shredder. The wind wafts past Fairchild Hall, a hive of 250 classrooms, 45 science labs, and 13 lecture halls. It chases cadet units—the wing is divided into 36 squadrons—off the Terrazzo and into Mitchell Hall, the three-story, 1.5-acre dining area, one of the largest mass-dining facilities in the world, where the entire cadet wing of 4,000 men and women assemble to consume meals in 20 minutes flat. The wind swirls over the gym and field house, the library, and the quarter-mile-long dorm, Vandenberg Hall—white, monolithic shapes in the academy's gargantuan geometry, the scale designed to make the individual feel subordinate to the institution at all hours, from reveille to taps.

As if the place itself weren't formidable enough, the rules and regulations that were still in place when Beth Davis arrived in Colorado Springs could make life nearly unbearable for a new cadet, or "four-degree." These procedures have been eased somewhat this year as the academy has sought to reform itself, but up until this summer all four-degrees, also known as "doolies," lived under the complete domination of upperclassmen, especially sophomores, called "three-degrees," whose job it was to train the newcomers. Juniors ("two-degrees") and seniors ("first-degrees," or "firsties") ran the squadrons, meted out punishments, and controlled everyone beneath them. The four-degrees, male and female, spent their first nine months in a state of constant hazing. The resulting terror, humiliation, and powerlessness were made all the harder for standout cadets of both sexes and especially for pretty young women such as Beth Davis—a tall brunette with long hair, big blue eyes, a soft voice, and the clear, honest innocence of a girl from a nice rural family who had grown up on a small, quiet farm.

At 6:30 every morning, with boots shined and rooms spotless, doolies were subject to Draconian inspections, the worst coming on Saturdays. Before meals they stood at attention in their dorm hallway and, in a carefully synchronized chant called "minutes," shouted out the schedule: "There are eight minutes until the first call for the breakfast meal formation! Menu for the meal includes scrambled eggs and sausages! Cereal! And orange juice! Uniform is blues!"

From Monday to Thursday, all cadets wore "blues." Originally created in 1956, the uniforms were designed by Cecil B. DeMille Studios in Hollywood. The lines of the blue suit were drawn with barrel chests and stiff, straight backs in mind. Expertly pressed and worn with pride, a cadet's uniform received special scrutiny throughout the doolie cycle. Even at mealtime in the galactic din of vast Mitchell Hall the four-degrees were subject to a strict code. Doolies had to eat at attention, "squaring" their forks by using the utensil to cut a perfect right angle in the air as they took food from the plate and brought it to their mouths.

They were permitted to chew no more than seven times before swallowing. Doolies also had to memorize the preferred beverages of their superiors and serve them accordingly.

Rules followed doolies day and night. They were not allowed to walk into a dorm area other than their own. On the Terrazzo, they had to run, not walk. They could never initiate a conversation with an upperclassman, much less strike up a friendship; if they tried, both would be accused of "fraternization," or "frat." The worst of all frat offenses was sex between a four-degree and an upperclassman. Despite coed dorms and the natural urges of 4,000 college-age, hormonally charged students, consensual sex was officially prohibited on-campus, though the rule was often disregarded. "Falcon love," or "doing blue"—sex between two cadets—was accomplished by "creeping," sneaking into each other's rooms.

Doolies, however, rarely had time for that. Twenty-four hours a day they were at the beck and call of their superiors. On a whim, doolies could be summoned to an upperclassman's dorm room or, more common in recent years, to their computer screens to answer an instant-messaging (I.M.) request, no matter how trivial. If they displeased an upperclassman, doolies, also called "smacks," could be made to submit to physical punishment, called "beat-downs," during which, in cycles lasting up to an hour, a three-degree would scream "up-down" orders in their ears: push-ups one minute, jumping jacks the next. Even the word "doolie"—taken from the Greek word *doulos,* for slave—institutionalized their servility.

The hell had an end to it. In March, just before spring break, the doolies were "recognized" and finally allowed to become equal members of the cadet wing. There is, of course, a method to all this. In order to achieve its mission of transforming outstanding individuals (the average S.A.T. score for the class of 2007 is 1290, the high-school grade-point average 3.9, and 84 percent had been varsity athletes) into a team of highly motivated career officers dedicated no longer to personal desires but to a lifetime of duty to the air force, the academy believes it has to break its trainees down and then build them back up by inculcating a value system designed to instill one quality above all others: trust.

According to this covenant, Beth Davis, in order to do what was expected of her, in order to endure the severe physical and emotional toll of her initiation, would have to trust her superiors. She would have to trust that the upperclassmen putting her through these nine months of hell would be guided by the academy's vaunted honor oath and a strong moral sense.

At first, Beth liked the structure of the academy because the discipline was not unlike that required to run the family farm on Maryland's Eastern Shore; she was used to waking up every morning at five to feed the animals before going off to school. Even as a girl she had wanted to fly fighter planes. Her uncle had flown P-3s for the navy for 20 years, and Beth had set her sights on the Naval Academy, in nearby Annapolis. She wanted the challenge of landing jets on aircraft carriers. Due to the high number of students applying from her area, Beth's application to Annapolis was also forwarded to Colorado Springs, and while the Naval Academy accepted her only for its one-year prep school, which some students attend to prepare for the academic rigors of Annapolis, she was admitted to the Air Force Academy in full. She decided to go, sight unseen.

In June, new cadets start basic training. During "in-processing," Beth's long brown hair was chopped into a bob just like all the other women's, but owing to her bright-blue eyes and delicate features she still stood out, and she was apparently picked on more than other female doolies. Tan lines where her rings had been, along with the highlights still in her hair, compelled the three-degree cadres to nickname her Prom Queen and Daddy's Little Girl. But Beth didn't let the hazing get the better of her. She held her own on the long rifle runs and grueling obstacle courses, and, though 5 percent of her fellow four-degrees washed out by August, Beth survived basic training and was placed in a dorm with the No. 13 squadron, "Bulldawgs."

She was severely restricted in her personal possessions. Doolies were allowed no more than two items (typically a framed family photograph and a personal memento) in their rooms. E-mail and letters were un-restricted, but telephone use was confined to Sundays and cell phones forbidden. Except on the very rare "blue weekend," when doolies could venture off-campus, the outside world was forbidden. Television, music, movies, and civilian clothes were considered contraband.

According to Beth's account of her doolie year, contraband was what first introduced her to a three-degree named Chris (not his real name). Soon after Beth moved into his squadron, Chris sent out an e-mail to all doolies in the squadron offering to hide their contraband in his room, where he said it would go undetected. On Parents' Weekend, in early September, when Beth's mother and father realized the extent of her privation, they tried to spoil her with several CDs, DVDs, and a pair of blue jeans. Beth hid the banned items in her laundry bag and decided to take Chris up on his offer.

She had never met him before. He was sitting at his desk when she entered with her laundry bag, but he didn't look up. Curiously, he kept his gaze averted from her throughout their first exchange. Beth said, "What would you like me to do with this, sir?" Chris said, "Don't call me 'sir' again. Put it in the cabinet above the door." Beth tried several times but could not reach the cabinet, and the bag kept falling down. Chris never got up to help her; he told her to leave the laundry bag on his bed.

Soon after that Chris e-mailed Beth on her computer to ask if she had instant messaging. He wanted her screen name. She felt reluctant to share this information, but at the same time she had been taught that the consequences of refusing such a request from a superior would be an hour of murderous calisthenics. She replied with her screen name, and Chris started I.M.-ing her.

At first he seemed to want to get to know her, but as Beth kept up her part in the exchange, she dutifully observed protocol, address-ing Chris as "sir," which infuriated him. Then, even more dismaying to Beth, he started asking about her sexual experience, and, though she would later say that there wasn't much to tell, she avoided Chris's questions. The instant messaging became constant. "I felt like every time I walked into my room—even if the hallways were empty—he would know I was there and a message would pop up," she later said. Adding to the eerie feeling of being watched and controlled was the fact that she rarely saw Chris in person.

By early fall, he was attaching pornographic images to his e-mails, cataloguing sex acts he wanted Beth to perform. In particular, she recalls, "he wanted me to 'suck him off'—those were his words." Disgusted, Beth nevertheless did not feel free to turn off her computer and pull the plug on Chris. To alienate him in any way was to risk angering a superior. "That is your job as a subordinate," she remembers thinking. "You're supposed to make your superiors happy."

One night in October, Beth says, Chris snapped. It was two in the morning, and he had kept Beth on a string in her dorm room, peppering her with instant messages. Trying once more to coax her to describe past sexual experiences, he suddenly lashed out at her when she refused. He told Beth he would turn in her classmates for drinking alcohol, and when they got into trouble she would be to blame. He said he would use the well-oiled machinery of the cadet rumor mill to tell her superiors that she was not the innocent farm girl everyone thought she was. He would blacken her reputation all over the academy. The smear would follow her throughout her air-force career. Even the long blue line of academy grads, or "ring knockers," would be talking about Beth Davis. Beth looked on, stunned, sickened, as a long line of crude names filled her screen: "Cocksucker . . . Dickface . . ."

The garish glow from the computer was the only light in the room. Beth stared at the screen in tears, unable to move, unable to understand how she had gotten herself into this situation. She says her roommate, who had been trying to sleep, heard her crying and told her to get off the computer. Suddenly, another message came through: Chris would be downstairs, outside the dorm, if she wanted to talk. Then he disconnected.

Thinking that she would reason with Chris and come to some kind of understanding, Beth sneaked downstairs and out into the chilly mountain air. She saw him standing in the dark outside Vandenberg Hall. Without a word, he started walking toward some trees. Beth called to him. Where was he going? What was he doing? He wouldn't answer. She trailed after him, but as soon as she came to the edge of a nearby grassy area she stopped. She decided she did not want to go any farther. Chris turned around and came back. As he approached, he ordered her to drop to her knees.

She just stood there, frozen. Facing her, Chris put his hands on Beth's shoulders and shoved her down to her knees. He lowered his pants. Later, she wished that at that moment she had jumped up and run away. He took her head in his hand and pulled it forward. She was now weeping, and as soon as he forced himself into her mouth she choked. "I had my hands on him, trying to push away. . . . I was gagging and really a mess," she later said. After he was finished, he pulled away quickly and left Beth where she was kneeling. But before he disappeared, he warned her to wait until he was inside the dorm before she returned to her room.

Like Beth Davis, Sharon Fullilove entered the academy with the class of 2003 and was singled out by upperclassmen because of her looks—large gray-green eyes, a button nose, full lips, blond hair. Like Beth, Sharon toughed it out through the hazing, not minding the loss of personal control. She had set her heart on becoming a cadet at the Air Force Academy and hadn't applied to any other colleges. While many cadets talked about "five and dive," leaving the service after performing the five years of active duty required to pay the air force back for a $300,000 education, Sharon wanted to make the air force her career. "That was part of the appeal. I knew where I was going for the next 20 to 30 years," she says.

Her mother, Michaela "Micki" Shafer, is an air-force colonel who met her second husband, an air-evacuation medic, Gary Shafer, in flight school. The air force had been her mother's and stepfather's lives. Micki, a Ph.D. in biomedical research, worked in air-force hospitals for most of her 20-year career. From January 2000, six months after her daughter entered the academy, through mid-August 2003, she served as the director of inpatient services at the academy hospital. When Sharon was admitted to the class of 2003, her mother was overjoyed. "It was very prestigious," says Micki. "We were proud as peacocks."

Sharon was in many ways the ideal cadet for the 21st-century air force. As a second-generation air-force woman who had set her sights on a career in the service, Sharon personified the mission that the academy had taken on since Congress, in 1975, giddy from the recent passage of the Equal Rights Amendment, forced all of the military academies—despite loud protest from military brass—to accept women. With the draft having ended in 1973, and the military now relying on an all-volunteer force, recruiters focused on a new generation of young women to fill more and more of its jobs. And as the composition of the military changed, so did the academies. Traditionally, they specialized in training officers to lead in combat. Now, in order to include the "weaker sex," who were not permitted to serve in frontline positions, Congress required the academies to alter their mission. As of June 1976, when the first class that included women began basic training, the academies would train not just combat officers but also career officers, who perform all of the other functions required of military leaders.

At the time, the air force limited the fields women could participate in. They could fly, but only on noncombat planes such as refueling tankers and personnel carriers. Colonel Debra Gray, the Air Force Academy's new vice commandant of cadets, was a member of that first class of women. "We were often confronted with the question: Women can't go into combat, so why are you here?" she says. "Our answer was O.K., maybe we can't fly [fighter planes], but we can go into other career fields, and when they do open things up, we'll be able to compete."

Fighter pilots run the air force and the academy. They are the commanders, the generals, the men who have stars on their epaulets. It was not until 13 years after Gray had graduated that the Pentagon changed combat restrictions and allowed women inside the cockpits of fighter jets. Today, 99.7 percent of all air-force jobs are open to women—a higher percentage than in the army (67.2 percent) or the navy (94 percent). By 2001, according to the Pentagon, there were 114 female active-duty fighter and bomber pilots in the U.S.

That was Sharon Fullilove's goal, to become a fighter pilot. At Parents' Weekend, she told her mother and stepfather about the McDonnell Douglas F-15E, a tactical fighter plane bristling with laser-guided munitions and cluster bombs used on deep interdiction missions. "That," she announced, "is the plane I'm going to fly." In the meantime, she thrived in basic training and endured the hazing, understanding as if it were her birthright the compact she had made with the Air Force Academy. She was in exceptional shape, so the physical rigor didn't faze her. She could knock off 100 push-ups with one hand. She made such good friends during the ordeal that she proudly told her parents, "I have 50 new brothers."

Everything changed the Sunday before Thanksgiving. Sharon called her mother during phone privileges. She was in hysterics. She begged her mother for permission to withdraw from the academy. Sharon would not say more, but Micki had an immediate and instinctive sense that Sharon had been raped.

This was not long after Beth Davis claims she was assaulted. To her immense relief, Chris's instant messages and e-mails stopped completely after the incident outside the dorm. Then, a week later, Chris sent a message telling Beth that she was lousy at oral sex, but that, for her own good, he would do her the favor of taking the time to teach her how to improve her technique.

Over the next five months, a pattern established itself. Chris, in a towering rage, would e-mail Beth and summon her to a study room in the dorm. "Being my superior, it meant all the diamonds in the world that he was mad at me," she later recalled. As soon as she had reported to him in the study room, he would step between Beth and the door and lock them in. Then, pulling up a chair, he would sit down and say, "You know what you have to do." Each time, Beth would say that she did not want to do it and could they please work this out. Chris would reply with silence or verbal coercion. "I was always in a position where I knew what was happening but couldn't do anything about it," says Beth. "It was always him getting infuriated and me trying to appease him, trying to make things better."

After each meeting the e-mails would stop for about two weeks and then start up again. Each time he summoned her, she would use any excuse she could think of to avoid going to the study room, but each time fear that he would turn in her classmates for drinking and spread rumors that she was a slut overwhelmed her. "I was so afraid of him," Beth said later. "It's a fear that you cannot describe to anyone who hasn't been [a student at the academy]." Supported by the cadet system of superiors and subordinates, "he could do whatever he wanted. . . . He had told me that he could get away with anything at the academy. That he knew how to work the system."

Finally, in March, just days before recognition, when she would no longer have to bow and scrape as a doolie, Chris forced her to a mattress that had somehow appeared in a study room, and penetrated her and sodomized her.

During that period, in which Beth Davis says she was sexually assaulted four times and finally raped, she kept her silence. She did not tell her roommates or her parents, and she did not report the incidents to any authorities.

At the beginning of her second year at the academy, she went running one night with a fellow cadet from her civil-engineering class. Their route took them away from the main part of campus. It was around 10, and as Beth and the young man kept running, the lights of the academy grew more and more distant. Beth felt an attack of pure panic overcome her. She dropped back and told her friend she didn't want to run anymore.

Incredibly, he guessed her secret. Sobbing, she told him the whole story. He encouraged her to report it and volunteered to help her find justice. "This is something," he said, "that needs to be reported."

Beth told her friend that she didn't want to lose her career over it. She also didn't want to be an example of why women shouldn't be in the air force. She felt that although women had been at the academy for two and half decades she was still a pioneer in this world, and she wanted to make it, she wanted to finish, and she wanted to succeed, even if her success was on terms other than her own. She knew that rape charges would ground her permanently, and like so many others, as it would turn out, she believed that she was alone in her torment. "I thought," she says now, "I was the only one."

Many female cadets say that the academy's aggressive, hypermasculine military culture, combined with the fact that women are such a small minority, makes for an inevitably alien environment for them. "They resent us being there, for taking away their pilot slots, for going on rifle runs and wearing their uniforms," one former female cadet says of certain male cadets. "Slowly but surely, like a storm, it starts to brew and it's just saturating. . . . There's a lot of pressure to do your best and be your best and be able to fit in."

Some female cadets react to the pressure by developing eating disorders. Women who gain weight are teased by the male cadets for having "Colorado hip disease" or "Terrazzo ass." Beth Davis remembers numerous women who suffered from anorexia, bulimia, or diet-pill addictions. She herself took diet pills when she was a cadet. Beth knew women who tried not to eat in front of the men in the dining hall for fear of being mocked. "In the middle of the night, you can see girls in the hallway picking food out of trash cans because they have these phobias against eating in front of guys in the lunchroom."

In 1999, the class of 1979—the last class before women were admitted to the academy—celebrated its 20th reunion. Known by their self-assigned initials, L.C.W.B., for Last Class With Balls or Last Class Without Bitches, the '79 graduates walked around campus with the letters printed on their hats. At the football game that weekend, L.C.W.B. was triumphantly flashed on the scoreboard for all 54,000 spectators to see. The graduates even spelled out L.C.W.B. in huge letters on a hillside visible from the Terrazzo. At first, Sharon Fullilove, who was a freshman that fall, didn't know what L.C.W.B. meant. "You'd ask people and finally they'd tell you. It was so ridiculous that they were proud of that. Unfortunately, it seems like the rest of the military is progressing and the Air Force Academy is stuck in 1965."

Sharon also noticed that the male cadets frequently accused the women of being products of affirmative action. "Guys would always say, 'A perfectly good male candidate didn't get in because of you.' " The fact that female cadets usually outpaced their male counterparts in both academic and military rankings never seemed to make a difference. In the spring of 1999, for example, 60.3 percent of the female seniors made the dean's list, whereas only 47.6 percent of the male seniors did. A higher percentage of women—39 versus 31—also made the commandant's list, which scores military performance.

Jeanette LeBlanc, an army veteran with a Ph.D. in management and administration, worked at the academy's Center for Character Development, serving for more than a year in the late 90s as the chief of human-relations-program evaluation. After conducting a series of "climate surveys" of the campus social environment, she came away with the strong impression that many of the male cadets believed the female cadets were receiving preferential treatment and benefiting from quotas. "A vast majority of the guys think these women are on their turf and are not as deserving."

Every year, without fail, the climate surveys would show a startlingly high rate of resentment and harassment of women cadets. In 2002, 63 percent of women respondents said they were the subject of derogatory comments or jokes by other cadets based on their gender. Thirty-four percent said they were avoided or shunned by other cadets because of their gender, and 57 percent felt generally discriminated against. When LeBlanc had tabulated the results of her 1998 survey (similar to those in 2002), she says she was shocked by the extent of the negative gender climate. But when she briefed the academy's superintendent and commandant on the survey, they seemed unfazed.

The Fowler panel has analyzed the climate surveys and concluded that on average one in five male cadets believes women do not belong at the academy. On the 2002 survey one cadet wrote, "Even with women in the Armed Forces, they should not be at the military academies." Another noted, "Women are worthless and should be taken away from the USAFA." As Tillie Fowler pointed out at a hearing, the cadets surveyed in 2002 hadn't even been born when the first class of women graduated from the academy. "These young men have no memory of an Air Force Academy without women, yet somehow they believe it should be that way," she said. "The warning signs were there but went unnoticed or were ignored." Indeed, the previous academy administration had dismissed the surveys because they were deemed statistically inaccurate.

The irony is that the air force is considered the most women-friendly of the military branches. "The air force has the highest percentage of women, and virtually all of its positions are open to women, including fighter pilots—the most prestigious," says Dr. Laura Miller, a military sociologist at the Rand Corporation. Miller, who studies the integration of women into the military, also served on the Fowler panel. "The air force," she says, "offers the nicest living conditions for its members, is more family-friendly than the navy, which sends sailors to sea for extended periods of time, and its jobs tend to contrast sharply with the heavy-labor grunt positions in the army and Marines." The incidence of rape at the academy, Miller believes, has nothing to do with the more corporate culture of the air force versus that of the navy, army, or Marines. "The real issue here is that the institution failed to respond to legitimate complaints. Inaction or, even worse, blaming the victim creates a climate in which rape, harassment, and general denigration of all women can flourish."

But the greater opportunities for women in the air force could be the very reason for the backlash female cadets feel at the academy. Women are a clear threat to the hidebound, male-dominated world of airmen. "The beau ideal at the Air Force Academy is to be a fighter pilot," observes General Bunting. "That person is deeply resentful of women who fly fighter aircraft." Says Lory Manning, a retired navy captain who studies issues involving women in the military, "The more accessible the jobs, the fiercer the protection."

By January 2000, Sharon Fullilove was at her parents' air-force-issued house on the academy grounds—a basket case. She slept all day, fell into random fits of tears, and quickly gained 30 pounds. It wasn't until March that Sharon finally confirmed her mother's suspicion. She told her that a two-degree in her squadron whom Sharon knew and trusted had taken her for a drive, pulled off a remote road, locked the car, and raped her.

Sharon explained that she didn't want to report the rape at the time, because she thought she would be forced to leave the academy. During basic training, at a sexual-assault-awareness briefing, some academy graduates had taken Sharon and a group of her classmates aside and told them, "If you get raped, don't tell anyone, because they'll find a way to get you kicked out." Sharon took the advice seriously. "I decided I would stay and not tell anybody," she said later. "The only thing I ever wanted to do was fly planes and so I tried to forget about it." But two days after she was attacked, when her rapist came to her room in an attempt to smooth things over, she realized that she would not be able to bury her fear.

Now that Sharon had left the academy, her mother argued that she didn't have anything to lose by reporting the rape. Moreover, by identifying her rapist, she might prevent him from assaulting other cadets. Micki took Sharon to the academy's Office of Special Investigations (O.S.I.), the equivalent of an in-house F.B.I., where Sharon was questioned for several hours by two investigators. "I had to type out my statement, and after I was done, they told me I had made the whole thing up," Sharon recalls. "Then they went into the hall and told my mother I was a liar because my story didn't match my stepfather's statement." What on earth did that mean?

It turned out that earlier that week, when Micki had called Gary at Wright-Patterson Air Force Base, in Ohio, where he was stationed as a reservist, to tell him that Sharon had been raped, she had not passed on the details. Enraged by the news, Gary went straight to Wright-Patterson's O.S.I. office. "I need some leadership here. I've got a big problem," Gary said. He was initially encouraged by the investigators' response. "We want to get this creep," they told him. "Now please write a statement telling us what happened." Gary said that he could not do that, because he didn't know any of the details. The agents talked him into writing a statement that Gary described as "pure speculation." He refused to sign the piece of paper.

When Sharon's story didn't check out with her stepfather's sketchy version of events, an O.S.I. agent told Micki he suspected Sharon was making the story up so that she could get back into the academy. "He asked why we couldn't afford to send her to a civilian college," recalls Micki. "It became apparent right off the bat that they were after her." A few weeks later, the investigation ended, and the Shafers never saw the report.

Micki—officially, Colonel Shafer—went on a mission. "I tried to talk to the superintendent, General Oelstrom, but he wouldn't see me. So I met with Brigadier General Mark Welsh, who was the commandant"—the academy's second-in-command. "My kids went to the same school as his kids. I spent two and a half hours in his office explaining what had happened to Sharon, and he never acknowledged that it was a problem on-campus beyond Sharon. He was sympathetic, but at one point he told me that I should get help," meaning psychiatric counseling. Micki became more and more frustrated and angry. "I would tell anybody who would listen what happened to Sharon. I was so sick of the cover-up. People in the military just would not believe that I would talk. They just bury their heads."

Beth Davis was having no better luck getting her story heard. Urged on by the friend to whom she had first unburdened herself, who assured her that it was the right thing to do, and motivated by the desire to protect other female cadets from Chris, Beth finally decided to report what had happened to her. In September 2000 she found herself crying once again as she recounted every sordid detail of the assaults to the agents at the Office of Special Investigations. The academy's victims' advocate, Alma Guzman, was also in tears, as was the O.S.I. commander who grabbed a tissue box and declared, "I'm not supposed to get emotionally involved in these things, but this S.O.B. is going to court. He's going to die."

"He kept preaching this," Beth says, recalling how the commander had announced that he was going to take the case himself because he felt it had to be done right. In fact, the commander did take the case, according to Beth. He interviewed almost 50 people, and computer forensic experts managed to retrieve many of the e-mails Chris had sent Beth. O.S.I.'s probe encouraged her; everything was moving forward. "I felt really good about it," she recalls.

Then, all of a sudden, about six months into the investigation, things started to change. "They brought me in one day and said, 'Chris passed the polygraph test.' I was floored. There were two or three of these agents sitting around a table." Beth noticed that the commander, who had begun the investigation and been so moved by her story, was not there. When they asked her to explain why Chris had passed the test, she theorized he must have convinced himself that the assaults hadn't happened. "They said they wanted me to run through the nature of our relationship prior to the first incident. I felt so odd about it. I felt like I had told them 50,000 times before. They had it in writing. They had my account."

Soon after that meeting, Beth was called in to the O.S.I. once again and given the news: the investigation was being shut down. Despite the e-mails the legal office at the academy had, Beth was told it had deemed the evidence in the case insufficient to prosecute Chris. Beth suspected she wasn't getting the whole story, so she checked with the legal office herself. A lawyer there told her that the office knew nothing about her case. Beth soon learned that the training-group commander, Colonel Alfred "Marty" Coffman, a top academy official who was known around campus for being a tough disciplinarian, had intervened and shut down the case.

"I went to Colonel Coffman," Beth recalls, "and he said that there was insufficient evidence and he thought I would end up looking just as bad as Chris." Beth had made friends with a couple of Chris's classmates in her squadron. One of them had seen some of Chris's e-mails and was so infuriated he offered to go and beat Chris up. Beth had mentioned these friendships to the O.S.I. agent, and now Colonel Coffman informed her that her actions amounted to fraternization. Beth knew that fraternization was not as grave an offense as rape, and that the academy had an amnesty policy dating back to 1993, when 13 female cadets had come forward to say they had been sexually assaulted. The amnesty was intended to protect victims from being punished for rules they may have broken at the time of their rapes. But now she could see that the amnesty policy did not seem to apply in her case.

Coffman punished Beth with three Class D "hits"—the most severe of four levels of offense. The first hit was for alcohol; Beth had known that Chris was buying alcohol for her classmates but had failed to report him. The second hit was for fraternization with an upperclassman. The third was the most unbelievable of all: sex in the dorms. The fact, as Colonel Coffman assured her, that Chris was getting more hits than Beth was cold comfort. Beth left his office in tears and disbelief, dejection quickly turning to rage. If she didn't appeal the punishment, she would be walking "tours"—marching back and forth underneath Vandenberg Hall, rifle on her shoulder, with all the other cadets who had gotten into trouble—every weekend until graduation day.

Nearly a year had passed since Beth made her rape allegation. Her grades had begun to suffer and so too her stamina. When her third year of classes started on August 8, 2001, she didn't go. She realized that she needed some time off, so she applied for an administrative "turnback," a form of leave that would allow her to remain on active duty and wouldn't be a blemish on her record. But when Beth handed in her papers, her A.O.C. (air-officer commander, the officer directly in charge of her squadron) told her that Colonel Coffman objected to her request. Instead of an administrative turnback, he wanted Beth to take a medical turnback. Beth knew that medical turnbacks, unlike administrative ones, gave the academy the opportunity to evaluate the cadet's status and find grounds for a discharge. "Colonel Coffman was almost belligerent about putting me on medical turnback," she says, "and he told me to report immediately to a psychologist on base. The psychologist was on the phone with Colonel Coffman when I walked into his office."

The psychologist casually went down a list of post-traumatic-stress-disorder symptoms and promptly diagnosed Beth with a chronic case as well as with anxiety and depression. "He showed the diagnosis to me, and I said I still didn't understand what was behind a medical turnback. So I went into another room and called an officer friend of mine, who said, 'Beth, he just took your pilot status and probably your commission away from you,' " the reason being that the air force doesn't look kindly on pilots or officers who supposedly suffer from crippling emotional disorders. Beth was furious. "I walked back into the psychologist's office and challenged him. He crumbled, saying, 'Please don't hold it against me—I was just following Colonel Coffman's orders.' " Nevertheless, she was forced to take a medical turnback. (The Pentagon would not make Colonel Coffman or any other official available to discuss specific cases.)

That September, Beth enrolled at the University of Tennessee, in Knoxville, for one semester, purposefully far away from home as well as the academy. Most of her family still did not know what had happened to her, and she didn't want to go home to face them. Meanwhile, a few weeks into the new semester at the academy, the school's medical board convened to evaluate her case under the terms of the medical-turnback protocol, and, finding Beth unfit for cadet status, recommended her for discharge. Beth appealed to the superintendent, and her discharge was repealed, but the damage was done. She knew her hopes of ever sitting in the cockpit of a fighter jet were gone forever.

––––––––––––––––

When change finally came, it came in a relative torrent. In September 2002, Lisa Ballas and Jessica Brakey, two seniors in what had been Sharon and Beth's class, met for the first time at a support group for rape victims set up by the academy's counseling center. "We went around the room and told our stories. All of the cadets were in despair and so frustrated," says Jessica Brakey. "Lisa and I were the only two who were pissed off."

"Aren't you angry he got away?" they asked the other women at the meeting. Jessica was amazed by the sense of defeat in the room, how listless and hopeless the women were. "They had given up on themselves," she recalls. Two years earlier, Jessica says, she had been raped by an upperclassman during field training exercises in a wilderness area. She kept the rape to herself. "I wanted to pretend like it never happened," she said later. It would take two years before she finally reported the rape. By that time, her attacker had already graduated.

After the meeting, Jessica and Lisa—each relieved to have met the other, a woman like herself with enough anger and guts to buck the system—banded together and decided that they would try to find out how many young women at the academy had been raped. Very soon, their list grew to 15 current cadets.

"I had so many people come talk to me and tell me their stories of how they were raped and were afraid to come forward," says Lisa Ballas. "I got tired of hearing them say, 'This happened to me, but I would never report it. You are so strong because you reported it.' They were afraid of getting punished for the rules they had broken at the time of the rape, like drinking—which made me so mad, because rape is a felony."

One of the few cadets who did report a rape during this period was Kira Mountjoy-Pepka. She claimed to have been assaulted the year before by DonCosta Seawell, the star of the academy's boxing team, but had kept the rape a secret for months, until she learned that Seawell had been charged with raping a civilian woman—this, she says, gave her the courage to come forward. But a few days after going to authorities, she was given a class-D hit for being too affectionate with her boyfriend.

Her rape case was dropped due to the lack of physical evidence—she had not had a rape examination performed directly after the assault. Later, after she asked the academy to enforce a no-contact order against Seawell (who, she claims, threatened her), she was called into the office of Colonel John "Lucky" Rivers, the vice commandant of cadets. "He told me I was a 'promiscuous little slut' and inferred that I deserved what had happened to me," she recalls. (In October 2002, Seawell pleaded guilty to one charge of "forcible sodomy" in the case involving the civilian woman and was sentenced to two years in a military jail.)

Lisa Ballas, meanwhile, had taken her rape case much further than most. When she was allegedly raped by a cadet named Max Rodriguez at an off-campus party in October 2001, during her junior year, she went to the hospital the next morning, had a rape examination, and reported the incident to academy authorities. Her case got as far as an Article 32 hearing, the military equivalent of a grand-jury proceeding, but the case was later dropped.

Lisa had lobbied the new commandant of cadets, Brigadier General Taco Gilbert, a '78 academy graduate, to take her case further and convene a court-martial. Gilbert agreed to meet with her, but instead of letting her state her case, he took the opportunity to berate Lisa. He told her that her behavior on the night of the alleged rape, when she had been drinking and playing strip poker, was "wrong and won't be tolerated." According to Lisa, he told her, "If I had my way, you'd be marching tours right next to Cadet Rodriguez." The officer said Lisa was responsible for her own actions that night: "You didn't have to go to the party, didn't have to drink that night, didn't have to play the card game, and didn't have to follow him into the bathroom." Lisa responded with "You know what, sir? He didn't have to rape me."

After the meeting with Gilbert, Lisa, who had grown up on an air-force base, and whose father was a '71 academy graduate, became deeply disillusioned with the system. "My whole world turned upside down. There was a huge paradigm shift in the wrong direction. I didn't know what was right anymore, what was real anymore." After exhausting all channels up and down the chain of command and not seeing any hope that changes would be made, Lisa and Jessica took a leap of faith and went public.

On October 29, 2002, Jessica clicked Send on an e-mail aimed at 150 media and government addresses. The e-mail read:

Dear Sir or Ma'am:

I am a senior at the air force academy . . . and since I have been here I know of many females who have been sexually assaulted (including myself) . . . and the academy has done close to nothing to provide recourse, assistance or aid to the victims. . . . The program they do have is inadequate, and fact is most girls who are raped end up leaving on their own after being "pushed out" by the system, or if they choose to stay endure so much political garbage that most of the time it deters them from reporting at all. The office of special investigations here has been known to purposely and negligently foil necessary evidence for rape victims . . . all in the name of protecting the academy's reputation. Is there anything that can be done? Can your office help some how? Thank you for your time.

The following Sunday morning, November 3, Jeff Harris and Kurt Silver, investigative producers for KMGH-TV, in Denver, drove south for an hour and a half to Colorado Springs. Though they were skeptical of Jessica's e-mail, the producers were curious to see if her story had legs. They sat down for breakfast at Mimi's Café with Jessica and Lisa. The two young women were noticeably nervous. Going to the press, Jessica told Harris, was "career suicide." Harris felt instantly that they had both been victimized. "You just knew it," he says. "There were things at the surface that were very painful to both of them." The two cadets told the producers that they were not the only ones; the other rape victims were just too scared to talk.

Together with the station's investigative reporter John Ferrugia,

Harris and Silver dedicated the next three months to tracking down current and former female cadets all over the country. Their goal was to find as many rape victims as possible to show that Lisa's and Jessica's were not isolated cases. "We thought that the story was not just about sexual assault at the academy," says Ferrugia. "The issue was: What does this mean systemically?" Ferrugia remembers making cold calls to women who had left the academy, introducing himself, explaining the project, "and before I could finish I would hear sobs on the other end of the line, and the woman saying, 'I thought I was the only one. I never thought anyone would believe me.' " In three months, Ferrugia, Harris, and Silver got similar accounts from 11 alleged victims of sexual assault. "What amazed me," recalls Ferrugia, "was that their stories were exactly the same."

When he finished his investigation in late January, Ferrugia contacted Colorado Republican senator Wayne Allard for comment. Allard, who serves on the Senate Armed Services Committee as well as the academy's Board of Visitors—the equivalent of a board of trustees—had been watching the academy closely; indeed, his staff had spoken to Beth Davis just a few days before Ferrugia's call. The problem, Ferrugia explained to Allard, was much bigger than just one or two isolated cases. On February 12, KMGH-TV aired the first in a series of three long pieces on the Air Force Academy. The first story, featuring Beth Davis, Jessica Brakey, and Lisa Ballas, ran 14 minutes—an eternity in television news. The piece closed with Allard and Senate Armed Services Committee chairman John Warner, an unlikely pair of conservative champions for women's issues, pledging to launch a major Pentagon inquiry into the allegations. [Allard was a senator until 2009 and has since become a lobbyist.]

That same week, by coincidence, Allard hired Victoria Broerman to help with health-care issues at his Colorado Springs office. Broerman, 38, a former emergency-room nurse, had spent much of her career counseling rape victims. Her arrival in Allard's office could not have been more perfectly timed, for just as Broerman had finished learning to operate the photocopier and placed a picture of her four daughters on her desk, the senator's phone started ringing off the hook. Ignited by Ferrugia's story, Air Force Academy cadets and alumnae were calling from all over the country, wanting to tell their stories.

The first calls came from graduates who had kept their secret for years. "When those women cadets went public, it was amazing to me that they had the courage to do it," says an '87 academy graduate who says she called Allard's office to report the rape she had experienced as a freshman. "There was such a code of silence for so many years, and they really blew it open." This particular graduate, who does not want to reveal her name, had endured the code of silence for two decades. When she returned to the academy in the 1990s as a faculty member, she found herself consoling several of her students who had also been raped.

Soon, word got out that Broerman had experience with rape victims and was a trained, sympathetic ear. Current cadets began to call, sometimes as many as six a day. Overnight, Allard's office became an ad hoc clearinghouse for information about academy rape victims. Other senators and representatives who had been working on isolated cases involving cadets who lived in their states sought help from the powerful Armed Services Committee member. Broerman and Andrew Merritt, Allard's state director, met with cadets and their families and began collecting drawerfuls of investigation reports and interview transcripts.

At an official event in Colorado Springs, just the sight of Senator Allard's name printed on the tag on Broerman's chest sparked a startling conversation. "A man introduced himself to me and told me that he was an academy grad, and his daughter also went there and was raped," Broerman recalls. "His daughter is an air-force pilot now, and her father confessed to me that he had advised her not to report the rape, because he knew how much she wanted to fly. Tears were falling down his face as he told me, 'I've lived with this burden for too many years.' " By September 2003, Allard's office had been contacted by 38 former cadets, 23 current cadets, and one civilian, all of whom said they had been raped by Air Force Academy men.

Any benefit from this outpouring would come too late for Jessica

Brakey, who by the time she sent her October e-mail was already on her way out of the academy. Stress from the rape, she says, had caused her to unravel emotionally, exacerbating problems that dated back to a turbulent childhood. An air-force psychiatrist had diagnosed her with a personality disorder, she was on academic probation, and she had been arrested by police for fighting with her boyfriend. Three days after she sent her e-mail, Jessica was forced to leave the academy with an honorable discharge. Lisa Ballas, who was in her final semester before graduation when the first news reports hit, turned out to be one of the victims who benefited from the publicity. "I got the looks and a lot of people were not talking to me," says Lisa. "But as far as overt retaliation, nothing happened. A lot of people said I did the most protective thing I could have done by talking to the press."

In March 2003, the top four academy commanders were "reassigned," and a new team moved in, charged with cleansing and changing the culture of the academy. When Brigadier General Johnny Weida, a decorated Thunderbird pilot, took over as acting superintendent, this past April, he began implementing a nine-page manifesto handed down by the secretary of the air force called the "Agenda for Change."

Weida's first step was altering the four-class system. The class of 2007, which started basic training in June, will have doolie status only until Thanksgiving, no longer through March. Doolies will not be trained exclusively by the three-degrees. Now seniors, trusted for their maturity and experience, will be in charge of the newcomers. "We have to teach them from day one what's a lawful order and what's an unlawful order. What's a professional relationship and what's an unprofessional relationship," Weida said last spring in an interview in his office, with its picture window overlooking snowcapped mountains and its walls festooned with photographs, paintings, and drawings of F-16s. "We have to do everything we can to prevent the coercive use of power. If there is anything in the environment that is subtly telling female cadets that they are not an equal part of the wing, it creates a culture that allows for sexual predators. . . . I say fix it, ruthlessly enforce our standards, and don't tolerate anything."

Weida and his number two, Colonel Debra Gray, the vice commandant of cadets, adopted the standards for handling rape cases that are used in the active-duty air force and at the other two military academies, which require rape victims to report to the chain of command. After the 1993 sexual-assault scandal, the Air Force Academy changed its policy by giving rape victims the choice of whether or not to report the crime. While this exception to military guidelines had benefits in that it gave power back to the victim and allowed her to preserve her anonymity, in the end it also allowed for rapes to go underreported and underinvestigated. "This is a crime, not an infraction," says Colonel Gray, who heads a new response team that meets every week to go over sexual-assault cases. "The old system handled the information in such a closed environment that no one knew who needed help," she says. "My goal is to take the shroud off this process." A compromise proposed by the Fowler panel that would allow for victim-therapist confidentiality is being adopted.

Colonel Bill "Trapper" Carpenter, the director of admissions for the past three years, acknowledges that the culture of the academy may not change until more women join the cadet ranks. "Service academies are tough, masculine environments," Carpenter, a '73 academy graduate, said in May. It's hardly a surprise that the Air Force Academy has had a hard time keeping its female cadets: through the 1990s, women dropped out at a rate of 33 percent, versus 28 percent for men, despite the fact that the women routinely performed better academically.

"I'd like to bring the percentage of women at the academy up to 25 percent," says Carpenter. That would equal the percentage of new female recruits for the air force at large; 25 percent of today's air-force R.O.T.C. candidates are also women. "I'm no expert at integration, but the more women we have the better," says Carpenter. "There is a cadet squadron right now with only two female doolies. What kind of environment is that? And how many [of the 36 total] A.O.C.'s are female right now? None. We need to have more role models out there."

Another of the Agenda for Change items that General Weida began enforcing requires air-officer commanders to get a master's degree in counseling. The A.O.C.'s are usually fighter pilots, and as the saying goes, "In the air force we man equipment—in the army we equip men." What that means is that, unlike in the army and the navy, where young officers lead troops or sailors, most air-force officers are in charge of manning planes, which doesn't necessarily equip them with the human skills they need for handling the problems of college-age students. (This is not to say that West Point and Annapolis do not have their share of problems with sexual harassment and sexual assault. A 1995 survey of the three academies by the General Accounting Office indicated that 80 percent of the women students at West Point and 70 percent at Annapolis had experienced sexual harassment on a recurring basis. The Defense Department inspector general is investigating the way all three military academies handle rape cases.)

Meanwhile, the Air Force Academy has stepped up its prosecution of current rape cases, and three are now pending. But the air force has recently admitted that 16 graduates who were accused of sexual assaults are currently serving as officers in the military. For current male cadets, the new scrutiny is disorienting. "There have been so many changes," cadet Ian Holt said with a sigh in early May during an interview in the academy library, "that I'm almost numb to them." Holt and many of his fellow cadets have reacted angrily to the bad press that has besmirched the name of their school and the reputations of its male cadets. Morale on-campus appears to be at an all-time low. "A lot of us feel like we are getting picked on by the press," said Holt. Adds Cadet David Vincent, "I feel like we've all been labeled as rapists. Maybe 1 percent are rapists, but unfortunately they are the ones who get represented by the media." Other cadets have reacted to the scandal with shock and disgust. "I find it weak and pathetic to have to coerce sex," says Ryan Roper. "You are not a man if you have to do that."

In July, with the Agenda for Change largely in place, acting superintendent General Weida stepped down and the school's new leader,

Lieutenant General John W. Rosa Jr., also a decorated fighter pilot, was sworn in. In September, the Fowler panel issued a blistering report to Donald Rumsfeld and to the Senate and House Armed Services Committees. After 90 days of research, the panel concluded that a serious failure of leadership "helped create an environment in which sexual assault became a part of life at the Academy." The panel also accused the earlier air-force general-counsel investigation of failing to hold anyone accountable and attempting to "shield Air Force Headquarters from public criticism." Blame was laid for the first time squarely on the heads of the former top four members of the academy administration.

While Congress decides whether or not to hold Secretary Roche ultimately responsible, and the Pentagon decides whether or not to discipline the academy's previous leadership, a group of seven alleged rape victims are considering filing a lawsuit against the institution. The former cadets have hired Jim Cox, a litigator in the Atlanta office of Greenberg Traurig, a firm that represented victims of sexual abuse in cases involving the Catholic Church, and Joseph J. Madonia, an entertainment lawyer and litigator from Chicago. "Our clients have lost their education and their military careers," says Cox. "They don't have jobs, they don't have counseling, their lives have been shattered." Adds Madonia, "It's time for them to get help putting their lives back together, and if it takes a lawsuit, then we'll do it."

Beth Davis, who is now engaged to be married to a civilian pilot and is living with her parents in Maryland, found that she was spending so much time fighting for her cause that she could no longer keep up with the classes she was taking at a local community college. She has yet to re-enroll.

Sharon Fullilove was at the University of Arizona studying to become an orthodontist, but could not afford the out-of-state tuition this fall and had to leave. The betrayal by her beloved academy is still hard to stomach. "It's a terrible feeling when someone does this to you and gets away with it, and then you report it and the system punishes you. It's almost worse than the actual act, that the system failed you."

"As a female officer," says her mother, Colonel Shafer, "I feel responsible to these girls who will get hurt. I can't get through to their mothers to tell them not to send their daughters to the academy." As for her daughter, who after three years of emotional instability has made a good recovery, "you're so happy to have your kid back, but you know they'll never be the same."

Jessica Brakey currently lives with a cousin in Denver and is working as a telemarketer. She sees herself as a sacrificial lamb. Reporting her rape and going public hurt her career, she believes, but she hopes she has helped other victims.

Lisa Ballas has remained in the air force. She graduated from the academy last May and is now attending an air-force flight school in Pensacola, Florida. She wants to fly an F-15E. "I would be honored to die for my country," she says. "That's my job. As far as I'm concerned, it's an occupational hazard."

POSTSCRIPT

(*Vanity Fair*, December 2006)

After Bingham's story hit newsstands, the Defense Department issued a report that blamed the scandal on eight high-ranking air-force officers and two legal counsel, but the brass were vindicated on the basis that they had not intentionally ignored red flags. However, the accountability issue was simultaneously addressed in a Pentagon-ordered review of the military's sexual-misconduct policy, and the findings determined that the D.O.D. needed a single point of responsibility. And so the Sexual Assault Prevention and Response Office was established.

Meanwhile, the Pentagon surveyed 4,200 military-academy students and midshipmen and discovered that only one-third of sexual assaults were reported to authorities. (Many victims feared punishment for assault-related behavior, such as under-age drinking, due to the military's mandatory reporting procedure.) Subsequently, the Defense

Department adopted a confidential policy, which enables victims to seek help without triggering disciplinary action.

And how has the Air Force Academy transformed? "It really boils down to two things," says Colonel Gail Colvin, the academy's vice commandant for strategic programs. "One is that we've launched a very successful, intensive education campaign that we hope results in [both] the prevention of any sexual assault and also in a cultural change. And then secondly . . . when an assault occurs, our primary focus is now on victim care." The changes seem to be working.

"THE PREP SCHOOL AND THE PREDATOR"

By Evgenia Peretz

MARCH 2015

It was the kind of article that might have gone unnoticed. Last summer, Mikaela Gilbert-Lurie, a sophomore at the University of Pennsylvania, posted a personal essay on the Web site xoJane.com, about a flirtation with a certain, unnamed English teacher at a certain unnamed high school. The relationship had culminated, she wrote, in the teacher's professing how attracted he was to her and touching her knee. When she complained to school administrators, all they did was require the teacher to undergo counseling. The essay was not long, the details scant, but within a day or two it went viral among graduates of Marlborough School, an elite all-girls private school in Hancock Park, Los Angeles, that for 126 years has been educating the girls of California's most prominent families—with such last names as Spielberg,

Goldwyn, Bloomingdale, Ahmanson, Booth (of the *Los Angeles Times*), and Munger (of Berkshire Hathaway). To the girls reading the article, there was no doubt about it. She was talking about Dr. Joseph Koetters, now 47, who had been head of the school's English department.

Eight other girls contacted Mikaela via Facebook with their own stories about Koetters. The basic pattern, according to the girls: he validated as brilliant their insights into human nature while pitting them against one another for his affection, bitching about his wife (a Santa Monica gynecologist) and kids, and finding reasons to have private meetings, which often climaxed with him putting his hand on a girl's knee. His yearbook photo shows a doughy blond resembling Conan O'Brien side-kick Andy Richter. But in person he evidently oozed charisma.

BuzzFeed broke the story about these girls (who remain anonymous), and the *Los Angeles Times* followed. Among current Marlborough parents, who came of age mostly in the 70s and 80s, the reaction, says one, "was 'Big whoop. These are 16- and 17-year-old girls. They're flirtatious and dramatic.' " But with sex abuse on campus dominating the national headlines, the school had a potential crisis on its hands. The board of trustees put together a "special investigative committee," consisting of five of its own members, that would look into and resolve the crisis.

Instead, everything went wrong. The committee noted that the investigation revealed a "pattern of misconduct by Joe Koetters," but it pinned the blame for how it was handled on one individual—Barbara Wagner, the beloved head of the school for 26 years. Meanwhile it absolved the board of all responsibility and downplayed the most explosive episode, which was far more damaging than anyone had imagined. The Marlborough community descended into name-calling, accusations of a cover-up, threats to withhold donations, and "gallons of tears. I've never been involved in such a firestorm," says investor and newspaper executive J. P. Guerin, 85, who belongs to one of the families (along with the Mungers and Booths) that are among the most generous donors to the school.

A sk most people who feel a strong connection to Marlborough and they will cite Barbara Wagner as the linchpin of their loyalty. Under her watch, the school became one of the best in the country. Thirty-seven percent of last year's graduating class was accepted by Ivy League colleges or Stanford, and the school ranked sixth for S.A.T. scores nationwide. By the accounts of her legions of fans, Wagner is awe-inspiring—polished, always on point, and tirelessly supportive of the 530 girls (grades 7 through 12) in her charge, stopping them in the halls to see if they need anything, or making last-minute calls while vacationing in far-flung areas of the globe to help get a student off a college wait list. Among the parents I spoke with, she drew comparisons to Hillary Clinton, "a mix of a Fortune 500 C.E.O. and supportive mother," and "the Dalai Lama." She treated the girls like her own daughters, say these sources, instilling in them a sense of empowerment. Integral to this approach was encouraging students to have strong one-on-one relationships with their teachers.

But some of those relationships, it now appears, crossed a line. For Mikaela Gilbert-Lurie, the flirtation with Koetters, she says, began during her junior year in 2011, when she e-mailed him, asking if she could interview him for an article she was writing for the school paper. "It's a date," he replied to his star student. According to e-mails obtained by BuzzFeed, he told her to be prepared for "evasive, non-committal answers which will invite gifts and favors that will seek to lure you into complicity in highly questionable endeavors."

"I'm a journalist," she wrote back. "I was born ready for that."

"Ahhh . . . then this could be quite special . . . possibly quite spectacular . . . the anticipation itself is quite tantalizing."

During one of their meetings, she says, he put his hand on her knee—his signature move. Though it made her uncomfortable, the e-mail exchange got more charged. Mikaela wrote him that she found herself at a "loss of words" in his presence and suggested that "with

time and, well something else, I'll get less self conscious around you."
He replied that "that inscrutable something else lingers in the air." During their next meeting, he told her that he was usually good at creating boundaries, but with her he just couldn't. Maybe it was the short skirt of her uniform that drove him so crazy. Alarmed, she told him in an e-mail that perhaps they could be "friends" later, and that she wanted to focus on her studying. He wrote back, "Ugh. Ok." But it wasn't O.K. According to Mikaela, Koetters started acting out, kicking her out of class one day and making provocative comments such as "You would never have gotten an A on that paper if it wasn't for your pretty eyes." Koetters was suddenly no longer a schoolgirl crush to Mikaela—he was a threat.

Mikaela was afraid to come forward because she felt ashamed by what she viewed as her complicity. But her brother persuaded her to show the e-mails to her parents, Leslie Gilbert-Lurie, a writer and philanthropist, and Cliff Gilbert-Lurie, a prominent entertainment lawyer who has represented, among others, Sandra Bullock. They sent the e-mails to the head of the upper school, Laura Hotchkiss. Wagner soon invited Mikaela and her parents into her office to discuss the situation. Leslie recalls, "She certainly *seemed* to take the situation seriously. She took notes. She said she would get back to us."

The Gilbert-Luries asked if any previous complaints had been made about Koetters. Wagner replied that there had not been, neglecting to mention that seven years earlier, in 2005, another girl had made similar complaints. At the time, Wagner hadn't given credence to them.

Wagner brought the matter to the attention of John Emerson, then the president of the board of trustees and an Obama fund-raiser. There was no policy in place about how to handle such allegations, but having worked as Gary Hart's deputy national campaign manager and Bill Clinton's California campaign manager in 1992, Emerson probably knew a thing or two about damaging accusations of sexual misconduct. According to Guerin, a Wagner confidant, Barbara's recollections were that Emerson told her that the board need not be informed, and that the situation should be handled internally. It was decided that Koetters would not be fired. Instead, it was decided, after consulting with Marlborough's legal counsel, that Koetters would be stripped of his department chairmanship and required to undergo sexual-harassment sensitivity training and to cease interacting with Mikaela, who would be moved to another English class.

Wagner informed Mikaela's parents of the consequences Koetters would face. But Koetters violated the guidelines by going into Mikaela's new English classroom and staring at her. Leslie recalls, "At one point I remember saying to Barbara, 'Mikaela still feels uncomfortable.' I said, 'How many conversations have you had with Joe Koetters about this situation to see how he's doing?,' and she said, 'Several.' And I said, 'How many have you had with Mikaela?' And she said, 'I'm not sure.' I said, 'Well, that's why Mikaela feels that she is not cared about in this situation.' . . . We felt like his comfort and well-being were taken into account ahead of our daughter's."

Koetters stayed on through the 2013 school year and was allowed to quietly leave to take a job in the English department at Polytechnic, a prep school in Pasadena. Marlborough told Polytechnic that the Mikaela business was an isolated incident.

PLACING BLAME

The Marlborough board's investigation into the events, the following summer, was led by two legal powerhouses: Christine Ewell, president of the board and a judge for the Los Angeles County Superior Court, and her friend and former boss, fellow trustee Debra Wong Yang, a partner at the law firm Gibson, Dunn & Crutcher. Yang's recent investigations included interviewing her good friend New Jersey governor Chris Christie as part of the internal review of Bridgegate which he himself ordered, and which cleared him and his current staffers of any wrongdoing. Backing them up on the Marlborough committee were more lawyers—Katherine Marik Thompson and Michael Gendler, an entertainment attorney—as well as financial consultant Michael Parks.

After five months, the committee issued its findings in an eight-page letter, signed by Ewell and Yang, to the members of the school community. The letter lauded its transparency. "It is only those institutions that conduct periodic and thorough self-examinations that can learn and improve over time." It was then announced that Wagner had "requested to resign effective June 30, 2015," and that the board accepted her resignation, apparently based on how she had handled Mikaela's case and failed to connect it to the similar complaint made in 2005. In reporting on the events of 2012, the letter acknowledged that Wagner had consulted with the president of the board and that there was no policy in place about how she was supposed to handle the situation. But the authors omitted entirely the name of former board head John Emerson, now the U.S. ambassador to Germany, and his role in handling the Koetters situation and that he chose to keep his own board in the dark. Which seems to leave only one mistake that could legitimately be placed at Wagner's feet: her neglecting to connect Mikaela's complaint to the one made in 2005.

The letter was viewed by many as an obfuscating, tone-deaf document. The bit about Wagner's choosing to resign struck many readers as nonsense—Wagner, they sensed, was pushed out because *someone's* head had to roll. Furious letters from parents, alumnae, and former board members poured into the school. "It is so like her [Barbara] to take upon herself all the blame even when there are others who should be held accountable," wrote past board chair Susie Donnelly. "It is clear to me that this statement was for the sake of distracting your readers from the fact that the Board Chair should have taken the information to the Board or to the Board's executive committee. Indeed, it is obvious that proper policies were not in place; that is not the fault of the Head of School. It is the fault of the Board! This grievous omission from your letter was a cover-up of your very own Board action. . . . Your omission of the Board Chair's name, John Emerson, is cowardly. . . . Your letter should have called out his inexcusable judgment and delivered his personal apology to the Marlborough community. . . . Your moral failure as a Board has brought shame upon Marlborough."

Sarah Gee, an alumna and daughter of a former board member, wrote, "It is unforgivable that you refuse to acknowledge your dysfunction and failure as the Board of Trustees and instead place improper blame on the very individual who has done more for Marlborough than any other single person in its history."

A recent graduate, who had pledged $75,000, wrote that she was considering sending her money elsewhere. "The real sex scandal here, in my opinion? How the Marlborough Board of Trustees just fucked the Marlborough community."

The special committee stood by its actions in singling out Wagner, however, and continued to tout its "transparency." Yet after *Vanity Fair* questioned Debra Wong Yang on key issues—such as Wasn't John Emerson at least partially culpable by advising Wagner how the matter should be handled? Why didn't he notify the board? Why is his name omitted from the report?—she had no comment.

And for all its talk about self-examination, the committee obfuscated the one story about Koetters and Marlborough that was the most scandalous. Within the eight pages, there's a passing reference to another girl, who was at Marlborough in the early 2000s, with whom Koetters engaged in "inappropriate physical conduct." The "inappropriate physical conduct" was, according to a former student, a full-blown sexual affair with her when she was a minor that resulted in her becoming pregnant.

ABUSE OF POWER

Holly, as we'll call her, kept her story secret for more than a decade. But when she read Mikaela's story, she thought it was time to deal with the damaging events she'd kept bottled up for so long. The seduction, she says, was incremental. It began in the fall semester of her junior year, with a paper on *Hamlet* she was struggling over. She was then 16. Koetters suggested they meet in private. One meeting led to another. During one, out on the lawn, he took it to another, thrilling level by putting his hand on her knee. "He made me feel like the smartest, funniest, most beautiful person walking the planet," says Holly over dinner near her office. Her demeanor is cool and standoffish, but the fragility is right there beneath the surface. By spring semester, she says, she was accepting invitations to hang out at Koetters's house, while his wife was at work. Soon, she says, they were having sex regularly. She was terrified that they'd be discovered, but he coached her through it, framing the affair, she says, as "fuck society, fuck social norms. This is something special, and we're entitled to pursue it as human beings. I was like, Sign me up. . . . I bought into the notion that our relationship was meant to exist in a little unconstrained bubble."

One day, during her senior year, all that changed. Holly had been late with her period—and, she says, a pregnancy test confirmed her worry. She went to his house to tell Koetters the news. "I remember sitting in his house, at the bottom of the stairs, shaking uncontrollably," she recalls. Koetters became clinical. He was intent on "handling it" and would make all the arrangements for her to get an abortion. "In the span of an hour, I went from being a cool, confident woman to being a kid. I was like, 'Fuck. I'm so in over my head. I've dug the deepest grave. I've never felt so small.' " As it happened, she miscarried two and a half months into her pregnancy.

Throughout it all—from the affair to the pregnancy to the miscarriage—Holly told no one. "I thought it was all my fault," she explains, despite the fact that she was a minor at the time. "The consequences of telling were unbearable." Though she ended up at a top college, "I came out of Marlborough the most self-loathing, self-destructive person ever." She has gone on to achieve professional success, but emotionally the last decade of her life has been defined by the damage Koetters caused. "If I have the capacity to bury something of that significance, I'm terrified of myself."

When she read Mikaela's article, Holly felt ill. She had e-mailed Koetters back in 2009, after she'd heard a rumor that he was involved with another girl, and he had denied it, writing back, "No . . . not even close. . . . I'm sorta flattered you could have heard such a thing about a fat old dude." Now, in 2014, with Mikaela's article, she had what she believed was evidence that he was a serial predator. She e-mailed him again: "Figured you were lying," she wrote. He replied that Mikaela's article was "full of lies." She contacted Mikaela, whom she didn't know, telling her that Koetters's actions were way worse than Mikaela knew. Mikaela told her about all the other girls she'd heard from. Holly was suddenly hit with an epiphany. "I'm old enough to be disgusted by how young a 16-year-old looks, and holy shit, I'm one of [many]? This is crazy. I was preyed upon and it wasn't my fault. . . . They're kids. I have to do something." She and Mikaela went to see the new head of Poly-technic to inform him of their respective stories. Holly says he planned to file a police report. Later that day, Koetters resigned.

Holly had only started releasing her rage. She wrote a letter to Bar-bara Wagner, in which she finally shared her entire Koetters story and castigated Marlborough for failing to protect Mikaela and the other girls like her: "I have been horrified to learn about all of it—how many girls Koetters has targeted, how poorly the school treated those willing to speak up, and—perhaps worst of all—that confronted with the knowl-edge that Koetters is a severely perverted and dangerous man, Marlbor-ough allowed him to preserve his career and reputation, and sat idly as he transitioned to Poly." (Koetters declined to comment.)

She added her own *mea culpa*: "I may never forgive myself—in a way my silence has made me complicit in allowing such a decrepit human being to continue his outrageously criminal behavior. For all Marlbor-ough taught me to stick my neck out, speak my mind, and act as a just and moral leader in my community, I have failed. But I'm no longer going to plow through this with my head down." Wagner promptly called her, sounding earnest, Holly recalls, and said that she too would need to file a report with the L.A.P.D. But Holly was in no state to feel it was enough. Last September, she sought out David M. Ring, California's go-to lawyer for victims of sexual abuse.

To Holly, it's pathetic, yet not surprising, that the committee would characterize her story in its report as "inappropriate physical conduct," given that they made minimal effort to contact her. "I never got any sense that Marlborough was interested in what she had to say," says Ring. "The school and its investigators hoped she would just fade away, that the story would dissipate, and things would then return to 'business as usual' for the school." He adds that the board "found a convenient scapegoat in the head of the school and yet intentionally left everyone with the impression that Koetters simply wrote inappropriate e-mails and made inappropriate comments. The school buried the real facts."

In Holly's view, this was more of the same. "Marlborough had an endemic problem," she claims. "As seventh-graders we knew about student-teacher relationships. There's no way they didn't know. No one is conditioned to think otherwise."

The wreckage at Marlborough is fairly devastating. Any day, the school will be hit with a lawsuit from Holly. Fund-raising efforts are believed to be hurting. Due to how the board handled the matter, "some people will never forgive the school and will change what's in their will or not react positively to the next fund-raising call," says Guerin. "I know all the major givers. They will stay loyal to the school, but it will be less."

Wagner is deeply hurt, presumably cognizant that at age 62 she's considered damaged goods. Finding a major talent to replace her may be tough. "Really competent people [offered the job] would wonder why the board would not support the head more appropriately," says Guerin. "Why would they put their career in the hands of a board they don't trust?"

Many of those who care deeply about Marlborough believe that it can power through, even without Wagner as its guiding light; it's been around for 126 years, after all. A helpful step, some suggest, would be for the chief members of the board to resign. Short of that, a statement acknowledging how badly they mangled things would be welcome. The members might be well served to take a cue from Guerin, Marlborough's longest-serving trustee, who retired from the board in 2008. "I feel some of the blame," he says. "I didn't pay attention to this when I was on the board. We *all* failed to notice that times were changing."

[In April 2015, Holly sued Marlborough. The lawsuit is pending. That October, Koetters pled guilty to charges that he engaged in sex acts with Holly and another girl and was sentenced to a year in jail.]

"ST. GEORGE'S HIDDEN DRAGONS"

By Benjamin Wallace

AUGUST 2016

High-school reunions are fraught occasions under the best of circumstances. Hairlines and waistlines are appraised, marriages and careers compared, insecurities awoken, changes in status noted, old wounds poked: normally solid citizens regress to their adolescent selves.

Then there are the worst of circumstances. Since December, when it broke into the open with a *Boston Globe* article and a televised press conference, St. George's, an elite boarding school in Rhode Island, has been engulfed by a scandal over alleged sexual abuse spanning decades, with at least 40 alleged victims and a dozen alleged staff and student perpetrators. In this, St. George's is only one among a snowballing list of prominent prep schools recently shaken by accusations of abuse, as one after another is forced to reckon with a shameful past. They include

Groton, Horace Mann, Deerfield, St. Paul's, Hotchkiss, Pomfret, Pin-
gry, and Exeter. "Elite boarding schools turn out an outsize number
of societal leaders," says Whit Sheppard, a Deerfield graduate who has
written about being a victim of abuse there and now advises schools on
handling similar crises (including, for a short time, St. George's). "This
is the part of the story that no one wanted to talk about."

Now they are being forced to talk about it. Across the archipelago
of prep schools clustered mainly in the northeastern United States, a
truth-and-reconciliation process is fitfully unfolding as school after
school sends letters to alumni acknowledging past abuse and asking if
they, too, were abused. At St. George's, the process has been especially
tumultuous, with a vocal, mobilized contingent of alumni calling for the
headmaster to resign amid a polarized atmosphere of mistrust. As the
school's annual reunion weekend approached in May, all-out bedlam
threatened to erupt.

In a private Facebook group, various St. George's alumni put forward
suggestions to hold "actions," perhaps cordoning off locations where
abuse had taken place with yellow police tape. One alumna proposed
bringing a gun and burning the place down, upsetting fellow graduates;
the alumna said she'd been joking. There was further talk of chaining
themselves to the school's front gates. After headmaster Eric Peterson
sent a letter to alumni in April announcing that the school would hold a
"Hope for Healing" event during reunion weekend to acknowledge the
abuse that had taken place at the school, some survivors reacted angrily
that Peterson hadn't consulted with them beforehand. Two days later,
the school backtracked and sent out another letter. This one, signed by
board chairman Leslie Bathgate Heaney, said the event would no longer
be held and that the school would consult with survivors about jointly
organizing an alternative event.

In a way, the same critical-thinking skills St. George's prides itself on
teaching had turned against their creator. This is a school that charges
$56,000 in annual tuition and boarding fees, and also one which, like
many of its peers, was founded not merely to educate but to provide

moral instruction, to inculcate that character-forming ethos known as muscular Christianity. Betrayals of the 1970s and 1980s—which among other things were a very expensive and damaging hypocrisy—are now forcing a privileged corner of America to wonder what went wrong. And looming over that question is another, voiced by Hawkins Cramer, principal of an elementary school in Seattle and a 1985 graduate of St. George's, who says he was abused there: "Where were the fucking adults?"

"ST. GORGEOUS"

St. George's has always stood apart from other New England boarding schools by virtue of its magnificent setting on Aquidneck Island, on a peninsula directly across from Newport. On the Hilltop, as the campus is known, a student standing on the columned porch off the main formal tearoom, looking out on the playing fields that slope down to the sea, might easily imagine himself as Jay Gatsby come to life.

St. George's is one of the so-called Saint Grottlesex schools (along with Groton, Middlesex, St. Paul's, and St. Mark's), bastions of the Wasp establishment founded in the late 19th century to educate the sons of the Gilded Age elite. Graduates have included Mellons and Vanderbilts, Bushes and Biddles, Astors and Auchinclosses. It was patterned, like many other American prep schools, on English institutions like Eton and Harrow, and the legacy is visible in the stone neo-Gothic Episcopal chapel that towers over the campus, in the mandatory uniform (coat and tie for boys), in the terminology (9th grade is third form, 12th grade is sixth form).

Over time, St. George's developed a reputation for producing clubbable Establishment heirs more than brainy members of the meritocracy. "It was a school where at one time very wealthy families would send their not so bright kids," says a late-80s graduate. "We're not talking about Nobel Prize winners here," echoes Daniel Brewster, a 1974 graduate. "If you're part of an entity that relies exclusively upon its reputation for its status in the world, that reputation will be protected at all costs. At St. George's, it was built on, frankly, the Social Register of a century ago. Otherwise you went to St. Paul's, Andover, or Exeter." F. Scott Fitzgerald described the students of St. George's as "prosperous and well-dressed," and by the 1970s, the school had acquired the nickname "St. Gorgeous," not only because of the school grounds but also because its admissions policy seemed to select for physical attractiveness.

Anthony Zane looked like he'd stepped out of the sort of oil portrait meant to be hung against wood paneling. Arriving at St. George's in 1972, he was a patrician, old-fashioned headmaster, a hale man of action more than introspection, his Dalmatian always at his side.

After the parents of a St. George's student reported to the school in 1974 that sports-car-driving associate chaplain Howard "Howdy" White had raped their son, Zane expressed shock that the relationship had been more than "paternal." He fired White but also seemed not to fully grasp the harm White had inflicted or the danger he represented. Zane didn't report White to the Rhode Island State Police or the Department of Children, Youth & Families. When White contacted him shortly thereafter, seeking help, Zane responded warmly, saying that he would pay him an additional month's salary and reimburse him for his moving expenses. He did add that "if you find yourself hard pressed in the future I suggest that you consider selling your Porsche. . . . I feel strongly that you should not be in a boarding school and that you should seek psychiatric help." He asked White not to return to St. George's "until one generation has gone through, that is, not for another five years." White didn't return, but he did go on to serve as dean and chaplain at Chatham Hall, a girls' prep school in Virginia, and then as rector at a church in North Carolina from 1984 to 2006; state police are investigating an allegation that he molested a teenage girl there, and the *Providence Journal* located at least one other alleged victim from that period. (White is now retired in Bedford, Pennsylvania, where he is under ecclesiastical review by the Episcopal Church. He has not commented on the allegations.) [White was removed from the Episcopal priesthood in October 2016. That

December, he pleaded not guilty to charges that he sexually assaulted a St. George's boy in 1973. His trial is scheduled to begin in 2017.]

St. George's began admitting girls as boarding students in the fall of 1972, Zane's first semester, but meaningful co-education would have to wait. When Anne Scott arrived as a sophomore five years later, boys still accounted for four-fifths of students. Little effort had been made to increase the number of female faculty, there was no girls' locker room (girls had to change for sports in their dorm rooms), and the culture remained starkly masculine.

The failure to diligently integrate girls was visible in the athletic training room, which despite serving both boys and girls was accessible only via the boys' locker room and was staffed by an older male trainer, Alphonse "Al" Gibbs, a small, gruff navy vet with the smashed nose of a boxer. It was a back wrenched playing field hockey that sent 14-year-old Anne Scott to see 67-year-old Gibbs in October of 1977. "I'll never forget the sound of the lock clicking," she says. Gibbs "would start with something remotely in the guise of treatment and work up from there. He'd change the narrative from treatment and the thing wrong with you to your developing body, as someone who was a helper, a carer of your whole body." Before the month was over, he had raped her, and he continued to do so for nearly two years. "I was that animal in the herd who got isolated out, and he was able to go really far with me." She started calling her parents, crying and wanting to come home, but wouldn't tell them why. She felt trapped. She didn't have the language to say what was happening. ("We're Wasps!") "He'd tell me not to tell anyone—I'd get in trouble." She says she developed an eating disorder and cut herself off from friends, sitting alone for hours in a place she'd found in the woods.

Anne Scott wasn't the only girl targeted by Gibbs. He smeared VapoRub on the chest of Kim Hardy Erskine (class of '80), then a sophomore basketball player, and at practices would "come up to his girls and kiss us in front of everybody, on the lips. He also gave me a gold necklace one year"—a chain with a heart on it. Joan "Bege" Reynolds, a sporty girl from a multi-generational St. George's family, was a 13-year-old freshman when Gibbs told her to undress and get in his whirlpool, groped her legs "up to the private area," smothered her with "really awful hugging and kisses," and took Polaroid photos of her naked under a heat lamp. Katie Wales, a three-sport athlete with a torn-up knee and back, had a similar experience: "He'd show you how to dry off: 'Lift your breasts, dry your private area. Let me make sure you're cleaning yourself properly.' It was awkward. But he has a medical patch on his shirt. He was a highly decorated medic in World War II. You figured he knew what he was doing." She, too, was Gibbs's photographic subject and had the additional humiliation of hearing things like "nice tits" from boys to whom Gibbs had shown the photos. Most of the girls didn't report Gibbs, but Wales says she went to Zane in tears, and he "dismissed it as my imagination." (Zane, now 84 and living in New Bedford, Massachusetts, has said it was he who approached Wales, after a senior boy happened to catch Gibbs photographing a naked girl with a towel over her face and reported him, and said that he never called Wales crazy.) In any case, on February 5, 1980, Zane fired Gibbs after a several-day investigation during which Zane interviewed a number of girls about their experiences with Gibbs. At least 20 students were abused by Gibbs during his seven years at St. George's. (Gibbs died in 1996.)

Why didn't the school catch on to Gibbs earlier? Clearly, there were rumors circulating about him, even if they were expressed jokingly: in the 1979 yearbook, a caption under a photo of Gibbs with a girl read, "Mr. Gibbs, get your hand off my . . . Elbow."

As he had done with White, Zane failed to report Gibbs to any state agencies. (Zane told *Vanity Fair* that he had not been aware of any legal obligation to do so.) Upon Gibbs's departure, Zane announced at a school assembly that the trainer had left merely because of a health issue. This may have been justified by concern for the privacy of the girls, but

shockingly, the school gave Gibbs a pension as well as a letter of recommendation which described him as "most certainly competent" and
attributed his departure from St. George's to a "medical leave." Gibbs
even reappeared on campus a few years later, attending a cocktail party
during homecoming weekend. "Zane pretty clearly was not interested
in rocking the boat," says Carmen Durso, an attorney representing a
number of the St. George's victims. "His idea was: You got a problem,
you make it go away."

A FACTORY FOR HOLDEN CAULFIELDS

If Gibbs was enabled by institutional misogyny, a second set of students fell casualty to a laissez-faire interpretation of the school's *in
loco parentis* mandate, which mixed harsh discipline with near anarchy.
At St. George's, suspensions and expulsions were common, often the
inevitable result of a tone set by the administration. "We bragged that
you could fit all the rules of the school on one side of an 8½-by-11-inch
piece of paper," says Bryce Traister (class of '86). "You could go down
to the beach and smoke pot and drink and have sex and surf," a late-80s
grad recalls. "It was heaven."

The school became a factory for Holden Caulfields, alienated kids
whose parenting had been outsourced to a not very nurturing place.
Freshmen and sophomores were effectively in the care of the seniors
who ran the dorms. It was a Darwinian environment, which several St.
George's alumni separately described to me as *Lord of the Flies*. Certain
years, the hazing got way, way out of hand. In the fall of 1978, a senior
made a freshman named Harry Groome stand on a trash can and pull
down his boxer shorts, whereupon the older student sodomized him
with a broomstick in front of several other students. It was neither a
secret incident nor one that was taken seriously by the school: a later
yearbook photo of Groome in a trash can was captioned: "It's better
than a broomstick!" Four years later, several boys experienced unwanted
nighttime visits from seniors trying to fondle them. After Charlie Henry

awoke one night during his third-form year, in 1982, to find a darkness-obscured figure touching him, he slept with a knife under his pillow for the remainder of the semester. The same year, some seniors took a freshman boy to a dorm basement, where they beat him up and raped him with a pencil. After the victim went to the administration, Tony Zane announced at Thursday chapel what had happened, and the seniors were expelled. "When their feet were held to the fire, they responded," says Ned Truslow, who was the school's senior prefect when he graduated, in 1986, but "how could these people have let this happen?"

CULT OF PERSONALITY

Franklin Coleman was big and tall, deep-voiced and pompous and kind and charismatic, a rare African-American teacher in a sea of whiteness, and the school's musical leader starting in 1980: organist, teacher of music theory and history, choirmaster at a school with a singing group serious enough to record albums and tour internationally. He often wore his choir robes around campus. A cult of personality surrounded him, and he played host to concentric rings of acolytes. The Kulture Vultures was a club of aesthetes who'd meet in Coleman's apartment in the Arden-Diman dorm, which he supervised, to drink soda, eat chips, and listen to classical music or jazz or watch a Hitchcock or Woody Allen film. A more exclusive group, the Colemanites, would receive floridly inscribed invitations to small soirées at Coleman's apartment; the boys wore black-tie. And then, at the center of these rings, according to alumni, was the small group of students in whom he had a sexual interest.

Coleman had a clear type: "that Brideshead, beautiful chiseled young boy" look, as a female ex–choir member describes it, and a predator's nose for wounded animals. Hawkins Cramer (class of '85) fit the profile, blond with a good voice, and his father had died of cancer the summer after his sophomore year. "I was devastated from that, and lost and sad and angry," Cramer recalls. "Franklin came in as the caring, avuncular guy that he is." Coleman could be generous, giving him a double tape deck, say, or a Christmas sweater from Barneys, but there was a push-pull. If Cramer's thank-you note was insufficiently long, he says, Coleman would become petulant and berate him, then apologize and pull him in for "a long embrace. Over time, he'd start pulling up my shirt, putting his hand under it, against my back. It became really uncomfortable, but you're already in this position where you just had to make this guy feel better—if I pull away now it will make it worse. So you carried on and tried not to think about it much."

Coleman took Cramer on a college tour the summer after his junior year, and the situation became increasingly fraught, with Coleman booking hotel rooms with a single bed and Cramer waking up with Coleman's arm around him. During a drive on that trip, Cramer fell asleep in the front seat and says he woke up with Coleman "massaging my genitals." Cramer froze, pretended he was stirring from sleep, and Coleman stopped touching him. Then Cramer opened his eyes and said, " 'I don't know what I've done to make you think I want that, but I don't. You can't do that sort of thing to me.' He pulled over, starts bawling and crying. 'I'm so sorry, you seemed so tense—I thought this would be something to relax you.' "

Another alumnus told me he was given marijuana and vodka by Coleman, and woke up naked in a bed in Coleman's apartment with no memory of what had happened. A third alumnus, "Ethan" (who has asked that his real name not be used), who is now in his 40s, was a Colemanite, blond and bullied and far from his home in the Bahamas when Coleman cultivated him, serving him Kahlúa ice cream and writing love notes. Over time, Ethan says, Coleman showed him gay porn videos, gave him a full-body Vaseline massage, and touched his penis. On Friday, May 6, 1988, Ethan told the school counselor, and the counselor told the headmaster, Zane's successor, the Reverend George Andrews, who fired Coleman the same day.

At least half a dozen alumni have reported that they were targets of some sort of advance or contact by Coleman. Even more than Gibbs, it's hard for many alumni to understand how Coleman was allowed to prey on students for as long as he did. Coleman's practice of sending invitations to handpicked favorites and posting them on a bulletin board for all to see, which today might be recognized as the grooming tactics of a predator, seemed troublingly exclusionary to some students but were evidently considered acceptable by the administration. A 1986 yearbook photo of Coleman was captioned "Frankie Say Relax," and there was bathroom-stall graffiti about "Franklin's organ" and someone sitting on "Franklin's Tower" (playing off the Grateful Dead song). "We all knew he was a perv," says one '86 graduate.

Decades later, the St. George's counselor would tell the school's investigator that in the early 80s he had informed Tony Zane about a student's supposedly receiving backrubs from Coleman, and Zane had responded that he didn't believe the student and hoped the matter would "go away." Zane himself told the investigator that he didn't remember this, but he had warned Coleman around 1983 or 1984 "not to give back rubs to any more students."

Innuendo and the fuzzy conflation of homosexuality and pedophilia in the mind of a 1980s teenager wasn't actionable knowledge of a specific incident or relationship. "There was a way in which the genteel homophobia of the school organized itself around Franklin Coleman, in a way that weirdly enabled his predatory behavior," Bryce Traister says, because it made Coleman's acolytes defensive around him and "also because it suggested it wouldn't be right to inquire too closely into what was really going on in these years . . . because that would suggest you were being homophobic or racist." A female member of the class of 1987 says she went to her adviser that year and reported that something untoward was clearly going on between Coleman and some students, and "someone needs to do something." The alumna says her adviser told her that unless she had evidence "you're in the same position I am. I said the same thing to the people in charge, and I was told to mind my own business."

When Andrews fired Coleman the following spring, he handled the matter much as Zane had handled Gibbs. The departure was presented as a "voluntary resignation" due to health reasons; the school, on the advice of counsel, made no report to authorities; and the school gave Coleman $10,000 and let him keep his health insurance for several more months, in return for not pursuing any legal claim against the school. Coleman moved on to working with school choirs at a church in Philadelphia, and by 1997 he was choirmaster at Tampa Prep, in Florida.

JANE DOE, UNMASKED

The year that Coleman was fired, 1988, a plaintiff using the pseudonym Jane Doe filed suit in November against St. George's School in federal court in Providence, alleging she had been raped by Al Gibbs. The plaintiff was Anne Scott, who had suffered in the eight years since she graduated from St. George's. She had finally started to talk about Gibbs with her therapist when she was a college junior, eventually informing her parents what she'd gone through. But while she had excelled academically, obtaining both an undergraduate degree and a Ph.D. in anthropology from the University of Pennsylvania, and later an M.B.A., she had been hobbled socially. She had spent much of her 20s living with her parents in Delaware, been hospitalized four or five times for an eating disorder, depression, and dissociation, and was on a number of psychiatric medications. As she entered her late 20s, and her Ph.D. neared completion, her parents were worried: about her marital prospects, her financial prospects (she was aging out of their health insurance), her future. They began to explore the idea of a civil suit against the school. "My parents aren't litigious people," Scott says, "but it was that motivation of, how do we provide for Anne, and what's going to happen when we're not around and she's not going to be able to live independently." Her family retained Eric MacLeish, whom another lawyer had recommended and who, as it happened, had attended St. George's for two years in the late 60s.

St. George's response to the lawsuit, which sought $10 million in punitive damages, was remarkably aggressive. Although the school was well aware of Gibbs's history of abuse, then headmaster Archer Harman (now deceased) wrote a letter that December to "Friends of St. George's," in which he stated that "we have no reason to believe that the alleged incidents took place." Besides trying unsuccessfully to have the suit thrown out on the grounds that the statute of limitations for a personal-injury suit had expired, lawyer William Robinson III, who now sits on Rhode Island's Supreme Court, argued for making Anne Scott's name public, suggested the sex might have been consensual (a suggestion that earned a withering rebuke from the judge), and tried to stop Scott from notifying other alumni. "They threatened to depose my parents' whole community," Scott says. (Robinson said in a statement in January, "I represented the client as an attorney must, zealously, ethically and to the best of my ability.") The situation produced tension in her family, and ultimately the pressure became too much for her to bear: "I just wanted it to go away. I didn't want money. I didn't want to lose my family. I dropped the case." St. George's refused to let her withdraw, however, until she signed a confidentiality agreement preventing her from ever discussing the case. MacLeish argued against signing it, but Scott was done. "I basically fled." She stopped therapy, "cut off everything," and moved overseas.

The school did, in response to the suit, finally stop providing Gibbs with financial support and report him to the Department of Children, Youth & Families (which responded that it had no jurisdiction).

THE CRUSADER

Over the next 20 years, America's understanding of childhood sexual abuse within institutions would evolve dramatically. Eric MacLeish was part of that movement. Anne Scott's case had been his first in the sexual-abuse area and had launched him on a career: he represented most of the victims in one of the first successful cases against the Catholic Church, in Fall River, Massachusetts, in 1992. MacLeish would become a key figure representing victims in the Archdiocese of Boston cases (in the movie *Spotlight,* he is portrayed, somewhat unflatteringly, by Billy Crudup). That work would take its toll: MacLeish experienced severe PTSD following the Catholic Church cases and gave up the law, lost 40 pounds, moved into a trailer in his in-laws' yard in Connecticut, remembered his own sexual abuse at an English boarding school he attended as a child (he also still has cane marks on his back from his time there), and began a romantic relationship with his psychotherapist. (His marriage ended, and he ended up filing a complaint against the therapist with the state, which revoked her license.)

As the Catholic Church scandal unfolded, a growing number of other cloistered institutions, including the American Boychoir School, in Princeton, and Groton, in Massachusetts, had to reckon with sex-abuse scandals. And a few St. George's alumni, still haunted by their experiences at the school, began to seek answers.

Ethan, after graduating in 1989, had wandered the world for 12 years as a sailor and "let strange men do things with me." He had become an alcoholic and extinguished a series of cigarettes on his own body, and he hadn't come to terms with what had happened to him at the school. (He is now married and living with his wife and son in Westport, Connecticut.) He approached the school in 2000. "I said, 'I'm not trying to sue, but I don't know why I have to pay for my therapy.' " He says he received a letter of apology, from then headmaster Charles Hamblet, and 23 sessions with the school counselor. Two years later, Harry Groome, reading about an abuse scandal at Groton, and newly the father of a son, was beginning to recognize the psychological impact of what had happened to him and found himself worrying about current students at S.G.S. and what was being done for them. He wrote to Hamblet and says he received a pat-on-the-head letter in response. (Hamblet died in 2010.)

The hiring of Eric Peterson as headmaster in 2004 prompted a new set of contacts by alumni. That year, Groome e-mailed Peterson and also the fellow graduate who had assaulted him. Twice a year, he'd see the perp's name in school mailings, because the man was an active alumnus, and he wrote him: "I said, 'I never forgot what you did to me; I see your name twice a year; in good faith please resign from that position.' He wrote back and said, 'I resigned—let's please talk.' I said no."

Hawkins Cramer now had a family and was the principal of an elementary school in Seattle, where he had recently dealt decisively with a teacher exhibiting grooming behaviors with students. Emboldened by that experience, in the spring of 2004, Cramer decided to track Franklin Coleman down. He found him working at Tampa Prep and called him directly. Cramer's palms were sweaty, his heart thumping. Reception put him through, and Coleman picked up after two rings. "At first he was 'Great to hear from you,' " says Cramer. "I said, 'I'm not calling because I'm interested in talking with you but to let you know that what you did with me was a terrible thing and you have no right to be around kids." Cramer told Coleman he was going to get him fired, then called the headmaster, told him everything, and suggested he call St. George's to confirm the information. Cramer says the headmaster thanked him and said he'd take it from there. Then Cramer called Peterson at St. George's and told him the story. "He said, Oh my God, that's terrible, that's awful, thank you so much." Cramer says he told Peterson he needed to call the Tampa school. "I hang up, think, That's great, I've done all I can do. Well, [Coleman] retired four years later from that job. So [Peterson] knowingly protected this guy who was a pedophile."

"Mr. Peterson's recollection is different," says Joe Baerlein, a spokesman for the school, in an e-mail. "During their conversation, Mr. Cramer said that he should expect a call from Tampa Prep and requested that he speak to them about Coleman. Mr. Peterson agreed to do so but did not hear from Tampa Prep." (Coleman now lives in Newark, New Jersey, and until recently had a page on Couchsurfing.com, a site where homeowners can offer free lodging to travelers, featuring pictures of himself surrounded by adolescent boys. He didn't respond to an interview request and has not responded to allegations in other news reports.)

In 2006, Ethan met with Peterson on campus, and Peterson, like his predecessor, wrote him a letter of apology and also promised 10 free psychotherapy consultations. In October of 2011, Harry Groome e-mailed Peterson a *Boston Globe* article about a scandal at the Fessenden School, in Newton, Massachusetts, heading the e-mail: "FYI—how another school is addressing past sexual abuse on campus. Time for SG to step up?" Peterson invited Groome to meet with him, and Groome gave Peterson a copy of the letter he'd sent to Hamblet in 2002.

In the spring of 2012, Eric MacLeish wrote to Peterson. MacLeish had found himself reading St. George's *Bulletin* and seeing story after story about "successful alums," he says. "The hypocrisy of it all was just overwhelming." MacLeish had always been haunted by the Anne Scott case. Over the years, he had tried to track her down, at one point even hiring skip tracers (akin to bounty hunters), without success. Thinking about Anne Scott and all the victims of Al Gibbs, MacLeish wondered, "Why can't there be an article about that conduct in the *Bulletin*?" He wrote Peterson that night, asking him to send out an alumni letter about Gibbs. MacLeish had eased back into mediation work after his time in the wilderness, but he wasn't representing a client then. Peterson invited him to come to the school, and they met and spoke. Afterward, MacLeish wrote to Peterson that the school had "an affirmative duty to act," but Peterson still didn't send out a letter to alumni.

A SORT OF HOMECOMING

In 2014, MacLeish was at a Christmas party in Lincoln, Massachusetts, where a fellow lawyer said he was in touch with someone MacLeish knew: Anne Scott. In the years after she left the country, Scott had ended up doing global health and development work for NGOs in Indonesia, India, Botswana, and the Palestinian territories, among other places. She found it healing to see people in impoverished countries showing grace, and being an expat had removed her from the painful context of her own culture, freeing her to be herself. In 2013, with her two sons, now teenagers (the marriage that produced them hadn't lasted: "holding on to friendships and intimate relationships is hard for me"), she decided to move back to the U.S. after a quarter-century abroad.

MacLeish called her that December, and when Scott received the phone message, she thought long and hard about calling him back. When she did, he brought her up to date—about how he'd reached out to Peterson in 2012, and how her case and its resolution had always bothered him—and asked her to speak to the school with him. She said that if it would help others and make the school a better place, she'd do it.

What happened next set the tone for everything that would follow. MacLeish, who in the past year has gotten back to doing trial work, asked Peterson to lift Anne Scott's gag order, and arranged for the three to meet. MacLeish also then sent, unsolicited, a draft letter for Peterson to send to alumni. It was an aggressive move, and at that point Peterson, a lawyer, said he wasn't so sure a meeting was such a good idea. Two weeks later, Peterson and then board chair Skip Branin sent a letter to all alumni, announcing that the school had become aware of past "sexual misconduct" by at least one employee, had hired an investigator to undertake "a full and independent inquiry," and encouraged any alumni who had been victims or had pertinent information to speak with the investigator. Peterson wrote that the letter and inquiry had their roots in another alumna's contacting him in 2012 about her Gibbs abuse experience, in the evolving best practices of independent schools, and in response to "other alumni" coming forward. (MacLeish believes that he forced Peterson's hand.)

In May of 2015, MacLeish, Anne Scott, Peterson, and a lawyer for the school met at MacLeish's office. Scott told Peterson her story and made several requests: the creation of a therapy-assistance fund, a release from her 1989 gag order, documents from her lawsuit (to help in her healing), and the removal of Tony Zane's name from the girls' dormitory. (Deerfield had agreed to a similar request, removing the names of two offending former teachers from a squash facility, an endowed chair, and a writing fellowship.) "Eric Peterson did apologize and acknowledge that it happened to me, and that was meaningful, and I'm grateful someone acknowledged it after all these years," Scott says. For a period, Scott felt good about the process. Then things started to go awry.

A FATAL COURSE

The details—how therapy reimbursement would work; whether or not survivors would have to sign confidentiality agreements; whether the school would release Anne Scott from her 1989 gag order; when exactly the investigative report would be finished—are less important than that, by the fall of last year, an adversarial dynamic had been established: Anne Scott, and a growing group of other alumni who'd stepped forward with stories of their own abuse, began to feel that the school was responding to profound pain with lawyerly caution and was more interested in protecting its reputation than truly making amends and ensuring that the problem had been addressed. Even as the school proceeded with its investigation and sent two more letters to alumni updating them on its progress, the survivor group became increasingly mistrustful, and they learned—only in December, MacLeish claims— that the investigator was a law partner of the school's outside counsel (as well as married to her). It's not uncommon for independent investigations to be conducted by an organization's outside counsel, but in light of the survivors' obvious trust issues, it's understandable that when they learned of the law firm's dual role, they felt betrayed once more.

The survivors' pivot from focusing on past misconduct to what they saw as present mishandling of the crisis would be hugely consequential in prolonging the scandal. Those who blame the school see a culture of cover-up and credit MacLeish with goading St. George's to act when it otherwise wouldn't have. Defenders of the school, even while acknowledging some missteps, say MacLeish riled up the victims, driven by his own demons. "I really think this is part of a personal-rehabilitation campaign for him," argues one former St. George's student.

MacLeish ramped up the pressure on the school. He is adept at working the media, and on December 14, *The Boston Globe* ran a front-page story about Al Gibbs's victims. On December 23, the school released its investigative report, but the survivors considered it woefully inadequate: among other flaws, it curiously didn't address any allegations after 2004, the year Peterson arrived, and it didn't delve into how the school had "passed the trash" (as the practice of letting a known abuser move on to another institution without alerting them is charmingly called). On January 5, in Boston, MacLeish held a lengthy press conference with Scott and two other victims, and also issued a 36-page rebuttal of the school's report.

The school had lost any control. An online petition by a Scott-led group called SGS for Healing, asking for a new, truly independent investigation and an independent therapy fund administered by a clinician, got nearly 850 signers. And the pressure yielded results. The school announced a new investigator and a therapy program that the survivors were happy with.

Meanwhile, a secret group on Facebook, open only to St. George's alumni, quickly collected more than 1,000 members, as students from the 1960s through 2016 hashed out the scandal. There were first-person accounts of abuse, expressions of solidarity with the victims, confessions of survivor guilt. The class of 1974 rescinded its yearbook dedication to Al Gibbs. There was considerable focus on the culpability of Tony Zane. (In a December 24 e-mail to friends, he and his wife, Eusie, defended themselves and bitterly attacked Peterson for, among other things, refusing to indemnify them and negotiating with MacLeish: "St. George's School has embarked on a fatal course, has embraced a viper, and thrown us under the bus." He told the school's investigator, according to the report received by the board, that he "wanted to make amends and help the students." Notwithstanding that, he sent another e-mail to friends, in which he wrote, "Anne Scott did not contract anorexia at St. George's; she arrived severely anorexic." Scott then wrote to him. "I said, 'Please stop. It's not true.' He didn't reply. . . . All the guy has to do is say he's sorry. 'I'm sorry it happened while I was there' would be a good start.")

The Facebook group got ugly, too. Some people were expelled from it; others, burned out, quit. People posted scurrilous rumors about family members of St. George's administration. Sometimes, when things really got heated, people tried to re-inject some perspective and recall some of the good things about their St. George's experiences. Jason Whitney (class of '90) found himself driving home listening to Led Zeppelin's "The Rain Song" and being transported back to the first night he'd heard it, which was at St. George's. He posted to the Facebook group: "Put the regrets away for a few hours. Now go cue up the Zep. Do it. Oh, and turn it way the fuck up too. Remember how epic St. George's could be." The post sparked more than 100 nostalgic comments.

As the second investigation proceeded, the survivors pressed a case against Peterson. Beyond what they viewed as his unresponsiveness to their early attempts to alert him, they were increasingly bothered by the absence of post-2004 allegations in the report released by the school, given that they knew of at least one that the investigator had been informed about. It was a matter involving a computer-science teacher and athletic trainer named Charles Thompson. In 2004, 18 students had made allegations that he'd touched their knees (he had a preoccupation with "sailor's knees") and pulled back a shower curtain in one case. It was "creepy," an administrator would tell the school's investigator, and parents of the boys in the dormitory received a letter from Peterson explaining the situation. Thompson was removed as a dorm master, suspended for several months, and given a psychiatric evaluation before being allowed to return. He later moved to the Taft School, in northwestern Connecticut, but after the St. George's survivor group alerted *The Boston Globe*, it ran an article about Thompson, and he was placed on leave by Taft. (Thompson remains on leave and did not respond to a request for an interview. Some St. George's alumni have suggested that the evidence against him is weak and that he's the victim of a witch hunt.) [Thompson has since left Taft.]

A CULTURE OF ABUSE

During all this, the school hunkered down, giving no interviews after the initial *Globe* story and hiring both the same law and crisis P.R. firms (Ropes & Gray and Rasky Baerlein) that had represented the Archdiocese of Boston. But a group of alumni and current parents defended the school on Facebook and in interviews. One of their main arguments, always couched with expressions of sympathy for the survivors, is that nonetheless St. George's is a "living school," and that present-day students and parents and faculty shouldn't be punished for the sins of the past. A current student assembled a spreadsheet showing how far the school had come in terms of gender equity, charting how many girls are now in leadership positions and how many female faculty there are.

And in the void of Peterson's public silence, some alumni and parents have stepped up to defend him. They point to the money he's raised and the programs he's championed, which have made the school a more academic place, as well as to his popularity among students and their parents and to his moral authority: there was, for instance, the decision a few years ago to forfeit a football game against rival Lawrence Academy, because Lawrence's team was stocked with 300-pounders. While this briefly turned St. George's into sports-radio fodder about the softening of the American male, others saw it as an act of courage. At a meeting in Newport in February, St. George's parents roundly expressed support for Peterson.

Tucker Carlson, the conservative commentator, graduated in 1987, married headmaster Andrews's daughter Susie (who now sits on the board) and has sent two of his children to the school: he thinks it's "disgusting" how people have gone after Peterson, who he believes has been unfairly scapegoated for things that happened long before he was there. Governor Howard Dean, the former presidential candidate and a 1966 graduate of St. George's, also supports the current leadership. "I was outraged when I first read about [the abuse]," he says. "I hate this kind of stuff. But the more I learned . . . what matters to me, classically institutions sweep these things under the rug, but in this case, I don't detect stonewalling. . . . My guess is they're trying to do the best they can by the victims. I don't see any evidence of this administration or this board, none of whom I know personally, that they're trying to shut it down. I don't know what else we can ask of them." Even Whit Sheppard, whose experience at Deerfield is cited by MacLeish as an exemplary response by a school to a case of abuse, says, "I firmly believe that Eric is a person who's genuinely interested in doing the right thing by survivors, for survivors."

Regarding the outward paralysis of the board of trustees, a current member of the school's advisory board offers a benign explanation: "No one's going into these conversations saying, O.K., tell me how to stonewall. They're saying, What do we do in a P.R. world where anything we say gets heavily criticized? How do we come across as ready, willing, and able to deal with issues raised without setting ourselves up for automatic failure or liability in the future? Those are tough things to navigate. And lawsuits are coming. No matter how well intentioned you are, you have to keep that in mind."

That still doesn't explain, though, why Peterson didn't send out an alumni letter before 2015, or why it took him seven months to release Anne Scott from her decades-old gag order. It's hard to avoid the sense that he either was dragging his feet and acting only when forced to, or was at the mercy of a board that wouldn't let him act. It's also hard to avoid the sense that the board did a bit of sanitizing of the first investigative report, a copy of which was obtained by *Vanity Fair.* The report publicly issued by the board was 11 pages, but the original pair of reports (a main one and a supplemental one) received by the board exceeded 100 pages. A reasonable case can be made for much of the winnowing that was done: a teacher who was a bit inappropriate, and was disciplined and investigated and ultimately cleared to work at the school again, arguably did not warrant inclusion in a report about sexual abuse. Other details that were excluded, like the facts that a former St. George's teacher is currently in federal prison for possession of child pornography and that another one told a male student that "you just need a good fuck," look more like a school sparing itself some embarrassment. It's unclear why the board didn't consider it important to disclose the investigator's finding that "the perception among many former members of the school community is that [a culture of abuse] did in fact exist decades ago at the school." More disturbingly, the published report excluded the investigator's finding that the school had given Al Gibbs a letter of recommendation and a stipend after firing him; had lied about having no reason to believe Jane Doe's claims were true; and had never attempted to alert White's, Gibbs's, or Coleman's later employers about their pasts.

"WHY WOULD THEY GET IT RIGHT?"

I visited St. George's on a Monday in early May, a week before the reunion weekend. It was a misty, overcast morning, but the handsomeness of the campus, with its abundant green lawns and looming stone chapel, all backed by the rolling surf of the ocean, was inescapable. First period was just beginning when I arrived at 8:30 A.M., and boys and girls and teachers were hurrying to their classrooms.

The school is larger now—50 percent more students than in the 1980s—with a new science building, a new library, a new arts center, and a state-of-the-art facility for the professional development of faculty. At an assembly I attended, run by the five senior prefects, the athletic director handed out awards for athlete of the week; a student group announced a project involving "design thinking," a concept Peterson had brought back from a continuing-education program at Stanford; and another club announced that Julie Bowen (class of '87), who plays a mother on *Modern Family*, would be speaking on campus the following week.

Then I sat down with Peterson in his office, a high-ceilinged space with wood paneling that is exactly as you imagine it. Peterson—a young 50, square-jawed, clean-shaven, earnest—wore a black St. George's fleece vest over a shirt and red tie. He had invited me to the school so that I could see St. George's as it is in 2016, but also said that he was constrained from speaking about its history of abuse. It was an odd set of circumstances that neatly encapsulated the situation Peterson finds himself in. Managing the greatest crisis ever to hit St. George's, and concerning events that mostly took place long before he'd set foot on the campus, he has had to simultaneously answer to trustees, to current students and parents, to faculty, to alumni, to survivors, to donors, all while a Rhode Island state-police investigation was ongoing (it has recently concluded with no charges being brought), the school's own second independent investigation was pending, and plaintiffs' lawyers were circling. Peterson also has a school to run. (And he's well paid to do so: $525,000 in 2014.) A strategic P.R. adviser sat between us.

We touched on the school's current anti-abuse precautions, on the wave of prep-school scandals, on the greater contemporary sensitivity to adolescent development. Peterson spoke of his pride in the school's more robust honor code (adopted nine years ago), in recent changes to student life ("We've established somewhere in the neighborhood of 40 new student traditions"), in the tone he's tried to foster. "I say to the students all the time, 'We don't do mean. Mean is a choice.' " I asked him about his decision to leave the law for teaching. "My heart was a teacher's heart," Peterson said. He talked about the continuing purpose of boarding schools. Peterson, who grew up in Laguna Beach, California, was the first person in his family to go to a private school, and his years at Deerfield had been "transformative. I didn't know what school could be until I went to boarding school."

While the survivors I'd talked to, and their allies, seemed mostly adamant that Peterson must go, there had recently been glimmers of détente—at least with the board. Just days after the uproar over the misbegotten "Hope for Healing" event, five survivors met with five trustees and a mediator in Boston. The trustees had agreed that the board would undergo training on the long-term impact of child sexual abuse and would also discuss "reparations" for survivors. The five trustees also agreed to consider survivors' criticism of Peterson and act on any issues raised about him by the report within 30 days of its release. The report was expected to be published in June, but its likely impact was pre-empted when, early that month, board chair Leslie Heaney announced in a letter to the school community that Peterson had recently told the board he would not seek to extend his contract beyond its end date in June 2017. The news did not appease survivors, who were disappointed that Peterson hadn't been explicitly fired, that he would keep his job for another year, and that his own letter to the school community alluded only obliquely to the scandal.

Many of the survivors and their allies see what's happening as an opportunity to help the school become a better place. They say they don't want to tear St. George's down but to rebuild it. Anne Scott, who after 25 years of being under a gag order was at first mortified to have the details of her life—her abuse, her hospitalizations, her medication—spilled on the pages of newspapers, has found meaning in this fight. "Our society has to start talking about this stuff," she says, "and maybe I can play a small part in that by putting my head over the parapet and talking about it and answering people's questions. A lot of what the school says is not evil, but it's ignorant and tone-deaf to survivors. But why would you expect them to understand something that's taboo and nobody gets any practice in talking about or understanding? Why would they get it right?"

[As part of the school's independent probe, investigators spoke with more than 150 witnesses and analyzed thousands of pages of documents, concluding that "the picture that emerges from this investigation is profoundly disturbing," but also noting that "St. George's School today is a very different place than it was in the 1970s and 1980s."]

FOLLOW THE MONEY

"RICH HARVARD, POOR HARVARD"

By Nina Munk

AUGUST 2009

Early last May, I attended a town-hall meeting of undergraduates at Harvard University in Cambridge, Massachusetts. The topic that evening: cost-cutting. As I settled into my chair, in Boylston Hall, student activists, members of the "Student Labor Action Movement," were making their way through the auditorium, handing out flyers. "Rethink. Resist," urged the bold black letters. It was a call to action. "NO LAYOFFS!" At the top of the printed page was Harvard's historic coat of arms: three small open books. Cleverly, the university's Latin motto—normally inscribed on the books as "VE-RI-TAS"—had been replaced with a near anagram, "AV-AR-ICE."

Ignoring the agitators as best he could, Michael Smith, dean of the Faculty of Arts and Sciences, Harvard's biggest division, called the meeting to order. Sitting casually on a desk, wearing jeans and a short-sleeved polo shirt, Smith, a professor of engineering and applied sciences, and a former competitive swimmer, looked more like an athlete than an administrator. He got straight to the point: his division—which includes Harvard College, the Graduate School of Arts and Sciences, and the School of Engineering and Applied Sciences—was facing a budget deficit of $220 million.

That's a huge sum: $220 million! Nearly 20 percent of the Faculty of Arts and Sciences' current budget had to be cut. "That frightens me," Smith said forthrightly. "It should frighten you. We obviously can't sit around and do nothing. We've got to find a way to try and get the income back in alignment with the expenses."

Smith's audience listened intensely. Already, they had seen evidence of the cutbacks Smith was alluding to. All across campus, as a preliminary measure, thermostats had been lowered during the winter months, from 72 degrees to 68 degrees. Students and faculty were no longer entitled to free coffee at the university's Barker Center. The Quad Express, which shuttles students between the Radcliffe Quadrangle and Memorial Hall, would soon be running every 20 minutes, not every 10 minutes. More recently, despite loud protests from Harvard's athletes, among others, it was announced that hot breakfasts would no longer be served on weekdays at undergraduate residential houses. Instead of bacon, poached eggs, and waffles, students would have to get by on cold ham, cottage cheese, cereal, and fruit.

Such cost-cutting measures—"alignments" and "resizements," as Harvard prefers to call them—are painful for everyone involved. In the words of a university staff member, as quoted by *The Harvard Crimson*, "Harvard's the richest place around here. If they can't even afford the coffee, it makes us wonder, you know."

But this evening at Boylston Hall, Michael Smith seemed to be suggesting something bigger, more serious, than the absence of free coffee. "What will that mean for students in practical terms?" asked one cool-headed member of the audience. "Are we going to have fewer resources in terms of advisers? Are we going to have fewer office hours for our professors? Are we going to have fewer professors?"

Smith would not be specific. "The resizing that we've done is nothing compared to what we've got coming up," he said, hinting at imminent upheaval.

Someone else asked a tough question: Instead of cutting undergraduate budgets, why not cut the salaries of Harvard's top administrators?

Smith sighed. *If only it were that easy.* His colleague Evelynn Hammonds, dean of Harvard College, answered this time round: "I'd rather use the words 'reduction,' 'shifting things around,' 'reorganizing'— rather than saying something that says 'cuts,' which implies you whack the heads off flowers," she said. "What we're trying to do is make those kinds of priority-driven changes."

Smith looked at the audience. "Are we done?" he asked. Then, glancing at the clock, he stood up. It was eight o'clock. "We're done!" he concluded.

Outside, along the Charles River, the cherry trees were in bloom. In Harvard Yard, the wide grassy lawn was soft and green. To my left was a bronze statue of John Harvard, the university's first major benefactor, his shoe polished to a high gloss by passersby. Then something else caught my eye: discarded paper cups, torn and crumpled candy wrappers, an empty Evian bottle. The trash can in front of the stately, granite University Hall was overflowing. It was a bad sign.

"There are going to be a hell of a lot of layoffs. Courses will be cut. Class sizes will get bigger," conceded a Harvard insider, who, like every other administrator on campus, was not permitted to speak openly to me on the classified subject of alignments and resizements and belt-tightenings.

Radical change is coming to Harvard. Fewer professors, for one thing. Fewer teaching assistants, janitors, and support staff. Shuttered libraries. Less money for research and travel and books. Cafés replaced by vending machines. Junior-varsity sports teams downgraded to clubs. No raises. No bonuses. No fresh coats of paint or new carpets. Overflowing trash cans.

The recession has been hard on most Americans. We know that. At Harvard, however, adjusting to the end of the gilded age, the champagne age, is proving especially wrenching: the university's endowment has collapsed, donations are down, budgets are overstretched. With so many enormous fixed costs—and with much of its endowment restricted by the narrowly defined wishes of donors—there's almost no room left to maneuver.

What's more, the university is facing the onerous financial consequences of over-building. Consider this: Over the 20-year period from 1980 to 2000, Harvard University added nearly 3.2 million square feet of new space to its campus. But that's nothing compared with the extravagance that followed. So far this decade, from 2000 through 2008, Harvard has added another 6.2 million square feet of new space, roughly equal to the total number of square feet occupied by the Pentagon. All across campus, one after another, new academic buildings have shot up. The price of these optimistic new projects: a breathtaking $4.3 billion.

In Allston, a Boston neighborhood just across the Charles River from the school's main campus, you can view Harvard's billion-dollar hole in the ground, a vast construction pit. It's the foundation of Harvard's most ambitious project of all: the sprawling Allston Science Complex, once scheduled to be completed by 2011 at a cost of $1.2 billion—but now on hold.

It's become a symbol, that vast hole in the ground, yet another indication that Harvard University is facing the worst, most dangerous financial crisis in its 373-year history. Adding to the instability: the university is on its fourth president in eight years. And every few weeks, or so it seems, Harvard announces the departure of yet another administrator—most recently the university's executive vice president, Edward Forst, who just last year came to Harvard from Goldman Sachs and intends to step down on August 1. [Katherine Lapp has since assumed Forst's position.]

"They have to do what businesspeople do—they have to make hard decisions," one Harvard business professor told me, referring to the university's administrators. But, of course, Harvard is not a business, nor is it being run like a business; it's a distinguished, high-minded research university, arguably the greatest university in the nation. "Balancing their budget is going to be very traumatic for them," the professor added, in case I'd missed his point.

Already, the inevitable recriminations and backbiting have started. Harvard is in trouble, and no one can decide who's to blame, or what to do next. In reporting this story, I found myself caught up in a nasty, self-serving whisper campaign: back and forth, "on background," Harvard's hostile fiefdoms are pointing anonymous fingers, each accusing another of "pulling the trigger" on this and that high-ticket capital project. They disagree about who made the flawed investment decisions in the first place, insisting that they themselves had never been consulted on the matter, or had been overruled, or pushed aside and ignored. Invariably, somebody else had the "ultimate fiduciary responsibility."

Meanwhile, the campus itself is in turmoil. Faculty members are angry. Students feel betrayed. "Why haven't the faculty been asked to sacrifice at all?" reads one typical comment posted on the *Crimson*'s Web site. "The lowest paid professors make over 150k+, and yet they have the nerve to tell students to suck it all up."

"Were the judgments we made reasonable ones?" a former top Harvard administrator asked me, rhetorically, addressing the sharp increase in expenses and capital commitments of the last decade. "At the time, I think they were reasonable judgments. It turns out, with the benefit of hindsight, you might have preferred less ambitious plans." (Which is not to say that the administrator in question accepts a grain of responsibility for those judgments.)

Incensed, one member of the board of Harvard Management Company, the fund that manages Harvard's endowment, told me, "This story is about leadership. It isn't about money." He may be right. At some point in the last five years, the men and women who run Harvard convinced themselves that the endowment would grow at double-digit rates forever. If Harvard were a publicly traded company, those people would have been fired by now.

"Apparently nobody in our financial office has read the story in Genesis about Joseph interpreting Pharaoh's dream—you know, during the seven good years you save for the seven lean years," remarked Alan Dershowitz, a professor at Harvard Law School since 1967. "And now they're coming hat in hand, pleading to the faculty and students to bear the burden of cutbacks. It's a scandal! It's an absolute scandal, the way Harvard has handled this financial crisis."

Once upon a time—that is, the fiscal year ending June 30, 2008— Harvard's endowment stood at $36.9 billion, way, way up from $4.8 billion in 1990. No other university endowment in the world comes close to matching Harvard's. Yale's endowment, the second-largest in the nation—$22.9 billion for fiscal 2008—is nearly 40 percent smaller than Harvard's. Stanford's is less than half the size: $17.2 billion, as of last year.

Then came the Great Recession. In the second half of 2008, even more quickly than it had taken off, Harvard's overheated endowment collapsed. Last December, in a letter written to the university's deans, Harvard's president, the historian Drew Gilpin Faust, and its executive vice president, Ed Forst, revealed that Harvard's endowment had lost $8 billion, or 22 percent, in the first four months of the fiscal year, from July through October 2008. To put that number in context: $8 billion is greater than Columbia University's entire endowment ($7.1 billion as of fiscal 2008). Not since 1974, when Harvard's endowment shrank by 12.2 percent, had the university seen losses of such magnitude. Anticipating more dire financial news, Faust warned her deans to expect a 30 percent loss in the endowment for the year. Other universities were showing big losses in 2008, but at Harvard, given the scale and size of its endowment, the numbers seemed inconceivably large.

Right away, some commentators said that Faust was being far too optimistic. On the Huffington Post, the financial journalist Edward Jay Epstein argued that, adjusted for the true value of Harvard's illiquid assets—that is, its private-equity partnerships and other assets that don't sell on the open market—the endowment's losses for those first four months alone were closer to 50 percent, or $18 billion. *Forbes* magazine, noting that Harvard faces a staggering $11 billion of unfunded commitments—money promised, but not yet paid, to various private-equity funds, real-estate funds, and hedge funds—concluded that the university was in a kind of death spiral, forced to sell healthy portions of its portfolio just to stay afloat.

If Harvard were a serious business facing a liquidity crisis, it would have done something drastic by now: fired senior employees, closed departments, sold off real estate. But Harvard, like most other leading universities, is stubborn and inflexible. "None of these schools has the ability to cut expenses fast enough" is how a hedge-fund manager who counts Harvard among his investors explained the problem. Running the numbers for me, proving how impossible it is for a shrinking endowment to keep up with the university's bloated, immovable costs, the hedge-fund manager concluded, "They are completely fucked."

Here's what we do know about Harvard's response to the crisis: at some point in the fall of 2008, Harvard Management Company tried to sell off a big chunk of its private-equity portfolio, about $1.5 billion worth of investments that were locked up in such long-term buyout funds as Apollo Investment Fund VI and Bain Capital Fund IX, among many others. The planned auction was a fiasco: no one was willing to pay anywhere near the asking price for those assets.

A money manager I spoke to described his meeting late last year with Jane Mendillo, who in July 2008 became president and chief executive officer of Harvard Management Company. Knowing that Mendillo was trying to unload assets, he offered to buy back Harvard's sizable stake in his private fund. As he recalls, the surreal dialogue went something like this:

HE: "Hey, look, I'll buy it back from you. I'll buy my interest back."

SHE: "Great."

HE: "Here, I think it's worth—you know, today the [book] value
is a dollar, so I'll pay you 50 cents."

SHE: "Then why would I sell it?"

HE: "Well, why are you? I don't know. You're the one who wants
to sell, not me. If you guys want to sell, I'm happy to rip your
lungs out. If you are desperate, I'm a buyer."

SHE: "Well, we're not desperate."

Was Harvard desperate then? Is Harvard desperate now? One clue
is this: last December, the university sold $2.5 billion worth of bonds,
increasing its total debt to just over $6 billion. Servicing that debt alone
will cost Harvard an average of $517 million a year through 2038, ac-
cording to Standard & Poor's.

To be clear, even if you'd tried hard, you could not have picked a worse
time to sell bonds than December 2008; that was the precise moment when
credit markets seized up. But Harvard, it seems, had no choice. Unwilling
to sell its assets at fire-sale prices, it needed immediate cash to cover, among
other things, what my sources say was approximately a $1 billion unrealized
loss from interest-rate swaps. That's a staggering figure: $1 billion, roughly
a third of the university's entire operating budget for last year.

Those swaps, put in place under Harvard's then president, Lawrence "Larry" Summers, in the early 2000s, were intended to protect,
or hedge, the university against rising interest rates on all the money it
had borrowed. The idea was simple: if interest rates went up, the swaps
would bring in enough money to cover Harvard's higher debt payments.

Instead, interest rates went down. And for reasons no one can explain to me, even as interest rates were plunging in 2007 and 2008, the
university simply forgot, or neglected, or chose not to cancel its swaps—
with the result that Harvard wound up facing that $1 billion loss! Whose
responsibility was that? Where were Harvard's chief financial officer and
treasurer while all this was going on?

In the financial press, it's been suggested that Larry Summers is
to blame for the interest-rate swaps crisis, despite the fact that he left

Harvard in 2006, long before interest rates plunged. The university flatly refuses to speak publicly on the subject. Which leaves journalists free to turn Summers into a scapegoat. But that's too easy: the real story of Harvard's financial catastrophe, and of Larry Summers, is far more nuanced.

In the days when Harvard's endowment provided only a fraction of the university's operating budget, a loss would have been unfortunate, but not tragic. In recent years, however, Harvard's soaring endowment has become the engine fueling the university's growth. In 2008 alone, so-called distributions from the endowment were $1.2 billion, representing more than a third of Harvard's total operating income, up from around 16 percent two decades ago.

During the boom years, it was assumed without question that the value of Harvard's endowment would keep rising. Trusting in that false certainty, the already profligate university went wild, increasing its annual operating budget by 67 percent, from an inflation-adjusted $2.1 billion in 1998 to $3.5 billion in 2008—this, even as the number of students remained constant. While I was reading through Harvard's financial reports from the past decade, the word "delusional" sprang to mind. So did "unsustainable." It was like feeding an addiction, having access to so much quick and easy money.

Harvard's biggest operating expense is salaries and benefits, which eat up almost half the operating budget. In the past year alone, that single expense jumped 7.5 percent. Today, on average, a full professor at Harvard earns $192,600, before benefits; that's more than he or she would make at any other school in the nation. (At Yale, for example, the average salary is $174,700. At the University of California, Berkeley: $143,500.)

Harvard is also generous with its financial aid to students. In the past decade, the cost of subsidizing students has increased nearly threefold, from $125 million a year to $338 million.

Officially, the university charges $48,868 a year for undergraduate tuition, room, and board—that's an increase of 50 percent over the last 10 years—but only a small number of students actually pays that much. Back in 2004, under growing pressure from Washington, and in response to outsiders who accused the school of (a) elitism and (b) hoarding its immense wealth, Larry Summers shook up the world of higher education by announcing that students whose parents earned $40,000 a year or less would be able to attend Harvard gratis. Two years later, that cutoff was increased to $60,000, a figure well above the median U.S. household income.

Still, Harvard pressed ahead in its efforts to ease the growing burden of tuition. In December 2007, declaring that "excellence and opportunity must go hand in hand," the university's new president, Drew Faust, made another stunning announcement: henceforth, students whose parents earn as much as $180,000 a year would pay no more than 10 percent of their family's annual income in tuition fees.

"Harvard's new financial aid policy is the boldest move yet to mitigate the soaring costs of a college education," applauded an editorial in *The New York Times*.

No one could have known it then, but two months before Faust's munificent offer to the upper middle class, the Dow Jones Industrial Average had peaked. By the time Harvard's new financial-aid initiative took effect, last September, right at the start of the school year, Lehman Brothers had filed for bankruptcy and the stock market was in a sickening free fall. By year-end, the Dow Jones Industrial Average had plunged almost 40 percent from its 2007 high, dragging with it Harvard's overheated endowment.

Years ago, when I was a reporter for *Forbes*, we revered Jack Meyer, the man who ran Harvard Management Company from 1990 to 2005. Together with his competitor David Swensen, Yale's long-serving chief investment officer, Meyer had transformed the way universities manage their endowments.

When Meyer arrived at Harvard, the endowment was in a deep rut, going nowhere. Walter Cabot, who'd run Harvard Management Company since its founding, in 1974, had survived the stock-market crash of 1987 magnificently. But afterward, weakened by a heart attack, Cabot remained cautiously on the sidelines, even as the market took off again. His time was up. Meyer, then 45, a Harvard M.B.A. and the former chief investment officer for the Rockefeller Foundation, was hired to take charge.

Meyer was a pioneer. He was daring, or reckless, depending on your point of view. Instead of abiding by the old, prosaic rule of 65/35 (whereby 65 percent of your portfolio is invested in U.S. equities and 35 percent in bonds), Meyer and his team of portfolio managers moved Harvard's money into all sorts of things: private equity, real estate, oil, gas, fixed-income arbitrage, timberland, hedge funds, high-tech start-ups, foreign equities, credit-default swaps, interest-rate swaps, cross-currency swaps, commodities, venture-capital funds, junk bonds. As if all those exotic, illiquid investments weren't enough to amplify the returns, Meyer added a heap of leverage. It was dizzying, Harvard's portfolio.

The best money managers in the country dreamed of working for Meyer. "It was an intellectually charged place," recalls a portfolio manager who worked at Harvard Management Company in the 1990s. "They were the brightest people that I have ever met," I was told by another portfolio manager who worked under Meyer.

If outsiders viewed the money managers at Harvard Management Company as cowboys—and they did—it may be because Meyer demanded performance above all. "Jack basically said he had no use for anybody who couldn't contribute value," said an admiring Frank Dunau, who worked for Meyer until 2001. "Unless you can beat the S&P, there's no reason for you to be here" is how Meyer put it, according to Dunau. "I mean, if you're not adding value, why am I paying you?"

For a long time, Meyer's daring strategy worked flawlessly. Between fiscal 1990 and 2008, Harvard's endowment boasted an average annual growth rate of 14.3 percent. That's a spectacular performance. The Wilshire TUCS index, which tracks the performance of 1,200 U.S. foundations and endowments, grew by a median annual rate of only 9.7 percent over that same time frame.

For all that, the long-term performance of Harvard's endowment doesn't tell us the whole story. What really happened is that somewhere along the line, around the year 2000 by most accounts, Harvard Management Company, like the university itself, lost its way.

In droves, the best portfolio managers started to leave Harvard Management Company. For most of them, the issue was money, pure and simple. Under Meyer, what Harvard paid his people was based on performance—in most cases, about 10 percent of what they made for the university. As the endowment got bigger, their incentive bonuses got bigger, too. And before long, the (mostly) men at Harvard Management Company were by far out-earning any administrator or professor at the university they were working for.

Jon Jacobson, age 34, was Harvard's top earner in 1995. He made $6 million that year, roughly 25 times more than what the university's then president, Neil Rudenstine, was being paid. Two years later, in 1997, Jacobson, a former trader at Shearson Lehman Brothers, made $7.6 million. By 1998, Jacobson was making $10.2 million.

Resentment followed. At first, articles criticizing Harvard's well-paid or overpaid money managers were limited to *The Harvard Crimson* and *The Boston Globe*. Then *The Wall Street Journal* got its hands on the story. Soon after that, in 1998, and backed by $500 million of seed capital from Harvard's endowment, Jacobson quit to start his own hedge fund; no one had to know how much money he was earning.

Complaints about excessive compensation at Harvard Management Company gathered force, like an avalanche or a mudslide. By the early 2000s, Harvard's top moneymen were making as much as $30 million to $40 million a year. Finally, in 2003, seven members of Harvard's class of 1969 wrote a strong letter of protest to the university's president, Larry Summers. They spoke out loudly, publicly, informing any member of the media who would listen that compensation at Harvard Management Company was "obscene."

At other American universities, where investing money for the institution is regarded as a kind of public service, Harvard's swagger raised deep suspicion. "Harvard became a bunch of mercenaries," the chief investment officer of another big private university told me.

One day in late April, I visited Walter Cabot—Harvard College class of 1955, first president of Harvard Management Company, and a descendant of one of Boston's most distinguished First Families. Almost 20 years have passed since Cabot was pushed out of Harvard Management Company and replaced by Jack Meyer. He's now 76 years old and semi-retired. "I always told people I had the greatest job in the world," Cabot said, nostalgically. "I could've probably made a lot more money doing something else, but my goal was to do something unique and different for an institution that I went to."

For nearly two hours, as I sat in his modest office in Wellesley, Massachusetts, Cabot reminisced, in monologue. Again and again, he kept returning to the subject of money and its discontents: "I mean, unlike New York, I guess we weren't greedy. We didn't know any better." Wearing a blue oxford-cloth shirt and khaki trousers, Cabot moved slowly across the room, supported by two metal canes. "We tried to run an honest, simple business. We tried to abide by the rules," he continued. "Obviously, we weren't there to go to the poorhouse, but you were there to do an honest trade and work hard and produce results and take pride in what you did. And money for the sake of money, or power, or whatever money is, was really not the objective."

Under Jack Meyer, making money was the sole objective of Harvard Management Company. That was its job. Located in a modern skyscraper in downtown Boston, well insulated from Harvard's right-thinking campus, on the other side of the river, Harvard Management Company resembled a typical Wall Street trading floor. That its portfolio managers were being paid according to the rules of Wall Street should have surprised no one.

In response to the growing protests about "obscene" compensation,

Meyer tried to reason with the Harvard community. If Harvard were to outsource its portfolio to various hedge funds, instead of managing its money in-house, he argued, the fees would amount to at least twice what he paid his traders. The end justified the means: consider the billions of dollars that his team was earning for the university!

Meyer's pragmatic line of reasoning was ignored. Meanwhile, more of his best people left in disgust. "You get to the point where you just don't want the ugly calls or the press coverage," I was told by one of Meyer's former portfolio managers. "I just said enough's enough."

There were other pressures on Meyer. Ever since Larry Summers, a renowned economist who'd served as secretary of the Treasury under Bill Clinton, had become president of Harvard, in 2001, he'd been questioning Meyer's investment strategies. Meyer, who was used to running things his own way, was insulted. Something else: Summers implied that Meyer was encouraging his top money managers to strike out on their own. By investing Harvard's money in their new hedge funds, and allowing them to keep their deferred compensation, Meyer was making it far too easy for his best traders to quit. "I think Larry is largely responsible for blowing up the place," one Meyer loyalist told me, still bitter at the memory of Summers's meddling. "Harvard Management Company worked perfectly when the board left them alone!"

Another critic should be cited: Robert Rubin, Summers's mentor and his predecessor as secretary of the Treasury under Bill Clinton. Rubin—a powerful member of the Harvard Corporation (the university's executive governing body), a former director of Harvard Management Company, and a graduate of Harvard College, class of 1960—was contemptuous of Meyer's daring investment strategies. As one person put it to me, Rubin was on the "warpath." To anyone who would listen—Harvard's board, Wall Street, Larry Summers—Rubin kept chipping away at Meyer's credibility.

By 2005, Jack Meyer had had enough. After 15 years at Harvard Management Company, frustrated by the circular fights about compensation, and sick of justifying himself to Summers and Rubin, he walked out and started his own giant hedge fund. Shamelessly, he took many of Harvard

Management Company's best people with him, about 30 portfolio managers and traders, along with the chief risk officer, chief operating officer, and chief technology officer. Harvard's trading floor was decimated. It was "like a Ferrari without the engine," I was told by a portfolio manager who arrived after Meyer left. Rubin, for one, was furious, according to someone who knows him well: "In Rubin's opinion, Meyer crippled the institution."

It took almost a year for Harvard Management Company to find someone to replace Meyer; few qualified people wanted the job. Meanwhile, under an interim manager, Harvard invested more and more of its money passively, in pools of stocks, bonds, and commodities intended to mirror the performance of the markets as a whole. It was safer that way; as long as Harvard's portfolio managers didn't underperform the broader stock market, no one could blame them for making bad calls.

But the bigger issue for Harvard was timing: Meyer's departure coincided with the peak of hedge-fund mania. With a reduced staff, and no particular investment strategy, Harvard foolishly sank huge sums of money into the latest, most glamorous hedge funds: notably, $500 million went to Old Lane Partners, a "multi-strategy" fund co-founded by Vikram Pandit in early 2006.

Some of these investments were a disaster—Old Lane folded last year after posting giant losses. Moreover, like other investors late to the game, Harvard was paying its outside managers preposterously high fees: typically an annual management fee of 2 percent of assets under management, plus a performance fee equal to 20 percent of that year's return. Harvard Management Company agreed to other conditions—conditions that contributed to Harvard's frantic scramble for cash late last year: long "lockup periods," whereby investors can't take back their money for five years, more or less, and "gate provisions," which limit how much money investors can withdraw at the end of the lockup period.

Finally, in February 2006, Meyer was replaced by Mohamed El-Erian, an economist with a Ph.D. from Oxford, whose most recent job had been overseeing $28 billion in emerging-market debt at PIMCO, the big money-management firm. Hoping to improve relations with his bosses across the Charles River, El-Erian lectured at Harvard Business School; he also spoke regularly with the editors of *Harvard Magazine*, and he created a Web site devoted to news and information about Harvard Management Company.

In terms of his investment strategy, El-Erian largely followed Meyer's aggressive approach to Harvard's portfolio. In fact, in some respects, El-Erian turned up the dial on risk: moving heavily into emerging markets, for example, he invested in a fund with EFG-Hermes, an investment bank based in Cairo that specializes in the Middle East and North Africa. At the same time, guarding against a possible downturn, he put in place more and more "tail-risk hedging," insurance against risk. In El-Erian's book *When Markets Collide,* written during his time at Harvard, he describes his hedging strategy as "Armageddon protection."

El-Erian stayed at Harvard for less than two years. In September 2007, having barely settled in, he announced that he was returning to his former employer, PIMCO, as co–chief executive officer. According to a friend, El-Erian felt suffocated at Harvard and couldn't wait to get out.

Under El-Erian, Harvard's endowment climbed 23 percent in fiscal 2007, comfortably above that year's 20 percent increase in the Dow Jones Industrial Average. Despite that success, El-Erian, an outsider, quickly became the subject of unsubstantiated attacks, many of them based on rumor and malice. Harvard tends to be like that. He was "a complete fraud," a former Harvard Management Company employee assured me. He "wrecked the place." "He's not an investor," opined someone else. *He didn't belong.*

On July 1, 2008, after a drawn-out search for yet another leader, Jane Mendillo took charge of Harvard Management Company. Having spent 15 years there, from 1987 to 2002, working for Walter Cabot and then Jack Meyer, Mendillo was a safe choice, a well-connected insider. That said, her only experience running an endowment was at Wellesley

College, where for six years she capably oversaw the school's relatively modest endowment, helping it grow from $1 billion to $1.6 billion.

Congeniality and competence may or may not be assets in the money-management business. If they are, no one I've spoken to has a bad word to say about Mendillo. "She's a very pleasant and analytic person," attested Scott Sperling, co-president of Thomas H. Lee Partners, who worked with Mendillo at Harvard Management Company in the 1980s and 1990s. Said someone else who used to work with Mendillo, "You know, she was someone that always was there early, always there late. I think she was very dedicated." A third person: "She's very orderly. She's organized."

Is Jane Mendillo the right person to lead Harvard Management Company? It's too early to tell. During the crisis of the past year, she's performed as inadequately as everyone else; nor has she given her nervous public much in the way of reassurance. We do know that she's laid off about a quarter of her staff and that she's cautiously moved more of Harvard's portfolio into cash, even as the market climbs. Otherwise, there has been no news, good or bad, from Harvard Management Company since late 2008. [Mendillo left Harvard Management Company at the end of 2014.]

On May 2, at the annual gathering of Harvard's Committee on University Resources—a privileged group of donors who have given $1 million or more to the university—Mendillo was the luncheon speaker. According to one discouraged alumnus who was present, Mendillo used nothing but empty rhetoric and dodged all the tough questions. A "pep talk" is the way her speech was described to me.

Any week now, Harvard will be releasing its final year-end results. One of my sources on the board of Harvard Management Company reports the endowment is down less than predicted and in line with losses at other universities: in the range of 23 to 25 percent. Give or take a few percentage points, however, what really matters is that Harvard's endowment is way down, and, more, thanks to (1) the unhappy arithmetic of investing and (2) the need to withdraw money from the endowment to fund the university's operations, it will probably take more than a decade for the value of the endowment to return to where it was in the heady days of 2008.

Let's back up for a moment and return to more prosperous times. It's 2001 and Larry Summers has just been named president of Harvard University. Unapologetically combative, Summers is determined to lead (or force) the university into a glorious renaissance. Gazing into the future, Summers envisions smaller class sizes, a more diverse student body, a younger and more energetic faculty, a revitalized core curriculum, cooperation among Harvard's balkanized divisions, and a greatly expanded campus. Above all, at a university best known for its focus on the humanities, business, and law, Summers hopes to make science a priority. Belatedly, Harvard will match and even surpass the lavish investments that Princeton and Stanford have plowed into the sciences over the previous decade.

As Summers recently remarked to one of his colleagues, "I held out the hope that Boston would be to this century what Florence was to the 15th century."

Harvard's soaring endowment was the key to Summers's blueprint for the future. Instead of promoting fiscal restraint, he argued, Harvard should loosen its purse strings. The endowment should be used for "priorities of transcendent importance," he proclaimed to *The New York Times* in 2008, after resigning as Harvard's 27th president. "There is a temptation to go for what is comfortable," he added, "but this would be a mistake. The universities have matchless resources that demand that they seize the moment."

Caught up in the exuberance of the new millennium, and guided by Summers's transcendent vision for the university, Harvard embarked on a plan of action. In September 2003, Summers cut a crimson ribbon marking the opening of the $260 million New Research Building, at Harvard Medical School: at 525,000 square feet, it was the largest building in Harvard's history. The previous year, construction had started on the 249,000-square-foot Center for Government and International Studies (CGIS). Designed by Henry N. Cobb, architect of Boston's John Hancock Tower, CGIS, with its two identical buildings covered in fragile terra-cotta panels, ended up costing a reported $140 million, more than four times what the planners had first anticipated.

The New College Theatre came next—a beautiful 272-seat space, built on the site of the Hasty Pudding Theatre of 1888 and retaining, at great expense, the Hasty Pudding's historic façade. A few months later, in November 2007, Harvard's Laboratory for Integrated Science and Engineering was completed. Its vital stats: 137,000 square feet, an internationally esteemed architect (1996 Pritzker winner Rafael Moneo), and a $155 million price tag, funded almost entirely with debt.

To be fair, when the Laboratory for Integrated Science and Engineering was still in the planning stage, Harvard intended to defray the cost of the building by selling naming rights. Nevertheless, for some now hazy reason, construction was well under way before a willing donor had been secured, and by then it was too late to seize the moment. "It is a lot harder to raise money for a building that has already been built" is how a former dean of Harvard College explained the situation at the time.

Where in the world were the voices urging restraint? "Some people really wondered at the expanse of the new buildings and the pace at which it was happening," I was informed by Everett Mendelsohn, a professor emeritus in the Department of the History of Science, who's been at Harvard since 1960. "Periodically, discussions would take place at the Faculty Council, and one of the deans or the presidents would come, and there would be questions asked. But there wasn't a regular give-and-take. . . . I'd say there was a sense that the critics were not being heard."

Even today construction is going on at Harvard. The polished 520,000-square-foot Northwest Science Building, designed by Skidmore, Owings & Merrill, has just opened. Over at Harvard Law School, a $250 million project, designed by the firm of Robert A. M. Stern, is a work in progress: a giant limestone building with a 700-car underground garage.

On the subject of Harvard's billion-dollar construction pit in Allston: over the years, quietly, the university had been assembling and buying hundreds of acres in the Allston-Brighton area, more land than it owns in Cambridge. Once home to slaughterhouses and stockyards and stench, Allston seemed the most likely place for Harvard to expand. In a 2006 interview with *Harvard Magazine,* Summers described Allston as "the launching pad for something new that reflects the dreams of the most creative young scientists in the world."

The university's master plan called for a "seminal" transformation of 220 acres in Allston over the next 50 years: in place of broken pavement and abandoned warehouses, Harvard would build new walkways and bicycle lanes. A paved piazza would be surrounded by theaters and museums. A new pedestrian bridge would span the Charles River. Here and there, landscapers would plant abundant, well-tended gardens. Small, charming shops would be adjacent to outdoor cafés. All that and more was the Utopian plan.

After decades of planning, construction began in Allston in 2007. Part one was to be the $1.2 billion Allston Science Complex. At 589,000 square feet it would include four buildings designed to house the Harvard Stem Cell Institute, the Harvard Medical School's Department of Systems Biology, the Department of Stem Cell and Regenerative Biology, and the new Wyss Institute for Biologically Inspired Engineering.

Earlier this year, however, when it became clear to everyone at Harvard that the effects of the global recession would be profound, construction at Allston was abruptly stopped. Not, mind you, that the verb "to stop" is part of Harvard's current vocabulary—the project is being "reassessed" and "recalibrated." Once its mammoth foundation has been poured (for otherwise the unstable mud walls could cave in), the Allston Science Complex will be suspended. [New architectural renderings for the Allston Science Complex were unveiled in January 2017 and construction has resumed. The complex is expected to open in late 2020.]

Meanwhile, as Harvard pauses to recalibrate, five huge and silent cranes, like prehistoric relics, like monoliths, dominate the local skyline— or at least they did when I was there in May. Residents of Allston are furious; they think they've been double-crossed. YOU DIRTY RATS, screamed a cover of the *Boston Herald*, referring to Allston's growing rodent problem and, subversively, to "rats" at Harvard jumping ship.

In theory, Larry Summers, who now heads the National Economic Council under Barack Obama, may have been the right person to lead Harvard into a glorious renaissance. In reality, however, when Summers was president of Harvard, he alienated just about every faculty member who crossed his path. Instead of being admired as a visionary, he was said to be arrogant. Instead of being recognized as a bold and fearless leader, he was perceived as a cerebral bully. That Summers suggested women lacked a natural ability for sciences did not help matters one bit. Nor did his very public feud with the professor of African-American studies Cornel West, who decamped for Princeton. In early 2006, anticipating a vote of no confidence by the Faculty of Arts and Sciences, Summers resigned.

"The fact that they fired him is a symptom of everything that's wrong with Harvard," one of Harvard's big donors told me. "He's not politically correct or diplomatic—he's incredibly provocative. What he really got fired for was attacking waste and abuse in the Faculty of Arts and Sciences."

Above all, what Harvard needs right now is stability. "Harvard, institutionally, never had change when I first came here," the law professor Alan Dershowitz told me. "It was like the old baseball teams; you were born here and you died here. . . . But the turnover now has become like corporate turnover—and that always takes a toll."

The need to restore calm may explain why the unprovocative Drew Gilpin Faust, a well-respected academic and the founding dean of Harvard's Radcliffe Institute for Advanced Study, was installed as Harvard's president in 2007 (following a year in which former president Derek Bok temporarily left the university).

Faust is not known as a visionary. In fact, outside of academia, no one I've spoken to has any idea who Drew Faust is or why she got the job in the first place. One undergraduate I spoke to described Faust as "expressionless." An alumnus, having recently attended a dinner where

Faust was the guest speaker, told me she was exceedingly dull—so dull he was reminded of those animated Peanuts cartoons from the 1970s, the ones where adults appear offscreen as so many disembodied, insubstantial "voices" that say nothing but "wa-wa-wa."

To leave her imprint on Harvard, and possibly to distance herself from Summers with his tight focus on the sciences, Faust has dedicated herself to elevating the arts. Last December, outlining her vision of the future, Faust released a written statement: "In times of uncertainty, the arts remind us of our humanity and provide the reassuring proof that we, along with the Grecian urn, have endured and will continue to do so."

Of course Harvard will endure—but in contrast to Keats's Grecian urn, which is poetically frozen in time, Harvard must change. Aside from making speeches and releasing inspirational statements about the permanence of art, what is Drew Faust doing to change things in Cambridge? What is her vision? According to Dershowitz, "Her vision at this point is preserving the university. She's in a defensive posture."

A s you may have guessed by now, Harvard refused to cooperate when I was reporting this story. At first, the university's public-relations apparatus ignored me. Week after week, e-mail after e-mail, I'd be assured that someone or someone else was unavailable—in meetings, or on vacation, or away from his desk, or out of the office, ill. When I did manage to track someone down, I was thrown a sop of evasive prose. ("I don't feel we've made a decision about how to best engage for your piece," the vice president for public affairs told me in an e-mail.) A formally scheduled interview with the dean of the business school was canceled at the very last minute. ("Glitch" was the subject heading of an e-mail informing me that the meeting was off.) Even requests for basic, public financial information were bungled. When I asked him a simple question about Harvard's debt, one of the university's many communications directors stonewalled: "I'm not a numbers person at all," he said, wide-eyed.

One day, desperate for someone in authority to talk on the record, I caught up with Michael Smith, dean of the Faculty of Arts and Sciences, as he was leaving the town-hall meeting of undergraduates at Boylston Hall. Unaware that I was *persona non grata* on the Harvard campus, he talked openly to me.

I walked with him from the meeting to his car. How did the university get into this mess? I asked as we cut across Harvard Yard. Smith stopped. "First of all," he remarked, reinforcing what I already knew, "the endowment growth did not keep up with the expenses. We hired faculty faster than we really should have. . . . We put up buildings based on debt financings—not fund-raising. And we decided the right thing to do was this financial-aid package, even though, again, we didn't have new finances behind it to actually do it."

A popular professor with an undergraduate degree from Princeton and a Ph.D. from Stanford, an expert in computer architecture, and co-founder of a data-security company called Liquid Machines, Smith, 47, is a driven and dedicated man. Yet even he conceded that his current job has been taxing. He's held the position for less than two years; still, as he remarked to me, it "seems like forever."

We were in the parking lot, Michael Smith and I. The sun had set. Smith looked tired. It can't be easy to be charged with cost-cutting at a university that refuses to use the term "cost-cutting" and instead goes on about "alignments" and "resizements." He added: "The hope was that the endowment would continue to increase, and we could get some support from our alumni base to help pay for those changes in the program."

He paused. "And then, of course, the bottom fell out of the market."

[Harvard's endowment is $35.7 billion, the biggest in the world. Harvard Management Company plans to lay off roughly half of its staff by the end of 2017.]

COLUMBIA'S ST. ANTHONY HALL

"HALL OF SECRETS"

By John Sedgwick

NOVEMBER 2015

I t was nearly midnight and drizzling outside Columbia's Saint Anthony Hall fraternity, and I was trying to sneak into its annual Halloween party. Before me, the building's giddy Beaux-Arts façade glowed in the lamplight. I was keen to move among the beautiful young things as they writhed to a D.J.'s beat. But mostly I just wanted to get inside.

I had come with an out-of-towner who was genetically St. A's— "Probably the 10th or 12th member in my family," he told me, conveying the tone of the place, then adding nervously, "Just don't use my name." He had arrived wearing New York black, no costume, but I had brought along an owlish mask, the closest thing I could find to the scarlet number in the Venetian-orgy scene in *Eyes Wide Shut*. I'd heard the stories: about the rivers of alcohol, the stacks of 20s by the backgammon board, the supposed drug use, the hot tub on the roof, the beauties reared back against the antique billiard table. An Asian slave was rumored to be kept in the basement to do laundry for what is referred to as The Membership. As part of their initiation, new members were said to be required to buy and then burn a plane ticket to China.

As my friend pressed the front doorbell, I peered through the glass into a deep, dimly lit foyer that led to some stone steps. There was the creak of an opening door, then a soft tread. A young woman with dark, Pre-Raphaelite hair came toward us.

"NO COMMENT"

It is fitting to enter St. A's in disguise, for nothing here is quite as it appears. I had come to investigate a crime that may seem like something out of the game of Clue. But the scandal created an uproar in the Hall that has tarnished its image, caused heavy soul-searching among some members, and led to prison time. The crime? Grand larceny, inside job. Upwards of $650,000 stolen by the genial, erudite Walter Perry, a devoted member with a Ph.D. in classical Greek whose heavy eyebrows, slim mustache, and glittering eyes suggest a kindly but perhaps unreliable uncle. By universal agreement, Perry kept the Hall together with Krazy Glue for three decades, serving as chief undergraduate officer, then as a trustee, and finally as president of the board, often doubling as treasurer and secretary when those gentlemen failed to show up. He worked out of a small office off the front hall at St. A's, just inside the doorway. For all this time, Perry says, he was the resident historian and keeper of the secrets; a bill collector; a scrutinizer of accounts; a fixer for several varieties of "girl trouble"; and a chauffeur for the alcoholically disabled.

Then there was the matter of the 362 checks Perry wrote to himself on a Saint Anthony Hall account, which led to an internal investigation and ultimately to criminal prosecution, the outcome of which landed Perry in the Ogdensburg Correctional Facility, in upstate New York.

Did he steal the money? When I asked him, his face tightened, like that of a prizefighter about to deliver a punch. "It wasn't there!" he told me firmly. "The whole question is absurd." He insists that the finances of the organization were so tight that, if he had stolen $650,000, the organization's bills couldn't have been paid and he would have set off alarms all over the place. Perry maintains he has said the same thing every time he's been offered a chance to confess his guilt in exchange for leniency, and then has gone on to say a lot more, with elliptical baroque flourishes. A better answer might just have been "No." This is not Perry's way, however, and that, as much as any crime, may be what got him into so much trouble. It may also be why nobody believes him, making Perry about the loneliest man on the planet. "Everybody has left me," he says. "Everybody."

But everybody is not always right. Being a secret society, the Hall initially declined to respond to any specific questions about the case, instead furnishing a one-page official statement followed by a two-page legal reiteration. At my request a loyal brother tried, through a St. A's intermediary named John Dawson, an investment adviser with LDR Capital Management, to interest members of the board of trustees in speaking to me. Dawson replied that the whole Perry business was "very sad," but no. When I called Dawson directly, he replied "No comment" to each of my questions.

Here were some of the questions I had: What happened to the two boxes of financial records—potentially exculpatory material that Perry says disappeared from his office—when the case broke? Is it true that two board members arranged, over Perry's objections, to get a third member onto the board, creating the coalition that ultimately led to the audit that in turn resulted in *The People of the State of New York* v. *Walter Perry*? And why, after everything Perry had done for the Hall, did the Hall send the matter to criminal court rather than to civil court, where the fraternity would have had a shot at quietly getting back its money?

And there was something else. The Hall first took the matter to Manhattan district attorney Robert Morgenthau, in 2008, but the office issued no indictment until Cyrus Vance took office, two years later. The son of a former secretary of state, Vance had attended Groton School, as did Perry and his younger brother, Proal. Vance had once been close to Proal—who is a wine importer in the Fort Lauderdale area—and had always been friendly to Walter. Until "the cops showed up at six A.M.," Perry recalls bitterly, to roust him out of bed, arrest him, slap him in handcuffs, and take him to the Tombs, a jail in Lower Manhattan and one of the more miserable places on earth.

A SACRED BOND

There are other Saint Anthony Halls, about a dozen of them, most notably at Yale and M.I.T., but Columbia's is the first, the alpha chapter. It is the model for the raucous, hyper-elite Hamilton House in *Gossip Girl*. Drawn from the same source, all St. A's chapters follow more or less the same practices. Members call one another Brother (or, now, Sister), timing weekly meetings to the slant of the sun; installing hidden rooms in their elegant chapter houses; calling the true president, his name known only to members, "Number One," and the titular president "Number Two"; and ending most get-togethers with the members insentient and horizontal. Details of the rituals are closely held, but at Princeton they are said to involve an oath of loyalty to a hooded figure known as the Most Noble Archon, along with the recitation in Latin of a vow from Scripture, with the speaker agreeing to give all his possessions to the poor. (St. A's members have not been known to follow through.)

Saint Anthony Hall was founded in the mid-19th century by a 15-year-old English schoolboy, Edward Forbes Travis, who had come to Columbia with an odd fascination for St. Anthony the Great, the gnarled fourth-century mystic who wandered the Egyptian desert and inspired early monks with his soul-purifying asceticism. In 1847, on the saint's feast day—January 17—Travis introduced a friend to certain rituals he'd brought from England. The two students forged a sacred bond that was soon extended to others, the appeal being not so much the invented mysteries as what underlay them: the age-old collegiate yearning for bromance. In its high-Victorian moment, St. A's also cultivated something of a literary flavor: members would spend hours reading essays to one another for general critique or amusement.

When the fraternity was founded, Columbia was down by Wall Street. Then it moved to Midtown. When Columbia moved to Morningside Heights, a St. A's man got advance word, because he was a Columbia trustee, and, on the cheap, snapped up a very desirable piece of property on Riverside Drive with a Hudson view. The jaunty clubhouse was designed by another Saint Anthony Hall member, Henry Hornbostel, who also designed the Williamsburg Bridge.

The various St. A's are like franchises—all the same but all a little bit different. Collectively, they have produced an impressive list of members: Charles Kuralt, of CBS; Lewis Lapham, the longtime editor of *Harper's*; the baseball writer Peter Gammons; the cartoonist Jeff MacNelly—and those are just the ones in the media world. Other members include the diplomat Strobe Talbott, World War II's Admiral William "Bull" Halsey, C.I.A. troublemaker Cornelius Roosevelt, and E. Digby Baltzell, the sociologist who coined the term "Wasp." Unlike the usual campus fraternities, most of the St. A's own their buildings, making them little worlds unto themselves. Think of them, perhaps, as a cross between Skull and Bones and a Princeton eating club, with a large heaping of Society and more than a dash of *Animal House*. It is an open question how much a university can interfere with admission policies at any of the St. A's. At Columbia, the answer seems to be: very little. In New York, the Hall rises six stories, from the mysterious basement crypt (the staircase to which is hidden behind a secret panel) to the three residential floors at the top. St. A's members live there, in rooms that house about 20 people of both sexes. Members eat their meals at St. A's. Two full-time employees are there to serve them, a steward and a cook. There is a library, a well-stocked bar, and a ballroom, whose chandelier graced the cover of the group Vampire Weekend's first album. The financial picture is not public, but a few years ago, when Perry was still in charge, each semester's dues ran to just $400. The meal plan added another $1,800 per semester, and the residential fees per semester could run to $2,200. Despite many efforts, there is little by way of an endowment.

Of late, the Hall has become slightly more multicultural, but for the longest time it was 200-proof Wasp, its 40 or so undergraduate members drawn not just from the elite boarding schools—Andover, Exeter, St. Paul's, Choate, and the Cate School, in California—but from the secret societies of that elite. More than anything else, the distinguishing characteristics of a St. A's member are two: an extremely rich mother and father.

A LITTLE DIGGING

I know Walter Perry, or at least I think I do. We went to Groton together, where he was two years ahead of me. I remember him as brainy and a little aloof. He was smallish and southern, with an accent you didn't normally hear in New England, and he celebrated Robert E. Lee's birthday every year with cake and candles. I recall an afternoon when we stayed together at the table after lunch—he wanted to show me how he was going to do away with the Pentagon (a popular notion back then). He made a pile of sugar, bent down, and blew. Then he smiled as he looked up. It may be for this reason that a Groton friend calls him a "shape-shifter." I hadn't seen him again until I bumped into him at a school gathering at the Colony Club, in Manhattan, almost two years ago. I asked him what he'd been up to.

"I've been in prison," he said, above the din of cocktail conversation. He might have said he'd been in California. It was either the neutrality of the utterly innocent or the neutrality of the utterly not innocent. I couldn't quite tell. I didn't pop the obvious question, "What the hell happened?" Instead, I let it go for a full year, until we met again at the same event and picked up where we'd left off. This time, he offered a few details of his experience—about St. A's and about the Tombs, with its mingling of drug dealers and subway pickpockets, and about the toughs he lived among at Ogdensburg. After that, I had to know more, and I arranged to meet Perry in various places—in the coffee shop of the Gershwin Hotel; near the clock at Grand Central Terminal; at the fourth-floor apartment he shares with his wife, on 157th Street; and finally on a park bench by the Hudson, the nearest he could come to Saint Anthony Hall without violating the terms of his parole.

If I was being played, I was being well played, for I liked Perry—his astounding politeness, his good-humored forbearance, and his astonishingly broad learning. All of our conversations were delightful, a bit like talking to an Oxford don who knows as much about Herodotus as about the unique action of a Remington rifle. I also came to appreciate the fact that, while Perry and St. A's were irreconcilably at odds, they were well matched too, which may be why Walter had made the place his second home, if not his first, for so much of his adulthood. Both aspired to something better, and both worked hard to keep up appearances.

To get at the truth of Walter Perry takes a little digging. To start with, you have to understand his father, Walter Emmett Perry Jr., and to understand him, you need to understand *his* father, Walter Emmett Perry Sr. That first Walter Perry was a Birmingham prosecutor who, in 1957, took on six Klansmen for castrating a black man named Edward Aaron with a razor blade. Two of the men confessed and were given suspended sentences. The other four were found guilty and sentenced to 20 years. "A magnificent old pillar of the law," says our Walter Perry III.

No one would say that about his father. Walter Perry Jr. served in the Alabama legislature during the George Wallace years, and, with his barrel chest and booming voice, he could fill the entire chamber with his charm. The charm gradually dissipated as alcohol flooded in.

Walter junior sent "Sticks," as he called his son, to Groton. There was no scholarship—Walter junior just never paid, and the headmaster for a while decided the whole thing was amusing. Walter III woke up to reality the summer he turned 13, when he got out of bed to discover that most of the family's possessions had suddenly been seized by state marshals. Young Walter was stupefied, his father cavalier. Later, in bank-ruptcy court, the opposing counsel asked Walter junior, "You mean to tell this court you own nothing but the clothes on your back?" Perry replied in his courtliest tones: "Oh no, sir. I do not own these clothes. Or any clothes at all. My wife is simply accommodating enough to own a selection of clothes in my size which she permits me to borrow from time to time."

To Walter III, his father consisted of "two sets of facts that never touched." One was designed to show his magnificence, the other to demonstrate his absolute lack of net worth. But Walter III could never quite tell which set of facts was the true measure of the man.

THE GRAY CLOUD

Walter's life fell apart when he was thrown out of Groton a few weeks before graduation. He and two classmates were caught in town, a hanging offense in those years of upheaval. Walter regularly made the honor list and was a devoted Grotonian. He'd been admitted to Harvard, but that was off now. He'd have to settle for Columbia, but not before the fabled Harry Coleman, Columbia's dean of students, had him in for a little talk about "his values and purpose in life." Coleman believed in second chances. Incredibly, he'd once been shot five times by a deranged student upset for being suspended because of his grades, but Coleman reappeared at his desk, his arm in a sling, a few weeks later—and never pressed charges. Coleman, a St. A's alum, was favorably disposed toward the studious, well-mannered Walter Perry.

As a Groton boy—Greek ace in need of redemption—Perry was per-fect for a high-end frat, but Perry himself wasn't so sure about St. A's. It wasn't exactly a literary society anymore, what with everybody drinking themselves silly. But he took a room on one of the upper floors, acquired a few close St. A's friends, and gradually made the Hall his home. He got married a few weeks after graduation, to a former Manhattanville student of distinguished lineage named Mary Gamble Kennard. Walter took Mary to Trinity College, Dublin, where he studied for a Ph.D. in classics with the reigning Homeric scholar at the time, William Bedell Stanford. Back in the U.S., he discovered that the degree wasn't good for much and had to settle for teaching Latin at the Hackley School, in Tarrytown, New York.

Then the fidgets set in. He jumped to a Manhattan securities firm called Laidlaw, which was kept afloat at times by the hefty backgammon winnings of the chairman, Bob Clayton. Backgammon couldn't carry Laidlaw forever, and, in 1983, Perry shifted briefly to the investment firm Rooney Pace, whose chairman would later be indicted in a $100 million fraud scheme. Perry then teamed up with a partner to buy a small company that developed computer systems to assist foreign firms with regulatory compliance. Fiduciary Automation, it was called. That one clicked, and he made a good bit of money. In 1997 he joined with another St. A's man to get in on the dot-com boom with Net Dot Uniqueness, which offered a database for business transactions. It wasn't actually a dot-com, but come 2001 it imploded all the same.

By then Walter had created a sweet life, with a charming house in Short Hills, New Jersey, four children he'd soon put through college, and a cherished spot in the Social Register. He had also returned to Saint Anthony Hall, at first just to keep in touch, then to help out, and eventually to do everything imaginable. One of the major draws of the place was John Shurtleff, known universally as Boly, who had attended Groton and was thought to have been a member of the society called the Raven, but such secrets were not to be divulged. At Harvard, Shurtleff had majored in Sanskrit, then settled into life as general counsel for Empire Blue Cross Blue Shield. It's not clear what made so many people worship Boly, but it is plain to see what got to Perry: he was the respectable version of his father.

Boly introduced Walter to a higher realm of Hall mysteries and lured him into them. It was all about the Gray Cloud, a secret cluster of national Saint Anthony Hall eminences so exalted that their names were never written down, but their powers were thought to be unbounded.

Boly apparently was the current supreme ruler of the Gray Cloud; before him, the art historian Winslow Ames, of the Boston Ameses, had held the invisible scepter. Someday, Walter dreamed, the job would be his.

Perry could not get enough of Boly. They spoke on the phone every day they didn't huddle in person at the club. When Boly drank himself legless at the Hall dinners, as he sometimes did, Walter would be the one to drive him home. But now that Boly was pushing 80, Perry was dismayed to learn that the Gray Cloud was to be replaced by something called a "policy committee." Was nothing sacred?

Perry's father died in 2001, under shocking circumstances, slamming his car into a bridge abutment at 80 miles an hour. "Eight o'clock on a Sunday morning," Perry says in a kind of trance. "Clear road. Bright sunshine." And no skid marks. Two years later Perry's wife succumbed to cancer. Boly died a year after that. By then Walter had moved to 105th and Broadway to be closer to the Hall, which became home once more. "It was my anchor to the city," he says. "It was also my anchor to youth, to youthfulness." Perry was already president of the St. A's board. Now, in effect, he was also Boly. He married again, to a woman named Lilian Chance. The wedding was held at Saint Anthony Hall, and Perry spent some of the honeymoon in Paris at a storefront Internet café with coin-operated computers, doing St. A's business.

Perry's reign was not entirely glorious. It was in fact a near-total pain, because the St. A's members weren't just drunken louts; they were immensely entitled drunken louts. He describes his job as "cleaning up after irresponsible children who haven't been toilet-trained." I'll leave aside his comments about sex and drugs. Many tasks were mundane. One year, the sprinkler system froze, bursting the pipes, because an undergraduate had left the oil bill unpaid. Later, when Perry found another one unpaid, he himself drove a check over to the oil company in Queens.

THOSE 362 CHECKS

And so it went until the fall of 2006, when the graduate treasurer, Vance Thurston, with whom Perry had been close, sensed that there was something amiss in the accounts. It tells you a lot about how the place was run that Thurston lived in San Francisco and almost never attended the trustee meetings in New York. But no one else would do the job at all. Thurston coped by leaving it to Perry to produce the financial numbers every month. He later told the story at Perry's trial. Thurston had just been diagnosed with cancer (erroneously, as it turned out), and he felt it prudent to add backup signatories to the Hall's various bank accounts. He asked Perry to switch his transactions from the Chase account that Perry primarily used—ending with the numbers 6363—to one of the new accounts so everything could be consolidated. Months went by, and Perry still had not complied. At one point, Thurston tried to get into the 6363 account himself, but he had only Boly's old ID number, and it didn't work. Meanwhile, the Hall got together an audit committee to derive some firm numbers of its own. Perry told Thurston he was furious about that. Some "Young Turks" who weren't really doing any work of their own were undermining him. Finally, in March of 2008, Thurston got word from Chase that the 6363 account was being summarily closed. Thurston called up Perry to find out what was going on, and Perry told Thurston he didn't like the audit committee snooping around. When Thurston insisted, Perry gave him the codes to the account so he could pull the records.

That's when Thurston found the first check. It was for $30,000, and it was made out to W. E. Perry, signed by Walter Perry, and endorsed by Walter Perry. There were many more such checks—$90,000 worth that one year. Ultimately 362 checks were found, totaling about $650,000.

Perry was summoned to an emergency meeting of the board, overseen by Brian Maas, a criminal-defense lawyer since 1986. The board figured it would need that sort of expertise. In the official statement furnished to me, the board maintains that Perry was given every chance "to explain his actions and restore the missing funds." Perry says that he was immediately cut off from contact with anyone at the Hall, and that he would not have accepted the offer in any case, because he wasn't guilty. In his indignation, he declared that the board was complicit in any financial improprieties, and demanded that the board vote "up or down" on whether the Hall should even continue to exist. Instead, Perry was asked to resign from his position as president, which he did. Ultimately, the board was advised by Maas to hand Walter Perry's case over to the D.A.'s office for further investigation. And in May 2011 the Perry case got under way in the New York County Courthouse, in Lower Manhattan.

If a lawyer who defends himself has a fool for a client, that must go double for a non-lawyer who defends himself. In the trial transcript, all 3,500 pages of it, Perry plays the brilliant fool, the man who knows everything about legal theory but nothing about how to ask a witness a simple question. By going *pro se*, as it's termed, Perry wanted to avoid the hammy theatricality of the law in favor of something more intellectually satisfying. Plus, he relished the prospect of facing down his accusers. But it was hopeless.

A dozen members of St. A's testified over the course of the month-long trial, and each landed a heavy blow. But it was Thurston who finished him off by describing in detail the hundreds of checks that Perry had made out to himself. Perry would contend that the 6363 account was always intended to be personal, and that the deposits from the Hall were reimbursements for funds that he himself had put into St. A's to cover its ordinary operations. Aside from $40,000 he seemed to have paid a contractor to renovate the windows, most of his contributions had dated from the Boly era, when the Hall was run much more like a private house than a proper institution. But the records that might prove his core contention—that the money he took out replaced money he had put in—were the very ones, Perry claimed, that had disappeared from his office.

Unfortunately for Perry, the prosecutor had plenty of information about Perry's spending habits—his hefty American Express–card payments; his memberships in the Knickerbocker Club and the Downtown Athletic Club; a $21,000 wedding for his daughter; a $16,500 wedding ring for Lilian.

When it was time for Perry to cross-examine, after Thurston's testimony, he had to take a moment to collect himself; he was too choked up to speak. During his opening defense, Perry had turned on his accusers, invoking "a coordinated, biased attack against me by members of a cult." And his friend was one of them. It was Perry's only display of grief at the trial, and he never repeated it with me. A brother had taken him down.

Perry was sentenced to two to six years in prison. He served one year at Ogdensburg, up near the Canadian border, then did another year on work release in Manhattan. In November 2013 he was released on parole. For a time he was denied a bank account and a credit card; with his record and at his age, he does not have much chance of an ordinary job. (He has his own business designing software.) The state is demanding $20,000 annually for 35 years in restitution, and the federal government is after him for back taxes. He has been filing appeals. By way of vengeance he harbors an unlikely ambition, if he can ever exonerate himself, of running against Cyrus Vance for D.A. in 2017. [Perry did not run.]

He must stay away from Saint Anthony Hall. Perry was in Ogdensburg when he received notice that St. A's was planning to drum him out—a ritual, he knew, that involved members putting on robes and then reciting the words that would end Perry's affiliation. Still loyal to St. A's, Perry would not tell me what these words are, but he acknowledged that he was the "custodian of all that ritual and procedure for many years." ("It's your basic bell-book-and-candle excommunication," he told me.) Perry was allowed one last chance to plead to stay on, and scrawled a long, begging letter in pencil, the only writing instrument he was allowed. His plea was rejected.

"ONTOLOGY OF MONEY"

It wasn't until I was deep into the Perry matter that the board furnished me with a "source close to the board" to tell me what the trustees themselves had refused to divulge, namely why it had gone after Walter Perry so hard. The short of it was, the board had no choice. Once it appeared that Perry had spent "a lot" of Saint Anthony Hall money without a good explanation, and then got indignant at a demand for restitution, the board believed that it was obliged to take the matter to the district attorney's office. Ultimately, it was the D.A.'s call to prosecute, not the Hall's. As for the idea of a vendetta, the source dismissed that as ridiculous. "Nobody said, 'We want to get this Walter Perry guy. Let's crucify him.' " And, he added, where's the logic? "If I'm sitting on the board of Saint Anthony Hall, and I know Walter Perry knows something really bad about me, the last thing I am going to want to do is turn him in to the criminal authorities."

Is Walter Perry guilty? I look at him from a certain angle, and I think, Yes, of course. Then I look at him from another, and I think, No, absolutely not. It may be that, like his father, he encompasses two sets of facts that don't overlap. One thing is clear: he did write those checks. But (you could argue) the very obviousness of his guilt may be the clearest proof of his innocence. Was Walter Perry so stupid as to think that nobody would ever notice that he'd cashed 362 checks to himself? Or was this one of those banal cries for help one reads about? Perry has created plenty of spreadsheets with the intention of showing there was no money to steal. Annual revenues during his time amounted at most to about $300,000, barely enough to keep two people on staff, plus pay for meals, parties, utilities, and maintenance. All the bills are known to have been paid, leaving not much by way of surplus to siphon off. So maybe Perry has a point, though the court did not think so. But he can go on, and I do know that when he starts using the phrase "the ontology of money" I want to drive him back to Ogdensburg myself.

Knowing what I do about the mysterious and seemingly inept operation of the Hall, I don't feel my heart warming to that crowd. At Columbia, "St. A's" is sometimes translated as "St. Asshole," and its smugness has earned the scornful envy that is the burden of the young rich everywhere. Could the critical records that might prove "money in" to pay for the club's expenses really have been deep-sixed by people who didn't like Perry's attitude or his pencil mustache? Noting that his wife sometimes calls him Malvolio, Perry acknowledges a puritanical streak that may not have gone down too well at a frat. If Perry was on both ends of the checks, it may be because of the nature of a shoestring operation he ran largely by himself. It doesn't help that Boly Shurtleff, the one witness who might have understood, is dead.

The Hall, in the end, is a place of secrets. I'd hoped to penetrate some of them that drizzly Halloween night, to see the thing up close. But my friend had it wrong—or perhaps he'd meant to get it wrong. The party had been the night before. The dark-haired woman who answered the door was welcoming, though. My friend acted like a member, and that was good enough for her. I put my mask in my pocket. She didn't care. When I got inside the Hall, I understood that, as is so often the case, exclusivity concealed a certain suppurating shabbiness. Saint Anthony Hall is, by nature, a fraternity, a place for beer kegs, blasting music, hookups. It was sparsely furnished with leather couches, a piano that was out of tune, a drab dining-room table. The French windows didn't look out on anything much. Maybe the scene seemed forlorn because there were just two people in evidence, the woman who had let us in and her boyfriend, a smooth, likable guy keen on finance. She intimated that he was the club's "Number One." There was no nimbus of authority around his *GQ* hair. The glory of yesteryear was on the pockmarked walls—an oil portrait of a former club member, an etching of the U.S. Senate, a print of a cricket match. Perry had occupied the tiny office, like a bellman's, off the foyer, trying to make St. A's more than it could be.

The alpha chapter lost a large number of seniors to graduation in 2013 and of late has frankly been pitching "diversity" to replace them. A recent crop includes a Korean, an Austrian, a Mexican, a German, and a former U.S. Marine. The members continue to be people with money. In its newfound desire for "decorum," the club has turned to athletes, primarily rowers. It also tried to summon its literary heritage at least once a semester. One event included a visit from D. T. Max to talk about his biography of David Foster Wallace, a writer who might well have had sport with St. A's. Other events in recent years have raised money for such causes as research on tick-borne Lyme disease and, according to a Hall summary published in *The Columbia Lion,* "children embroiled in the Arab-Israeli conflict." But the Hall will party on to the 40s swing-band sound of Lester Lanin for its annual Valentine's Day Black-Tie Gala. It remains committed to the core values of "intellectual rigor, literary exercise, secrecy, constancy, and devotion."

That is to say: I hadn't missed anything on Halloween. At Saint Anthony Hall, the party is always last year.

"BIG HAIR ON CAMPUS"

By William D. Cohan

JANUARY 2014

Donald J. Trump has 2.43 million followers on Twitter, making him the 670th most followed person in the global Twitterverse. Last fall he was sandwiched there between Lonny Rashid Lynn Jr., better known as the Chicago-born hip-hop artist Common, and Alejandro Fernández, or El Potrillo, the Mexican singer.

The Donald likes to tweet about his many triumphs and to re-tweet exhortations for him to run for president and save the country. On October 29, he re-tweeted a boast from his daughter Ivanka—who has more than 1.5 million followers—that the yet to be completed Trump International Golf Club, in Dubai, was voted by the International Property Awards "the Best Golf Development in the Middle East." That same day, he revealed that his Virginia winery had been awarded the "coveted" Virginia Double Gold Medal.

One project The Donald isn't crowing about on Twitter—or anywhere else, for that matter—is the public-relations problem known first as Trump University and then as the Trump Entrepreneur Initiative, his effort to teach the great unwashed (for as much as $35,000 a head) his vaunted investing techniques. If Eric Schneiderman, the New York attorney general, is to be believed, this particular (now defunct) Trump enterprise was nothing short of out-and-out fraud. Touré, a host of *The Cycle* on MSNBC, appears to agree. He tweeted to The Donald, "Why did you rob all those Trump University students out of their money?"

Schneiderman thinks that's a good question, and he wants a good answer. Last August the attorney general's office filed suit against Trump and his associates for more than $40 million in New York State Supreme Court, claiming that between 2005 and 2011 they "intentionally" misled "over 5,000 individuals nationwide," including some 600 New York State residents, who paid to "participate in live seminars and mentorship programs with the promise of learning Trump's real estate investing techniques." Schneiderman asserted that Trump personally made about $5 million from the endeavor—although Trump said he intended to donate any profits to charity. (Now he says that between legal fees and refunds no money is left to do so.)

At a press conference announcing the suit, Schneiderman claimed that "Mr. Trump used his celebrity status and personally appeared in commercials making false promises to convince people to spend tens of thousands of dollars they couldn't afford for lessons they never got."

Trump wasted little time in responding, hitting the airwaves to call into question Schneiderman's character—he's a "political hack," Trump told *Fox & Friends*—and his motivation for filing the suit. Trump claims that Schneiderman cooked up the lawsuit after visiting with President

Obama—the target of much of Trump's political ire (recall Trump's birther non-bombshell)—in upstate New York. They met on a Thursday and Schneiderman filed the lawsuit that Saturday, leaving Trump incredulous. "It's a helluva coincidence," he tells me. "You meet and then you immediately file a lawsuit and the lawsuit is filed not on a Monday or Tuesday but on a Saturday? . . . I've had a lot of litigation. I have never heard of a lawsuit being filed on a Saturday."

Schneiderman responds, "I assure you I have many more important things to talk to the president about than the fact that we busted this penny-ante fraud. . . . [Trump] seems to be the kind of person who goes to the Super Bowl and thinks the people in the huddle are talking about him." As to why the suit was filed on a Saturday, Schneiderman says that Trump and his attorneys asked him to hold off until the weekend, allowing Trump to leak in advance his side of the story to the Saturday editions of the *New York Post* and *The Wall Street Journal* and "to whip up this strange Web site attacking me."

Trump says Schneiderman came to him hat in hand for a campaign contribution in 2010, when he was thinking about running for office. On one of the three visits that Trump alleges Schneiderman made, Trump gave him $12,500: "He said, 'Can you fix me up with some people?' I set him up with people. Now you can make the case 'Isn't that wonderful that there's somebody who helped him that he'll screw.' But you could also say he's a real disgusting human being."

Trump elaborated in a recent letter to Graydon Carter, the editor of *Vanity Fair*: "He wanted to settle and I didn't. . . . During settlement negotiations, he was asking for campaign contributions. He's a sleazebag and a crook who is driving business out of New York City." To Trump's charges, Schneiderman responds, "The fact that he has a larger megaphone than most fraudsters is what gets all the attention here, so I would expect that he would attempt to distract the court, unsuccessfully. . . . It is true that he did not support me in the Democratic primary when I ran in 2010, and, after I won the primary, he gave me one contribution, which is the only contribution he has ever given me."

Schneiderman fought back with an opinion piece in the *Daily News*, as well as with numerous TV appearances. "Trump has answered with outlandish accusations," he wrote. "That's not surprising for a show-man who has built a career around bluster and hype. But I am not in the entertainment business; I am in the justice business." He conceded that Trump could have settled the case—as another for-profit school did for $10 million—"or answered the charges in a dignified manner through his attorney. Instead," the attorney general continued, "he chose to try the case in the press."

"I went to the Wharton School of Finance," Trump says. "I have a great feeling for education and for knowledge and learning. . . . I love the idea of helping people, because I've had a lot of experience with real estate, to put it mildly."

Trump and his associates Michael Sexton and Jonathan Spitalny formed Trump University as a limited-liability corporation in 2004. The original business plan was to focus on long-distance, Web-based learning, but they would also be "experimenting" with offering "live instructional programs" to paying customers, according to Sexton's sub-poenaed deposition.

The following spring, the New York State Department of Education sent letters to both Trump and Sexton notifying them that Trump University was in violation of state law by calling itself a "university" when "it was not chartered as such" and because it had not been properly "licensed" by the state.

In a series of follow-up conversations and e-mails between Sexton and Joseph Frey, then a state education official, Frey explained that Trump University could avoid the "licensure" provision of the state law if it were to re-incorporate outside of New York State and if it ran no physical seminars in the state. But "Trump University failed to abide by any of these conditions," the attorney general wrote.

Schneiderman claims the "university" continued to use 40 Wall

Street—one of the few buildings in Manhattan that Trump actually owns—as its principal corporate address, including in numerous advertisements. It furthermore conducted "at least fifty live programs in New York between 2006 and 2011." Schneiderman noted that "Trump University LLC" was finally renamed, on May 20, 2010, "The Trump Entrepreneur Initiative LLC."

In his deposition Sexton admitted that the failure to comply with the stipulations was "an oversight" and something he and Trump "forgot" about.

Also misleading, according to Schneiderman, were the claims made in Trump's advertising. In one, published in 2009, Trump looks resplendent in a blue suit while standing in front of one of the buildings that bear his name—but not his ownership—on Manhattan's West Side. "Learn from Donald Trump's handpicked experts how you can profit from the largest real-estate liquidation in history," the ad promises. (He was presumably not referring to the Chapter 11 filings of the three highly leveraged hotel and casino properties he once had a stake in.) The ad pronounced Trump "the most celebrated entrepreneur on earth. He's earned more in a day than most people do in a lifetime. . . . And now he's ready to share—with Americans like you—the Trump process for investing in today's once-in-a-lifetime real estate market."

This was followed by a quotation from The Donald: "I can turn anyone into a successful real estate investor, including you."

Schneiderman argues that Trump University's advertisements, Web site, and promotional materials were just an elaborate ruse. The initial "free seminars," according to the lawsuit, were "the first step in a bait and switch to induce prospective students to enroll in increasingly expensive seminars starting with the three-day $1495 seminar and ultimately [for] advanced seminars such as the 'Gold Elite' program costing $35,000."

"We're going to have professors that are absolutely terrific—terrific people, terrific brains, successful, the best," Trump claimed on videos shown at the seminars. "We're going to have the best of the best. And honestly, if you do not learn from them, if you do not learn from me . . . then you're just not going to make it in terms of the world of success."

That was good enough for June Harris, of White Plains, New York, who had previously taken an online Trump real-estate investing course and found it useful. After the free June 2009 session at a hotel in Stamford, Connecticut—where participants were told to keep $1,000 in their pockets at all times as "a confidence builder for wealth"—Harris signed up for the three-day seminar, which cost her $747.50. She spent the weekend of June 19 at the seminar, where she was encouraged to call her credit-card company and increase her line of credit. "They said that we should invest in property without ever touching our own assets," she wrote in a September 2012 affidavit. "The instructor said if we surmounted the fear of losing money then we would actually make money."

She was then encouraged to sign up for the "Trump Gold" mentorship program—at a cost of $35,000—described as a yearlong group of seminars and private consultations with Trump instructors. When Harris declined, "The agent was very upset and quickly hung up the phone on me," she wrote in her affidavit.

Bob Guillo, from Manhasset, New York, and his son, Alex, fell hard for the Trump line. After the free seminar and the three-day course costing nearly $1,500—and which he graded as "excellent" in his evaluation—Guillo signed up for the Trump Gold Elite program and paid nearly $35,000. He was told he would be part of a select "in-the-know group" and among "insiders" who would have access to proprietary real-estate deals. "For example," Guillo wrote in an affidavit, "where Mr. Trump would be involved in building condominiums, we would get first choice at purchasing an apartment and then would be able to immediately sell it at a profit."

Guillo wrote that at the first day of the Trump Gold Elite program he "began to realize I had been taken" because the information conveyed seemed to be coming from Zillow.com, a real-estate Web site, or from the I.R.S. Web site. In August 2011, Guillo wrote George Sorial, an assistant general counsel in the Trump Organization, to request a refund. But he never got his money back. Instead, "Trump staff promised to set me up with their best mentor," Guillo wrote. He declined the offer. He just wanted his money back.

Guillo, now 74 years old and a retired legal-document processor, says he attended every one of the seminars his $35,000 bought him and at every one the Trump instructors did the same thing. "They tried to solicit more money from us," he explains. "I got a picture of myself with a Trump cutout and basically very, very little else."

Trump is unmoved by the people who have complained. He and his legal advisers set up a Web site, 98percentapproval.com, which contains video testimonials from satisfied customers, as well as more than 10,000 attendee surveys, many of which give Trump top marks. "It's like Harvard," Trump tells me. "You know Harvard doesn't have a 98 percent approval rating." Alan Garten, an executive vice president of the Trump Organization and litigation counsel, interjects, "When you take into account the fact that the attorney general's been looking at this case for what, two-plus years, 46 [negative] affidavits is [nothing]."

Trump quickly picks up on Garten's observation. "Of those 46," The Donald says, "most of them have signed a letter saying how great it was. . . . They complained that they weren't given refunds, except they were."

What about Bob Guillo, who has not received a refund? "I had many conversations with Bob Guillo," says Sorial. "He could not articulate one thing that was wrong with the course. And I just got the impression that this was a guy who read about this frivolous lawsuit and was saying,

'Hey, look. I'm going to try and get some money back.' Especially because he signed up for multiple courses in multiple years, and had multiple, very positive evaluations."

Schneiderman is not persuaded by such arguments. "All the promotional materials, many of which featured Mr. Trump, made numerous false statements," he explains. "He never 'handpicked' experts to teach people. These people weren't experts. They weren't even certified as teachers by the state of New York. They didn't learn any real-estate secrets from Trump, because he never participated in developing the curriculum." (Trump says he personally reviewed the résumés of many but not all of the teachers.)

Trump is especially miffed that he is being tarred as a fraud. "I really did this because I thought we could really help a lot of people, and we did help a lot of people." He is determined to make the attorney general pay politically for his accusations and says his legal response "will blow Schneiderman out of the water."

Schneiderman responds, "I have no idea how he thinks his strategy is going to work." He adds, "The lawyers in my office are going to pursue it. I am quite confident we're going to prevail, and the rest of it is just distraction."

[In 2016, Trump agreed to pay $1 million in penalties to New York State for violating state education laws. In March 2017, a federal judge gave final approval of a $25 million class-action settlement between Trump University and more than 3,700 former students. (Trump admitted no wrongdoing in either case.)]

ACKNOWLEDGMENTS

EDITOR	GRAYDON CARTER
V.F. BOOKS EDITOR	DAVID FRIEND
MANAGING EDITOR	CHRIS GARRETT
EDITOR-AT-LARGE	CULLEN MURPHY
EDITORIAL ASSISTANT	SARAH BRACY PENN

Editorial guidance was provided by Chris Dixon, Hilary Fitzgibbons, Ben Kalin, Matt Kapp, Mike Sacks, and Robert Walsh.

We gratefully acknowledge our partners at Simon & Schuster, including Jonathan Karp, Cary Goldstein, Zachary Knoll, Kristen Lemire, and Jackie Seow.

And we sincerely thank *Vanity Fair*'s publisher and chief revenue officer Chris Mitchell; Dan Gilmore and Camille Zumwalt Coppola (*Vanity Fair* Business Office); Christopher P. Donnellan, Tamara Kobin, and Matthew Barad (Condé Nast Contracts and Rights Department); and Andrew Wylie and Jeffrey Posternak of The Wylie Agency.

CONTRIBUTORS

CLARA BINGHAM is the author of three books: *Witness to the Revolution* (2016); *Class Action* (co-authored with Laura Leedy Gansler), which inspired the 2005 feature film *North Country*; and *Women on the Hill: Challenging the Culture of Congress* (1997). Her *Vanity Fair* article on the Air Force Academy rape scandal, included in these pages, won a 2004 National Women's Political Caucus Exceptional Merit in Media Award.

BUZZ BISSINGER is a Pulitzer Prize–winning journalist and contributing editor at *Vanity Fair*. In 2015, he wrote *V.F.*'s July cover story, "Call Me Caitlyn," which was the first journalistic profile of Caitlyn Jenner. Bissinger is the author of six books, including *Friday Night Lights*, which inspired the film and television series.

WILLIAM D. COHAN is a special correspondent at *Vanity Fair* and former Wall Street banker. He is the author of four books, including *The*

Last Tycoons: The Secret History of Lazard Frères & Co., which won The *Financial Times* and Goldman Sachs Business Book of the Year Award. His latest book, *Why Wall Street Matters*, was published in February.

SARAH ELLISON is a special correspondent for *Vanity Fair* and frequent contributor to the Hive, the magazine's digital daily. She chronicled Rupert Murdoch's takeover of *The Wall Street Journal* in her 2010 book, *War at The Wall Street Journal*. Previously, she was a reporter for the *Journal* in Paris, London, and New York, and for *Newsweek* in Paris.

JOHN FALK is a freelance journalist. His piece "Anti-Sniper," for *Details*, was adapted into the HBO film *Shot Through the Heart*, which won a Peabody Award. He is also the author of a memoir, *Hello to All That: A Memoir of Zoloft, War, and Peace*.

JESSE KORNBLUTH, formerly a contributing editor at *Vanity Fair*, is the author of nine books, including *Married Sex: A Love Story* and *Highly Confident: The Crime and Punishment of Michael Milken*. His work has also appeared in *New York, Architectural Digest, The New York Times*, and *The New Yorker*. He has served as editorial director of AOL Networks and now edits HeadButler.com.

DAVID MARGOLICK is a contributing editor at *Vanity Fair*, contributor to *The New York Times Review of Books*, and former legal-affairs correspondent for *The New York Times*. His books include *Elizabeth and Hazel: Two Women of Little Rock; Strange Fruit: The Biography of a Song; Beyond Glory: Joe Louis vs. Max Schmeling, and a World on the Brink*; and *Undue Influence: The Epic Battle for the Johnson & Johnson Fortune*.

BRETT MARTIN, author of *Difficult Men: Behind the Scenes of a Creative Revolution, From The Sopranos and The Wire to Mad Men and Breaking Bad*, is a correspondent for *GQ*. His work has appeared in *Vanity*

Fair, The New Yorker, The New York Times, and *Bon Appétit,* and on *This American Life.* He is the recipient of two James Beard Journalism Awards.

NINA MUNK joined *Vanity Fair* as a contributing editor in 2001. She is the author of *The Idealist: Jeffrey Sachs and the Quest to End Poverty; Fools Rush In: Steve Case, Jerry Levin, and the Unmaking of AOL Time Warner;* and *The Art of Clairtone: The Making of a Design Icon.* Her work has also appeared in *The Atlantic, The New York Times Magazine, The New York Times, The New Yorker, Forbes,* and *Fortune.*

EVGENIA PERETZ is a screenwriter and *Vanity Fair* contributing editor. For *V.F.,* she has covered a diverse range of topics, from social history to political personalities to a cheating scandal at her mother's alma mater, Miss Porter's School. In 2011 she co-wrote the film *Our Idiot Brother,* starring Paul Rudd, and she executive produced last year's documentary *Theo Who Lived.*

TODD S. PURDUM, a senior writer at *Politico,* joined *Vanity Fair* in 2006, where he is a contributing editor, after having been at *The New York Times* for 23 years. His last *Times* assignment was as a correspondent in the Washington bureau, where he also served as a diplomatic and White House correspondent. From 1997 until 2001, Purdum was the Los Angeles–bureau chief. He is the author of *An Idea Whose Time Has Come: Two Presidents, Two Parties, and the Battle for the Civil Rights Act of 1964.*

ALEXANDRA ROBBINS is a journalist, lecturer, and *New York Times* best-selling author, having written seven books, including *Secrets of the Tomb: Skull and Bones, the Ivy League, and the Hidden Paths of Power.* Her work has appeared in *Vanity Fair, The New Yorker, The New York Times, The Wall Street Journal, The Atlantic, The Washington Post,* and other publications.

JOHN SEDGWICK has written approximately 500 magazine pieces. His stories have appeared in *Vanity Fair, The Atlantic, GQ, Newsweek, Esquire,* and elsewhere. He has written *War of Two: Alexander Hamilton, Aaron Burr, and the Duel That Stunned the Nation* and *In My Blood: Six Generations of Madness and Desire in an American Family.*

MICHAEL SHNAYERSON is a contributing editor at *Vanity Fair,* for which he's written more than 80 articles. Two of his *V.F.* stories, "The Widow on the Hill" and "Murder in East Hampton," were made into movies. He is the author of six books, including *The Contender,* a 2015 biography of New York Governor Andrew Cuomo.

ALEX SHOUMATOFF, a former contributing editor to *Vanity Fair* and accomplished author, was a founding contributing editor of *Condé Nast Traveler* and *Outside.* Shoumatoff has covered stories for *V.F.* around the globe, including the 1986 article about Dian Fossey's preservation of the gorilla community in Rwanda, which helped inspire the film *Gorillas in the Mist.*

SAM TANENHAUS, the journalist and historian, has contributed articles to *Vanity Fair* since 1999. He was the editor of *The New York Times Book Review,* as well as the *Week In Review,* and is now a writer-at-large for the *Times.* The author of several books—including *Whittaker Chambers: A Biography,* a finalist for the National Book Award and the Pulitzer Prize—Tanenhaus is writing the authorized biography of William F. Buckley Jr.

BENJAMIN WALLACE is a contributing editor at *Vanity Fair* and *New York.* He is the author of *The Billionaire's Vinegar: The Mystery of the World's Most Expensive Bottle of Wine,* a *New York Times* best-seller. In 2011, he won a James Beard Journalism Award.